from the archives of Maclean's

CANADA ON ICE

50 Years of Great Hockey

edited by
Michael Benedict
and
D'Arcy Jenish

VIKING

VIKING

Published by the Penguin Group
Penguin Books Canada Ltd, 10 Alcorn Avenue, Toronto, Ontario, Canada M4V 3B2
Penguin Books Ltd, 27 Wrights Lane, London W8 5TZ, England
Penguin Putnam Inc., 375 Hudson Street, New York, New York 10014, U.S.A.
Penguin Books Australia Ltd, Ringwood, Victoria, Australia
Penguin Books (NZ) Ltd, cnr Rosedale and Airborne Roads, Albany Aukland 1310, New Zealand

Penguin Books Ltd Registered Offices: Harmondsworth, Middlesex, England

First published 1998
10 9 8 7 6 5 4 3 2 1

Copyright © Maclean Hunter Publishing Limited, 1998

Every effort has been made to locate the original copyright owner. If you have any additional information on the copyright owner, we would be happy to include it in any revised edition.

All rights reserved. Without limiting the rights under copyright reserved above, no part of this publication may be reproduced, stored in or introduced into a retrieval system, or transmitted in any form or by any means (electronic, mechanical, photocopying, recording or otherwise), without the prior written permission of both the copyright owner and the above publisher of this book.

Printed and bound in Canada on acid free paper ∞

CANADIAN CATALOGUING IN PUBLICATION DATA

Main entry under title:

Canada on ice: fifty years of great hockey

Articles originally published in Maclean's magazine.
Includes bibliographical references.
ISBN 0-670-88037-X

I. Hockey – Canada – History. I. Benedict, Michael, 1947– .
II. Jenish, D'Arcy, 1952– .

GB848.4.C3C36 1998   796.962'0971   C98-931546-0

Visit Penguin Canada's website at www.penguin.ca

Contents

Foreword   ix
    PETER GZOWSKI
Preface   xiii

Hockey's Holy Cities

Montreal's Grey-Flannel Hockey Cartel *December 3, 1960*   3
    TRENT FRAYNE
The Maple Leaf Money Machine *March 21, 1964*   12
    PETER GZOWSKI

Stars, Heroes and Innovators

Lester Patrick's 50 Years on Ice *March 1, 1950*   25
    BRUCE HUTCHISON
Foster Hewitt: Play-by-Playboy *April 1, 1950*   34
    TRENT FRAYNE
Conn Smythe: That Man in the Greens *January 1, 1952*   41
    TRENT FRAYNE
How They Broke the Heart of Howie Morenz *October 15, 1953*   50
    TRENT FRAYNE
The High Spots of a Lifetime with the Red Wings *January 28, 1961*   58
    JACK ADAMS *with* TRENT FRAYNE

Mr. Hockey

Gordie Howe: Hero *December 14, 1963*   67
    PETER GZOWSKI
Gordie Goes Home *October 15, 1966*   78
    JOHN ROBERTSON

The Miracle Worker *January 23, 1978*   84
ROBERT MILLER
Memories of a Time that Never Changes *February 8, 1993*   91
ALLAN FOTHERINGHAM

The Rocket

Maurice Richard off the Ice *May 9, 1959*   97
JUNE CALLWOOD
The Strange Forces behind the Richard Hockey Riot *September 17, 1955*   105
SIDNEY KATZ

Stars of the Original Six

Is Jean Beliveau the Best Ever? *March 3, 1956*   127
TRENT FRAYNE
Nobody's Too Big for Ted Lindsay *October 26, 1957*   134
TRENT FRAYNE
The Awful Ups and Downs of Terry Sawchuk *December 19, 1959*   142
TRENT FRAYNE
Viva Mahovlich! *February 25, 1961*   149
PETER GZOWSKI
Bobby Hull: Hockey Hero *January 22, 1966*   153
TRENT FRAYNE
The New Eddie Shack *February 5, 1966*   161
SUSAN DEXTER

The Turbulent Seventies

Who Is Bobby Orr? *February 20, 1965*   169
TRENT FRAYNE
The Dead-End Kid who Wants to Be a Superstar *November, 1969*   176
STAN FISCHLER
Dr. Jekyll and Mr. Hull *March, 1973*   184
JACK BATTEN
Coaching Scared *November, 1974*   194
TRENT FRAYNE
Good-time Harold *September, 1975*   200
ROY MACSKIMMING

Farewell to Greatness *February 21, 1977*   209
  ROBERT MILLER
A Flower for All Seasons *October 16, 1978*   213
  ROY MACGREGOR
King of the Kings *March 24, 1980*   221
  ROY MACGREGOR

Hockey Goes Global

Team Canada in War and Peace *December, 1972*   231
  JACK LUDWIG
The Deck Was Stacked *October 4, 1976*   246
  MICHAEL POSNER
Exploding the Myth *February 26, 1979*   249
  HAL QUINN
Greatest Show on Ice *September 29, 1987*   254
  HAL QUINN
Henderson Scores! Recalling 1972 *September 29, 1997*   257
  JAMES DEACON
The Russians Remember *September 29, 1997*   263
  MALCOLM GRAY
Hockey Meltdown *March 2, 1998*   268
  BRUCE WALLACE

The Great One

The Best in the World *January 25, 1988*   275
  PETER GZOWSKI
The "Royal" Wedding *July 25, 1988*   279
  MARK NICHOLS
Gretzky Inc. *December 5, 1994*   288
  JAMES DEACON

Lemieux, Lindros and Other Legends

Like Father, Like Son *March 18, 1991*   301
  D'ARCY JENISH
Lucky Lindros *September 9, 1991*   305
  BRUCE WALLACE

Broadway Mark Messier *March 20, 1992* 312
    D'ARCY JENISH

Mario Lemieux: The Reluctant Superstar *April 8, 1996* 317
    JAMES DEACON

In the Name of Greed *January 19, 1998* 325
    JANE O'HARA

Has Don Cherry Gone Too Far? *May 18, 1998* 332
    JAMES DEACON

Postscript

The Holy Grail *April 26, 1992* 343
    D'ARCY JENISH

Photo Credits 346

Foreword

Peter Gzowski

June, 1998—Scratch a Canadian writer, I'm pretty sure, and you'll find a hockey fan. Not just the scribes who cover the endless grind of the National Hockey League, either—a breed, in fact, that grows more cynical every year about the money, intimidation and rampant Americanization of the game they love (if those aren't all the same thing)—but just people who like to write, to seek some kind of truth, to find some insight in the quotidian pastimes of Canadian life. Or, as sometimes happens, simply to have some fun.

At first glance, hockey may seem a curious pursuit for the writerly mind. If for no other reason, it's too damn fast. Except perhaps for a long lob from the defensive zone that skitters agonizingly toward an empty net, there is scarcely a play that can be described on paper and read about in anything resembling the time it takes to occur—witness in these pages my own struggle to set down on paper, in 1988, the magic wrought by Wayne Gretzky and Mario Lemieux to score the goal that, for the time being anyway, put Canada back on top of the hockey world. By contrast, the rhythms of baseball or golf suit themselves perfectly to both the writer's ability to transcribe and the reader's to absorb, which is, of course, one of the reasons each of those sports has spawned a literature that dwarfs hockey's. The only real equivalent I can think of in the Canadian lexicon is curling, but if anyone has written a book that captures the flavor and strategy of that intriguing game, I'm not aware of it—though I do remember a lively instalment of the department *Maclean's* used to call "For the Sake of Argument," in which the illustrious editor (and reformed sportswriter) Ralph Allen decried the fact that the game he had looked forward to mastering in creaky middle age had been taken over by muscular young *athletes* who eschewed strategy for smashing take-outs and slides that took them halfway into the waiting beer hall.

But for all the difficulties, we try. Hockey is more than a sport for us; it's in our blood. Other people may beat us in some world tournaments and even (sigh) in the

Olympics, but even when they're playing it more stylishly than we are, it isn't their game, it's ours. If we didn't play it as kids—and, in my time at least, any boy who didn't grow up in Vancouver did—you listened to it on the radio, with Foster Hewitt broadcasting to Canada, Newfoundland, all the ships at sea (see Trent Frayne's lovely evocation in these pages) and you, huddled under your blankets dreaming of Foster's voice describing the thrills as the kid from Galt or Moosomin or Musquoidobit broke in alone on goal in the dying seconds of the Stanley Cup, faked left, faked right and...

Sometimes I would think in later years, as I swapped memories of shinny with sticks worn down to toothpicks and cross-sections of inner tubes holding up our stockings and, of course, a frozen horse-bun for a puck, there was only one long continuous game, which started somewhere in the salt spray of the Atlantic and ran through the winter twilight across pond and tickle and river and slough to the foothills of the Rockies, no raising, no body checks and an automatic goal when you threw your stick to stop a breakaway.

Now, in so many ways, all that has changed. I remember a winter Saturday morning in the early '80s, being on the road to promote the book I'd fashioned from a year with the then young and electrifying Edmonton Oilers—they had yet to win their first Stanley Cup—and driving past the park in what had been my Ontario boyhood home of Galt, but was now part of the larger municipality called Cambridge. The outdoor rink where I'd scored so many Cup-winning goals was long gone. In its place was an enclosed, heated arena, and as I parked across the road, memories of dawn-to-dusk games tumbling through my head—sometimes we played two games at once, one with the men and older boys soaring end to end while the little kids wobbled happily across the middle, the two patterns kept mutually distinct by the differing white initials on their pucks—a steady stream of cars disgorged boys in padded pants and brightly striped stockings, toting duffel bags of still more equipment. From each of their carefully taped sticks, slung across their shoulders, dangled a pair of rigid-looking skates that alone would have cost their parents more than I'd paid for all the gear I ever wore. Inside, I knew from my own attempts at coaching the teams my sons had played on in a similar building in mid-town Toronto, each boy would be lucky to get 12 minutes of ice time before a whistle blew and someone else's father changed the lines.

There's much to be said for all the changes. Improved equipment, better diet and certainly better coaching have meant an even faster game played by bigger and, to be honest, better athletes. (People who have worked with old film footage and modern technology have ascertained that even Howie Morenz, whose tragic death is chronicled in these pages, could scarcely have kept up with today's journeymen.) Social and political changes have brought women into hockey (I doubt there is a kid I used to play with on the outdoor rinks of Galt who could make third-string defensive forward on today's national Canadian women's team) and hockey to the world; nearly half the players in the NHL today, and alas, as the Nagano Olympics showed so dramatically, a far higher proportion of the most skilled skaters and puckhandlers, if not the grinders and the clutchers and holders, come from the United States and Europe. Television, too, has changed the game of my youth, not only in the raucous half-time shows and the constant interruptions for commercials, or the steady Americanization of the NHL (Foster himself must be spinning in his grave at the prospect of a team called the Mighty Ducks or pucks that glow in the dark), but in the very comportment of the players. Inside all those heated arenas, kids now slap each other with high fives after every goal and are more concerned about the prospect of scouts in the stands and the relentless cries of their coaches—or, sometimes, parents—than in the pleasures of the game they're playing.

And money, money is everything. For a measure of how much the arithmetic has changed, see (again) my own apparent astonishment, when I reported, in 1964, that players were pulling down as much as *fifteen thousand dollars* a year.

But still what brought us to the game remains: the speed, the grace, the kaleidoscopic patterns, the feel of the wind through your hair or billowing your sweater, the crunch of skates against ice, the thud of the puck.

And still we write. The standard that was set by Trent Frayne, the dean of us all—Bill, to almost everyone who knows him, for who, as he says, could consider a sports writer named Trent?, who rightfully is the most prolific contributor to this anthology—has been (and is) carried on by new generations of observers, including the elegant stylist Roy MacGregor. Along the way, the experts have been joined by writers whose reputations were built in other fields: the great political oracle Bruce Hutchison; Sidney Katz, the distinguished scientific journalist (among other coups, he broke, in *Maclean's*, the story of LSD); the incomparable June Callwood, in private life Mrs. Trent Frayne, and arguably the greatest all-round magazine writer of us all; and, later on, such generalists as Jack Batten, Jack Ludwig, Susan Dexter and Mark Nichols.

Maclean's, for most of its life, has been a writer's magazine—a *Canadian* writer's magazine. We wrote about what we knew and loved, even when we viewed what was happening with a sense of loss or dismay. And when we had a chance, we wrote about our game.

Peter Gzowski worked at Maclean's *from 1958 to 1964, the last two years as managing editor, and then returned to the magazine as editor for nine months in 1969. His book on the Edmonton Oilers,* The Game of Our Lives, *was published in 1982.*

Preface

June, 1998—Earlier this year, the *Hockey News* asked 50 veteran hockey experts a question that has sparked heated debates since the first puck was dropped: Who is the best player in hockey history?

In the post-war era, Canadians first argued that question in terms of the comparative merits of Maurice "Rocket" Richard and Gordie Howe. In the early 1960s, the spotlight had shifted to Bobby Hull and Frank Mahovlich, then the two best young players in the game. A decade later, Bobby Orr soared so far above his peers that the argument became more like: Who's second best, Guy Lafleur or Marcel Dionne? By the late 1980s, it was back to: Who's the best? Wayne Gretzky, Mario Lemieux or one of the stars from the Original Six?

These arguments can never be resolved by polls or turning to the record books to see who scored the most goals, collected the most assists or led the league in shutouts. Hockey is too much a game of style and character for that. All the great ones of the modern era, from Richard and Howe to Gretzky and Lemieux have been generals on the ice. They have all excelled at leading their teams to victory in the big games because they were full of confidence, devoid of fear and rock solid under pressure.

As Canada's magazine of news and current affairs, *Maclean's* has been intertwined with the game of hockey and the debate over the greatest player ever. Over the past 50 years, particularly, *Maclean's* has assigned the country's best writers—Bruce Hutchison, Trent Frayne, June Callwood, Peter Gzowski, Roy MacGregor, Allan Fotheringham and Jack Batten, to name a few, as well as renowned U.S. hockey writer Stan Fischler—to probe Canada's game and its relation to the national psyche. These writers have watched from press boxes, stood at rinkside, hung around dressing rooms, followed the players home, caught up to them during the off-season, and interviewed their wives, parents and children. Collected here, the result is polished articles on the greatest players of the times—Richard, Howe, Hull, Orr, Gretzky and

Lemieux, all of whom made the *Hockey News*'s all-time Top 10 greatest. *Maclean's* has also written about Hall of Famers like Mahovlich, Lafleur and Dionne, Jean Beliveau, Terry Sawchuk and Ted Lindsay, and contemporary stars such as Eric Lindros, Mark Messier and Brett Hull. Included in this collection, as well, are pieces on the game's rogues and more colorful characters, from Eddie Shack through Derek Sanderson and Harold Ballard to Don Cherry and the recently disgraced Alan Eagleson.

Timely and relevant when first published, the articles still sparkle with insight, engaging anecdotes and classical tales of young men who transcended humble backgrounds to become hockey legends. Although they were all published after 1950, the pieces provide a snapshot of hockey throughout the entire 20th century. Bruce Hutchison, a giant of Canadian journalism best known for his political coverage, captures the flavor of the game's early years in a retrospective look at the career of Lester Patrick, one of hockey's great pioneers. Trent Frayne, whose work still graces the pages of *Maclean's* more than half a century after his first piece appeared in the magazine, displays his mastery of the game in a wide range of articles, from a touching 1953 tale of one of the game's first superstars, Montreal Canadiens' centre Howie Morenz to a profile of a pre-NHL Bobby Orr. And in stark contrast to a simpler era, *Maclean's* current sports editor, James Deacon, describes, in a groundbreaking December, 1994 profile of Wayne Gretzky, a purely contemporary phenomenon— the hockey hero as business tycoon.

Throughout the decades, *Maclean's* has been there when hockey history was made. Sidney Katz's reconstruction of the Richard riot in March, 1955 is a riveting and revealing account of one of the most violent and shocking incidents in the history of Canadian sport. The magazine has also probed the major developments of the postwar era—NHL expansion and international competition, starting with Canada's heart-stopping win over the Russians in 1972 and later taking an astute look back at that series a quarter of a century later.

While the *Hockey News* experts chose Gretzky as the game's greatest ever, the editors of this collection feel the debate cannot—and should not—be so easily resolved. Instead, we have compiled a series of stylish portraits and essays in the hope that, by capturing the lives and character of some of hockey's greatest players, the discussion will become timeless.

Many of the articles were shortened, but otherwise they underwent very little editing. Biographical information on the subjects and the writers who profiled them is added at the end of most pieces. This information was compiled and checked by free-lance writer Steve Brearton.

From the magazine's current staff, many worked hard to bring this project to fruition, especially associate photo editor Kristine Ryall, researcher-reporter Ruth Abramson, library technician Mary Jane Culbert and editorial administrator Sean McCluskey. Sports editor Deacon provided support and sage advice.

Michael Benedict
Editorial Director of New Ventures

D'Arcy Jenish
Senior Writer

CANADA ON ICE

OCKEY'S
HOLY
CITIES

Montreal's Grey-Flannel Hockey Cartel

Trent Frayne

December 3, 1960—The rich, thoroughly organized, mass-produced Montreal Canadiens have brought the corporate image to hockey, with a resultant domination of their game that has been matched in sports only by the rich, thoroughly organized, mass-produced New York Yankees in baseball. Last April, in running their five-year playoff record to 40 wins in 49 post-season games, the Canadiens swept the semifinal and final rounds of the Stanley Cup playoffs in the minimum of eight games, to win their fifth straight Stanley Cup.

The Canadiens, the oldest organization in hockey, have a long proud record. But nothing they have achieved in the dimming past compares with their monstrous domination of the game today. The questions naturally arise: How did they get that way? Is the end in sight?

The answers relate directly to Frank Selke, the managing director, a one-time Kitchener, Ont., electrician who quit the front office of the Toronto Maple Leafs in the mid-'40s when his relations with the Toronto boss, Conn Smythe, became intolerable, and took over the Canadiens on July 26, 1946. A trim and gloomy man of perhaps five foot five with a funereal mien, a soft high voice, a habit of rubbing his hands while he talks, rimless glasses and thin short-clipped hair, Selke is the incongruously colorless architect of the flaming Habitants and their farm system, the finest and most extensive in the game and the best explanation of their present position in it.

Selke has built this club with an idea he evolved in Toronto in the early '40s. "I realized that young players in the services would not return to hockey as probable stars," he says. "The years that would have improved their ability were being spent in the army."

In the absence of Conn Smythe overseas, he got permission from director E.W. Bickle "to sign the best 16-year-olds around." These included Jimmy Thomson, Tod Sloan, Joe Klukay, Fleming Mackell and Gus Mortson, all of whom eventually blossomed into enduring National Leaguers. Also Selke traded a defenceman, Frankie Eddolls (to the Canadiens, ironically), for 16-year-old Ted Kennedy, who became one of Toronto's great centre players. Smythe sent a cable to the executive saying that the deal should be cancelled, Selke says unemotionally. "I think Kennedy saved the Maple Leafs."

Selke believes that when Smythe returned from overseas he was told that Selke was trying to usurp his power at Maple Leaf Gardens, information that Selke brands completely false. His relations with Smythe worsened, and Selke resigned with no job to go to. Three months later, he received a letter from William Northey, a director of the Canadiens, asking if he were interested in moving to the Forum. "I wrote back and said I couldn't work with Gorman," Selke recalls, referring to Tommy Gorman, then general manager of the Canadiens. "Mr. Northey said the idea was to replace Gorman," Selke relates. "I didn't answer that letter. My experience at Toronto was too recent."

Then Senator Donat Raymond, president of the Canadiens, telephoned Selke. "He told me he was going to accept Gorman's resignation," Selke says. "I told him that when Gorman was gone I would consider his offer."

In the summer of 1946, Tommy Gorman moved to Ottawa and Selke joined the Canadiens, who had won the Stanley Cup that spring. Nevertheless, Selke foresaw a dark future for the champions, he says now. "When the team hit the ice I asked for an executive meeting," he recalls. "I told Senator Raymond that no other team could come up with six players as good as his top six—Bill Durnan, Ken Reardon, Butch Bouchard, and the Punch Line of Elmer Lach, Toe Blake and Rocket Richard—but that there were no reserves in sight."

Raymond asked for his solution. "I'd like to inaugurate a farm system, with a team in every province to build up young reserves, as in Toronto. The players there will be haunting me for years." Raymond gave him carte blanche. "We owe the people of Montreal a good hockey team," he said. "Go ahead and build an empire."

Selke did, throwing Montreal funds into teams all across the land for the rights to young players. The Canadiens spent $300,000 one season to keep the system going since many of their affiliates lost money. "It cost us $70,000 to bail out the team in Quebec City," Selke says.

As he predicted, Toronto players haunted him for years. The Leafs won the Stanley Cup four times in the next five years, aided by the youngsters he'd signed in his Toronto days, but then the fruit began to come in from the Montreal farms. Beginning with the spring of 1951, the Canadiens have reached the Stanley Cup final through ten straight seasons and have won the trophy in six of them. And the notion that the end of their flight is not in sight is Selke's. "Canadiens will be the team to beat for the next 10 years!" he observed in a rare exclamatory outburst last spring. "I would be foolish to predict that we'll be in first place for that length of time, because we don't know what the other teams have in the way of kids coming up. But we'll be the team to beat because we have the players."

He rewards them lavishly. Six players in the Montreal lineup this season have basic salaries of $20,000 a year or better, and that doesn't include playoff money worth $4,000 a man if the team finishes first in the standings and goes on to win the Stanley Cup. The Habitant payroll for the 1960–61 roster is $300,000 and, in addition, Maurice (Rocket) Richard is being paid $25,000 for not playing. This is reward for services rendered in his 18 stormily productive seasons and balm for the Rocket's retirement at thirty-nine last fall so that he won't blemish a magnificent reputation on legs that may no longer match his fierce pride.

There's more to the Canadiens' prowl of conquest than mere money, however. Last September, they played a meaningless intra-squad exhibition game in the Forum in which the Reds defeated the Whites 5 to 1. As it happened, team captain Doug Harvey was lined up with the Whites. When the game ended he sat disconsolately in the dressing room chatting with *Montreal Star* columnist Red Fisher. "They shouldn't have beat us that bad," Harvey grumbled, although the game meant nothing. They talked about it while Harvey changed his clothes and then they went to a restaurant for Chinese food. Harvey was still downcast. "I should have stayed home in bed," he said to Fisher. "I wasn't any help to anybody."

Here was the attitude of a player many believe to be the finest defenceman in the history of hockey. The opening of his 14th season in the NHL was still three weeks away, and Harvey, one would think, had won too many awards to be concerned about an exhibition. He has been named on the first all-star team in eight of the last nine seasons and has won the James Norris Memorial Trophy as the game's top defenceman in five of the seven seasons it has been in existence, but defeat, even in an intra-squad game, still distresses him.

Harvey was asked recently why the Canadiens never seem to grown complacent, why they never let down in mid-season, say, knowing they're the class of the field. "There's no use playing this game if you're not trying to win," he replied. "For one thing, it's more fun winning than losing, eh? You should never say tomorrow we'll be

Dickie Moore (left) and Jacques Plante (right) carry coach Toe Blake after the Montreal Canadiens defeat the Detroit Red Wings to capture the Stanley Cup on April 10, 1956.

all right if you lose a game or two, because the first thing you know the season's over and it's too late. It's tonight's game that matters."

Harvey, an unruffled man of 35 who was a gunner on the merchant ships during the war, says the Montreal fans have a good deal to do with the team's urge to win, though not necessarily the fans who comprise the idolatrous Forum legion and shower down their teeming support. "The boys are pretty well known in Montreal," he says of the players. "Any time we lost a game, even on the road, people on the street want to know what the hell happened—in two languages. It's the same all summer; you can have a pretty good summer when you win in the spring."

Young players moving into the Canadien lineup, spotted expertly by coach Hector (Toe) Blake and given salubrious experience under fire, keep an enduring balance and depth that offsets injuries of seasoned players, and this keeps the team strong. Since the Selke farm system became productive there has rarely been a moment when burgeoning young players aren't sitting on the bench, waiting hopefully for somebody to catch some trivial incurable disease. This keeps the stars alert, too. Last season, for example, Rocket Richard was edgy in his 18th season because Toe Blake was employing four forward lines for a time instead of the usual three. This was giving less jealously guarded ice-time to Richard—only one turn in four, rather than one in three. Dickie Moore, who'd been scoring champion for two years in a row, was crestfallen when Blake moved him from the power-play alignment for a brief period last season. All that was bothering Moore was two sprained wrists.

But beneath the surface there's more to the Canadiens than an eager desire to play and a long strong bench. There is the pride of belonging to something tall that augments an individual's ability and makes him taller. There is the sense of achievement in having been good enough to move with the best, and this brings out the best. "When you've played here, you just don't want to play anywhere else," says Floyd (Busher) Curry, a former right winger on championship Canadien teams who now coaches the Habitant affiliate, the Montreal Royals in the Eastern Professional Hockey League. "When I was nearing the end of the line, Mr. Selke called me into his office and asked me if I'd like to be traded to another NHL club, that there wasn't room on the roster for me. I decided against being traded. I didn't want to play against this club; we'd always had good times together. So I retired. In my time, guys who did choose to be traded in these circumstances used to come up to me and say, 'You lucky so-and-so, playing with this club.'"

There are no cliques on the Canadiens. Frank Selke has molded the two religions and the two nationalities so that they do not exist, as such. Only the Canadiens matter. Occasionally Selke goes hunting deer with Rocket Richard and when they've bagged one they take it to Butch Bouchard's restaurant and a banquet is held for the players and their wives. Each Christmas, Selke holds a skating party at the Forum for the players, their wives and their families, and this is followed by the Christmas turkey. There is a camaraderie about the Canadiens, unquestionably stimulated by these affairs.

Selke, his undertaker's bearing curiously misplaced in a game rife with pop-offs, has more than the respect usually accorded an employer. Rocket Richard worships him and after all these years still calls him Mr. Selke out of his presence. Bert Olmstead, whom the Canadiens let go to Toronto three seasons ago after nearly eight full seasons with the Habs, says that in all his time there he never knew a teammate who didn't have an abiding respect for the solemn little boss. Selke, it would appear, is a sort of father-figure to the Canadiens in addition to being the silent perceptive builder.

The Flying Frenchmen, curiously, had their genesis in a conversation between a Scottish baker and an Irish contractor one December night in 1909. There was only one professional league in the country, the Eastern Canada Hockey Association. To strengthen it, James Strachan, the manager of the Montreal Wanderers, a Montrealer whose family was prominent in the baking industry, made a thoughtful remark to young Ambrose O'Brien of Renfrew, Ont., whose father had made a good deal of money as a railway contractor. "A club composed entirely of French-Canadian players in Montreal, with its 70 per cent French-Canadian population, is bound to be a success," Strachan said.

O'Brien, at that moment, wasn't interested. He wanted his home-town team, the Renfrew Millionaires, to win the Stanley Cup and made application to the Eastern Canada league for its admittance. When the application was refused, he remembered Strachan's remark and set out to form his own league. He founded and financed the Montreal Canadiens on Dec. 10, 1909, depositing $5,000 in a St. James Street bank to guarantee players' salaries. They got a series of postdated cheques that could be stopped at the bank if any player defected. He commissioned Jack Laviolette, an itinerant hockey player and owner of a restaurant in Montreal called Jack's Cafe, to put together a team for the $5,000.

To round out his league, O'Brien urged James Strachan to transfer his Montreal Wanderers to it, brought in the Renfrew Millionaires, and financed two teams in the booming mining belt of northern Ontario, at Cobalt and Haileybury. He called the league the National Hockey Association. It turned out to be the forerunner of the NHL.

The move by O'Brien caused an upheaval out of which the Ottawa Senators and the Montreal Shamrocks withdrew from the Eastern Canada league and joined the NHA, bringing an end to the tottering Eastern league. The season began on Jan. 5, 1910, with the Canadiens playing Cobalt in a tiny noisy smoke-filled firetrap called the Jubilee Rink. They attracted just under 3,000 customers who watched seven-man hockey in two thirty-minute periods. And the Canadiens were indeed comprised entirely of French-Canadian players, among them Jack Laviolette, the cafe owner; goalkeeper Joe Cattarinich, who later, with Leo Dandurand as his partner, became co-owner of the club; Newsy Lalonde, the greatest lacrosse player of the era, and Didier Pitre, who'd been paid $2,000 for a season with Renfrew a few years earlier but signed for considerably less to be with the new club. For that first game, Newsy Lalonde, who still lives in Montreal and is a bubbling, energetic man in his 70s, believes he was the highest-paid Canadien on the ice. He got $1,300 for the season, which the Canadiens launched with a 7-to-1 victory.

O'Brien made a 50 per cent profit on the Canadiens even before the season ended. He sold the franchise for $7,500 to a Montreal wrestler and wrestling promoter who called himself George Kennedy. Actually, Kennedy's name was Kendall, but his father, a dour Scottish sea captain, was so outraged when his son told him of his wrestling ambitions that George altered his surname. Kennedy, "without once raising his voice or using an oath," according to Lalonde, cajoled Canadiens to their first Stanley Cup in 1916.

In the spring of 1919, the Canadiens were involved in the only Stanley Cup final ever suspended. They were playing the Seattle Metropolitans in the Pacific coast city during an influenza epidemic and Kennedy and all but three of his players caught the flu. Joe Hall, a brilliant centre player, was seriously ill. Hall's roommate, Newsy Lalonde, kept imploring him to go to bed. Hall refused, and wore his Canadien sweater until he dropped. He died two days later. Kennedy himself never fully recovered. He died two years later, at the age of 41.

The club was put on the auction block in October, 1921. Out of a flurry of bidding that started at $8,000, Leo Dandurand, Louis Letourneau and Joe Cattarinich, who were then operating a race track at Cleveland, had their representative, Canadien coach Cecil Hart, buy the club for them for $11,000. It took them three years to build another Stanley Cup winner, employing the haphazard scouting methods of the era. Cattarinich, on a trip to Chicoutimi, Que., saw an amateur game one night in 1922 and was impressed by the goalkeeper, Georges Vezina, a tall solemn fellow so cool that after Cattarinich casually signed him for the Canadiens he became known everywhere in hockey as the Chicoutimi Cucumber. Vezina, in whose name the trophy for NHL goalkeeping is awarded, played in the best Canadien tradition—he collapsed during a game in November, 1925 and died a few months later.

Sylvio Mantha, the Canadien most recently elected to the Hall of Fame, was found in Montreal idly playing shinny on the school rinks of a working-class district called St. Henri. Dandurand happened to run into George Boucher, an Ottawa star, at a racetrack in the summer of 1922. Boucher said he'd been impressed in a game against the Saskatoon Sheiks of the Western Canada league by a slim elusive rookie named Aurel Joliat. Dandurand incensed Canadien fans by trading the idolized Newsy Lalonde for the unknown Joliat. He got so many telephone threats that he had the phone disconnected. Of the trade Lalonde says, "I was getting $2,000 a season at Montreal. Leo knew I was over the hill, but he made Saskatoon pay me $4,500. I was delighted, for heaven's sake!"

Almost as casually as he'd met George Boucher at the track, Dandurand saw a referee, Ernest Sauvé, the morning after a junior game. Sauvé advised him to look closely

Montreal's Grey-Flannel Hockey Cartel

at Howie Morenz, a young Stratford, Ont., player. The Toronto St. Pat's also were interested in Morenz, but the immortal Howie later admitted he signed with the Canadiens because Dandurand paid a $45 tailor's bill and gave him $300 to settle a number of small debts. His salary for the 24-game schedule was $3,500 and the contract was signed July 7, Dandurand's birthday. Accordingly, Dandurand assigned Morenz sweater number 7. Eleven years later, in the autumn of 1934, when Dandurand traded a crestfallen Morenz to Chicago, he tendered him a going-away dinner and announced that no other player would ever wear Morenz's number. None ever has.

A year later Dandurand sold the club to the Canadian Arena Company headed by Senator Raymond, for $165,000. Raymond brought back Morenz and just when it appeared he was making a strong comeback Morenz broke a leg. He died in hospital, apparently of a heart attack, on March 8, 1937. His body was placed at centre ice in the Forum and Canadien players formed a guard of honor as 15,000 people moved slowly and silently into the rink for the service. Outside, 25,000 more stood with heads bared, tightly packed for blocks.

Morenz was a symbol of a time when the ice heroes were a rough-hewn lot. To the millworkers and tram drivers and off-duty cabbies who jammed the north end of the Forum and called themselves the Millionaires, he was a superhuman figure. Their battle cry, *Les Canadiens sont là!*, never reached such frenzy as when Morenz hurtled down centre, burst through the defence and crashed the puck past the goalkeeper.

Today, by comparison, the players are smartly attired young businessmen off the ice, though on it they can still incite a riot. Which, indeed, they did on St. Patrick's Day in 1955. Rocket Richard had been suspended for hitting a referee, and vociferously objecting fans broke up a game between the Canadiens and the Detroit Red Wings by hurtling a tear-gas bomb on the Forum ice. Outside, those who couldn't get in on the festivities indoors did $30,000 damage.

Richard was a hothead for a decade while the late Dick Irvin was coaching the Canadiens. Irvin was a tough and remorseless needler who left the Canadiens after the 1954–55 season and was replaced by Toe Blake, the incumbent. With the arrival of his old linemate Blake, Richard mellowed considerably through the last five years of his career, the long stretch of complete Canadiens domination that shows no sign of abating.

There are those who feel that a comparatively recent draft law in NHL legislation will work against the Flying Frenchmen, but it's likely they're sympathetic alarmists from Montreal or wishful thinkers in the five other NHL cities. The draft is aimed at the strongest clubs. By it, each of the six teams enters an annual draft meeting with 20 players—18 forwards and defencemen, and two goalkeepers—on a so-called protected list. None of these can be drafted by another club, but all other professional players in the farm system can be, at $20,000 each. Thus, a club like the Canadiens can either sell players before the draft meeting at a higher price or wait for them to be selected at it, and in the last 18 months Frank Selke has sold Bill Hay, Murray Balfour and Ab McDonald in pre-draft deals to the Chicago Black Hawks; all three of them have helped that once pathetic organization to move into comparative contention. Earlier, Eddie Litzenberger and Dollard St. Laurent were shipped to the Hawks. Selke says Chicago has been his market because the Hawk owners, James Norris Jr. and Arthur Wirtz, "have lost millions trying to give their fans a good team and they've never complained."

Significantly, though, the Canadiens have not yet lost a player in the draft itself who has come back to distress them noticeably. Accordingly, there seems no reason to assume that Selke and his aides—Ken Reardon, the club's vice-president, Toe Blake, the coach, and Sam Pollock, who guides the farm system—will suddenly be struck with myopia in spotting their potential stars when they name their proctected 20. Similarly, it would seem reasonable that they'll be as adroit in plucking other teams' star prospects, if they choose, as the others may be in fingering theirs.

The team's present president, Senator Hartland Molson, who bought the Canadiens in 1957 for reportedly more than $1 million, has continued the carte-blanche policy with Selke that was originated by Senator Raymond. Add all this up and on the record it would appear that if there is any embarrassment over players in the future it will be an embarrassment of riches.

Montreal lost to Chicago in the semifinals that year to end their string of Cups at five and Selke retired as general manager of the Canadiens at the end of the 1963–64 season. He had helped create two hockey dynasties, in Toronto and Montreal, and was associated with nine Stanley Cup winning teams—six with the Habs and three with the Maple Leafs. A member of the Hockey Hall of Fame, Frank Selke faithfully watched games at the Forum from his seat behind the net until just before his death at age 92 in 1985.

One of the deans of Canadian sports writers, Trent Frayne wrote his first piece for Maclean's in 1941 and has contributed hundreds of pieces to the magazine since. He is the winner of numerous awards and has written 14 books, including six on hockey. Frayne lives in Toronto with his wife, fellow writer and frequent Maclean's contributor June Callwood.

The Maple Leaf Money Machine

Peter Gzowski

March 21, 1964—One Sunday evening this winter, I decided to have a look at my favorite hockey team, the Toronto Maple Leafs, away from their usual setting of Maple Leaf Gardens, and I went down to one of the six Toronto movie houses where their match in Detroit with the Red Wings would be visible, live, on a giant television screen. Tickets, I had read in the paper, were $1.25, $2 and $2.50. I bought one at $2. This put me in the "blues," for exactly half the price I would have paid the evening before to see the Leafs in living color from a blue seat at the Gardens. By curtain, or faceoff, time the house was about three-quarters full, and when Frank Mahovlich scored after five minutes of the first period there was a loud roar of appreciation. The theatre I had chosen was in the Italian district of Toronto, and I heard someone in the greys behind me yell, "*bella* goal!"

The second period was scoreless and a little dull. I began to wish I'd bought a $1.25 ticket, since my position in the blues, about ten rows from the front, gave me the feeling I was watching a television set attached to the end of my nose. Sometimes the picture flopped, and all our heads bobbed in unison. Early in the third period Detroit tied the score (the game ended in a tie) and for two or three minutes the theatre rocked with rhythmic clapping, as several hundred adults tried to encourage the ghostly, flickering image of a hockey team playing two hundred and thirty miles away.

Enthusiasm for hockey in Toronto is so great that Famous Players will not be able to meet the demand for seats—even at $2.50—this year. Already some of the thirty-two games they will project have been sold out. By next year the theatre owners may well have people lining up for season's tickets—a situation that already applies at Maple Leaf Gardens, where there hasn't been an empty seat for a hockey game since February 27, 1946, and where the waiting list is now nearly 10,000 names long.

The Leafs are a national institution. They are the co-stars of the most popular television program any Canadian has yet thought up, *Hockey Night in Canada*, on which they alternate with the Montreal Canadiens. (Southern Ontario sees the Leafs *every* Saturday night on the CBC, and all of their Wednesday night games against Canadiens are on private television as well.) If the sale of sweaters patterned after those of NHL teams is a measure of popularity, the Leafs are not quite *the* national hockey team of Canada—Canadien sweaters outsell theirs by a slight margin—but they dominate the area they're centred in; 80 per cent of the sweaters sold in Ontario are theirs. Many of their players are popular luncheon-club speakers and nearly all of them have at least one commercial product to endorse. Sixteen Leafs, for instance, recently lined up for a certain razor-blade ad—and got their $50 each without even having to shave with one blade. Their coach has a weekly TV show in Toronto and is the author of a book of hockey tips available from a cereal company, and even their trainer is so famous he is pictured in some ads for the cars he sells during the off season. The Gardens sells Maple Leaf pennants (in three designs), serving trays (with engraved autographs), crests, pins, lighters, mascot dolls, team pictures, souvenir pucks, sticks and miniatures of the Stanley Cup, which the Leafs won last year.

The Leafs began turning a profit almost as soon as Conn Smythe put them together, in 1927, out of the remnants of the old Toronto St. Patrick's team. The Gardens, which is to the Leafs what Buckingham Palace is to the Queen, was built in 1931, at a cost of about $1.5 million, and by 1934, right in the eye of the Depression, it paid a dividend to its shareholders. It has not missed a year since, and the total of dividends paid is now over $3 million. With the advent of pay-TV, which adds nothing to hockey's overhead but will add greatly to the Leafs' income, there is every prospect of the Gardens raising dividends in the future.

In the world of sports promotion, where nearly everyone loses money and where even the winners have off-years, this makes the Gardens—whose profits are unaffected by war, peace, the national economy, or how many goals the team scores—appear to be the original money machine.

Sports "promotion," however, as it is applied by the Gardens toward the Leafs, involves almost none of the cigar-smoke-and-baloney aura the word usually conjures up. (*Almost*, I said. There are a couple of points to be raised later.) What the Gardens has been selling, over the years, is a package, and the wrappings have usually been as businesslike and even dignified as it is possible to make the violent, and often brutal, game of hockey appear. As just one tiny example of the impression that the Leafs' owners have striven to give the public: Conn Smythe would sometimes introduce his great centreman Syl Apps (who is, incidentally, now a member of the Ontario legislature) as "our captain, who doesn't smoke or drink." The Gardens building itself is kept just a trifle cleaner than St. James Cathedral, and people going to a hockey game directly from dinner at the King Edward Hotel do not look overdressed.

The packaging of the Leafs extends into the players' lives. When they show up for practice at the Gardens they must be wearing a jacket and tie, as, indeed, they must when they appear anywhere on the road. (Although at Tam O'Shanter, the suburban curling and golf club where they practise when the Gardens is full of rodeo dirt or other obstacles, they are allowed to dress casually.) And it also extends to *Hockey Night in Canada*. The television rights to the Leafs are owned, through a complex and long-standing arrangement, by MacLaren Advertising Co. Ltd., on behalf of the two companies that sponsor the Leaf and Canadien games, Imperial Oil and Molson's Brewery. Theoretically, the Leafs and their management are not in the television business at all. But it is unlikely, to say the least, that a barrage of critical comment about hockey will ever be launched from a broadcast originating in the Gardens. For one thing, Ed Fitkin, the personable commentator who brings us the "videotape highlights," is also the public relations director of the Gardens, and it's hard to picture him saying, "Well, the Leafs sure stunk up the joint in that period," even when the Leafs, as they sometimes do, stink up the joint. *Hockey Night* is not in the fair comment business; it is an entertainment package, and that concept so pervades every minute the show is on the air that I imagine if Bill Hewitt, the play-by-play announcer, were to say, "We're having a dull game here tonight," television sets all over the country would explode.

Something *almost* exploded this season when Johnny Bower, the Leafs' remarkable and immensely popular goaltender, was being interviewed between periods during a Molson's segment of the program. "What do you do in the summer?" the interviewer made the mistake of asking him. "I work for the John Labatt Brewing Company," said Bower. Neither Bower nor the interviewer lost his job.

This apparently makes it more acceptable to undercut the sponsor—if inadvertently—than to commit the infraction that the men who run hockey call "knocking the game"—even off television. In 1962, Scott Young, the Toronto *Globe and Mail* columnist and, at that time, between-periods *Hockey Night* commentator, wrote in the *Globe* that the story put out by the Leaf ownership about selling Frank Mahovlich for a million dollars was pure hokum, calculated to get the Leafs some newspaper space during the football season. The three principal shareholders of the Gardens, according to one of them, John Bassett, felt "extreme concern." "We took our case to the people responsible for the program," Bassett said not long ago. "We told them, A, what Young had

Johnny Bower makes a save off Gordie Howe in Game One of the Stanley Cup finals in Maple Leaf Gardens, April 11, 1964.

written was detrimental to hockey, and, B, he was an inefficient television personality. At the end of the season, I guess they saw our case." Young was fired.

Hockey, of course, is what makes the Maple Leaf money machine go, and the atmosphere of serious business that surrounds the Gardens and its management is also evident in the way the Leafs play. Most of the Leaf players simply don't appear to enjoy the game quite as much as the other teams in the league. The Chicago Black Hawks, for example, when they're having a good night, seem almost to explode down the ice, and there is an air of sheer joy about their young star Bobby Hull when he's skating well. But when the Leafs are going well, there's a doggedness about their play, they forecheck ferociously; they knock a lot of people down at the blue line, and they grab and hold a lot more people in front of the goal mouth. They seem to be a group of men getting a job done—which, of course, they are—more than a bunch of healthy males playing a game, which they also are. Defeat, as the famous sign in their dressing room says, does not rest lightly on their shoulders, and neither does anything else. They are very serious fellows.

It is not only hockey that they are serious about. Nearly every regular on the Leafs has an outside interest, usually in business, in which he capitalizes on the name he has made in hockey or the time it allows him between seasons, or both. Many of the younger Leafs are studying at university in the off season, and Bob Pulford completed his BA at McMaster in Hamilton last summer. With the income from their outside activities, together with their team salaries and bonuses (minimum NHL salaries are now $7,000 a year), there are probably very few established Leafs making less than $15,000 annually, and certainly some making more than double that.

Allan Stanley is one of the few Leafs in history who have flunked in politics; he once tried for the provincial Conservative nomination in Timmins, Ont. The latest of a line of successful Leaf politicians—which has included Bucko MacDonald, Howie Meeker and Syl Apps—is Red Kelly, the Liberal Member of Parliament for York West, in Toronto. Kelly's lives sometimes get intertwined. After one game the Leafs played in New York this season, an American fan bearded him in the dressing room. The fan gave him a folder full of information about the labor troubles on the Great Lakes. Kelly took it with him on his hurried flight to Ottawa the next morning. He was still carrying it when he entered his Parliament Hill office, and when he heard his secretary say, "Oh, Mr. Kelly, there's a lady on the phone for you now," Kelly took the call. The woman's voice said, "Why on earth does that Punch Imlach always blame Johnny Bower when the Leafs lose?"

One of the reasons for the kind of hockey the Leafs play, and the kind of public figures they appear to be, may simply be Toronto. Only four of the current Leafs were not born in Ontario and one of *them* went to school in Toronto, as did, by my count, eleven others. This naturally gives them a much stronger feeling of playing for the old home town than any of the NHL teams except the Montreal Canadiens, who, as the national team of French Canada, are another special case. The Leafs are a part of the community, recognized everywhere, and carry the reputation and tradition of their team with them wherever they go. This is another fact that doesn't hurt their business careers. Andy Bathgate, for instance, was the highest-scoring New York Ranger in history, and one of the most lustrous stars in the NHL for the past five or six years, but was seldom able to cash in on his abilities in New York. Now that the Leafs have acquired him in a late-season trade, Toronto may expect to see his name in newspaper ads slightly less often than Eaton's.

Another reason why the Leafs play the kind of hockey that has won them the last two Stanley Cups is named Bert Olmstead. Olmstead was 32 years old when the Leafs, who had finished last the year before, drafted him from Montreal in 1958, and he'd already put in more than eight years in the NHL. On the ice he was a workhorse, a tireless checker and one of the most effective men at getting the puck out of a scramble in a corner ever to play in the league. His aggressive play was one of the reasons the Canadiens won four Stanley Cups. Off the ice, too, he was a tough guy, who was once charged with assault for flattening a critic in a tavern washroom. He was a pusher, and between periods he would lash anyone he didn't think was pulling his weight. In those days many of the men who are now the mainstays of the Leafs—Pulford, Brewer, Keon, Baun—were just getting used to big-time hockey. When Olmstead told them in the dressing room to "get off your butt and start playing hockey or I'll stuff this stick down your throat," they would usually start playing hockey. Olmstead had a particular influence on Bob Pulford, with whom he roomed, and it is not entirely coincidental that Pulford's energetic, persistent play has been one of the most enjoyable aspects of the Leafs' games for the last four seasons.

Olmstead left the Leafs in 1962, and, although they had their best season since 1948 last year, winning both the league championship and the Stanley Cup, they have not been quite the same team without him. They lack a leader on the ice, the one man who can inspire the whole team, as Beliveau does Montreal, Howe does Detroit, and Hull does Chicago. The player they have counted on to be their "big man" for the past three or four years, Frank Mahovlich, a much vilified athlete of enormous talent, has had problems getting the lead out recently, and has turned out to be a "big man" who doesn't score very many goals and who can't, or won't, check. And it is still too early to see if Bathgate, who was the fourth-highest scorer in the league when the Leafs got him but is nearly as undetermined a checker as Mahovlich, will provide the lift they need.

Just as Mahovlich and Bathgate are exceptions to my generalization about doggedness, there is it least one notable exception to the ones I made earlier about complete seriousness and propriety. Eddie Shack, one of the most exciting skaters in hockey and by all odds now the most popular player in Toronto, is one of the least serious people in the world. He enjoys skating, travelling, yelling, shooting, kidding—life. He arrived in the NHL at the age of 21 as a functional illiterate, but he has been going to school and his native stupidity is roughly equal to that of the former Roy, now Baron, Thomson. He is an adept trader-upper of automobiles and a wily buyer-and-seller of just about everything anyone he meets wants to buy or sell, and he is a very foxy euchre player indeed.

But the Leafs, as a team, are more mechanics than artists, and the big problem for the man who has to make them win is getting them what athletes call "up" for enough games a season. Since there is not a great deal of difference between the NHL teams with the most physically gifted athletes and those with the least, a team that *is* "up"—or alert, and hungry to win—can often knock off a physically superior team that simply isn't in the right frame of mind that night. The Leafs' frame of mind is in the care of Punch Imlach, their coach and general manager. Imlach is one of the few men who have taken over the reins of a big-time professional team without having made it in the big time himself. But it's difficult to imagine what he might have achieved as a coach if, as a player, he'd been another Rocket Richard. He is a bald, superstitious man of 46 whose manner can be friendly and domineering at the same time. His single purpose in life, for the moment anyway, is to win hockey games. If he has to ride roughshod over some personalities to do so, well, he rides, and the hockey games, in the main, have been won. Professional sport is one of the few walks of life where a man's success or failure can be measured instantly: What kind of day did you have at the office? Well, not too bad, I guess, but that secretary problem is really getting me down, etc. But: what kind of night did you have at the *hockey rink*? We won. This factor of instant measurement, surely, is one reason why the men involved in sports are so wrapped up in them: you can't just do your job, you have to win at it, and that takes a great deal of attention.

Imlach took over the Leafs in 1958. They had finished last the year before and were apparently well on their way to finishing out of the playoffs again. But he souped them up for a roaring finish, got them into the Stanley Cup finals, and in the next few years steadily built their personnel and morale until, last spring, they were the best hockey team in the world.

One of Imlach's most effective ways of tinkering with the money machine has been to add to it well-broken-in players from other teams in the league. Among veterans who have come to Toronto to play out their careers in recent years have been Bower, Kelly, Stanley, Bronco Horvath, Eddie Litzenberger, Larry Regan and, most recently of all, of course, Bathgate and Don McKenney from New York.

Imlach's system is one of needling the players who must be angry to play well and coddling those who give their all anyway—Dave Keon, the Leafs' quick, brilliant little centre, for instance, is often excused from Monday morning practice when the Leafs return from a road trip. Imlach does use a number of gimmicks that seem to be strange ways to treat grown men. Before a trip to Montreal in February, he gave each member of the team a copy of *The Power of Positive Thinking*, by Norman Vincent Peale, whereupon they went and got themselves positively clobbered by the Canadiens. He has been known to send five defencemen out on his power play just to humiliate his forwards. His statements to the press are often carefully tailored for the ears of the team—he does not seem to mind criticism of himself, but sometimes thinks the writers are unfair to his players. And he slaps on fines that would make adults quit nearly any other job in the world; $25 for being late for practice is one example. But he is convinced that all his acts help him win hockey games, and who are we to argue with him?

I was with the Leafs on the weekend they played their worst game of the year Saturday night and probably their best one Sunday. In the first game the Boston Bruins, a physically inferior team, edged them 11–0. The next night the Leafs beat the Chicago Black Hawks 2–0.

The Leafs had been heading for some sort of nosedive for a couple of weeks before the Boston game, losing one here and one there, winning a couple by luck, but generally playing sloppy hockey—by their standards anyway. They were still in a tight three-way race for first place, though, because Chicago and Montreal were idling too, and it just might have occurred to the Leaf players that they could finish on top without putting in too much effort. In the Boston game, they were terrible. The Bruins' good, workmanlike rookie, Gary Dornhoefer, scored 53 seconds after the opening faceoff, and the Leafs never seemed to notice they were behind. Before the first period was half over, the score was 4–0 and the crowd was ironically cheering every save made by the Toronto goalie, Don Simmons.

Without the one big man to inspire them, the Leafs, when they collapse, collapse as a unit. On the ice as well as off it, there are no cliques among them—they are a *team*—so that when an outbreak of lethargy hits a few of them, it can quickly become epidemic.

We outsiders did not find out how defeat rested on their shoulders that night. After the game, the Leafs packed quickly and in near silence, and went off in twos and threes to Union Station where a CNR train was waiting to whisk them to Chicago. The players headed straight for their sleeping car, and the rest of the group travelling with the Leafs—the reporters; Imlach and his assistant King Clancy; Foster and Bill Hewitt; a 13-year-old boy who had won a trip with the Leafs in a Gardens' draw and who had lost a nickel on the game; the boy's brother-in-law; and a Gardens public relations man—all sat in the lounge car.

Imlach and Clancy pored over a master sheet of what they both call "statistics," and shook their heads.

"It has to be a joke," Clancy said.

"It's the worst —— beating I've ever taken," Imlach said. Imlach uses a distressing number of ——'s when he talks. The 13-year-old was at the other end of the car. "I've got to tell them about it."

I said that most of the players would already know. "I can't take that chance," Imlach said. "I've got to make —— sure they know how bad they were."

The Leafs had used a youngster from their junior team, the Toronto Marlboros, in the Boston game. He had not played noticeably worse than the veterans. "I told him in front of the team," Imlach said, "that I wasn't taking him on this trip, because I wouldn't humiliate him by making him play with a team like this."

"We've got one line that didn't get a hit, didn't get a shot and was on the ice for five of their goals," said Clancy, who counts every body contact and every shot each player gets, and picks his own, private, three stars after every game. He carefully kept the statistics sheet hidden from me.

"The breaks were all against them too," said Foster Hewitt, perhaps not realizing he was not on the air.

"Breaks ——!" said Imlach.

"I was going to ask you what you thought was the turning point of the game," one of the newspapermen said to Imlach. Imlach laughed. "When we skated out onto the —— ice," he said, and we all went to bed.

In Chicago, the Leafs spent Sunday as they do most days on the road. The devout went to church, the rest killed time. Some had eaten on the train, and the others gathered in the hotel coffee shop. The public relations man introduced the team's 13-year-old guest to the players in the restaurant. Told the boy had lost his nickel bet the night before, George Armstrong said, "We'll try to win it back for you tonight," which may come perilously close to the league's rule against fraternizing with gamblers. The players were restrained after their performance the night before, but not morose. However heavily defeat may have been resting on their shoulders, they were bearing the weight.

By mid-morning, most of the players had gone to their rooms to rest or catch up on sleep missed on the train. They take rooms even when they're not staying overnight. Most have roommates on the road, but a few, like Ron Stewart, who snores, have single rooms.

Early in the afternoon Imlach called a team meeting in the suite he was sharing with Clancy, and, presumably, told the players how bad they were. He also told them that he was putting it squarely to them; he was bringing in the goalie from the Leafs' farm team in Denver. If they were scored on heavily tonight, they must take the blame themselves. If not, Simmons could be held responsible for the catastrophic score of the night before. (Bower was along on the trip, but had an injured catching hand.) Suddenly the phone rang, just when many of the players must have been thinking that Simmons, having fallen, ought to be given a chance to ride the horse again immediately. Imlach answered, and learned that the aircraft carrying his goalie couldn't land in Chicago, and was turning back to Des Moines. Simmons was under the gun.

The Leafs, looking thoughtful, came down from their meeting for a communal steak. At around five they began making their way over to Chicago Stadium.

Imlach had invited me to travel in the team's car on the way back to Toronto, and about half an hour before game time I dropped into the dressing room to leave my bag. It was as silent as a library, with the players, some of them still not completely dressed for the game, sitting on the benches that ringed the room, contemplating their equipment bags as if they were going to paint pictures of them.

Every NHL team plays 70 games a season, and while all of them play some games as if they were what athletes call "laughers," it is a rare player who doesn't tighten up with excitement before he is on the ice. One of the oldest veterans in the league is still sick with tension 70 times a year. I left, feeling as if I had interrupted the service of a church I didn't understand, and went to get a beer and a program, and take my seat.

Watching a hockey game in Chicago is like watching the Christians against the Lions, except that in Chicago most of the animals are in the stands. When Reg Fleming, one of the Black Hawks' tough guys, was injured in a fall he took untouched by a Leaf, the crowd started chanting, "We want Howie," a call for Howie Young, who was then the Hawks' even-tougher guy. They got him, later, but by that time the game was as rough as it was going to get. At one point, Brewer, the Leafs' bad man, speared Stan Mikita, which is to say he rammed the business end of his hockey stick into Mikita's stomach. It was as vicious a spearing as I had ever seen. Mikita, a dirty but exceedingly effective hockey player, clutched his stomach and fell as if axed, and another Hawk, young Autry Erickson I think, swung his stick at Brewer's skull. Brewer ducked behind the net, and then backed into a corner, four Hawks surrounding him with their sticks at slope arms. With the crowd, most of whom had seen Brewer's spear, yelling for blood, I thought perhaps I was about to see hockey's first killing. As the Leafs moved in to Brewer's aid, Mikita, who is almost as good an actor as he is a hockey player, got quickly to his feet and joined his teammates, with his stick up too. Later, Brewer was to say, "I wasn't really afraid because I knew none of those guys coming at me first would really hit me, but when I saw Mikita coming around behind me, I thought there'd be real trouble." As for his own spear: "Mikita had been doing it to our guys. Just before I got him he'd given me a really wild one in the groin. You just can't let anyone get away with that." As the Leafs piled from behind into the Black Hawk war party, the sticks came down. There were a few minutes of fist fighting, with no clear decisions, and the game went back to relative peace—except that a few fans, if that is the word, threw pieces of their chairs onto the ice, and one hit Brewer's shoulder pad.

The Leafs played determined, hard hockey, knocking more Black Hawks down in the first period than they had Bruins in the whole game the night before, according to Clancy's hit charts. The Leafs have the best defence in the league: Allan Stanley, who falls short of being the fastest skater in the NHL by roughly a 108 players, but whose poke-check is a work of art; Carl Brewer, who may be the *fastest* defenceman and who is almost as good at his specialties of shoulder-fakes, lob-shots and holding sweaters as Stanley is at his; Bob Baun, a punishing body-checker; and Tim Horton, a wise, tough veteran who was playing so well through the first half of this season he almost became the inspiration the whole team needs. They have a complete squadron of capable, seasoned forwards, and when everyone is knocking opponents down they look unbeatable—but whether this is a cause of their problems this year or just a symptom, no one can say.

On the train back they were relaxed and chatty, sitting around the smoking room at either end of their car, wearing underwear or pyjamas, soaking up the apparently innumerable soft drinks they had bought at the station. A euchre game in one smoker went on past three until the last tension drained out of the last players. No one talked much about the hockey game. At one point, Shack looked at Mahovlich and said, "Man, you were really playing tonight," and Mahovlich, who really had been, just grinned.

The Leafs finished third that season, but went on to win the Stanley Cup, defeating Detroit in the finals.

Peter Gzowski was managing editor of Maclean's *when he wrote this story, but left eight months later to work as a writer and editor. Gzowski returned to* Maclean's *in 1969 for a nine-month stint, this time as editor, and then went on to become one of Canada's best-known television and radio broadcasters.*

Stars, Heroes and Innovators

Lester Patrick's 50 Years on Ice

Bruce Hutchison

March 1, 1950—It is curious, when you come to think of it, that the most vivid symbol of Canadian life consists of a game in which 12 overstuffed men on artificial feet use an artificial wooden arm to propel a piece of artificial rubber along a stretch of artificial ice. Yet, Canadians play hockey, talk hockey and dream hockey as naturally as they breathe. Hockey, better than any other thing, expresses Canada. It is, perhaps, our only truly national expression which cuts across language, race, age and distance.

But hockey has become much more than a game. It is a myth. By now the myth has produced its first mythological figure. His name is Lester Patrick.

Lester has marched across the world (on skates) only to be sucked back to his original home, having accomplished nothing but an epic. He is home again in Victoria, after 50 years of hockey—a powerful, white-haired and handsome old gentleman of 66 who could pass for 50. The epic will not be recounted in detail since most Canadians know it already—the lean, gangling Montreal amateur with a face like an eagle and a body of structural steel who invested the family wealth, hardly short of disaster, in the hockey teams and rinks of the Pacific Coast, played spectacular hockey himself until he was on the edge of 50, managed five world championship clubs, sold his teams just in time to the National Hockey League and climaxed his public career managing the New York Rangers.

All the exploits of a figure who was part athlete, part tough businessman and part adventurer have made Lester one of the most famous Canadians of his time. His reputation is largely caricature, for under the public fantasy (which Lester tolerated because it was good business but never liked much) lies in fact an extremely simple Canadian, highly domesticated, God-fearing, studious, businesslike—essentially a family man and small-town citizen with a single aberration, a boy's love of hockey.

What follows is not a profile of Lester but an attempt to distill what he has learned about hockey, and about Canadian life which it reflects, since he cut his first crooked stick in the woods and played shinny on the icy sidewalks of Montreal.

After many days of talk, with Patrick leaping across the floor behind an imaginary puck, thrusting an imaginary stick in the listener's face and scoring imaginary goals from the blue line and after digesting his scrapbooks that weigh 48 pounds 12 ounces, I can tell you what the man who made that epic thinks of hockey. He thinks hockey is better today than ever. To old hockey players and to most Canadians over 40 this statement will come as a shattering heresy. And inevitably, to prove that hockey has become a sissy game, they will retell the legend of Cyclone Taylor, who used to bet that he could score goals skating backward and win his bets every time.

Lester played with Taylor and thinks him the greatest hockey performer in history, but he saw the original incident from the ice and herewith deflates the legend for the first time: "In 1909–10, Taylor and I were playing for Renfrew. Taylor had played for the Silver Seven of Ottawa (what a team!) and now he was back in Ottawa to play against his old teammates. He was a modest fellow and still is, and a very fine gentleman, but he liked to joke in those days. And in the old Windsor Hotel, before the game, some sports writers asked him how he expected to get past the Ottawa defence. Taylor laughed—that contagious boy's laugh of his. 'Why,' he said, 'I can score on those fellows skating backward.'

"Well, of course he didn't mean it seriously. But on one of his rushes the Ottawa defence stopped him cold and turned him around with his back to the Ottawa goal. He flipped the puck, back-handed. It nosed past the goaltender. I was on the ice and saw the whole thing and we went on playing. But by the time the sports writers had finished with it you'd have thought the Cyclone had deliberately won a bet, and you'd have thought he repeated this performance just about every night afterward. The Cyclone didn't make the legend. The public did."

It is staggering and rather sad for a Canadian to hear the truth about Taylor's famous goal. It is like being told that Laura Secord had no cow, that Sir John A. was a teetotaller. Fortunately no one will believe the truth. "And in case you're disappointed," said Lester, "I'll tell you something still more amazing that Taylor actually did, and I saw him do it. (Patrick began to demonstrate by skating across the living room floor.) I forget just when it was but I can see the Cyclone now—taking the puck down the entire rink, being forced behind the opposing goal, slipping out with the puck, skating all the way back and around his own goal, and then down the ice all the way again, through the whole opposing team and scoring, without the help of anyone! Skating backward," said Lester, retreating zig-zag across the room, "was nothing to the Cyclone. He could skate faster backward than almost anyone else could skate frontward. But taking the puck twice down the ice, holding it all the way and finally scoring—that was special, even for him."

The truth, as Lester sees it, is that there are few if any hockey stars today as good as such immortals as Hod Stuart or Tom Phillips and few, he might have added but didn't, as good as Lester Patrick. There is none, he says, as good as Taylor. But the game is better, faster, more scientific and more spectacular.

This is indeed a heresy but Lester is entitled to utter it, for his experience in the actual play of hockey, apart from its management, is unequalled. He played in the East in his teens and twenties and had won a Stanley Cup virtually single-handed before he moved out to Nelson, B.C., to work in his father's lumber camps and mills. He returned to the East in the winters to play his first professional hockey and then, tired of such migrations, established with his father, Joseph Patrick, and his brother, Frank, the rinks of Vancouver, Victoria, New Westminster and later Seattle into which the whole Patrick fortune was plunged and almost lost. And all those years, east and west, he was playing hockey himself as one of the greatest defencemen of all time, first because it saved a player's wages and, second, because he couldn't live without a hockey stick in his hands.

Comparing modern with ancient hockey, you have to remember, says Lester, that a seven-man team used to play 60 minutes—no substitutions allowed unless a player was knocked out completely—and by the end of the game every player was exhausted. That cut down speed. Lester himself invented the substitution of an entire forward line in the famous Stanley Cup series of 1925 in Victoria and revolutionized hockey overnight. "The Canadiens came west and those easterners who came with them in their hard derby hats bet their last dollar that an upstart team in Victoria (Victoria, the city of flowers at Christmas) couldn't stop them. Who could stop Morenz and Joliat and Boucher? Who could score on the great Vezina? But I knew we'd win because our second forward line would just tire them out, and it did. "From then on, with three, then four interchangeable lines spelling each other, the game speeded up and it's immeasurably faster now than ever."

A defenceman's job in the old days was to get the puck and hurl it up to the other end of the rink. When Lester stopped off at Brandon, Man., in the fall of 1903 and was persuaded to play hockey there—working in a laundry all day—he was expected to stay where he belonged, on the defensive as point. (The defence then consisted of the point and cover point, one in front of the other and the rover in front of them.) In the first game Lester rushed down the ice and scored, and the local management rushed with similar speed into the dressing room and almost fired him for spoiling the team's strategy. After a few more goals it realized that Lester had something and allowed him to rush as he pleased.

Soon all the defences began to rush until Art Duncan, a defenceman, became the leading scorer of the world champion Vancouver Maroons. That change of tactics also meant speed. However, the biggest revolution in hockey, Lester thinks, was the Coast League's introduction of the blue lines and the forward pass in the season of 1913–14. Lester's brother, Frank, thought them up when he saw a game between Vancouver and Victoria interrupted every minute or so by an offside whistle. At first the eastern leagues wouldn't hear of the new rule. Now, Lester asks, who would abandon it? This alone speeded up the game about 50 per cent, he says.

After he and his brother had established the Pacific Coast teams, they set out to win the Stanley Cup. They had to do it on finances vastly inferior to those of the eastern teams which they raided for players, paying high salaries to lure such stars as Taylor westward. In such a process a man learns management as well as hockey. In 1926, the Patrick empire, so glittering on the outside, had no negotiable asset but its teams. The game was expanding into the United States; Lester had the only teams ready to fill the American arenas and he knew it. So he waited and the eastern Mohammed, as he expected, came to the western mountain, desperate not for individual players but working hockey machines. The Patricks sold their playing property for a quarter of a million and cut the losses of their original investment to a round hundred thousand. They were glad to escape so easily for, better than anyone, they know how money can be lost when it is put on ice.

Comparing present-day hockey with the past, Lester says, for example, that no better team than the Montreal Wanderers of 1905–06, 1906–07 and 1907–08 ever touched the ice, but he admits his old age and prejudice. Everyone who pretends to know Canadian history remembers that the Wanderers, captained by Lester, won the first game of the 1905–06 Stanley Cup series by 9 to 1 in Montreal. At Ottawa three nights later, in the two-game total goal final, the Wanderers quickly made it 10 to 1. And then came the strangest catastrophe in the annals of hockey—Ottawa scored nine goals, one after the other, evening the score. Young Captain Patrick saw his team fall to pieces before his eyes. He doesn't know to this day what happened to them. He remembers vaguely that he picked up a loose puck at his own goal, started down

Lester Patrick at age 66.

the ice and saw the puck sail into the Ottawa net. He repeated a few minutes later. That has been called the greatest single performance in a Stanley Cup series—a legend only second to the Cyclone's back-skating goal. Lester is old enough and scarred enough—50 inches of stitches on his skin—not to be boastful or overmodest. That famous game, he said, shows how hockey has improved. No modern team would let nine goals past it in about 30 minutes, said Lester.

Lester speaks as a professional player and manager, the most experienced in the business. But he had played a lot of amateur hockey before three telegrams reached him in Nelson, B.C., one day in November, 1909, the first inviting him to play professionally for Ottawa, the second with the same invitation from Montreal and the third from Renfrew, Ont. Lester's father, the late Joseph Patrick, was against professionalism, advised his son to stay in the lumber business with him. The only lumber that really interested Lester was that used in hockey sticks. Being of age and, as he thought, in his right mind, he offered to play for Montreal for $1,200 because he liked Montreal, asked $1,500 from Ottawa because he wasn't attracted to it and as for Renfrew—who had ever heard of Renfrew? To make sure he wouldn't go there Lester asked $3,000, which no one would pay.

Within an hour back came a telegram from Renfrew asking him what he was waiting for. Lester put up one last defensive play—he would play for Renfrew if he could bring along his brother, Frank, at $2,000. Renfrew wired the two Patricks to catch the first train. That was how Lester became a professional, drawing a salary of $3,000 a season.

Not long afterward, Frank proposed to his father that he invest the proceeds of his lumber business, something under $350,000, in a hockey league on the Pacific Coast. At a family conference called to consider all such decisions, Lester voted against the venture. Yes, unbelievable as it seems, Lester voted against hockey. He thought it wouldn't pay. (He was right.) His father sided with Frank. The rest is public history—the creation of the Pacific Coast league, the raid on eastern teams, the travels of the Stanley Cup from the East to Vancouver, Seattle and Victoria.

Lester speaks with authority as a manager. Managing the Victoria and Seattle teams, his family's own property, was relatively simple—apart from the fact that in those early days of professional hockey he was constantly on the edge of bankruptcy, simply because the coast cities could not support the kind of hockey Lester was giving them. But when he had sold his teams to the National League and thought he was through with hockey only to find himself invited by the New York Rangers to take charge of their club, he was playing with other people's money in the big town.

Applying his own small-town methods to a big-town team, he found that they worked—not only to win championships but to attract crowds and make money for his employers. They worked so well indeed, that the New York capitalists, who had hired him for his hockey brains entirely, found that they had hired at once an able businessman and an impresario with a flair which excited the dull appetites of the metropolis. Out of the lessons of those years Lester concludes that while the ideal raw material for a star is a boy with a fine body and a rather simple, uncomplicated and easy-going brain which concentrates on hockey, you can't be sure this combination will work. "Look, I'm in the dressing room before the game. I've given my last instructions. Some of the boys are sitting calmly, looking at the floor or the ceiling, thinking about nothing and worrying about nothing. Then I look at a great star like Bill Cook. Is he at ease? No, sir, he's on the edge of the bench, he's rocking back and forth and it's all he can do to hold himself down.

"The calm boys I can rely on for their usual steady game, but for super-hockey that wins championships I have to rely on the Bill Cooks. It isn't an invariable rule but in general, if you find a great player he'll be as tense before a game as a race horse at the post."

What does a great player need next to a good body and the instinct called hockey brains? Lester answers without hesitation: "Courage. Above all, courage. And I don't mean just physical courage—no one plays hockey long without a lot of that—I mean moral courage."

Given physique, character and harmony with his teammates, what is the next essential ingredient of a great player? "Quick reflexes. What makes a quick reflex I don't know, but I do know that a hockey player must react more quickly than any other athlete."

There are a few other obvious ingredients. A boy must be able to skate, and most boys never learn how, for hockey purposes. He doesn't have to be a speed champion. He must have learned stickhandling in his boyhood for it can never be learned afterward. He must have a fair shot, though this can be improved with practice. He must have, above all, the capacity and willingness to learn.

When does the average player reach his peak? At 30, Lester calculates. "You never lose your skill, but at 35 you suddenly find your legs getting unaccountably heavy. They're the first thing to go. When I was playing at 37 and then again at 42, it got mighty tough on the old man's legs. The rest of me seemed as good as ever."

A player at his peak may have every other quality and lack the odd quality called color. "In hockey Cyclone Taylor had color—what color, like a neon light!—and Morenz, Nighbor, Shore, Moose Johnson, Ching Johnson, Frederickson and dozens more I could mention. Jack Walker, who made the hook check famous, was one of the greatest players who ever lived and not far short of the brainiest I ever knew, but somehow, no matter how brilliant he was, he didn't bring the crowd to their feet. He lacked color. So did his teammate Frank Foyston, and there were few better in centre ice. Why? You'd better ask a psychologist. I'm only an ex-hockey player," says Lester.

In Patrick's book, the greatest player in history was the one and only "Cyclone." "He was," says Lester, "as near perfection as we shall probably ever see. He had the speed of Morenz, the grace of Bun Cook, the poke check of Frank Boucher, the shot of Tom Phillips. He began as a defenceman in the East and when he came West my brother, Frank, said to him, 'I'm going to make you the greatest centre-ice man in history.' The Cyclone laughed and thought it was crazy. But Frank was right."

The bulk of good players come from the poorer groups of society, not from the well-to-do, Patrick has found. "The reason is obvious when you come to think of it. On average, the boy in a rich or even a moderately prosperous home is inclined to take it easy. He's driving a car instead of walking. He's playing golf or tennis rather than hard team games. He probably gads around a lot at parties. He may drink a bit. His food is soft and rich. His body and, more important his attitude, is softer than a poor boy's. He doesn't have to be hard, as the poor boy does to survive.

"A poor boy is thrown up against the tough side of life from the start. He's toughened physically, and equally important, mentally. There will always be good hockey players in college and in well-to-do families, but on average they will come mostly from a poor environment."

That, Lester adds, is what makes hockey one of the major factors in the democracy of Canada—it is pre-eminently a poor boy's game, played on every pond and creek and flooded lot across the nation, and on the ice every boy is equal.

Patrick's training rules for his players are pretty simple—plenty of sleep, no dissipation, good digestible food. What if the player breaks the rules? Every man who has played under Lester in the last 40 years knows what happens then—the offender got the famous Patrick silent treatment.

In the spring of 1926, the world champion Victoria Cougars were riddled with injuries and in a slump. Lester, at 42 years of age, returned to the ice after five years of retirement. He was giving a pretty good imitation of himself and his scoring helped to lift the team from the basement into the western playoffs. On the prairie tour which would decide the western championship, a famous Cougar star seemed to crack up. He couldn't find the goal and he had stopped fighting.

One night in Saskatoon, Lester told his team to be back in the hotel by 11 at the latest. Most of them were in bed before 10. But the star had not turned up. Lester sat in the hotel lobby, waiting and at 2 a.m. the missing player reeled in with two friends, all equally high. Lester didn't even look at him. He stretched, yawned and walked upstairs to his room. For two days he simply ignored the offending player.

Before the decisive game of the series the player came to Lester in tears to ask forgiveness. "For God's sake, Lester," he cried, "why don't you talk to me? Tell me what you think of me, say anything you like to me, but say something!" Then Lester talked, without raising his voice, without change of expression and he made that young giant cringe. "And if you want to talk to me again," Lester concluded, "you get out on that ice and play some hockey." That night, the boy scored three goals and practically assured Victoria its place in the playoff series. He and Lester have been fast friends to this day.

The silent treatment worked equally well on another star who had held out, demanding more salary. Lester didn't argue, and left the fellow alone, stewing for weeks. Finally, the two met and it turned out that the player thought he was underpaid because he did not receive the salary of $3,500 paid to the great Frank Frederickson (a huge sum in those days). "Look," said Lester, "you don't have to play. I can replace you. But if you'll come to the opening game and stand in the crowd while everyone's cheering Frederickson, and if one fan, just one, ever mentions the fact that you're missing from the lineup, I'll double your salary."

"Give me your pen," said the player. "I'll sign."

Lester Patrick is also renowned for an incident in 1928 when, as the coach of the New York Rangers, he himself replaced his injured goalie to preserve a playoff win. Patrick spent his retirement in Victoria where he died in 1960 at age 76.

Bruce Hutchison, one of Canada's most respected journalists and public commentators, won three National Newspaper awards and wrote many books. A frequent contributor to Maclean's, *he died in Victoria in 1992 at age 91.*

Foster Hewitt: Play-by-Playboy

Trent Frayne

April 1, 1950 — There aren't many sports columnists in Canada who haven't observed at one time or another that there are two hockey games in Maple Leaf Gardens in Toronto on a Saturday night: the one on the ice and the one on the air.

The observation seldom is meant as a compliment to Foster Hewitt, who is fairly generally regarded as the most entertaining play-by-play announcer of them all, but it is, nevertheless, backhanded tribute to his artistry with a microphone. Bad game or good, Hewitt's method of describing what he sees spellbinds an audience estimated by surveys conducted by his sponsor, the Imperial Oil Company, at five million people in the United States and Canada. He has been doing it since 1931 and he will be doing it during the next couple of weeks as the annual Stanley Cup playoffs unwind.

Hewitt has become the best-known hockey announcer in the world. Everything he says about a hockey game is accurate but it's what he doesn't tell that sets him apart. He has the talent of eliminating the meaningless scrambles beneath his gondola and he gives voice only to developments of consequence. Thus, while the spectator absorbs the ragged and the brilliant, the listener hears only what is pertinent and significant. If it's a dull game the spectator is bored; the listener is entertained by its highlights.

Although Hewitt has been broadcasting hockey nationally for 20 years, employing all of the game's standard clichés ("It was a rousing first period with neither team asking quarter or giving it," "He had the goalkeeper at his mercy and made no mistake," "They came from behind in an uphill battle," etc.) the listening public, far from falling off, has increased annually, particularly in the United States which now, surveys show, has as many listeners as Canada.

Hewitt does broadcasts in which his fee is waived to charity yet his price on his services chases more prospective sponsors whimpering back to their vice-presidents' chairs than anyone else's. Conversely, he turns down lucrative assignments on other sports because he says he feels the public gets enough of Hewitt on hockey ("We don't want to saturate the air.") Hewitt, when he is talking about himself, says "we" more frequently than "I."

It is doubtful if more than a small fraction of one per cent of the five million listeners would know Hewitt if they talked to him. His flamboyant voice with the trenchant tones of an evangelist belongs to an almost embarrassingly modest, retiring and colorless paradox. Hewitt's conversational voice is not the voice Canada hears on Saturday. Inflections are similar but the volume and energy he puts into his broadcasts are missing.

"We speak from here," he explains, pointing to the base of his breastbone. "That's the only place we feel the effects of a broadcast, a dull pain here." His throat has never bothered him although there have been reports for years that he's had cancer. "There's never a trip around the country but somebody doesn't sidle up to me, peer solicitously for a moment and then softly enquire about my throat. Why, one night one of the Leaf doctors took me aside and asked me if there was anything he could do!"

He is tremendously conscientious about his broadcasts. He used to lose up to 20 pounds over a season but right now, at 160, he weighs more than he ever did. By play-off time his nerves become so jumpy that he can't eat the day of a broadcast. He doesn't smoke or drink that day, either, indulges moderately at other times.

When he's working he leaves his long, narrow, picture-lined office on the third floor of Maple Leaf Gardens about 8 o'clock, goes down a flight of stairs to begin a long trek to his gondola. He opens six doors and climbs 89 concrete steps in a long, twisting trail which leads to the catwalks in the rafters. The slender broadcasting booth is only 56 feet above the ice surface but seems much more than that. It is suspended directly over the rink-boards at mid-ice and offers an unobstructed view of the playing surface. When the Gardens was built in 1931, Foster selected the location because it was far enough away to give him an overall picture of the action and close enough to permit instant recognition of the players. Hewitt uses the first period (which is not broadcast) to acquaint himself with the trend of play and the characteristics of new players. He uses no notes or diagrams, says he never refers to players' numbers for recognition purposes; rather, learns their styles and mannerisms. He works bare-headed, though wearing a topcoat, keeps a jar of mineral oil near him for occasional gargles. He makes a quick pass at the jar just before he goes on the air at the start of the second period, hunches low over his microphone and talks in a deliberate, unhurried manner, his jaw working feverishly.

A criticism that Hewitt frequently faces is that he is partial to the Toronto Maple

Foster Hewitt during a radio broadcast.

Leafs. It is hissed by some that his excitement in reporting a Toronto goal far surpasses that which accompanies a goal by the visiting team and critics insist that even in these latter descriptions his enthusiasm is synthetic and forced. Hewitt admits all this but denies it proves he is partial. "We let the game and the crowd carry us," he explains. "As the noise swells the voice rolls higher. If the play culminates in a goal the noise and the excitement are at such a pitch that the voice must reflect it. Since the vast majority of our games are done in Toronto it naturally follows that there is more excitement accompanying a Toronto goal. If the visiting team scores there is no such crowd reaction and in an effort to be fair and make one goal sound as exhilarating as the other the voice, of the fans, quite possibly sounds artificial at times. It's an actual fact that we do the same thing in playoff games in Boston, say, or Detroit; we reach the most natural pitch in describing goals by the Bruins or the Red Wings."

Hewitt regards himself as an official must regard himself. He admits he has favorites but, like the referees, he feels he must be impartial. If players are hurt, he says, he must be tactful; he must neither condemn the offender nor condone the offence. "I try to sell hockey," he says. "The man who sells his product, not himself, is valuable to his sponsors."

Hewitt can sell a product, whether it's hockey (a game which he loves and attends whether or not he's working it), motor oil or binoculars. At one point in the war, the Royal Canadian Navy was short of binoculars and the Navy League tried several unsuccessful methods of raising them. Then the League asked Hewitt if he would try. He mentioned the need for glasses once. The response was so great that the Navy League had to ask him to tell the kind people to stop. In less than two weeks, 1,116 pairs were forwarded from all over Canada.

Hewitt declines to reveal his income; he says that anyone who makes less than $100,000 a year is not a celebrity and that the income of anyone less than a celebrity is of no public interest. There are those who feel that he is a celebrity, however, and one of these, a friend of Hewitt's, estimates he is worth around $250,000. From various sources, it is possible to estimate his annual income from sports at $25,000. An exact breakdown of this figure is impossible because, in return for the broadcasting concession, Hewitt splits his fees with the Gardens. These fees come from three major sources—a 15-minute sports roundup which he does every Friday night on a CBC sustaining program; his Saturday afternoon junior hockey broadcasts over CFRB, a Toronto independent; and the Saturday night coast-to-coasters over the CBC. In effect the stations and sponsors rent Foster's voice from the Gardens, and the rent comes high—an approximate average of $500 a game for each Saturday night NHL performance and $200 a game for the afternoon Junior broadcasts.

Hewitt writes occasional magazine articles and has a 30,000-word book called *He Shoots, He Scores*. At this writing the book has sold more than 14,500 copies, has been on the market five months. It follows an earlier book called *Down the Ice*, a history of hockey written in 1933 which covered radio's place, coaching tips and player instruction. He denies reports his books and articles are ghost written. He does not regard himself as an author and neither do critics who reviewed *He Shoots, He Scores*. "The book wasn't written for the critics," he says off-handedly, "it was written for boys."

Any discussion of the Hewitt income must necessarily include his interest in mining in Northern Ontario and in oil drilling in Alberta because he says he realizes more from these than from his broadcasting. He owns a considerable amount of stock in Maple Leaf Gardens.

Hewitt is not what might be called one of the boys. He doesn't frequent the bar or club which often becomes a forum for sports writers, promoters, the occasional retired hockey player and devotees of the turf. He feels that he can't afford to fraternize with team officials, players or, in some instances, the writers who follow one particular club lest he lay himself open to charges of prejudice. If there is an inference here that Hewitt is a stuffed shirt it ought to be quickly allayed. He simply isn't gregarious. A close friend, Waldo Holden of CFRB, says Hewitt is shy of crowds, tends to clam up when confronted by a roomful of people he doesn't know, thereby leaving an unfavorable impression. "His idea of a good big party," Holden says, "is about six people he's known for 20 years."

He has a cottage near Beaverton on Lake Simcoe where he spends his summers with his family, has become an ardent vegetable gardener and enjoys getting outdoors with an axe or hatchet to clear underbrush. He owns a handsome 14-room house in Forest Hill Village, one of Toronto's more plushy suburbs.

Foster's father, W.A. Hewitt, was sports editor of the *Toronto Star* when Foster was a cub reporter there in the early '20s. The young man also looked after a radio column and frequently went on the air for the *Star*'s station, CFCA. In 1928 he mentioned in one broadcast that if listeners would send 10 cents to cover handling they could receive a copy of the small Maple Leaf hockey program. The response to the announcement over the small Ontario network was fantastic. Bag after bag of mail was piled around the tiny desk he used at the *Star* and Hewitt believes that response, more than any other factor, sold Conn Smythe, now president of Maple Leaf Gardens, on the value of radio broadcasts. When the Gardens was built in 1931, Smythe gave Hewitt the broadcasting rights and to this day no other announcer can work in the Gardens without Hewitt's okay.

During his eight years with CFCA, he broadcast the arrival of the dirigible R-100 at Montreal, the docking of the Empress of Britain on her maiden voyage and the great days of the Canadian National Exhibition marathon swims. He did hockey interviews which now are conducted nationally every Saturday before NHL games by Wes McKnight, gave the job to McKnight when the hockey broadcast became an exacting enough evening's exercise. This little item alone is reportedly worth $125 a week and is being conducted today in the same cut-and-dried pattern Hewitt originated.

One of his best sports was football which he broadcast from stadium roofs to which he was strapped. During one game at Queen's University at Kingston, Ont., Hewitt was frozen to the roof. People pulling on ropes pried him loose after 20 minutes but the seat of his pants declined to accompany him to safety.

Hewitt has never missed a broadcast; has done approximately 500 NHL games in his 20 years in the Gardens' gondola. Only once has he come close to missing. That was in 1936 when the Maple Leafs were trading stitches with the old Montreal Maroons in a Stanley Cup playoff. When Foster awakened on the morning of the final game and opened his mouth to speak all that came out was something like static on an old crystal set. His doctor diagnosed laryngitis, said it wasn't serious and that his voice would return in three or four days. Croaking like a turkey, Hewitt conveyed the importance of the evening's mission and the doctor set to work. He rigged up a pail of steaming water and balsam and placed it at the foot of a chair. He sat his patient in the chair, his head bent forward over the pail. Around his shoulders the doctor teepeed a blanket. "Stay in there the rest of the day," he ordered. "Don't open your mouth and keep that water steaming."

At six o'clock there emerged a shaken man. He drank coffee, bundled himself into heavy clothes and went to the Gardens. A Montreal announcer had been flown to Toronto and was ready to make with the monosyllables. Hewitt had lost eight pounds by 15 minutes before broadcast time and the nervous tension, always high with him, was practically unbearable. Millions of people were waiting to hear him and after 12 hours as an absolute mute in a sweat box, frantic Hewitt didn't know if he had a lilt in his larynx.

The seconds ticked away. He got his cue, opened his mouth. "Hello Canada, and hockey fans in the United States and Newfoundland..."

In recollection, he smiles: "I nearly went nuts in that last 15 minutes but when we went on the air it was all right. The voice was shaky at first but as the game wore on we got warmed up."

The Hewitts (Foster) are a hockey family just as were the Hewitts (W.A.). Foster's 22-year-old daughter, Anne, is a statistics addict. Knows the records of most modern players, and 16-year-old Wendy, a student at Bishop Strachan girls' school in Toronto, also can tell the players without a program. A young fellow named Bill Hewitt, 21, has worked on Ontario stations at Owen Sound, Kenora and Barrie. He has appeared each Christmas on the Young Canada Night broadcasts to report part of the play-by-play. In Canada's hockey it seems, there'll always be a Hewitt.

Foster Hewitt's dramatic telecasts continued for 28 more years. By his final broadcast on Nov. 15, 1978, the 75-year-old had described the play-by-play of more than 3,000 games. After NHL expansion in 1967, Hewitt soured on the game, calling it an absurd copy of the sport he had loved and seldom went to games after he stopped broadcasting. The man who made famous the expression "He shoots, he scores!," proved to be as successful in business as he was behind the mike. He owned two radio stations, was a director of several mining companies and a part-owner of the Vancouver Canucks. Hewitt suffered from Alzheimer's disease in his later years and died in Toronto at age 82 in 1985.

Conn Smythe: That Man in the Greens

Trent Frayne

January 1, 1952—Constantine Falkland Cary Smythe, the most successful hockey executive in the world, is a paradox. Although he was a poor hockey player and has not laced on a skate since he failed to make the University of Toronto senior team more than 30 years ago, he has consistently produced one of the most colorful and, over the years, the best professional team in hockey. At the height of the Depression, in 1931, he built Maple Leaf Gardens, the finest indoor arena on the continent. He has made hockey so respectable that it is right up there with ballet in the social scale in his native Toronto, yet some people blame him for turning the game into a ruffianly burlesque of what it used to be and others regard him as an ogre and a dictator. He condones players who draw penalties and preaches fire and brimstone to his Toronto Maple Leafs before a game. He neither smokes nor drinks and has little patience with those who do. He fought like a catamount to get into the last war and then spent a fair proportion of his time fighting the army he had sought to join; just before his discharge he helped precipitate a national political crisis by risking a court martial to denounce the army's recruiting methods.

An army acquaintance, Major Zooch (Pete) Palmer, of Hamilton, who succeeded Smythe as officer commanding the 30th Light Anti-Aircraft Battery near Caen after a shell fragment struck Smythe's spine, commented with admiration recently that he'd never seen a group of army men quite so well trained as Smythe's battery. "There was the most remarkable discipline I had ever encountered."

There are many who contend that Smythe, a millionaire, could have been a success at anything and, for a fact, he hasn't missed much. On a shoestring he bought a small share of a sand-and-gravel business 30 years ago. Today, 60 trucks with C. Smythe for Sand emblazoned across their sides in white churn in and out of a property worth about $300,000. He is the largest single shareholder in Maple Leaf Gardens (no individual owns controlling interest) now valued at better than $4 million. He has owned a stable of race horses and, as treasurer of the Ontario Society for Crippled Children in Toronto, has been described by one of the board members as "the difference between success and failure of the whole venture."

Smythe, who will be 57 next Feb. 1, has the body of a man 30 years his junior. He is well-muscled and flat-stomached, although his activity has been slowed by the effects of the war wound. His right leg is considerably slimmer than the left because the splinter severed a nerve in his spine and he walks slowly and with a slight limp. He is able to play golf, however, and to swim twice a day during his annual six-week winter vacation in Florida through January and part of February and at his summer home at Orchard Beach, Lake Simcoe.

Smythe is stocky, five feet seven, has a sandy complexion and pale penetrating blue eyes which his secretary, Madeleine McDonald, swears turn steely grey when he is annoyed or angered. The Smythes live in a spacious nine-room house in Toronto's west end which they built in 1929 and recently remodelled. He prefers plain good food and finds it hard to believe that some people enjoy caviar or other exotic tidbits. Smythe drinks neither tea, coffee nor milk; in fact he sips stronger liquid only after the Leafs have won a championship and fill the Stanley Cup with champagne. Mostly he drinks ginger ale.

Smythe has a son, Stafford, with him in the sand business who also helps his father greatly in administering the Leafs' amateur system. Another son, Hugh, is a doctor. There were two daughters but one of them, 10-year-old Patricia, died suddenly about six years ago. The other girl, Miriam, is married to Jack Hoult, employed in the Gardens box office.

Smythe has been hockey's most publicized figure for almost a quarter of a century —partly because he discovered early in his career that feuds with rival teams made good newspaper copy, both at home and on the road. Though many of these have started with tongue in cheek, some turned out to be completely genuine. For instance, through one 12-year period he and Art Ross of the Boston Bruins did not speak to one another and for the last two years he and Jack Adams of the Detroit Red Wings have not exchanged words.

Smythe has said that he detested Ross because the Boston boss seemed to have devoted his life to making a fool of Smythe. "He stationed two longshoremen near our bench in the Boston Garden and their instructions were to goad me into a fight," Smythe said recently. "He wanted to have me put in jail." One night as he was making his way toward the Toronto dressing room after a game, the longshoremen began pushing him and insulting him. Smythe shouted back at them and then he saw Ross nearby, obviously angry. "He started after me but little Frank Selke, then my assistant, saw him coming and dove at him with a flying tackle that knocked him down. We got out of there fast but not before I yelled at one of the longshoremen, 'When your boss gets up tell him I can't waste my time with anybody that a man as small as Selke can lick.'" Smythe now watches home games with relative calm from the green seats, high up in the Gardens.

But one time Ross did succeed in getting Smythe behind bars. It was in Boston on a December night in 1933 that Irvin (Ace) Bailey, Toronto's right winger, was tripped by Boston's boisterous defenceman, the great Eddie Shore. Bailey almost became the first fatality in the league's history. When his feet were pushed from under him from behind he went into the air and fell to the ice. His skull was split at both temples. While he lay unconscious on the ice his teammate Red Horner sought out Shore, hit him with a roundhouse right on the chin and when Shore fell his head also hit the ice and he, too, was knocked unconscious. The Boston arena began to rock with a roaring cacophony. Smythe, leading the way while Toronto players carried Bailey to their dressing room, heard a fan shriek, "Fake, fake! The bum's actin'." Smythe wheeled and swung. He struck a bespectacled spectator who he believed had shouted. Blood spurted from the fan's face and rink policemen took charge of Smythe and escorted him to jail. The fan charged assault and battery but according to Smythe, Art Ross, who originally had instructed the fan to lay the charge, demanded he withdraw it when the seriousness of Bailey's injury became apparent. Smythe was released at 2 a.m. Meanwhile, Bailey lay unconscious in a hospital and it wasn't until 15 days and two delicate brain operations later that he regained consciousness. He was in Boston for six weeks, during which Smythe never left the city. He arranged to send Bailey's wife and daughter to a Boston hotel and when the player recovered sufficiently to return to Toronto Smythe arranged a benefit game between an All-Star NHL team and the Leafs. He raised over $20,000 for Bailey, who is completely recovered today although he never played hockey again.

Smythe and Ross have since made up too. The Toronto fireball explained to a friend not long ago: "His two sons both served overseas with excellent records. I figured anybody who could rear two boys like that must be all right."

Smythe was born a hundred yards from the present site of Maple Leaf Gardens, the only son of Albert Ernest Stafford Smythe, a newspaperman who, though poor, managed to send the boy to boarding schools after his mother died when he was seven. One of the first things he did was to shorten his imposing collection of Christian names to just plain Conn. He discovered an outlet, in sports, in which he excelled. When he threw his weight around violently enough he discovered he got what he wanted and at the University of Toronto he was a belligerent 118-pound centre for the Varsity junior hockey team.

He was a 19-year-old undergraduate when war was declared in 1914 and early in the following year he went overseas an an artilleryman. Smythe was captured by the Germans and he spent 14 months in prison camp, alternately endeavoring to escape (he made it twice and was recaptured both times) and playing bridge.

Back in Canada, after the armistice, he felt like an old man, an old man of 24 who had lost four years out of his life. In 1927, the last year he coached the University of Toronto team, they won the Allan Cup. The following year, as the Varsity Grads, they represented Canada at the 1928 Olympic Games in St. Moritz and won the world championship. The team's earlier showing in intercollegiate games with Boston College, Harvard and Princeton in the old Boston Garden, and Smythe's handling of the players, had impressed the Garden president, Charles W. Adams. When in 1926 the NHL began to expand and New York, Chicago and Detroit were admitted into the league, Adams recommended Smythe to Col. John Hammond, president of the New York Rangers, as the man to assemble and coach the Rangers.

Smythe agreed verbally to a salary of $10,000 but before the team played a game Hammond decided to replace Smythe with an older, more experienced hockey man, Lester Patrick. He offered Smythe $7,500 in settlement which Smythe accepted while protesting hotly, insisting he had earned the full $10,000. He stomped out of Hammond's office to watch the Rangers engage in their first league encounter in Madison Square Garden. They were playing the Montreal Maroons, then world's champions, and before the game Smythe ran into Hammond's boss, the late Tex Rickard, famous fight promoter and then Garden president. He told Rickard that Col. Hammond owed him $2,500. Rickard escorted him to Hammond's office, listened to the details of the agreement and then told Hammond to write a cheque for $2,500. He wagered it, while in Montreal en route home, on the University of Toronto to beat McGill—and he won. He then wagered these winnings on the underdog Toronto St. Pats to triumph over the Ottawa Senators, and won again.

A year later, with two Toronto brokers, the late Peter Campbell and E.W. Bickle, he bought the St. Pats, who were an NHL team, for $160,000. He got two good hockey players out of the lot, Hap Day and Ace Bailey, a trainer named Tim Daly and

Conn Smythe shares champagne with Maple Leaf wives after the team's 1951 Stanley Cup triumph.

a National Hockey League franchise in a small rink called Mutual Arena. Smythe changed the team's name to the Maple Leafs, striving for a national appeal, and he added new players in a building program that gradually attracted fan interest.

In 1930, Smythe set to work to build a $1 million rink. He wheedled capital from bankers and businessmen. The architect went on the cuff; contractors took part payment in stock; even the carpenters, masons and electricians got part of their wages in stock. One of Smythe's greatest strikes was in eliciting the interest and support of the late J.P. Bickell, a mining man and one of the country's richest. Bickell, sold on Smythe's drive, enthusiasm and determination to succeed, used to phone his friends, tell them who was speaking and casually inform them they had just bought $10,000 worth of stock in a place called Maple Leaf Gardens. It was built within a year and at the beginning it was no gold mine. Smythe refused to scrimp, however, and his tireless efforts to give the fans a winner finally won them over in large numbers.

Smythe has sold his product so well that there was not an empty seat in Maple Leaf Gardens for any NHL game between Feb. 27, 1946 and Nov. 7, 1951. Seating capacity is 12,586 seats and about 9,000 of these are occupied by people who subscribe for a full season of 35 games. There is a waiting list (currently 5,018) for subscribers' seats and this season the Gardens was able to accommodate the last of those who placed their names on the list during 1947. At that rate a man who goes on the waiting list today will quite likely have the privilege of watching all of the Maple Leafs' home games in the 1955–56 season.

To do this, Smythe has first of all produced a winner. Since Maple Leaf Gardens was finished in 1931, the Maple Leafs have missed the playoffs only once. The Leafs have won the trophy seven times and have been in the finals, and lost, on seven other occasions. No other team comes close to these figures.

Unlike many less successful gamblers, the man who built the Maple Leafs is not a creature of impulse, although he often pretends to be. Behind everything he does is a meticulous and calculating mind and away from the public view, in the confines of his richly, though conservatively, appointed office on the second floor of the Gardens, he becomes as fussily efficient as a bookkeeper. He keeps charts on every conceivable aspect of his players' performances; how many minutes each player is on the ice, whether he is on when his own team scores, when the opposing team scores, how many goals he scores against inferior opposition as opposed to his record against the top teams, his every move, check, shot and pratfall.

Smythe's was the first team in the league to keep a movie record of every home game and Smythe and his assistants, coach Joe Primeau and assistant general manager Hap Day, spend hours studying the films to get a better line on the merits and deficiencies of every player in the league. He rules Maple Gardens and its 120 permanent employees plus an additional 229 gatemen, ushers, and concession workers like a martinet. Almost all of them fear him in one form or another but every one of them has the profoundest respect for him.

Before his war wound slowed his activity, Smythe used to use the aisle in front of the box seats as a one-man race track and he'd charge around shouting at players and officials from behind both goals and from the sides of the rink. One of his favorite forms of self-expression was to ride the referee from his own bench, leaning across the boards and shouting at the poor fellow, then galloping around to the other side of the ice to shout at him some more. Nowadays he makes very few road trips and at home sits high in the $1.75 seats and, superficially at least, views the games impassively. He generally is flanked by a scout or a player, such as the spare goalkeeper or one temporarily sidelined by an injury, and he usually keeps this aide hopping from his seat down to the Maple Leaf bench with verbal instructions to the coach. By and large, though, his coach runs the club, the instructions from the greens serving mostly as reminders of pregame strategy or a suggestion accrued by Smythe in his lofty vantage point.

But while Smythe is busy keeping his fans provided with a good hockey team, he is just as often providing them with reading matter. His occasional press conferences are carefully planned and when he calls one he usually has something to say. He is a glib talker and these affairs are generally redolent of high good humor and the hard work he puts into their preparation is reflected in the space they command on the sports pages. It is a fact that the Gardens' vice-president, George McCullagh, is publisher of two Toronto newspapers but even so, it would be impossible for any hockey writer to miss the news significance of most of Smythe's statements. An illustration of this point is the flood of space he is accorded by American interviewers during his visits around the NHL circuit.

During the worst of the winter he goes to Palm Beach, Fla., and runs the club by remote control. He flies back for important games and between times runs up a $600-a-month telephone bill. After every game his secretary phones him and gives him a complete rundown on the scoring and Primeau and Day give him a synopsis of play. The calls are made from the press room in the Gardens which is adjacent to the Leaf dressing room. Near the phone is a large blackboard on which a period-by-period scoring summary of all NHL and AHL games is chalked. Smythe is as interested in the progress of his Pittsburgh farm affiliate in the American League, in this regard, as he is in the Maple Leafs' progress. It was from Florida last winter, in fact, that he issued a directive which was received with great unpopularity in all marriage clinics. This was his order that Johnny McCormack, Leaf centre, be demoted to the Pittsburgh farm because he got married in mid-season. The decision brought a flood of indignation in the papers and one columnist pointed out that Smythe was running everything else and now was trying to govern love.

Smythe's Gardens, though it was built 20 years ago, still has the fresh clean appearance of a building a quarter its age. Cleanliness is a Smythe fetish, and costs the Gardens about a $135 after every attraction when a maintenance staff comes in, even before the last patron has left, to get busy with broom, mop and duster. The ladies' powder rooms have uniformed attendants. A year ago, after Smythe's office had received numerous complaints about the quality and quantity of the food-stuffs sold at the refreshment stands, Smythe took over those concessions himself. Nowadays

Smythe makes periodic unannounced trips to the booths to sample the soft drinks and hot dogs which he personally detests but which he'll test to assure himself they're top grade. His meticulous approach to the game helped sell it to well-to-do people who sit in the reds, or $3.50 seats, in their mink coats and Lily Dache originals and even in evening dress—much as they would attend a horse show, because Saturday night at the Gardens has become a sort of social event, too.

Smythe is happy with his role as a big man in hockey but he is far from egotistical about it. "Something I learned a long time ago was that a smart man surrounds himself with the best men in the business," he remarked recently. "I wanted to be a smart man so look what I've got; there aren't two smarter hockey men anywhere than Day and Primeau, Henry Bolton is the best box-office man in the league, Ed Fitkin does the best job on publicity and it's that way right through the organization. That's why we build winners."

Smythe originated another method of building winning hockey teams. He moved sprouts from their homes to Toronto where their academic schooling was continued and where they played minor amateur hockey under the tutorship of Smythe or of coaches in his organization. These included boys from the prairies like Nick and Don Metz and such Ontario youngsters as Pep Kelly and Art Jackson, all educated at St. Michael's College, where they played junior hockey before graduating to the Maple Leafs. "People in hockey are often criticized for stealing babies from the cradles," Smythe remarked not long ago, "and yet look at those Metz boys. Both of them grew prosperous because of hockey and now they are well-to-do farmers in Saskatchewan. There are any number of successful businessmen around today who owe their start or their contacts or their business opportunities to hockey."

Smythe long has maintained he is not interested in hockey players who don't play to win. They can take penalties but they've got to be giving everything. His dressing room dressing-downs are celebrated, although at least one former Maple Leaf, Charlie Conacher, feels their effect is over-rated. "Sure, he pops off a lot between periods," Conacher once remarked, "but we never used to pay too much attention to him. We were grown men; we were doing our best and I don't think his hollering made much difference." Smythe feels there is great purpose in his dressing-room rantings and virtually all of them are carefully calculated. "Everybody has an incentive," he says, "and if you can bring out that incentive you've got a winner. A lot of people go their best when they're mad so your job is to get them mad."

With most hockey players, Smythe has observed, the incentive is money and he recalls an incident in which he believes that knowing it won him the Stanley Cup in 1942. The Maple Leafs were opposing the favored New York Rangers and they started briskly, and then the Rangers started to come on. The Leafs were ahead three games to two and the score was 1–1 in the sixth game with time running out. Smythe had the feeling that if the Leafs dropped this game they'd drop the series and with only a few seconds to play he saw Nick Metz grab the puck inside the Toronto blue line and start down the ice with only one Ranger player to beat. In a twinkling Smythe recalled that Metz was saving his money to buy a farm for his father in Wilcox, Sask., and as the player skated past him Smythe cupped his hands to his mouth and shouted until he thought his lungs would burst: "Remember the old man in Wilcox, Nick!" Metz went straight down the ice like a startled fawn and fired a low line drive into the net to win the series. "Nine times out of ten," Smythe has laughed in recollection, "Nick would have passed the puck to Syl Apps or Gordie Drillon, who were tearing down with him. This time, I guess he thought of the old man's farm."

Conn Smythe sold the Leafs in 1960 to a consortium that included his son Stafford and Harold Ballard. Smythe maintained a box at the Gardens, but rarely went and condemned the state of hockey following expansion. He spent most of his time raising money for charity and pursuing his interest in thoroughbred racing. His horses won 147 stake races in Ontario, including two Queen's Plate victories. Smythe died at 85 in 1980 of a heart attack at his farm in Caledon, Ont.

How They Broke the
Heart of Howie Morenz

Trent Frayne

October 15, 1953—Sixteen years have passed since Howie Morenz died on the floor of a hospital room in Montreal. There are some who believe this greatest of hockey players died of a broken heart.

Howie Morenz was more than the best hockey player that ever lived. He became part of the nation's folklore, a symbol of a hockey era that is now only a memory, of a time when the ice heroes were a rough-hewn and sometimes hard-drinking lot, fiercely loyal to their team. Even the smoke-filled rinks in which they played had a warmer look and smell than the antiseptic palaces of today. Then, the millworkers and tram drivers and off-duty cabbies who jammed the rush end of the Forum in Montreal and called themselves the Millionaires said Morenz was a superhuman figure. Between periods they toasted him surreptitiously in homemade gin. Their battle cry, *"Les Canadiens sont là,"* never reached such frenzy as when Morenz started winding up behind his own net with a queer little bouncing jig that sent him hurtling down the ice with an exhilarating moment of excitement that reached its crescendo when he threw himself between the defencemen and crashed the puck past the goalkeeper.

For the 12 years he wore the uniform of the Canadiens Morenz was an idol. Since the bleak March night in 1937 when he died he has become a legend.

Morenz was far more than a Canadien hero. To youngsters all over Canada he was to hockey what Babe Ruth was to baseball and Jack Dempsey to boxing—a fairy-tale figure who could do things no one else could do and against greater odds. When Morenz duped a defenceman it was David slaying Goliath for Morenz was a small man as hockey stars go and defencemen were big and menacing with battle-scarred faces.

Once he received a terrible bodycheck from Rod Horner, of Toronto, the league's bad man who weighed 210 and stood six feet two. The check knocked Morenz 30 feet across the ice into a corner where he lay still for a moment. Then he climbed to his feet, skated shakily toward his own end of the rink and retrieved the puck. He bounced into stride, catapulted directly toward Horner, faked a swerve to deceive the defenceman and leaped nimbly past him to score.

When Canadiens were hard-pressed it was usually Morenz who brought the hoarse roar from the Millionaires and the happy nods from the millions who followed his exploits by radio or through the newspapers. During the 14 seasons he played in the NHL the schedule progressively increased from 24 games to 48. The 270 goals he notched were scored in the equivalent of nine present seasons.

Morenz led the Canadiens to three Stanley Cups and won the Hart Trophy three times as the league's most valuable player. He took top scoring awards in two seasons and was among the five best scorers in no fewer than eight seasons. But his value lay not merely in the number of goals scored. He had a way of getting payoff goals when the Canadiens needed them most. One night in 1930 the Chicago Black Hawks, with their superb goalkeeper, Charlie Gardiner, plus strong defensive tactics, held Canadiens to a tie until 10 minutes to two in the morning—the longest overtime game up to then. Finally Morenz barged past big Taffy Abel and beat Gardiner with the goal that eliminated Chicago from the Stanley Cup playoffs.

Howie's speed was a defensive asset too. Once in Ottawa a defenceman, Alex Smith, got a breakaway against Canadiens and had a 50-foot start on Morenz. But Howie caught him, batted the puck into a corner, picked it up, passed Smith going the other way and flipped to Aurel Joliat for a goal before the Ottawa team knew what hit them.

Howie's skating was as spectacular as it was fast—in fact even more so. His flying arms and bouncing stride made him look like the whirlwind he almost was. Actually he was only *one* of the fastest skaters in the NHL. Once in a match race at the Forum, Hec Kilrea, of Ottawa, circled the rink carrying a puck in slightly faster time than Morenz. The incredulous Millionaires dismissed it with, "*Enfin*, Howie let him win as a kindness." Morenz's juvenile fans throughout Canada did not try to explain it— they just didn't believe it.

Morenz was the most sought-after player in the game. After one thrilling contest in New York in 1926 in which he scored the winning goal in overtime, the Rangers offered $60,000 for him. Montreal Maroons heard of the offer and bid $75,000. Leo Dandurand, owner of the Canadiens, declined both offers. "Morenz," he said, "is beyond price."

Morenz, who was called the Stratford Streak because it was in that western Ontario town that he made his early impression in hockey, was born in nearby Mitchell, Sept. 21, 1902, the youngest in a family of six that included brothers Wilf and Ezra and sisters Erma, Freda and Gertrude. His German descent, the Canadiens' management felt, might not be good box office, so he was publicized as a Swiss. His mother had hoped he'd be musical and made him take piano lessons but he often skipped these to play hockey on the Thames River with homemade sticks and chunks of coal.

He started as a goalkeeper, wearing shin-pads improvised of magazines stuffed into his stockings. In his first organized game in the Mitchell rink, Howie gave up 21 goals; instantly he became a forward. When Howie was 14, the family moved from Mitchell to Stratford where his father worked in the shops of the Grand Trunk Railway and he won the centre's position on the junior hockey team. He filled in with the intermediates, too, and when he was 19, he played regularly with the juniors, the intermediates and the Grand Trunk Railway's commercial league team. In one period of 11 days he played 12 games and travelled 2,000 miles. One night in Montreal he scored 11 goals for the intermediates and the next night he scored six for the juniors in Kitchener.

Although young Morenz lived for hockey he apparently did not think he was good enough for the NHL. On a trip home from Montreal he stopped in Toronto to watch the professional St. Pats, ancestors of the Maple Leafs, play the Ottawa Senators. "You don't have to worry about me becoming a professional," he told his mother when he got home, "those fellows are far too good."

If he didn't have confidence in his ability to play professionally, the pro teams did. Charlie Querrie, of the Toronto St. Pats, offered him $1,000 to play in the team's five remaining games of the 1922–23 season. Dandurand offered him $2,500 for the 24-game season of 1923–24 and grew concerned when Lou Marsh, a referee and sports writer, telephoned that the St. Pats were hot after Morenz. Canadiens dispatched coach Cecil Hart to Stratford with a pocketful of cash. Later Morenz admitted he signed with Canadiens because Hart paid a $45 tailor's bill and gave Morenz $300 to settle a number of small debts he had run up.

When Stratford fans and officials heard about it they begged Morenz to reconsider. Letters of protest were sent to Dandurand and a minister wrote to a Toronto newspaper decrying the audacity of the Canadiens in "luring an under-age boy to the wicked city of Montreal." Upset by the fuss Morenz wrote Dandurand on Aug. 10, 1923:

I am enclosing check and contract to play hockey with your club owing to several reasons of which family and work are the most to consider I find it impossible to leave Stratford. I am sorry if I have caused you expense and inconvenience and trust you will accept the returned contract in a sportsmanlike way.

Dandurand learned that Morenz was getting $800 a year as an amateur and threatened to "blow the lid off amateur hockey," if the Ontario Hockey Association didn't persuade Morenz to honor the contract. Howie made a trip to Montreal to plead personally with Dandurand. He spent an afternoon with the Dandurand family, had dinner with them and agreed to join the Canadiens.

At training camp in Grimsby, Ont., Morenz was tried out between Aurel Joliat and Billy Boucher. Odie Cleghorn, the regular centre, never was able to win his job back. Howie's rink-length dashes and wicked shot led the Montrealers to the Stanley Cup that season; and the next year when the Canadiens lost to the Victoria Cougars in the final Morenz figured in every Canadien goal.

Though his personal glory grew, the team's success meant more to Morenz than his own. In a playoff against Boston he faced off in overtime against Cooney Weiland, of the Bruins. The puck flew in the air as their sticks clashed, Weiland took a half-swing and bounced it into the Canadien net for the winning goal. At four o'clock next morning Elmer Ferguson, Montreal sports writer, answered a knock on his hotel-room door and found Morenz there. "He was in complete despair," Ferguson recalls. "He'd been walking the streets since the game ended, berating himself for Weiland's goal."

Morenz's ceaseless drive did not stem from a physique comparable with the majority of hockey stars. He stood five feet eight and weighed 165 pounds. But he looked heavier than that because as Charlie Conacher once put it, "all his weight was in his face." He had a wide high forehead from which thinning hair lay smoothly back, wide-set brown eyes and the suggestion of jowls on his dark-whiskered cheeks. But Morenz, with his comparatively small frame, never backed up from the big men. He loved the violent exchanges, the speed and the competition of the game and the roars of the fiery partisans who shouted his name in the Forum.

In an era when hockey players were far less carefully coddled than today, Morenz was a companionable free-spender, an easy mark for panhandlers and acquaintances who often wrote him hard-luck letters. In summer he played golf nearly every day, or worked in the pari-mutuel wickets at the racetrack. In the spring of 1926 he married Mary McKay, of Montreal. The day before the wedding he lost $1,500 at the races and cheerfully borrowed on next year's contract to pay for the honeymoon. Few people in Montreal were better known than Morenz and he had a happy smile and an expansive wave for everyone who greeted him.

Life was a song for the boyish, exuberant Morenz with money in his pocket, hundreds of friends and seemingly eternal youth. One Saturday afternoon he sat in Elmer Ferguson's house drinking beer and eating limburger cheese with onions. "When we ran out of onions Howie switched to garlic," the newspaperman recalls. "My wife couldn't stand the smell so she brought us some turkey legs. 'You stink,' I laughed at Howie, 'and you're full of beer. You'll never play hockey tonight.' He laughed right back at me and scored three goals that night."

His great shot made him the scourge of goalkeepers. "He could shoot harder than anybody I see nowadays," insists little Roy Worters, who played for the New York Americans. He recalls Morenz, who wore No. 7, as the fastest skater he ever saw. "When he'd wind up behind that net he wasn't No. 7," Worters says, "he was No. 777—just a blur."

Then came the day when Morenz was no longer a blur to his opponents, when the great strides became a fraction slower and the whizzing shot a shade less lethal. It didn't come quickly and it wasn't always perceptible but by the spring of 1933 Morenz had fallen to ninth place among the scorers and the Canadiens were lagging in the standings. Finally the long-famed line of Aurel Joliat, Johnny Gagnon and Morenz was broken up and Pit Lepine replaced Morenz at centre. Morenz brooded over the demotion. By the spring of 1934 Howie hadn't regained his form and his spirits hit a sickening bottom one night in the Forum when part of the Montreal crowd booed him. Cheers from the loyal Millionaires quickly drowned the boos but Leo Dandurand recalls that Morenz came to him after that game "sobbing like a child."

Dandurand faced one of the most difficult decisions of his life. The idea of selling Morenz to another team had been unthinkable during Howie's magnificent years. Yet Morenz was visibly slipping and the prospect of the volatile fans turning on a man who had meant so much to the Canadiens made Dandurand writhe. In the summer of 1934 he made his decision; he traded Morenz to Chicago.

Morenz couldn't believe it. The Canadiens were his life, the Millionaires were as close to him as the players who'd been his teammates for 11 years. He walked the streets of Montreal trying to convince himself it wasn't true. One night he returned home to his sleeping family. His wife found him sitting in the living room staring blankly at the floor. Tears were flowing slowly down his cheeks. Later Morenz reacted as he'd always reacted to a body blow—violently. He denounced Dandurand as a heartless club owner influenced by what Howie insisted had been merely a bad year. He wasn't through; he was far from through.

But in Chicago things were scarcely better. The barnlike Chicago Stadium with its raucous callous fans was a different world from the familiar old Forum and the warm excitable Millionaires. He couldn't get along with Major Frederic McLaughlin, the rich and irascible Chicago owner. After Canadiens beat the Hawks, 2–1, one night, McLaughlin stomped angrily into the dressing room. He stopped in front of Morenz, pointed a finger accusingly at him and charged him with being responsible for the defeat.

Through the next two games Morenz sat on the bench. Then he went to McLaughlin. "Could you sell me or trade me?" he asked. "I'm not helping you, sitting on the bench, and I might be going stale." A few days later McLaughlin made a straight-trade with the New York Rangers for a run-of-the-mill forward named Glenn Brydson. This seared Morenz's pride.

In 1936 Cecil Hart, Morenz's great friend and coach for 10 years, who had been replaced by Newsy Lalonde the year Morenz was traded to Chicago, came back to the Canadiens. His first move was to buy back Morenz and re-create the famed Morenz-Joliat-Gagnon line. Morenz was 34 but to the surprise of most hockey men he began to get back in stride immediately. Again in the beloved Forum, with the shrill cries of the Millionaires once more cascading down on him, Howie had compiled 16 scoring points by Jan. 28. On that fateful night his skate caught in the boards as Chicago's Earl Seibert body checked him. His left leg twisted under him and he broke three bones in the ankle and one in the leg.

It was the tragic climax of Morenz's career. After 11 years of success and adulation and two years of disillusion and dejection he'd started on the road back. Now, in a hospital bed with his leg in a plaster cast, came the realization that he was through. He had lived high and spent his money as fast as he made it. He'd provided little insurance for his family. His one major investment, a restaurant on Ste-Catherine Street in Montreal, had gone sour and lost him a considerable outlay.

Players from visiting teams went to St. Luke's Hospital to see him frequently and Montreal friends streamed into his room. Almost always they brought a bottle and to drown his depression Howie drank with them, too many of them. By day he

Montrealers jam the Forum for the funeral of Howie Morenz, March 11, 1937.

chatted animatedly with his visitors, made them autograph his cast. At night doctors gave him sedatives to relieve his physical pain and mental turmoil. He never admitted to his visitors that he knew his hockey career was ended but close friends insist that this knowledge, together with the original shock of having been traded away by the Canadiens, left scars that never healed.

After he'd been lying in bed for a month, pale and drawn and fretful, his nerves gave way. But, as he'd always done, he battled back and he still insisted to visitors that he'd be wearing No. 7 again next season, better than ever. There was something wistful about the way he said it, though, and a friend who visited him after he'd been on his back for almost six weeks remembers that Howie turned his head quickly into the pillow and suddenly began coughing to cover his emotion.

On the night of March 8, 1937, he could stand his confinement no longer. Heaving his leg in its plaster cast off the bed he forced himself upright, took one faltering step, then slowly crumpled to the floor. He was dead.

The death certificate said the cause was "a cardiac deficiency and acute excitement." Complicated, perhaps, by a broken heart. Many of his friends believed that drugs and alcohol helped weaken his once rugged constitution. When he died something died in the Millionaires. It was a strangely quiet crowd that watched the game the night after Morenz died. The Canadiens were going to cancel the game but

Howie's wife, weeping, telephoned the Forum the afternoon of the game. "Don't call it off," she whispered. "He wouldn't want that."

On March 11, Howie's body was placed at centre ice in the Forum and Canadien players formed an honor guard as thousands filed past. Fifteen thousand people moved slowly and silently into the Forum for the service and 25,000 more with heads bared packed the streets outside. Thousands more lined the long route to the cemetery up the snow-covered slopes of Mount Royal. The casket was covered by a huge floral "7," Howie's uniform number. It was the final tribute of his teammates. No Canadien player ever again wore the number.

The High Spots of a Lifetime with the Red Wings

Jack Adams with *Trent Frayne*

January 28, 1961—The turning point in my life came one morning late in the spring of 1935 as I walked without enthusiasm to the Olympia. This was the Depression era, the rink had gone into receivership, and there were rumors the hockey club would fold.

The girl on the switchboard greeted my glum face with a smile. "There's a long-distance call for you from Chicago," she told me. "The new owner wants to talk to you."

"New owner!" I exclaimed. "Who?"

"Mr. James Norris, the grain millionaire," she said.

Several hours later I went to the trust company in Detroit that had taken over the rink. Mr. Norris had arrived from Chicago to meet the bankers. I was shown into an office where a big bald gruff man with heavy black eyebrows, round features and a wide nose was sitting behind a desk.

James Norris Sr. introduced himself and told me to sit down. He said hockey had long been a favored sideline of his, dating from his early years in Montreal, where he'd played for the Montreal Amateur Athletic Association, the famed Winged Wheelers. "We'll call this team the Wings," Mr. Norris said, "in fact, we'll call it the *Red* Wings. Our emblem will be a winged wheel. That will be appropriate in Detroit. And I'll give you a year in your job—on probation."

We didn't sign a contract—in fact I've never had one in all my 33 years at Detroit. But what I got from Mr. Norris, instead, was a bankroll and one boss—a welcome change from the multiple ownership that used to debate team policy in the broad lounge of the Detroit Athletic Club, worrying about costs, going deep into debt, and finally failing.

In the early years of the Depression we were lucky if we drew 80,000 people a season. The team travelled in day coaches and munched sandwiches on the trains. The team was called the Cougars then, a legacy from the Victoria Cougars whose franchise was transferred to Detroit when the Pacific Coast league folded in 1926. It wasn't a popular name and when one of the newspapers conducted a contest we selected Falcons. Any good that might have done was voided by mediocre teams and hard times.

In that bleak period we were literally giving our tickets away. It wasn't that the game itself was unpopular, it was simply that people had no money. This was illustrated early in the '30s when we played an exhibition game to help a fund being conducted by Detroit's mayor, Frank Murphy. There was no admission charge, as such; people delivered food or clothing to the firehalls and got tickets in exchange. We attracted a capacity crowd of around 13,000. Just before game time we heard there was a guy driving up and down Woodward Avenue outside the rink. He had five bags of potatoes and wanted in. We took his potatoes and gave him standing room.

So Mr. Norris's arrival in 1935 was the turning point in Detroit, although I must say that the fastest and maybe the best deal I ever made came a matter of weeks before he bought the club. One cold March morning in Montreal, I was standing on the steps of the Windsor Hotel with Frank Patrick, who was running the Boston club then. They'd been eliminated from the playoffs, our bunch hadn't even made them, and Frank and I were in Montreal to watch the old Maroons play Toronto in the Stanley Cup final. The wind was howling up the Windsor Street hill from the station below the hotel, but we were oblivious to it. We were talking hockey, oddly enough. "If I had Cooney Weiland," Patrick said of our slick little centre, "my club would be in this final."

"If I had Marty Barry," I said of Boston's big solemn centre, "Detroit would win the Stanley Cup." We looked at each other for a moment, then we chuckled. We shook hands to seal the bargain, a couple of free-wheeling paupers. I never made a better deal. We put Barry with Herbie Lewis and Larry Aurie to form a line that led us to the Stanley Cup the next season, as I'd predicted with more bravura than conviction on the hotel steps. The Norris money didn't hurt us in the climb from obscurity to the championship. I paid $35,000, a fortune in those days, to get a player I'd long admired, Syd Howe, from the St. Louis Flyers, and we paid about half that to Toronto for Hec Kilrea. With these changes we won our division and qualified to meet the Montreal Maroons, who'd won the other division. The mid-'30s was an era of two sections in the NHL, the Canadian and the American, with the top three teams in each qualifying for the playoffs. Our playoff with Montreal was the most unforgettable of any preliminary in my time.

The series opened in the Montreal Forum with Normie Smith, the little acrobat in our goal, engaging the big black-browed stoic Lorne Chabot in the longest scoreless game on record. Regulation time produced marvellous work by the pair, and then the game settled into a test of endurance, hour after hour. Since the first goal scored would end the game, the tension in the smoky Forum rose and fell and rose again, time after time. One o'clock came and then 2 o'clock and by now the ice was slashed and chipped and brutal on the players. At 2:25 I looked along our bench for the strongest legs and I broke up lines to send out Syd Howe, Hec Kilrea and young Mud Bruneteau. "Boys," I told them, "let's get some sleep. It's now or never."

Bruneteau got the goal that ended the longest game ever. The puck went into the net after 16 minutes and 30 seconds of the sixth 20-minute overtime period, just three and a half minutes short of three full games. The teams had played 176 minutes and 30 seconds in their six hours in the Forum. The goalkeepers were skillful but I'd have to say that poor ice conditions contributed most to the record.

While I was riding in a cab along Ste-Catherine Street the following night for the second game I winced at the possibility of a repetition. There wasn't one that night—we beat the Maroons 3 to 0 in regulation time—but I realized we had a problem: Bad ice produced bad hockey that could be an ordeal for spectators as well as players. It was two years before I solved this problem, and I got the idea in Paris, of all places. We toured France in the spring of 1938 with the Montreal Canadiens and one evening we went to a restaurant where the tables lined a sheet of ice for a curling exhibition. Afterward, attendants swept the ice with sheepskin brushes and then flooded it for the next show. That turned on the light. I discussed the ice-flooding plan with governors of the NHL and by the 1940–41 season flooding between periods was the rule. This, with such legislation as the centre red line in 1943, speeded up play to an extent that convinces me there'll never be an approach to our overtime record. The game is simply too fast now and too wide open to permit long scoreless stretches. Great as the modern goalkeepers are, you rarely see even a goal-less period and scoreless games are virtually extinct.

In the season of the long game we won our first Stanley Cup, capping my first—and last—year as a probationary coach and manager.

The bitterest blow of my career came six years later, again against Toronto in the

A young Gordie Howe with Jack Adams.

Stanley Cup final. We won the first three games and were leading in the fourth with 15 minutes to play, but lost it by a goal after some of the most incredible refereeing I have ever witnessed. Don Grosso, our centre, told me that the referee had said to him, "I'll make damned sure that you guys don't win this game." In those first four games our club was assessed 135 minutes in penalties. We weren't a particularly rough club that year. In the whole 48 games through the season we drew 440 minutes, only a fraction more than nine minutes a game. Yet the average leaped to almost 34 minutes in the playoffs.

When that fourth game ended, three of my players, Eddie Wares, Grosso and Sid Abel, surrounded the referee, Mel Harwood, at the exit gate. I went across the ice after them to pull them away and was charged with belting the referee. Actually, I didn't get within 10 feet of him in the scuffling. But the league president, Frank Calder, suspended me for the balance of the series, and fined Wares and Grosso $100 each. Toronto won that game and took the next three, the only time a team ever won the Stanley Cup in a series in which it had lost the first three games. To me, the series seemed to be controlled by the Toronto newspapers and Conn Smythe. Their influence on Calder provided my darkest moment in hockey. At the next NHL governors' meeting I turned to the president. "You're through persecuting me, my boy," I told Calder. "I'm through being your patsy."

We expect to get penalties, all right, because we're a rugged kind of hockey club. I'm not much for having on our club winners of the "gentleman's prize," the Lady Byng trophy. I like guys with the hard glow of dedication—men like Sid Abel, our present coach, and Gordie Howe, whom I call My Guy. Abel illustrated the kind of thing I mean in the Stanley Cup final of 1950 when the Rangers came up with a real hot club.

Abel was clearly played out as we went into a seventh game against the Rangers. Also, he was missing Gordie Howe on his right wing. Howe had been critically injured two weeks before. The Rangers were fired up for that seventh game in Detroit and they had a 3-to-2 lead with a few minutes left to play. I sent out Abel and Ted Lindsay and Gerry Couture, who'd scored 24 goals that season. Sid was sagging. I figured he might set up the other two, tired as he was.

Abel showed the heart I've been talking about. He was knocked to his knees in front of the Ranger goal when a rebound came off Charlie Rayner's pads. Unable to climb to his feet, Sid scored the tying goal on his knees. That kept us alive, and we won in overtime on a goal by Pete Babando.

Howe, as I've said many times, is the greatest all-around player I've ever seen. I'm a strong admirer of Rocket Richard. He'll go down as one of the greats. But for pure versatility, high purpose and team contribution, my guy is the greatest. He has a marvellous temperament and he never changes. He'd have been a standout in any game he'd chosen. His build and his razor reflexes are ideally suited to athletics. Even now he occasionally works out with the Detroit Tigers and looks right at home on the baseball diamond.

In 1952 when Gordie was shooting for 50 goals to tie Rocket's record, I told Tommy Ivan to put him out there every chance he got in our last few games. Tommy did, but Gordie kept passing the puck to Abel. Finally Tommy asked him what the hell he was up to. "Ol' Boot has a bonus for 20 goals, you know," Howe told him, using Abel's nickname, Bootnose. "If he's in front of that net he's gonna get the puck." They both missed. Abel got 17 and Gordie wound up with 47. The next year he got 49.

It's a miracle that Howe is playing at all. Before we played the Rangers in that 1950 final we met Toronto in the semi-final, a tight and vicious series. Near the end of the first game in the Olympia, Toronto's Ted Kennedy was carrying the puck near the boards. Howe sped toward him, cutting diagonally across the ice. A fraction of a second before the impact, Kennedy drew himself up, and Howe crashed headlong into the boards. Gordie lay limp on the ice, bleeding from his nose and eye. Later, in hospital, there was every indication he was dying. He was unconscious, vomiting, had a broken cheekbone and nose, and a brain specialist operated, boring a hole into his skull to remove fluid pressing on the brain. We paced the corridors all night. Even the next day his condition was critical.

But then he rallied and, incredibly, 12 days later, when we played the Rangers in that seventh game, Gordie was able to watch in the Olympia. And when Pete Babando scored the overtime goal that made us champions, the cheers during the Cup presentation were for Gordie. "We want Howe!" chorused some 14,000 people, again and again.

With his head swathed in bandages, Howe made his way carefully across the ice to the presentation. People were cheering and crying in that pent-up emotional binge as Howe stood there, a little awkwardly, his head held at a self-depreciating and evasive angle that is typical of him every time the cheers ring down. It's a tableau I'll never forget.

Howe is one player who'll be at Detroit as long as he wants to stay. I know I've said that of two other players in the past, Ted Lindsay and Red Kelly, but in their cases things had a way of changing. I'm sure they never will in Howe's instance. When Lindsay came to us from the Toronto St. Mike's juniors in 1944 he was a fine boy, and he and Abel and Howe made a great forward line. Eventually, though, it became a question of whether we were going to run the club or he was, and in Lindsay's last two seasons with us he and I didn't have much to say to each other. After his 13th season with our club I decided to send him to Chicago where he had three more good years before retiring last fall. When you make changes, you know down in your heart that you're right even when the players involved have been around for a long time.

Kelly was in his 13th season, too, when it became apparent that he wasn't the defenceman he'd once been. We were battling for that fourth playoff position late last season when an opportunity arose to acquire Bill Gadsby from the Rangers. I figured Gadsby, a first-team all-star the year before, could give us the defensive strength we needed in our late run. By coincidence, when Toronto offered us Marc Reaume for Red we were ready to do business because Reaume is seven years younger than Kelly and I figured he'd help us. I've often said that being a general manager is not a job in which you win friends. You do the best you can and if you satisfy your boss and sleep nights you've done all right.

It's true that no team in this game comes close to the Red Wings in the magnitude of big-name deals and in the sheer numbers of players peddled. I've broken up championship teams and we've gone right on winning. For instance, of the 22 players on our 1950 Stanley Cup team, 14 were gone when we won again in 1952. One year I even traded two first-team NHL all-stars, Lindsay and Glenn Hall, the goalkeeper. That was unprecedented. A couple of years ago we looked over the rosters of the six NHL clubs and their minor-league affiliates and discovered, even to our own surprise, that 96 players in the leagues had been Detroit property at one time or another.

I got the nickname Trader Jack by carrying out a club policy we stress to every kid we sign. We tell him that if he has NHL ability, he'll make the NHL, that if he doesn't make it with us he'll make it with one of the other clubs. We don't keep 'em buried down on the farm, and if we have to choose between a boy of 22 and one of 27, we'll keep the kid every time.

There's a second important point to our trading philosophy: we're in the entertainment business. The four American teams in our league don't have the soft touch they have in Toronto and Montreal, with the built-in interest of a national game. We have to sell our product, game by game. Since each club comes into the Olympia seven times a season, a bad team can chase away customers. Sometimes, making a trade to sell our product, I've lost some good boys.

I figure I'm responsible for starting 99 per cent of the trades we make. It's seldom that anybody approaches me first. And, anyway, I have an answer for my critics; no team in hockey can match Detroit's 12 league championships over the last 25 years, and nobody, not even the current Montreal Canadiens with their five straight Stanley Cups, is even close to our record of seven successive league championships from 1948–49 through 1954–55.

Jack Adams left the Wings in 1961 to become president of the Central Pro League. He was 72 when he died in 1968 at his desk of a heart attack at the Central League offices in Detroit.

MR. HOCKEY

Gordie Howe: Hero

Peter Gzowski

December 14, 1963—Gordie Howe, 35, now in his 18th season with the Detroit Red Wings and generally regarded as the finest hockey player there has ever been, is a hero of our time, but he doesn't look very heroic. A six-footer, Howe weighs almost exactly 200 pounds when he is in playing shape, which is most of the time. This makes him the seventh-heaviest man in the National Hockey League, but hardly a giant in the measurements of modern sports. In street clothes, he looks quite slim, an impression heightened by his long arms, rather long neck and narrow face. His most outstanding physical characteristic is the slope of his shoulders; his trapezius muscles—the muscle you feel if you stretch your arm out to one side—rise into his neck at an angle not far from 45 degrees, while his deltoids, at the top of the arm, look scarcely better developed than the average dentist's. The enormous strength he displays in hockey flows from him, rather than exploding, and the easy grace with which he moves on the ice, and which has given so many hockey fans pleasure over the years, is also evident in his loose, almost lazy walk.

Howe goes through life much as he goes through a hockey game. He's a quiet man, at once relaxed and in control, very cool. His success has sprung from both his great natural gifts and his dedication to his job, and he seems to take it as his due, and to exploit it, but not to be overwhelmed by it.

A while ago he was talking about an experience he had had on the highway going to the Detroit suburb where he lives with his wife, Colleen, and their four young children in a $60,000 house. "A police car pulled me over, and the guy said I'd made an illegal pass. I said I had not, but he said I'd gone past a truck on the right a few miles back. Well, everybody does that, eh? I told him I'd been doing it for 20 years. But he just started to write me up. I said I guessed *he'd* be pretty popular around the station. I've been giving about five days a year to that police department's kids' work, at their picnics and that, and I said he could tell the gang that he was the fellow who stopped *that*. A $10 ticket would just run them about two dollars a day for getting rid of me. But he just wrote me up, and I drove over to the station to pay it right then."

Howe told this anecdote mostly as a joke on himself and on his inability to buffalo the cop. He quite patently was *not* going to stop helping with the boys' work. But at the same time a listener could sense that he really *had* expected to be recognized, and, because he is Gordie Howe, to be let off a traffic ticket. He is at the top, a man who is known and admired. This role affects him as a man, and it should also affect the people he encounters. (In one of its more interesting experiments, the CTV program *Telepoll* recently flashed on its screen the names and pictures of a dozen famous Canadians. Then its researchers asked a thousand people who had watched the show which of the dozen they could identify by occupation. Howe came in second, being recognized by 88 per cent, behind Lester Pearson's 96, but ahead of such figures as Georges Vanier, Charlotte Whitton and Jean Lesage.)

A couple of days after Howe told the traffic-cop story, he drove across from Detroit to Windsor to catch a plane for Toronto. The rest of the Red Wings had gone the day before, but Howe was nursing a minor injury and had stayed on at home for extra treatment. Howe was driving, and in the car with him were the team doctor, the Red Wings' publicity man, and I. Our examination at the border consisted solely of a customs officer saying, "Are you going to play tonight, Gordie?" Gordie—as nearly everyone in the world seems to call him—said he was, and we went on through. Someone in the car said, "Next time you're coming across I've got a little white powder I'd like you to take with you." Howe was not amused. Being recognized and let through is part of being The Best. Howe could no more imagine using his exalted position to smuggle something across the border than he could really fink out on some kids because a policeman didn't know who he was.

Hockey players—like most professional athletes, I suppose—live in a world of their own. They are boy-men, many of whom have never done an honest day's work in their lives, and because they play a game for a living they often seem to make all life into a game. They joke mercilessly and incessantly among themselves, but they close ranks against outsiders, and they are often quick to express their contempt of people who are not "in the game." It is difficult to blame them for this tendency. Much of their contact with the public comes through sports writers, men who hang around the outside of their world, having to report every day about a game that few of them have played. In between game-days a writer facing a deadline has to think of *something* he can say, and many sports-page stories cover some of the most striking non-events of all time. And although hockey players do make fatuous remarks about "only playing one game at a time," they do not confine their conversations solely to such remarks, as anyone reading most sports pages would believe they do. And the result is that not many players hold writers—i.e. the fans—in very much respect. Howe, however, is something of an exception to this rule. Although he is in on all his team's bantering, his jokes, unlike those of most of his colleagues, are almost never directed at someone's person. He is as close to being utterly unassuming as it is possible, after 17 years in a steadily increasing limelight, to be. He seems willing to answer the most banal questions as seriously and fully as he can, and he presents a shy and grateful attitude to the many fans who approach him nearly everywhere he goes. Although he is still a boy-man, in that he still plays a boy's game for a living, he is a mature one.

There is, in fact, very little about Gordie Howe that isn't admirable. His off-ice personality is something that might have been designed by Lord Baden-Powell. He swears, of course. Listening to a hockey player talk without swear words would be like watching him play without his stick. He has been known to consume an entire can of beer in an evening, and to smoke a whole cigar between seasons, but he is not what is usually described as a rake. His most serious sin seems to lie in the wicked number of crossword puzzles he goes through. In Detroit, he is almost more popular than hockey; it is not the game that seems to sell tickets there so much as Howe's domination of it. He gets roughly three times as much mail as the rest of the team combined (typically, he tries to answer all of it himself, and even enlists his wife's help on occasion) and, although Detroit newspapers don't take hockey seriously enough to send their own men on every road trip, as papers in Montreal and Toronto do for their teams, a minor skate cut he suffered this fall was a daily story, with pictures of his foot and lengthy bulletins from the medical department.

For all his fame, Howe is still astonishingly shy. The nervous blinking of both his eyes that is apparent when he is interviewed on television is much less evident in private moments, and when he is relaxing in a pinochle game with teammates it all but disappears. Part of his shyness he covers with his warm, disarming wit, and it is evident that all the people who are in frequent contact with him, from his bosses at the Red Wings to his partners in business to his neighbors' children, whom he sometimes smuggles into the Olympia to go skating, like him as much as they respect his ability to play hockey.

On the ice, though, Howe can be as cruel and vicious as he is personable and generous off it. He is not the most penalized player in the NHL—although only seven men

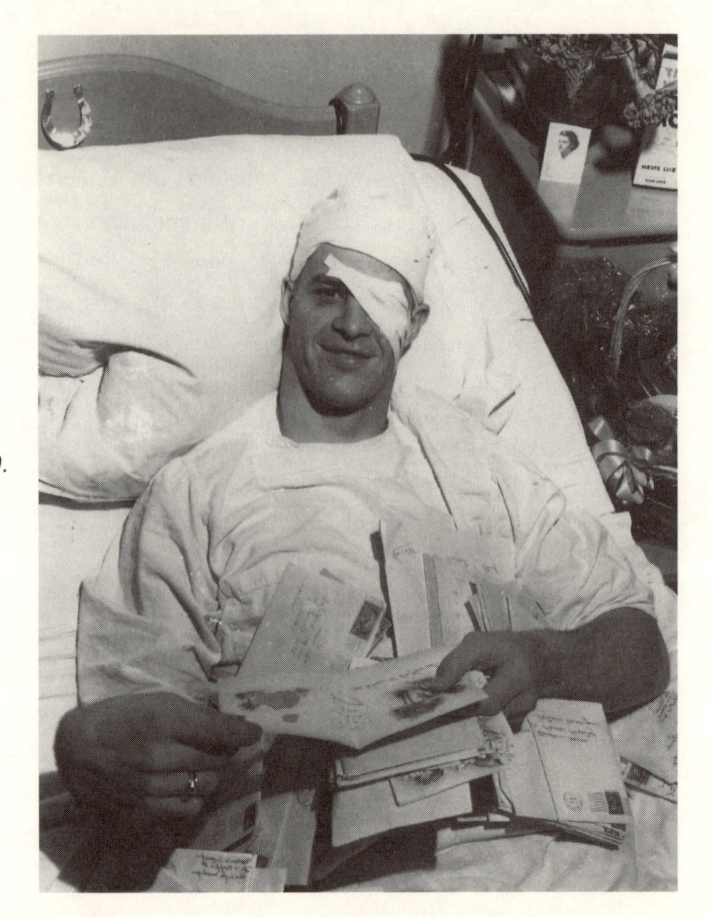

Recovering from his near-death crash into the boards, April, 1950.

had more penalties last year—but he is the acknowledged leader at getting away with things that would draw penalties if the referees saw them. His illegalities are as controlled as his play. He seems able to deal out punishment and pain with a complete lack of passion. In one game a couple of years ago, Howe and Carl Brewer of the Toronto Maple Leafs fell together in a tangle behind the Toronto goal just as play was stopped. Brewer was on top. "ok, ok, Carl," said Howe. "Play's over." Brewer resisted the temptation to give Howe a last one in the clinch, and rose. In the next period, the same two ended another play in another tangle. This time Howe was on top. When the whistle blew, Brewer, thinking a standard of gentlemanliness had been established for the evening, relaxed. Pow! Howe gave him one in the ribs.

"He's always at the outer edge of the rule-book anyway," says Eric Nesterenko of the Chicago Black Hawks, a veteran who has played frequently against Howe man-on-man. "You never know when he's going to slip over into what's dirty." Ted Lindsay, who was Howe's linemate with Detroit for a dozen years and his opponent with Chicago for three more, says, "Gordie gets away with more than anyone else in hockey." Andy Bathgate, the New York Ranger star who was fined by the league in 1960 for writing an article called "Atrocities on Ice," for *True* magazine, has accused Howe of deliberately inflicting head cuts, of deliberately raising the puck at other people's heads. About the only crimes Howe is not generally accused of are the heinous ones of "spearing"—the art of jabbing the business end of a hockey stick into an onrushing opponent's unpadded belly—and "butt-ending," another manoeuvre with a stick that takes place in flurries around the goal mouth or in the corners. He is a recognized master of "high sticking," an action that is almost impossible for the fans or even the referees to separate from an accident, and which has carved his signature on a good many faces around the league.

To the players who suffer most from its effects, Howe's cruelty is a thing to be admired rather than disliked. It is, simply, part of his superiority at their game; violence and intimidation are a facet of hockey, and Howe is good at *all* facets of the game. Furthermore, Howe *has* to be dirty. Because he is so much the outstanding performer on his team, he is—or would be if he allowed it—the most closely checked player in the league: stop Howe and you have stopped Detroit. But a man who holds Howe or clutches him or chips away at him for an evening's play is not likely to come out of that game unscathed. "Sure you're a little scared," says Nesterenko, one of the few frank players in the league. "But you admire him for the way he can keep you off. It's your job to stay with him and keep him under control, but unless you keep thinking about it all the time, you're inclined to stay a step or so away from him."

Still another aspect of Howe's cruelty, of course, is his strength and ability to fight. Red Storey, the former all-around athlete who watched Howe from a referee's vantage point for nine years, has said that if Howe had wanted to, he could have been the heavyweight champion of the world. He is without doubt the heavyweight champion of the NHL. When Howe first broke into the league in the 1940s, Ted Lindsay recalled not long ago, "he seemed to think he had to beat up everyone one at a time." But Jack Adams, then the Red Wings' general manager, took him aside and told him to take it easy. In recent years, Howe hasn't fought very often. He hasn't had to, since not many people want to take him on. But in 1959 he made it clear that he had not relinquished his title by default.

Throughout the 1958–59 season, New York Ranger coach Phil Watson had assigned Eddie Shack, then a bumptious rookie, to stick with Howe when the

Rangers played Detroit, and for the first several games Shack did a remarkably fine job. In New York one night, though, the predictable occurred. Shack emerged from a skirmish with Howe with a face cut that needed three stitches to close. Lou Fontinato, who was then the Rangers' "policeman"—the man charged with retaliating for any indignities his teammates might suffer at the hands of opposing bullies—drew a bead on Howe at the first opportunity and smashed him into the boards. Both Howe and Fontinato dropped their gloves. Fontinato went low, for Howe's body. Howe grabbed him by the sweater with his left hand and, with his right, administered the most famous single punch in NHL history, shattering Fontinato's nose. That week, *Life* magazine ran one full-page photo of Fontinato in the hospital, his nose a wreck and his eyes swollen and bruised, and another of Howe in the dressing room, with his shirt off and his muscles rippling. In a nice summary of the importance of a man playing a body-collision sport like hockey not only *being* tougher than his opponent, but *appearing* to be tougher, the Rangers' coach Watson said later that the heart went out of his team not when Howe threw his mighty punch but when the two contrasting photos appeared for the world to see: the Red Wings' cool Goliath had made a patsy out of their champion. The Rangers finished a bad last that year.

But even Fontinato, a likeable ruffian who has unfortunately been lost to hockey through a serious injury, could not hold Howe's victory over him as a *personal* grudge. Scott Young, then writing his excellent sports column for the Toronto *Globe and Mail*, happened to be present when Howe and Fontinato met for the first time off the ice after their match. "I guess you know Gordie Howe," Young said to Fontinato. "I guess so, but I'm not sure I should lower my hands to shake hands with him," Fontinato said, and then smiled and did so.

"Baseball," goes one of the most common clichés in sports, "is a game of inches." So is hockey. But in hockey the inches, since they are covered a lot more quickly, are not so evident to the casual observer. All the men who play in the NHL—the best 120 or so of the hundreds of thousands of Canadian boys who play hockey in every generation—have completely mastered the fundamentals of their game. By the time one of them has reached that plateau, he can skate, shoot, pass and check nearly as well as he is ever going to, so that the only things that separate those who are going to remain journeymen from those who will rise to stardom are such natural qualities as physique, desire and what might be called hockey sense. Howe has all three in abundance, and in various combinations they have given him a tiny but real advantage over virtually every player in the NHL in virtually every department of the game.

He is so well co-ordinated that he could almost certainly play with the best at any sport he chose to take up. A few years ago, in fact, he became friends with a few of the professional baseball players who live in Detroit and, mostly for conditioning, he worked out with the Detroit Tigers occasionally. Bucky Harris, then manager of the Tigers, saw him in the batting cage one day, pounding balls out into the bleachers with the strongest of Detroit's long-ball hitters, and was heard to remark that it would take only a few months to turn Howe into a regular in the big leagues. And Howe has been seen at a Red Wing practice standing beside the goal, holding his hockey stick like a baseball bat and knocking back many of the hardest shots his teammates tried to fire past him.

Howe's co-ordination, however remarkable, probably does not set him so far apart from the average professional hockey player as his strength does. He can shoot a puck from near one goal and make it rise into the seats at the other end of the rink—an impossible feat for nearly anyone else in the league. One man whose shot comes close in speed to Howe's, which has been measured at a little better than a 120 miles an hour, is Bobby Hull, the glamorous and exceedingly talented star of the Chicago Black Hawks and the man who may some day succeed to Howe's mantle. (Significantly, Hull this year began wearing number 9 on his sweater, after having been 7 for his first six seasons: 9 is Howe's number, and was also worn by Maurice Richard of Montreal, when Richard was the biggest name in hockey.) But for Hull to take his fastest shot he has to raise his stick three or four feet and slap the puck. Howe can move his stick only a foot or so and actually *flick* the puck away at close to his maximum speed. Another curious similarity between Howe, the old bull, and Hull, the young one, is that Howe has for years been the only man in the league who can change the position of his hands on the stick from his natural grip, right-handed, to his unnatural one, left, and still retain most of his power, and now Hull appears to be the second one—although Howe's wrong-side shot is still stronger than Hull's. This technique of switch-hitting, as it were, gives Howe an advantage of an inch or more over anyone who's trying to check him. When he first broke into the league, in 1946, he played against Dit Clapper, who had stayed in the NHL for 20 years, a record Howe is almost certain to match. For all his age, Clapper still had surprising speed, and he was able to stay with most of the young forwards who came scooting in on him. One of the first times Clapper checked the young Howe, though, Howe changed his hands on his stick, thus putting his body between Clapper and the puck, and getting a clear shot on the Boston goal. "I think that's when Dit decided he'd quit hockey," Ted Lindsay says.

Except for his exceptional shot, Howe doesn't move *quickly* on the ice. His motions are graceful and economical; he never seems to waste energy. As one result, he has not only played more NHL games than any other player in history (more than 1,100), but he has frequently been able to put in as much as 45 minutes in a single game. Most forwards average perhaps 25. Howe often comes off the ice exhausted, and he can lose as much as six pounds in a single game, but anyone watching him on the bench will notice that no matter how he droops when he first hits his seat, he always seems to be the first resting player to recuperate. In about half a minute, it seems, his head is up and he is studying the play as if thinking about what he can do during his next shift. Unfortunately for medical science, no one has yet tried to measure the source of Howe's remarkable endurance. His counterpart in basketball, Bob Cousy of the Boston Celtics, now retired, was once discovered by some Massachusetts scientists to discharge ten times as much of an adrenal hormone called epinephrine as any other basketball player they tested. It would be fascinating to see if Howe has similar characteristics, or if he secretes an exceptional amount of another adrenal hormone, norepinephrine, which is associated with "aggression, anger and competitiveness," and is sometimes called the hockey player's hormone.

Physical gifts aside, Howe brings to hockey a fierce pride and dedication that would probably have made him excel at whatever line of work he'd chosen. As it is, he applies it to bowling and golf, at both of which he can beat any of the people he plays with. Whatever he does, he must win, and in hockey he's been willing to work long hours to achieve his near-perfection. In their early years, for instance, Howe and his linemate Lindsay used to stay at practice well after lesser luminaries of the Detroit team had gone to the showers, and work on special plays. Once they discovered that if the puck were shot into the other team's corner at a certain angle it could be made to bounce out in front of the goal, but out of the goalie's reach. Howe and Lindsay worked on this play for hours, until they were able to use it in games, and for a season or two Lindsay received dozens of apparently fluke breakaways by going straight at the goal while Howe shot the puck into the corner. Now, of course, every team in the league executes this play (usually most effectively on home ice, since all boards react differently).

Howe's third talent seems, to some, almost supernatural. He appears to anticipate the puck—or his opponents—almost as if play gravitated toward him by some natural force. In fact, it is a result of many qualities: a thorough knowledge of the game, his ability to remain always in control of himself, and his high sense of timing.

Hockey at the NHL level is not so much a matter of *how* you make your move—since so little separates the good players from the mediocre in their ability to make it—but *when*. With his graceful control, Howe can appear to the man checking him to be relaxed, but if that man gives him so much as half a step, Howe will seize on the instant to send or receive a pass or get away a shot. In the same way, he can sense a play developing, and without giving away his plans to the man on his back, move toward the place he knows the puck must come, or shake his check for the brief instant that he will be in the clear. Situations form and disintegrate so rapidly when a hockey game is flowing back and forth at full tilt that a split second's advantage—an "inch" of ice—is all a player of Howe's certainty needs to appear to be all by himself. (Another reason Howe gets the puck a lot, of course, is that his teammates give it to him as often as they can, as who would not?)

In the opinion of the people who ought to be able to judge best, Howe is now not quite as fast a skater as he was a few years ago (he never was as fast a breakaway skater as Maurice Richard), although he can still move pretty rapidly when he gets loose. If he's lost anything in speed, though, he has more than made up for it in guile. Last season, when he led the league in scoring for the first time in five years (he did it five times in the '50s), and led Detroit into a surprisingly close Stanley Cup final, Dave Keon, the young Toronto Maple Leaf star, remarked: "There are four strong teams in this league and two weak ones. The weak ones are Boston and New York and the strong ones are Toronto, Chicago, Montreal and Gordie Howe."

Howe began to skate at about the age of five. He was the fifth of nine children of a family that had been farming in the district of Floral, Sask., in 1928 when Gordon was born. The family had moved to a two-storey clapboard house on Avenue L North in Saskatoon when he was an infant. From the time he got his first pair of skates, he recalls, he spent most of his winters on ice, skating across a series of sloughs to get to school, or playing hockey outdoors. As a boy, he played goal, and he recalls that one teacher told him "if I ever moved out from between the pipes I'd never get anywhere in hockey." (Howe thinks his season and a half as a goalie, holding his stick with one hand, has something to do with his ability to switch-hit as a pro.)

In the summers, young Gordie worked on farms around Saskatoon, putting in 12-hour days, and, he says, eating five big meals a day. His father was nearly as strong as Gordie is today. Gordie remembers straining to hold up one end of a giant boulder they were lifting together, and his father muttering, "Come on, boy, don't let me down." He weighed 200 pounds at 16. But talent bird-dogs from the professional hockey clubs had sniffed him out even before that. Fred McCrorry, a scout for the New York Rangers, talked him into going to the Rangers' training camp at Winnipeg the summer he was 15.

The camp was a miserable experience for him. On the first day of practice, the boy who had been assigned as his roommate was injured and Howe was forced to spend the remaining weeks by himself. He was too shy to join in the general scramble at mealtime, and occasionally missed eating. Homesick, he went back to Saskatoon.

The next year, though, a Detroit scout named Fred Pinckney was able to talk him into trying the Red Wings' camp at Windsor, Ont., and Jack Adams signed him to a contract to play with the Red Wings' Junior A farm team in Galt, Ont. This was an "illegal" transfer, taking a western boy to an eastern team, and Howe was forced to spend his first year away from home as a pariah, allowed on the ice only in practice games. (He did, in fact, play one league game, which the Galt Red Wings won but had to forfeit because of his participation.) His shyness affected his life in Galt, too. The Red Wings had enrolled him at the Galt Collegiate Institute and Vocational School. But, never a good student, he "took one look at the size of the campus and all those kids and decided not to go." Instead, he got a job at Galt Metal Industries, and suffered through his lonely winter.

The next year, 1945, the Red Wings sent him to their U.S. Hockey League team in Omaha, Neb., where he scored 22 goals and convinced his bosses that he would be ready for the big team at 18.

In Omaha, Howe had been so shy that he used to leave the arena by the dressing-room window rather than face the ardent fans outside the door—particularly a very ardent girl fan the Omaha players called Spaghetti-Legs. The Red Wings hit on a good antidote. They gave him, as a roommate, Ted Lindsay, a cocky, aggressive youngster from Kirkland Lake, Ont., who went on to become the game's third leading goal scorer, behind only Howe and Richard. These two vastly different personalities quickly became good friends and earnest allies in the Detroit cause, and to this day are mutual admirers.

Howe was slow to start in the NHL, although he scored a goal in his first game, and before his first season was over had won a fight with Maurice Richard and lost his front teeth. In his first three years in the NHL, he scored only 35 goals, but he hit his stride quickly after that, matching his total of 35 in his fourth season alone. Since then he has failed to score 30 goals only three times, and for one of those seasons, he was named the most valuable player in the league anyway. For the last 14 years, he has completely dominated the statistics of the NHL, never being worse than sixth in the league scoring, making eight first and five second all-star teams, being judged the most valuable player to his team six times. When he finally scored his 545th goal in league play this year and passed Maurice Richard's lifetime total, he completed a clean sweep of all the significant scoring records: most goals, most assists and, naturally, most points. Since he intends to play at least two more seasons after this one, he will undoubtedly run his record totals well out beyond the reach of anyone now in sight.

Hockey has been immensely good to Howe—almost as good as he has been to it. Through the years, he has suffered far fewer than his share of injuries. (Although he has had serious ones. In the Stanley Cup finals in 1950 he hit the boards after missing a check on Toronto's Ted Kennedy and slumped unconscious to the ice. For two days he was close to death, and an operation was needed to relieve the pressure on his brain. In the season of 1952–53, he broke his right wrist around Christmas time. But he had a cast put on, played the next game and went on to win the scoring championship. In 18 seasons, he's missed only 43 games.) He is now being paid $35,000 a year by the Red Wings, and his outside activities may well bring him nearly as much again. He is a partner in a commercial rink in Detroit called Gordie Howe's Hockey-land, and in another firm that sells ice-cream machines. He is known as a cool negotiator. He endorses a cornucopia of products from milk to shirts. This year, Campbell Soup has brought out a little hard-cover book called *Hockey . . . Here's Howe*, written by Howe and the Toronto writer, Bob Hesketh, from which young players who have a dollar and two soup carton fronts can learn the fundamentals. Howe also has a column in the *Toronto Star*.

Howe will likely stay in hockey when his playing days are over. The Red Wings have already named him an assistant coach, and it does not seem impossible that he will take over all the coaching when he retires, so that Sid Abel, now handling both that job and the general manager's, can concentrate on being manager.

There is some light on the horizon for the fans who will miss Howe's power and grace. At least one of his three sons—to avoid family jealousies no one is supposed to say publicly which one—has all the makings of a hockey player. He's big for his age, skates with long, strong strides, and has a powerful shot. But I suppose it would be too much to hope for another Gordie Howe.

The previous season was the last time Gordie Howe won a scoring title, and he placed fifth during the 1963–64 campaign. In the playoffs, the Red Wings beat Chicago in the semifinals, but lost the Cup to Toronto in overtime in the seventh game.

Gordie Goes Home

John Robertson

October 15, 1966—They were all there, every marching band that mattered in Saskatoon—the Fireman's Band, the Police Band, the Boys' Pipe Band—all puckering for effect and exchanging cacophonous bleeps and blares as they primed their brasses and woodwinds for the big blow. Equally resplendent, a block-long cavalcade of sleek new convertibles was glittering in the sunshine, growling through chrome teeth at parade chairman Alf Bentley as he gave the order to start engines. And in the last car, the profile was familiar, but Gordie Howe was not the burly imposing figure western TV hockey fans remember, but a fidgety father of four, rubbing his sweating palms together and making a brave attempt to engage in idle chitchat with his family—anything to help stem the mounting tension within him. All his adult life, he had earned a living performing under the critical scrutiny of thousands, but he could shut them out then, because he had been preoccupied with a stick and a puck. Now, just around the corner on this bright July morning, were 70,000 people—two-thirds of the entire population of Saskatoon—waiting along the parade route to stand him the emotional binge of his life: Gordie Howe Day in his old hometown.

Sitting there, beside his attractive blond wife, Colleen, Howe wore the expression of a nervous rookie about to take the ice for his first NHL game. He had confided to friends the night before that it was going to take all the stamina he could muster just to retain his composure throughout this day. Lavish tributes had always embarrassed him, and this mass eulogy was to last 14 hours. The parade was only the start.

The cavalcade was moving now, inching around the corner onto 21st Street, where the first phalanx of well-wishers were wedged tightly from curb to storefront, bobbing up and down for a better view, like so many tufts of prairie wheat. Soon Gordie's face began erupting in a succession of explosive grins as he swivelled to and fro to acknowledge the shouted greetings from people on both sides of the street. Periodically, his head would bow, and the corners of his mouth would sag, as if in sombre

Signing autographs in Saskatoon on Gordie Howe Day, July 22, 1966.

reflection of the old days. There were no convertibles to ride in then. He and his boyhood pal Mike Yano were lucky if they had bus fare. But they didn't mind the subzero frost nipping at their ears and noses, or the squeaking snow underfoot as they walked over to the Hudson Bay Slough on those winter afternoons. It had all started for Gordie that day—a woman in a flimsy cloth coat stood on the front door stoop of the Howe house on Avenue L North, her bare fingers wrapped around a huge gunny sack. It was December, 1933, and she was shivering, but not from the cold. Mrs. Howe answered her knock immediately and invited her inside. "Can you help me out?" the caller pleaded. "My husband and baby are both sick, and we have no milk. If you'll give me a dollar, you can have everything in this sack."

Without even glancing down, Mrs. Howe went to the kitchen, dipped a hand into the jar that held her milk money, returned to the door, and pressed $1.50 into the woman's hand. When the woman was gone, Mrs. Howe took the sack and dumped its contents onto her linoleum floor. Among the items considered expendable for

Gordie Goes Home

milk that day was a pair of skates. Five-year-old Gordie quickly grabbed one, and his older sister had eagerly pounced on the other.

The next day, hand in hand, the two youngsters were off to the rink, wearing one skate apiece—size six and far too big, with rags stuffed in the boots to make them fit. A week later, Edna surrendered her skate to her little brother, and every night from then on they would stagger home from the rink for supper, tired and covered with snow from countless tumbles. But he was learning to skate. And one day, young Gordie Howe would skate and play hockey better than anyone else in the world.

His mother, Mrs. Catherine Howe, was tingling all over as she rode, quite erect, beside her husband, Ab Howe, in the car ahead of Gordie's and she glowed with pride as she saw and heard an entire city eulogizing her son. But more than pride was causing her to cherish this day. For the first time in 18 years all nine Howe children were together.

It was a rare occasion to reminisce about those days when Gordie was a mischievous little boy. When he was five years old, he used to scour the back lanes, looking for corn syrup labels in garbage tins. Then he'd get his sisters to send away for hockey pictures for him. "He was crazy about any picture or book on hockey," his mother recalled. "He couldn't read, but he'd thumb through them anyway." And he was always asking her, "Can I be a hockey player some day? Can I, Mom?" When he was six or seven he'd come home from school, and it was "C'mon, Mom, let's play hockey." Gordie would find her an old stick and they'd either play in the kitchen with old sealer tops, or go outside and shoot rocks against the shingled veranda.

As the parade was rolling past the halfway point on Second Avenue, one of the Howe youngsters made a face at a photographer and promptly received a cuff behind the ear from his dad. When he wasn't exchanging hellos and salutes with the crowd, Gordie's eyes flitted back and forth between huge placards, being hoisted by young children, emblazoned with slogans: "We love you, Gordie" ... "Long live Gordie Howe."

The presence of so many youngsters seemed to relax him a little. After all, he wasn't skating around now in front of millions of TV fans; he was just back home. And for all they cared, he could probably slip away later and take a few shots at the side of his old house if he wanted to. Ab Howe chuckled now when he thought of the beating those veranda shingles used to take. "The house wasn't ours ... and I was afraid we'd get kicked out. But every day, it was the same thing."

In the winter, Gordie would go down to the Hudson Bay Slough every weekend with a school chum named Frank Shedden, and they'd play hockey from morning until dusk. There'd be 30 or 40 boys on each side, and the final score would be something like 369 to 300. "There was no passing," said Shedden. "You just tried to get the puck. And I seem to recall we spent most of the time chasing Gordie."

Now the parade was over, and members of the cavalcade were gathering with civic officials at JD's restaurant, where Ernie Cole, the mayor of Saskatoon, read an official proclamation declaring July 22 to be Gordie Howe Day.

Gordie was feeling a bit jittery when he rose to make his first speech of the day. "I'd much rather be fishing than speaking here now," he said. "I'll be a nervous wreck by tonight. But this tops everything that ever happened to me… except my wedding."

Gordie went on, telling the gathering how he lacked sufficient education to make a proper thank-you speech. That apologetic explanation seems to be almost a reflex action every time he steps onto a public platform. As a speaker, he has developed a homespun delivery that generates warmth in any audience, mainly because he seldom strays from easily digestible anecdotes about hockey. But his poised manner now is a radical departure from the way his brothers and sisters remember him as a boy.

"I don't know how he got anywhere being so shy and quiet," said his sister Vi. But she could see it coming out in him then, the way he handled a hockey stick, as if it were part of his body. "Hockey seemed to be built right in him."

Gordie was scrambling just to keep his limbs intact later in the afternoon, when 4,000 youngsters converged on him as he stepped from the bus to mount a podium and officially dedicate Gordon Howe Park. It was really much more than just a playing area, because it contained a golf course, football field, baseball and fastball diamonds, a campsite and a hockey rink. "It's nice to be among fellow teen-agers," he said once he got to the microphone. "Things weren't that great here a few years ago. I used to sneak onto the golf course, and hide in a chicken house when the golf pro chased me." The youngsters squealed with delight as their god exposed his clay feet.

"He used to come home crying when the other boys pushed him around," Mrs. Howe recalled privately. "But he soon stopped that, when I pushed him back out and told him to learn to take care of himself."

Gordie stayed on to sign autographs for a full hour at his newly christened park, before he left to attend first a private family supper, then the big testimonial evening at the Saskatoon Arena. As he was boarding the bus, weariness was mirrored on his face. He turned to his wife and said, "This is harder on me than a playoff game."

Now it was evening, and 4,000 people, who had each paid $1 to $2.50 admission, were settling into hardbacked chairs at the Saskatoon Arena, looking forward to three hours of verbal tributes to Gordie from 14 hockey dignitaries, including NHL President Clarence Campbell. As he stepped onto the stage, Howe was looking refreshed by the quiet hours he had spent with his family at the dinner break. He was wearing his maroon Red Wing blazer and a pair of grey slacks. As he took his place beside wife, Colleen, and their four children—Marty, 12, Mark, 11, Cathy, 7, and Murray, 5—the people began springing from their chairs to give him a standing ovation. Two locally well-known broadcasters, Lloyd Saunders and Vern Prior, took turns introducing the speakers. Gordie stirred restlessly in his chair, bowing his head periodically and gripping the bridge of his nose with his forefingers as each superlative was punctuated by applause from the audience.

Pierre Pilote of the Chicago Black Hawks pointed out how Gordie brought out the best in everyone he ever played against; and John Ferguson of the Montreal Canadiens got everybody chuckling when he said, "I know I have to go back to Richardland after I say this, but Gordie Howe is the greatest of them all." Other tributes soon followed, and then it was Jack Adams's turn, and the former general manager of the Wings pulled a rumpled piece of paper out of his pocket and read a poem.

> Isn't it strange, that princes and kings,
> And clowns that caper in sawdust rings,
> And common folk like you and me,
> Are builders of eternity?
>
> To each is given a bag of tools,
> A shapeless mass and a set of rules,
> And each must make, ere life goes on,
> A stumbling block or a stepping stone.

"Gordie Howe was given a bag of tools and I don't have to tell you what he's done with them," Adams went on. "I know he's made my life in hockey."

Finally, as the arena clock was inching toward 11 p.m., it was time to hear from the Big Fella. He strode slowly to the rostrum, amid deafening cheers. His two smallest children, Murray and Cathy, tagged along on either side of him, tugging at his hands and digging into his jacket pockets, oblivious to the crowd. Tears welled in Gordie's eyes as he began, "I feel like a small lost boy... I don't know where to start thanking people... If I can live up to 10 per cent of the things said about me here tonight, I'll be a lucky man... I am a lucky man to have such fine friends and such a wonderful family. My ma?... well, she's just the apple of my eye..."

Then he was bowing his head and trying to compose himself as he hugged his two youngsters with those massive forearms. "It's been an unbelievable day... all you wonderful people... and those thousands at the parade. Listening to all these words has kind of gotten to me. I hope you don't mind if I shed a tear or two."

Now just about everyone's eyes were brimming, especially Mrs. Howe's, who had first carried Gordie into Saskatoon in a baby shawl. The family had moved to town from the nearby hamlet of Floral when he was just nine days old. She might also have been wondering what would have happened 33 years ago if Gordie's sister hadn't given up that other skate.

Gordie had stopped returning to Saskatoon for the summer 10 years ago, and there had been some under-current of resentment in the city when he chose to live year around in Lathrup Village, Mich., a suburb of Detroit. But that was all forgotten now he had shown the people of Saskatoon a side of Gordie Howe all children could freely imitate with full parental blessing—Howe the attentive, loving son; the doting, exemplary father; the living legend who still has a lot of little boy in him.

Longtime newspaper sports writer John Robertson has contributed numerous columns and articles to Maclean's.

The Miracle Worker

Robert Miller

January 23, 1978—It is late in a game long since won by the New England Whalers (final score: 7–2), but the inappropriately named Soviet All-Stars keep skating, skating, skating. As the Russians buzz around goalie Al Smith, the Whaler defence looks momentarily bewildered. Coach Harry Neale taps the famous sloping shoulder and Number 9 is over the boards, chugging into the action. Whap! Down goes a Russian. Crunch! Down goes another one. And suddenly, here's Gordie Howe, gliding sedately up the right wing, the puck his by the divine right of elbows. The Russians give chase and, over on the left wing, a young Whaler named Mark Howe cuts across the blue line, heading for the net. The pass, of course, is perfect. Mark Howe scores, with an assist from Dad. Later still: the Russians are again storming the Whaler net and, in the space of a few seconds, Number 9 goes down twice to block shots with his body, an assemblage of bone and muscle and scar-tissue so extraordinary that one day it surely must be cast in bronze or ensconced in the Smithsonian. The game ends, and Soviet coach Boris Majorov just shakes his head in wonderment while Number 9 stands there, grinning, blinking back the sweat.

Gordie Howe, in his 50th year, blocking shots against Russians? "Aw well," he says later, "you just kinda get into the game and it just kinda happens." And the body checks? "Yeah, well, I guess I drilled a couple of those guys." Drilled. That's Gordie Howe's word for what he's been doing to enemy players in various leagues ever since Black Jack Stewart was a household word, since the only murder done in Detroit happened in the Olympia during Red Wings games, since, in fact, the Russians were our allies. A thousand goals ago.

The night the Whalers played the Soviets in the Hartford, Conn., Civic Centre, Howe was honored in a pregame ceremony, for finally having scored number 1,000 (regular season and playoff, National Hockey League and World Hockey Association). The 10,000 fans gave him an ovation and two of his teammates presented him with a commemorative gold puck. The teammates, of course, were his sons—winger Mark and defenceman Marty. On and off the ice, the Howes like to keep it all in the family. And why not? It's quite a family. Gordie is a certified marvel, his sons Mark and Marty are certified professional hockey stars, third son Murray is a certified scholar as well as an up-and-coming hockey player himself, daughter Cathy is the certified apple of her father's ever-blinking eye as she completes her high school and plans a summer wedding, and wife/mother/chief cheerleader Colleen, well, Colleen is the glue that holds it all together.

Half a century on, Gordie Howe is having the time of his life. He's also playing some excellent hockey, albeit in what is a somewhat less-than-excellent league. As mid-season approached, the Whalers were solidly in first place in the WHA and Howe was the team's leading scorer, despite an injury-plagued 10-game stretch during which he was frustrated in his search for number 1,000. It came, finally, on a power play in Birmingham, Ala., which is in the heart of Dixie and which says something about what is happening to Old Man Winter's game these days.

For the Howes of Detroit, Houston and now Hartford, it has not all been fun. There have been hurts, both physical and mental, and feuds, both corporate and individual. The family left Detroit hurt, but hopeful. It left Houston angry, but determined. It has settled, now, in Connecticut—Gordie and Colleen live in a big house on a 16-acre estate—and claims to be happy at last. Fame, fortune and Gordie's elbows have sustained the family, and now the family as well as the New England Whalers sustain Gordie. "His whole life is there in the rink, in the dressing room," says Colleen. "He can't wait to get to practice, just to see what some of the younger members of the team will do or say next. Then, he can't wait to get home to tell me about it. There are a lot of characters on this team, and they're always poking fun at Gord. Why, the night he got his thousandth, (WHA president) Howard Baldwin asked Gordie to say a few words in the dressing room after the game, and do you know what they did? They *gonged* him! Gordie loved it."

Not surprisingly, the players love Gordie. It is quite incredible that only three members of the Whalers—centre Dave Keon, winger John McKenzie and goalie Al Smith—were even born when Howe scored number one against Turk Broda and the Toronto Maple Leafs, back in 1946. Says Keon, who is a pro's pro and who played against Howe in the NHL for 11 seasons: "He's a fantastic guy, not just as a hockey player but as a man. The kids on this team are really overwhelmed by his presence." McKenzie, who is 40 now, has polished a favorite line about Howe: "When I broke

With sons Mark (left) and Marty.

in with the Red Wings in 1959, I used to tell people Gordie was amazing for his age. In 1959! And here he is, still amazing." His coach, Harry Neale, says bluntly that Howe is the "greatest athlete any of us have ever seen."

Watching Howe in his green track suit, practising one morning in Birmingham, Johnny F. Bassett, president of the Birmingham Bulls, chuckles: "He's unbelievable, like a great big kid. Look at him out there. Never misses a practice." This particular morning, the team has divided itself into U.S. and Canadian citizens for a loose scrimmage. Gordie is playing defence, teasing the kids, tripping them up, giving them gentle elbow massages. They shout back fearsome and unprintable insults. Every time the U.S. players score on Gordie and the Canadians they line up on the blue line and sing *"The Star-Spangled Banner."*

Alas, the fun will soon be over for Gordie Howe, native of Floral, Sask., and subject of as many legends as he is author of goals. "This is definitely it," Howe says. "I won't play next year." A thousand goals and a million miles are enough. Next season he'll help the Whalers recruit and develop talent, spend some time selling steel for the Fitzsimmons Steel Co. of Youngstown, Ohio, and leave the playing to the kids. Of course, Howe has retired before, only to feel the itch again in September and to decide that maybe he ought to lace them on one more year and go out and drill a few people.

Other sports have had their geriatric marvels. One-time quarterback George Blanda was still kicking field goals for the National Football League's Oakland Raiders at the age of 49. Satchel Paige was still pitching big-league baseball in his 50s. Soccer's Sir Stanley Matthews led Stoke City into England's First Division in his late 40s. But no sport has ever had a performer as skilled and as old as hockey's Gordie Howe, whose physique is as responsible as his expertise for the high level of his game-in, game-out performance. Howe not only keeps up with players less than half his age; in spurts he can keep ahead of them. This is all the more remarkable when Howe says quite sincerely: "The game today is much better than when I broke in. The players are bigger, and they move a lot faster."

But do they? Or, as its many critics contend, has hockey regressed in the decade since the NHL expanded? Certainly when there were only six major-league teams there were only 120 major-league jobs. Now there are 26 teams calling themselves major-league, providing about 550 jobs. It seems clear that Howe's longevity, however much of a personal triumph it may be, is due in part to the dilution rather than the improvement of his sport. Facilities have improved and salaries have gone into orbit (the three playing Howes alone will earn roughly $400,000 this year). And the athletes are bigger and stronger, as Howe says. But the net result seems to be ennui, rather than excitement, for the fans, financial nightmares, rather than bonanzas, for most of the owners, and fretfulness, rather than fun, for many of the players.

North American hockey is not in good shape. The WHA has shrunk from 14 teams to eight, after its ill-starred attempt last summer to merge with the NHL. Alan Eagleson, hockey's Mr. Everything, who wears as one of his hats the executive directorship of the NHL Players' Association, says again and again that the NHL has too many teams skating over too much thin financial ice (Colorado Rockies, Atlanta Flames, Cleveland Barons, Pittsburgh Penguins, even the once-mighty Detroit Red Wings and Chicago Black Hawks are all box-office disaster areas). Despite its relentless efforts, the NHL has failed to find and maintain a U.S. television network deal of the type that so enriches football, baseball and basketball. With Bobby Orr gone, Gordie Howe going and Bobby Hull racing around rinks in such unlikely places as Indianapolis and Tokyo, hockey is hard-pressed to come up with the superstars so crucial to the mass popularity of any game today. Boston Bruins coach Don Cherry is unequivocal on the point: "The age of the superstar, except for Guy Lafleur, has passed." The reason: "Everybody's playing a system now." In pro hockey today, a system is quite simply a defensive-oriented, grind-out-a-win-and-never-mind-how-it-looks approach that inhibits the kind of freewheeling that the Howes, Hulls, Orrs, Jean Beliveaus and Rocket Richards used to display as a matter of course.

The idea that international hockey, which in 1972, 1974 and during the Canada Cup of 1976 so thrilled fans everywhere, might save the game and keep the fans happy is also fading. New York Rangers captain Phil Esposito, a true international star, grumbled about having to practise on Christmas Day in order to get ready for an exhibition game against a club team from Czechoslovakia. "The owners," growled Espo, "are greedy." Toronto Maple Leafs president Harold Ballard called the game his team lost to the same Czechs "utterly stupid... a waste of time," although he still found it in his heart to charge $13.50 for the best tickets.

If anything, this season there has been far too much international hockey. The Junior World Cup, in which Canada's best young players failed to make the final, was one legitimate event, even though it was a box-office failure. But much of the rest of this season's international play smacked, in Montreal goaltender Ken Dryden's words, "of plain old-fashioned barnstorming." Czech and Soviet teams, representing far from the best talent these countries have available, played their way through the WHA, losing more often than winning, during December. Two more Czech teams, Kladno and Pardubice, plus Russia's Spartak played 13 exhibitions against NHL clubs, winning more often than losing. The Soviet national team was preparing for a January romp through the WHA's buildings. The Quebec Nordiques went off to Moscow to be clobbered in the *Izvestia* invitational tournament. Bobby Hull and the Winnipeg Jets flew off to Tokyo to lose three straight games to the Russians over Christmas. Amid so much uncertainty, Gordie Howe's durability and consistency take on new importance: here, after all, is something real, something a fan can believe in, whatever the merits of the league he plays in.

Howe will be 50 on March 31. The Whalers have a game that night, against Indianapolis Racers, and Colleen and Howard Baldwin are planning a mammoth celebration. Colleen will organize it, just the way she organizes everything Gordie does off the ice. "He just hates paperwork and stuff like that," she says. "Over the years I've just naturally taken on more and more of it." Today, Colleen Howe, who recently passed her insurance agent's exam, does most of the contract negotiating for her husband and two sons. She does their public relations groundwork, handles the mail, prepares their itineraries, gets their airplane tickets for non-Whalers travel. She is a kind of family general manager, and she enjoys the work. "I'm smart enough to know when I need a lawyer or an accountant, and smart enough to hire them when I do," she says, anticipating a question. "I know people have criticized me, people like Ted (Lindsay, Gordie's old Red Wing linemate who this year took over as general manager of the Detroit team). But things have worked out pretty well."

It is easy, looking at Colleen Howe with her fluffy blond hair and attractive features and figure, to understand how a lonely farm boy plunked down in a big city could fall in love with her (they met in a Detroit bowling alley when she was 17, he 22, and were married three years later) and stay in love with her. "People say I'm henpecked," Howe says, frowning at such effrontery. "Well, let them say it. But Colleen likes doing things, and she does them pretty well, so I say let her carry on. She's done a great job raising the kids and keeping me going."

Besides hockey and the family, Howe's passions are crossword puzzles and bridge. "It used to be the hockey players played rummy or euchre or pinochle," he laughs. "Now everyone plays bridge." Howe's love of crossword puzzles, he concedes, is a direct outgrowth of his self-consciousness about dropping out of school at 15. "That's where I made my big mistake, I guess." But as Father Athol Murray, the late head of Saskatchewan's Notre Dame College and a man who proved an inspiration to so many young Prairie Canadians, once told Howe, every Canadian boy could go to school but no Canadian boy could play hockey quite like Gordie Howe.

Howe is demonstrably kind, signing autographs and joking with his public wherever he goes; making personal appearances throughout North America, to reminisce about the old days in pro hockey and marvel at the new ones. But that is off the ice. On it, he's still an intimidating presence. That's how he has survived. "I've been lucky with injuries," he admits. "I've had three knee operations, but they've all taken. Other guys, well... It's just a shame about Bobby Orr. I'd have to say he was the best player I ever saw." (Orr says the same thing about Howe.) Only once in his long career has Howe been badly hurt, and then he almost died after missing Maple Leaf captain Teeder Kennedy with a check and going head first into the boards.

His records are too numerous and too well known to list. Quite simply, he holds all the important ones. He's proud of them but not preoccupied by them. Even his 1,000-goal total, which would have once been considered as unreachable as the moon used to be, may eventually fall to Bobby Hull. But his achievement in playing 30 years of major-league hockey (not counting two years when he retired from the NHL and sat around a Red Wing office with nothing to do but go to banquets for Bruce Norris) and ending up his career on the same team as two of his sons is a record that should stand as long as the game is played. Meantime, until the WHA playoffs end in May or June, enemy players are advised to keep their heads up or Number 9 will drill them. Next year, they'll be able to relax. Unless, that is, Howe gets the itch again, come September.

Gordie Howe did play the following season and the next one — his 32nd — before retiring at 52. Mr. Hockey ended his career with 1,071 goals and 2,589 total points. When he hung up his skates in 1980, he was the NHL career leader in goals, assists, total points, games and years played. Howe now lives in Traverse City, Mich., about 400 km northwest of Detroit. He makes dozens of personal appearances each year and is heavily involved in charity work for children and youth.

Robert Miller worked as a senior editor at Maclean's from 1976 to 1978 and as a senior writer from 1983 to 1985.

Memories of a Time that Never Changes

Allan Fotheringham

February 8, 1993—In Saskatoon in winter, with the steam trails from the chimneys tracing the night air over the South Saskatchewan, the most pleasant place in town is Firehall No. 3. This is because—its great glass folding doors intact, its sliding pole from the second floor intact—it's a restaurant, lovingly restored and decorated by its new owners and called, cleverly, Firehall No. 3.

A stranger to town, chewing over his pork ribs with pleasant companions and gazing through the vast glass doors, suddenly spies across the road a scene out of a boy's dreams. A clutch of youths, perhaps eight or 10, ranging from six years to teen-age hulks, all in their favorite hockey jerseys, skating in the dark in those never-ending pickup games on a formless little rink, their breath hanging in the air.

To the stranger, it brings it all back. Skate after school, skate all night. Mothers pleading through the back doors to come in for homework or warmth or fear of frostbite and chilblains, all of the warnings meaning nothing since a future role as left wing of the Toronto Maple Leafs was surely in the future.

It's how Gordie Howe and Nick Metz and Bill Barilko and Elmer Lach and Toe Blake learned it, on a frozen pond, not some artificial rink in an arena with a Howie Meeker-trained coach and stage mothers sitting, hunched in the cold, watching their darlings.

The stranger finds it hard explaining all this to his pleasant companions, feeling like a dinosaur from the swamp, attempting to evoke an era when every boy on the Prairies, his Beehive Corn Syrup coupons going in to someplace in Ontario to return a stand-up photo of Bob Davidson—stick flat on ice, no helmet, no visor, hair slicked down like Rudolph Valentino—a guy who probably made up to $6,000 a year for being the checking forward to Apps and Drillon.

One wonders, as the wine flows, whether these tads outside the window dream in their reverie of wearing—some day!—the famous sweaters of the Anaheim Flying

Ducks? As they fly over the snowbank boards of their imaginary rink, do they lust in their hearts to be in some future heaven wearing the livery of the Tampa Bay Lightning?

Is there a single one of them, as their mothers call one last time from the back stoop, who want in their secret dreams to be a San Jose Shark? One wonders and ponders. Is there a juvenile left winger in Rouleau who seriously lusts to body check in Florida?

The young proprietor, who has the finely chiselled features of Montgomery Clift, is justifiably proud of his icon-cum-restaurant. Once the jewel of Saskatoon was the Capital Theatre, one of those wonders of the '30s that were the centres of culture and decorated in like manner.

The modern age, of course, rendered the property too valuable for such trivial pursuits, an insurance tower yielding much more to those to whom land is everything. As the cold city fathers put the theatre under the wrecker's ball, the firehall thinker and friends rescued the magnificent chandeliers, the cast-iron lighting mounts, and the fire station looks, well, elegant.

Old joke: two American matrons, in the 1940s, are doing a railway tour of the Great White North. Train stops in unknown station. Matron leans out the window to address a local lout, toothpick in mouth, leaning against the station, and asks him where she is. "Saskatoon, Saskatchewan," he offers. She turns to her companion: "Isn't that delightful. They don't speak English." Old joke.

The diner recalls a Canadian classic that is all about a hockey sweater. Roch Carrier's unforgettable story about the Quebec boy who receives in the mail, not the Montreal Canadien jersey his mother ordered, but the alien colors of the Toronto Maple Leafs and, to much derision and contempt, must wear it in the pickup games. There is Canada on ice. He reads the story on the Peter Gzowski show every so often in response to constant requests.

They are having some trouble with the wine list, as with all new restaurants. Firehall No. 3 opened on Nov. 10. They have had to put a protective shield around the fireman's pole on the second floor since on opening night two ladies—the wine must have been good then—insisted on sliding down it, with not entirely satisfactory results.

This very day, Saskatoon has been the venue for the largest protest rally of farmers ever held in Western Canada. Quiet and orderly, 12,704 farmers gathered to express their bitterness over their economic plight, brought about by an international

Playing shinny, 1998.

trade war between heavily subsidized French and American farmers that has driven the price of wheat to Depression-era levels.

The town of Floral, which spawned Gordie Howe, who will be 65 next month, is right outside Saskatoon. It is now 10 p.m. and, the last mother apparently having given up, there are two lone figures still on the rink, one goalie and one shooter, still eking the last fun out of the moon. Saskatchewan will survive.

Allan Fotheringham, a winner of both national magazine and national newspaper awards and a best-selling author, has written a regular column for Maclean's *since October, 1975.*

THE ROCKET

Maurice Richard off the Ice

June Callwood

May 9, 1959—Maurice Richard and his wife, Lucille, live with their six children in a 13-room stone house on the northeast shore of the island on which Montreal is built. Their living room windows overlook a strip of park, beyond which is the river where in summer the Richard boat is in constant use, towing the older children or their father on water skis.

In the winter Maurice is kept busy at his trade which is hockey. The man known as Rocket holds 16 individual scoring records, the greatest scorer the game has ever known. Only four players in the history of the National Hockey League have scored more than 300 goals; at midwinter this year Richard had scored 525 in season play and an extra 81 in playoff games. He has been named on all-star teams 14 years in succession; only severe injuries, a broken leg one season and cut tendons the other, kept him from stretching that record to 16.

This winter, in his 17th season, the Montreal Canadiens phenomenal right winger was injured again. He broke a bone in his ankle, an accident that reminded apprehensive fans that Richard at 37 is the oldest active player in the league and cannot be expected to withstand much more battering. Richard himself needed no reminders; for the past few years he has been thinking of little else; he is heavy with dread.

In February, while Maurice was still limping around with his left foot in a cast, I visited the Richards for *Maclean's* to discuss with them such topics as their marriage, which has a tenderness congruous with Maurice's reputation for taciturnity and temper; their children, whom they frankly indulge; hockey and French Canadians, fame and the future. The interviews were conducted in pockets of time over a period of three days and were laced through with the ringing of the telephone as many as five times to the half hour, with tumbling French exhortations to the children, who speak no English, and with Popeye (pronounced P'peye by the small Richards) rescuing his shrill lady friend with such volume from the television that Maurice's soft, accented answers were difficult to hear. Lucille was at home only the first day, departing that night to give birth to their sixth child, an almost 10-pound boy the Richards have named Paul.

Some of the appointments inside the Richard home could be transposed, just as they are, to a Maurice Richard wing on hockey's hall of fame. The wrought-iron frame of the mirror, in the front hall, for instance, is studded with 400th-, 500th- and 600th-goal pucks. The living-room mantel holds nine trophies, awards or mountings of other pucks. Several other trophies, including a small version of the Stanley Cup, are scattered through the room. Lucille has stored literally dozens of cups, statues and plaques in a glass-doored case in the recreation room, along with boxes of pucks—all identical in appearance—labelled to indicate that this one won a Stanley Cup playoff game and that one broke a scoring record. The scrapbook situation is almost out of hand and so is the number of paintings of Maurice that fans have made from photographs and sent to him. Several are hung in the living room, others in the recreation room. One, a real trial, is over six feet high and leans against a basement wall.

Many gifts have been of great value, among them a color television set, a freezer, a stove, a marble-statue floor lamp and four refrigerators. Lucille dispersed the abundance of refrigerators by putting the biggest one in the kitchen, another in the bar in the recreation room and two others in the back entrance vestibule. One of these is packed to the doors with beer, a reflection of an affiliation Maurice has with Dow Breweries, rather than of his drinking habits, which are only a notch above teetotalling.

Lucille Richard is a small, animated, pretty woman of 35 with mildly red hair and blue eyes. Only daughter of Mr. and Mrs. Lucien Norchet, the former a butcher of comfortable means, Lucille was raised in a warm, hearty household that was a gathering place for her friends and any number of people her two older brothers might happen to bring home.

The afternoon of the first interview was viciously cold in Montreal, 20 below zero with a wild wind. The Richard home was warm, sparkling clean and bright with sunlight. Lucille, greatly pregnant but untired-looking, explained that Maurice was away on an errand to the Forum, taking five-year-old André with him. "He often does that, when he must make a few calls," she added, leading the way into the living room. "He is so fond of the children that he hates to be away from them. When he telephones home while the team is away on a road trip he starts by saying, 'How are the kids?' I say, 'What about me?' He tells people that he loves his children and hockey, sometimes he remembers to put me in there. I come before hockey, but after the kids."

Being interviewed by June Callwood as son André watches TV.

She settled in a chair that caught the thin winter sunshine. As we talked, Lucille's parents arrived and were introduced, her father shyly removing himself to the recreation room and her mother joining us with the same air of uncritical interest that marks her daughter's attitudes. The maid, a timid, awed young girl, was working silently in the kitchen. "I met Maurice when I was 13," Lucille said, in answer to my question. "My older brother was playing hockey and he used to rave about Maurice Richard. Maurice was scoring four or five goals every game. Then he brought him home to meet us. Maurice was 17 then, so shy, so quiet. Remember, Mama?"

Mrs. Norchet chuckled. "I remember. His clothes were so, I shouldn't say, but not right. Not poor, but just... you know. My heart went out to him. He used to comb his hair straight back, very long. One day I took a comb and parted it on other side and combed it for him. 'There,' I told him. 'That's better.' He still parts it that way."

"Maurice had no girl," continued Lucille, "but he always came to our house after the hockey games with all the rest. We would roll up the rugs and dance and eat peanuts and potato chips and drink soft drinks. I was very young, but I taught Maurice to dance. After a while, he was very good at the rumba."

"Was Maurice popular?" Lucille was asked.

"Oh sure," she responded, "he was such a wonderful hockey player, everyone was talking about him and waiting to meet him. Except for hockey, he didn't have friends. He was so shy, so quiet. He just watched people."

Despite the image most people have of all French-Canadian families being close and jolly, the Richard family is a cool one and its members, with the exception of Maurice and his hockey-playing broth Henri, rarely see one another. Lucille says, "Maurice had it tough when he was young, really tough."

His father was a CPR machinist, out of work for a two-year period during the Depression. Maurice was the oldest of eight children. When Lucille first met Maurice, he was attending technical school, taking training as a machinist. Hockey was a hobby; he never considered it as a career. When she was 17 and he was well into his 20th year, Maurice proposed and Lucille accepted. Neither had ever dated anyone else. The Norchets approved of young Richard but were appalled at the couple's youth. Despite the objections, Lucille and Maurice were married the following year. "You should have seen her leave for the church," Mrs. Norchet recalled, grinning wryly. "Most brides are nervous but she was as gay as a bird, turned and waved like she was going to a movie. Me, *I* was crying."

It was 1942, and Maurice was earning $40 a week as a machinist in the CPR shops, making extra money in the winter playing for the Canadian Seniors. Neither spoke a word of English and when Maurice began to play for the NHL Canadiens the following winter, Lucille drank coffee with the players' wives before the games and was taught English. Maurice was learning from the players and from watching movies in the strange cities where the team travelled to play. He was wretched with loneliness, developing the protective veneer of cold hostility that he outgrew only recently.

The Richards' eldest daughter, Hugette, now 15, had been born shortly after their first anniversary and a son, Maurice Jr., followed. "He is another Rocket," the nurse told Lucille, displaying the new baby.

"Maurice waits at the hospital when Lucille is having a baby," observed Mrs. Norchet. "It doesn't matter how long it takes, he won't leave. Would you believe it, he cries. My sons never shed a tear when their wives are having babies, but Maurice weeps every time."

"He's supposed to be so hard," added Lucille, "but wait till you see him at home. He's so gentle and kind, so good to the kids. Too good, I tell him."

"We used to fight a lot when we were first married," smiled Lucille comfortably, "but not any more. He is much happier now, much more contented. He is living a good life and it makes him feel well, proud. He is wonderful to us. Last Christmas he gave me this diamond ring..."

"And a mink coat," prompted Mrs. Norchet.

"No, it was a stole. Christmas before it was a lamb coat. And in the spring he will get me a Pontiac convertible. Neat, eh?"

It's not all diamonds and cars. Lucille's nails are bitten to the quick from the nervousness she suffers before and during every hockey game. "The worry is when he is playing on the road and I am listening on the radio and the announcer says, 'Richard is hurt, he's leaving the ice.' I almost die."

Lucille Richard and young Rocket sit directly behind the visiting team bench in the Forum. Since league president Clarence Campbell often sits nearby, it's a position that strangles her natural exuberance. "I can't say what I think about the referees, everyone knows me."

The day of a game, Lucille tries to keep the children in the recreation room so the house will be quieter. Maurice goes to a players' meeting in the morning, returns and at three o'clock has filet mignon, medium, one potato, a vegetable, some tomato juice, maybe fruit or ice cream. "For 16 years, I have been fixing the same food, 16 years," Lucille murmured in gathering astonishment. "Sixteen years! Then Maurice goes down to sleep, but he doesn't sleep—he lies there. He comes out of the room around five or six. I say, 'Did you sleep?' and he says, 'No.' We don't talk much, just get ready and drive down to the Forum. All the wives go with their husbands and we drink coffee until the game starts and talk."

She was reflective. "I don't know what we will do when there is no more hockey. The first year is going to be terrible, just terrible for him."

The next day, Mrs. Norchet opened the door beaming. "You've heard the news? Lucille had a son last night, 10 pounds! It's been on the radio all day. Maurice is still at the hospital, he stayed all night with her. Come in, come in."

The telephone rang; although the number is unlisted, it was to ring all day almost as soon as the receiver was replaced. After a time, Maurice arrived. A thick-bodied, not tall, man, Richard normally has an expression of remote sadness and his black eyes are fathomless. "Lucille says you are too good to your children," I commented, when he had settled on the chesterfield and his two-year-old daughter, Suzanne, was comfortable on my lap. "They can have anything they want, anything at all," he agreed.

"Your childhood was very different." A closed look came over his face. "I don't want to think about the differences. If I do, it will be hard for me."

"What kind of rules do you have, raising your family?"

"Rules? I don't know. I want them home or else I want to know where they are and who they are with. That's the only rule. Rocket was going to a school where he hung around afterwards with the rest of the boys. I took him out and put him in another school. Now he comes home. And Hugette, she goes skiing on the weekends and the priest is along with them. If the children are at home or with good people, they are not getting into trouble, that's for sure."

"Why are the Canadiens so good?"

"They get along good," he said. "On the trips we all eat together, go to movies together. There's never an argument among our players. Some other teams have players who argue with one another even during a game. Not us, we are friends."

He paused. "It's been tougher for us to keep going the last two or three years. The younger guys on the Canadiens help me." His accent thickened. "It will be very hard on me when I quit hockey."

"Why do you love it?"

He gave himself time to consider. "It's because of the big thrill, before and after every game. Before, you keep wanting the game to start, but you're afraid, too. You're afraid of a bad injury, or not playing a good game. That's what I think about all day of a game. Then, when you start to play and begin to sweat, it all goes away and you feel good."

"Have you ever been satisfied with yourself?"

"Never," replied Richard immediately. "I've never played well enough to be pleased with myself. If I get three, four goals, I know some of them have been lucky ones. You can't be proud of yourself for that. It's impossible to be perfect. You try, maybe come close, but the next day it's over. It was just another game."

The next morning Maurice had a half hour to spare before attending the funeral of a former Canadiens trainer. We began by discussing the consequences of being famous. Lucille had mourned, "We can't go anywhere, can't eat in a restaurant, can't walk down in the street before somebody comes over to talk to Maurice. And he must smile and be pleasant, while his dinner gets cold." She too is recognized everywhere in Montreal. "I am looking over a table for bargains when I notice heads begin to turn and people whisper. I have to drop the bargain and buy something more expensive. I don't want people to say that the wife of Maurice Richard is cheap."

Maurice was embarrassed by my question about fame. "Sometimes I get fed up, but I can't let it show," he said uncomfortably. "It's not nice for kids to hear about me being sore at people."

"What's the angriest you've ever been?"

"The time in Toronto, three or four years ago, when I was fighting with Bob Bailey and he put his fingers in my eyes. When I first felt my eyes, I thought they were gone. I was yelling at the referee, so I got a match penalty. Funny thing about Toronto, I used to hate playing there. The rink was like a morgue. Now, you know what—the fans cheer me, cheer all the visiting teams. It's a good place to play now."

"They say you are the greatest in the world."

"I'm not," Richard said quietly. "Howe is better than me, Schmidt was better, Elmer Lach, lots of guys are better than me. Beliveau, Geoffrion, lots of guys on the Canadiens today are better hockey players than me."

"What is it then that you have got, if it isn't ability?"

Said Richard. "Desire."

The last meeting with Maurice Richard took place in an odd setting a few hours later. He agreed to meet at the Montreal Forum for a last question or two and suggested, when we met in the lobby, that we go into the rink. "There's no one there," he explained.

The rink was dark, with only a single light hanging over centre ice. Workmen had started to set up the ring at centre ice for the night's wrestling bouts: they had departed for their lunch. The empty tiers of seats stretched into darkness and our voices were hollow in the vast emptiness. We sat in box seats and Richard stared at the cluttered ice, where his hunched figure, skating raggedly with wounded-animal fury, has scored hundreds of goals and brought the entire arena-full of people to their feet, screaming his name in ecstasy. A sense of old ghosts made Richard speak heavily, slowly and sadly.

"I've thought about nothing but money, all my life. There's a lot I've missed. I don't read books, only magazines on the train. Lots of times I am ashamed because people are talking about things I never heard about. Every year I think I ought to get interested in another business, start a restaurant or something. But when the hockey starts, I forget about everything else. Maybe if I had other interests I wouldn't have lasted so long in hockey."

"Are you afraid of anything?"

Richard was quiet a long time. "Yes. I am afraid of the future. I am afraid to grow older. I never used to think of it, now it's on my mind every day. I will be so lonely when hockey is over for me."

"Can you coach, maybe?"

"No, I can't change the way a man plays hockey. Either he can play it or he can't. I can't help him."

He looked at the ice, his eyes moving up and down its length. "I give myself another day, that's all. I just count one day ahead to be able to play. For the last four or five years, I've been the oldest in the league. That's terrible for a man to think about."

We were both quiet again. "Nerves give you a lot of trouble, I hear."

He nodded. "My stomach nerves were very bad for a while. I still don't sleep maybe four or five hours a night. The rest of the time I lie awake. I don't know why."

The workmen returned and the lights came on with splintering brightness. They looked at the man in the dark overcoat, looked away, looked again. Richard didn't see them. "I've heard other hockey players say that this is their last season, that they think they will retire at the end of the year. I don't know how they can say it. I couldn't make myself say that. I love hockey so much, I couldn't say such a thing."

"Are you still playing as hard as you used to?"

"I pace myself. When I was younger I used to skate for nothing. Now I save it for a burst when I think I can score. I have to do it that way."

The brightness of the rink and the curiosity of the workmen suddenly embarrassed him. He rose and we left. In the lobby again, people lined up before ticket windows saw him and nudged one another in excitement. "I've got a little put by," Richard was saying, "but not enough to live on for the rest of my life. I'll have to work. But what can I do? I don't know anything but hockey." He shrugged, turned and limped away.

Maurice Richard would play only one more year for the Canadiens and won a Stanley Cup, his eighth, in that final 1959–60 season. Although Richard won the MVP trophy only once, he is known as one of the fiercest competitors ever to lace up skates. A prolific and timely goal scorer, he was the first player to score 50 goals in a season. The Rocket moved to a public relations job in the Habs organization after retiring, but left within the year. He has since held various business and public relations jobs in the Montreal area.

June Callwood is an award-winning journalist and author who contributed her first article to Maclean's *in 1947. Callwood has written over 15 books on topics as diverse as the law and living with HIV.*

The Strange Forces behind the Richard Hockey Riot

Sidney Katz

September 17, 1955—On March 17, 1955, at exactly 9:11 p.m., a tear-gas bomb exploded in the Montreal Forum where 16,000 people had gathered to watch a hockey match between the Montreal Canadiens and the Detroit Red Wings. The acrid yellowish fumes that filled the stadium sent the crowd rushing to the exits, crying, shrieking, coughing and retching. But it did more. It touched off the most destructive and frenzied riot in the history of Canadian sport.

The explosion of the bomb was the last straw in a long series of provocative incidents that swept away the last remnant of the crowd's restraint and decency. Many of the hockey fans had come to the game in an ugly mood. The day before, Clarence Campbell, president of the National Hockey League, had banished Maurice (The Rocket) Richard, the star of the Canadiens and the idol of the Montreal fans, from hockey for the remainder of the season. The suspension couldn't have come at a worse time for the Canadiens. They were leading Detroit by the narrow margin of two points. Richard's award for individual high scoring was at stake, too—he was only two points ahead of his teammate Bernie (Boom Boom) Geoffrion. Furthermore, it had been a long tough hockey season, full of emotional outbursts. All during the first period of play the crowd had vented their anger at Campbell by shouting, "*Va-t'en, Campbell*" ("Scram, Campbell") and showering him with rotten fruit, eggs, pickled pigs' feet and empty bottles.

At one time there were as many as 10,000 people—patrons, demonstrators and onlookers—packed around the outside of the Forum. Many of them rushed around in bands shrieking like animals. For a time it looked as if a lynching might even be attempted: groups of rioters were savagely chanting in unison, "Kill Campbell! Kill Campbell!" The windows of passing streetcars were smashed and, for no apparent reason, cab drivers were hauled from their vehicles and pummelled. The mob smashed hundreds of windows in the Forum by throwing bricks, chunks of ice and even full bottles of beer. They pulled down signs and tore doors off their hinges. They toppled corner newsstands and telephone booths, doused them in oil and left them burning.

When the mob grew weary of the Forum they moved eastward down Ste-Catherine Street, Montreal's main shopping district. For 15 blocks they left in their path a swath of destruction. It looked like the aftermath of a wartime blitz in London. Hardly a store in those 15 blocks was spared. Display windows were smashed and looters carried away practically everything portable—jewelry, clothes, clocks, radios and cameras. The cost of the riot was added up later: an estimated $30,000 worth of damage due to looting and vandalism; 12 policeman and 25 civilians injured; eight police cars and several streetcars, taxicabs and private automobiles damaged. "It was the worst night I've had in my 33 years as a policeman," said Thomas Leggett, Montreal's director of police.

But the greatest damage done was not physical. Montrealers awoke ashamed and stunned after their emotional binge. The *Montreal Star* observed, "Nothing remains but shame." The *Toronto Star* commented, "It's savagery which attacks the fundamentals of civilized behavior." Canadian hockey was given a black name on the front pages of newspapers as far apart as Los Angeles and London, England. "Ice hockey is rough," observed the London *News Chronicle*, "but it is now a matter of grim record that Canadian players are spring lambs compared to those who support them." A Dutch newspaper headlined the riot story: STADIUM WRECKED, 27 DEAD, 100 WOUNDED.

The newspapers and radio were blamed for whipping up public opinion against Campbell before the riot. Frank Hanley, of the Montreal city council, said that Mayor Jean Drapeau must accept at least some of the responsibility. Had he not publicly criticized Campbell's decision to suspend Richard instead of appealing to the public to accept it? Drapeau, in turn, blamed the riot on Campbell who "provoked it" by his presence at the game. Frank D. Corbett, a citizen of Westmount, expressed an opinion about the riot which many people thought about but few discussed publicly. In a letter to the editor of a local paper, he said bluntly that the outbreak was symptomatic of racial ill-feeling. "French and English relationships have deteriorated badly over the past 10 years and they have never been worse," he wrote. "The basic unrest is nationalism, which is ever present in Quebec. Let's face it... the French Canadians want the English expelled from the province."

All of these observations contained some germ of truth but no single one of them explains satisfactorily what happened in Montreal on St. Patrick's Night. In the case history of the Richard riot, the night of March 13, four nights before the Montreal outburst, is important. On that night, the Montreal Canadiens were playing against the Boston Bruins in Boston Garden. An incident occurred six minutes before the end of the game which set the stage for the debacle in Montreal. Boston was leading 4–2, playing one man short because of a penalty. In a desperate effort to score, the Canadiens had removed their goalie and sent six men up the ice. Richard was skating across the Boston blue line past Boston defenceman Hal Laycoe when the latter put his stick up high and caught Richard on the left side of his head. It made a nasty gash which later required five stitches. Frank Udvari, the referee, signalled a penalty to Laycoe for high sticking but allowed the game to go on because Canadiens had the puck.

Richard skated behind the Boston net and had returned to the blue line when the whistle blew. He rubbed his head, then suddenly skated over to Laycoe who was a short distance away. Lifting his stick high over his head with both hands Richard pounded Laycoe over the face and shoulders with all his strength. Laycoe dropped his gloves and stick and motioned to Richard to come and fight with his fists. An official, linesman Cliff Thompson, grabbed Richard and took his stick away from him. Richard broke away, picked up a loose stick on the ice and again slashed away at Laycoe, this time breaking the stick on him. Again Thompson got hold of Richard, but again Richard escaped and with another stick slashed at the man who had injured him. Thompson subdued Richard for the third time by forcing him down to the ice. With the help of a teammate, Richard regained his feet and sprang at Thompson, bruising his face and blackening his eye. Thompson finally got Richard under control and sent him to the first-aid room for medical attention.

Richard was penalized for the remainder of the game and fined $100. Laycoe, who suffered body bruises and face wounds, was penalized five minutes for high sticking and was given a further ten minute penalty for tossing a blood-stained towel at referee Udvari as he entered the penalty box.

Richard's emotional and physical resistance were at a low ebb on the night of the Boston game. It was near the end of a long exhausting schedule. The Canadiens had played Boston only the previous night in Montreal. Richard had been hurled against a net and had injured his back. The back was so painful he hadn't been able to sleep on the train trip to Boston in spite of the application of ice packs. On the morning of the game he confided to a reporter, "My back still hurts like the dickens. I feel beat." He never considered sitting out the Boston game. There was too much at stake. With three scheduled games left, the Canadiens chances of finishing first in the league were bright. Furthermore, Richard was narrowly leading the league for individual high scoring. If he won, he would receive a cup, $1,000 from the league and another $1,000 from his club. He was still brooding over an incident that had threatened his winning the top-scoring award. In Toronto the previous Thursday, he had been in a perfect position to score when he was hooked by Hugh Bolton of the Maple Leafs. Bolton was penalized but it still meant that Richard was deprived of a goal he desperately wanted.

Accustomed to the "win-at-any-cost" brand of hockey, some fans resort to violence of their own. Once in Boston, a woman jabbed Butch Bouchard, captain of the Canadiens, in the hip with a pin as he was entering the rink. Only a few months before the Richard riot, a Canadien supporter sprinkled pepper on the towels used by the Boston Bruins to mop their faces. Many observers feel that the Richard riot was merely another example of how lawlessness can spread from players to spectators. Team owners, coaches and trainers have promoted disrespect for law and authority in hockey by their attitude. They complain bitterly when referees apply the rules strictly. A few weeks before the Richard riot, coach Jimmy Skinner was using abusive language from the Detroit bench during a game. Campbell left his seat and approached him. "You've got to stop talking like that," he warned him. Skinner turned his abuse on Campbell. "Beat it, you ———," he is reported to have said. "You're only a spectator here."

In this new brand of hockey which permits rough play and often ignores the rules, the most harassed player in the NHL is Richard. Thirty-four years old, five foot nine in height, Richard weighs 180 pounds and is handsome in a sullen kind of a way. His dark-brown hair is slicked back, he has bushy eyebrows, a small mouth and his characteristic expression is deadpan. His intense, penetrating dark eyes seem to perceive everything in microscopic detail. Talking to him at close range, you sometimes feel uneasy. It's possible that Richard is the greatest hockey player who ever lived. Canadiens were once offered $135,000 for him—the highest value ever placed on a hockey player. Frank Selke, Canadien managing director, refused, saying, "I'd sooner sell half the Forum."

Opposing teams fully recognize Richard's talent and use rugged methods to stop him. One—and sometimes two—players are specifically detailed to nettle him. They regularly hang on to him, put hockey sticks between his legs, body check him and board him harder than necessary. Once he skated 20 feet with two men on his shoulders to score a goal.

His opponents also employ psychological warfare to unnerve him. Inspector William Minogue, who, as police officer in charge of the Forum, is regularly at the rinkside during games, frequently hears opposing players calling Richard "French pea soup" or "dirty French bastard" as they skate past. If these taunts result in a fight, both Richard and his provoker are sent to the penalty bench. Opposing teams consider this a good bargain.

Because of these tactics, Richard frequently explodes. But he is a rarity among men as well as among hockey players. He is an artist. He is completely dedicated to playing good hockey and scoring goals. "It's the most important thing in my life," he told me. In hockey, Richard has found a kind of personal destiny. "He's on fire inside all the time he's on the ice," says Frank Selke. "I've never had a player who tries so intensely." Even after 13 years of professional hockey Richard still approaches each game as though he were about to undergo a major surgical operation. He is in a brooding, uncommunicative mood. "I feel nervous the whole day," he told me. "I feel sick in the stomach. When we are lined up for the National Anthem I pray silently to God that I might play a good game." As soon as the game starts, however, he loses his queasiness and is unaware of the crowd. "I think of only one thing," says Richard, "scoring goals." He has never been known to miss a practice or to be late for one. He doesn't want to be anything less than the greatest hockey player. "No one will have to tell me when to stop playing hockey," he told me. "When I stop scoring, I'll quit. I wouldn't be able to take that."

He suffers mental agony after a game in which he thinks he's done poorly. He'll slink quietly into the dressing room and sit on the bench for half an hour before making an attempt to get out of his uniform. On some such occasions he's been known to burst into tears. "A poor game makes me feel bad," he explains. "I'll go home and not talk to anybody, not even my wife. I'll sit by myself and think, over and over again, about all the chances I missed to score. I try to forget about it but I can't. I won't get to bed till about three or four in the morning." On the road, he'll sit on the edge of his berth repeating to himself, "I was lousy." He never offers alibis or blames a defeat on others.

There are better skaters, better stick handlers, better checkers and better playmakers than Richard, but no better hockey player. He seems to have the power to summon forth all his strength at the very instant it's needed. "His strength comes all at once like the explosion of a bomb," says Kenny Reardon, an ex-hockey player who is now assistant manager of the Canadiens. Most of the time this concentrated outburst is channelled into the scoring of goals. But sometimes it is used to strike back at his tormentors—as it was in Boston on Sunday, March 13, when he assaulted Hal Laycoe and linesman Cliff Thompson.

On the night of the Boston fracas, Clarence Campbell was travelling from Montreal to New York by train to attend a meeting of the NHL board of governors where plans for the Stanley Cup playoffs were to be made. In Grand Central station next morning he read about the rumpus in the *New York Times*. Hurrying to his hotel, he phoned referee Frank Udvari and linesmen Sam Babcock and Cliff Thompson to get a verbal report. Disturbed by what he heard, he announced a hearing would be held in Montreal to ascertain all the facts and to decide on what punishment should be given to the players involved. The time set was two days later—Wednesday, March 16 at 10:30 a.m.

In the intervening time, the Boston incident was widely commented on. Dick Irvin was angry at his players. "What kind of spirit have we got on the Canadiens?" he asked. "There were four of five players on the ice and they hardly gave Richard any help!" He suggested that the Richard hearing be televised. Most of the comments were in a more serious vein. Richard's supporters contended that because of lax refereeing their hero had been badgered beyond his endurance. On the other hand, the *Toronto Star* described Richard as "a chronic blow-top and an habitual offender." Campbell was advised by many out-of-town newspapers to ground the Rocket long enough to teach him a lesson. Marshall Dann, a Boston columnist, said angrily that "if Richard is permitted to play one more game of hockey this season, Campbell should be fired. Richard is the most pampered player in the league. For his repeated misbehavior, he has drawn only mild wrist slaps or inconsequential fines from Campbell."

In January, 1954, in his regular column in the Montreal weekly *Le Samedi-dimanche*, Richard denounced Campbell as a "dictator" who was prejudiced against the Canadiens and who "gloated when an opposing team scored a goal against us." He was required to apologize and post a $1,000 bond for good behavior. In December, 1954, in Toronto, he charged into Bob Bailey with his stick, broke two of his front teeth, then turned and struck linesman George Hayes. He was given two 10-minute misconduct penalties and fined a total of $250.

And now, three months later, came the incident in Boston. Both Richard and Campbell refrained from making public statements until after the hearing. Richard, because of his head wound, spent most of the time under observation at the Montreal Western Hospital which was then located across from the Forum. On the morning of the hearing, March 16, he got dressed but did not shave. He looked pale and worried and wore a patch on the left side of his head. He walked across to the Forum where he picked up coach Dick Irvin and assistant manager Kenny Reardon. The three men got into a cab. On the way over to NHL headquarters about a mile away, Richard broke his silence only once to observe ruefully, "I always seem to be getting into trouble."

The NHL suite on the sixth floor of the Sun Life Building was a beehive of activity. A large group of young people from the adjoining offices, mostly girls, lined the corridors to catch a glimpse of their hockey hero. Reporters, photographers and TV cameramen had overflowed the outer office, sitting on the desks and monopolizing the phones. Richard posed unsmilingly for the photographers, forced a weak grin for the TV cameramen. When he entered Campbell's office with Irvin and Reardon, the other participants in the hearing were already seated around Campbell's desk: referee-in-chief Carl Voss, referee Frank Udvari, linesmen Cliff Thompson and Sammy Babcock, Hal Laycoe and Lynn Patrick, manager and coach of the Boston Bruins. The hearing was private.

It lasted for three hours. The officials read their reports of the incident and submitted to questioning. Everyone present was then invited to give his version of what happened. On some points, there were sharp differences. Campbell took notes busily. In defence of Richard, Irvin said that he had been temporarily stunned by the blow on his head and was unaware of what he was doing. Richard remained silent until asked if he had anything to say. "I don't remember what happened," he replied. Later, Richard told me: "When I'm hit, I get mad and I don't know what I do. Before each game I think about my temper and how I should control it, but as soon as I get on the ice I forget all that."

At 1:30 p.m. they filed out. They refused to comment to the 40 newsmen who had now gathered in the outer office. Richard returned to the hospital. Left alone, Campbell ordered a ham sandwich on brown bread and a cup of coffee and began studying his notes, preparatory to writing out his decision. "I had a hard time making up my mind," he told me later. By three o'clock Campbell had written out the first page of his decision. As each page was completed it was carried across the office by referee-in-chief Voss to a private office to be typed by Phyllis King, Campbell's secretary. He had made thousands of unpopular decisions—but none nearly so unpopular as the one he made public to the assembled newspapermen in his presidential office at four o'clock that March afternoon.

The attacks on Laycoe and Thompson were deliberate and persistent, he found. "An incident occurred less than three months ago in which the pattern of conduct of Richard was almost identical... Consequently, the time for leniency or probation is past. Whether this type of conduct is the product of temperamental instability or wilful defiance doesn't matter. It's a type of conduct that cannot be tolerated." The room was completely silent as Campbell then pronounced the punishment. "Richard is suspended from playing in the remaining league and playoff games."

At about 4:30 p.m., Irvin, Reardon, Elmer Lach, a former Richard teammate, and Elmer Ferguson, of the *Montreal Herald*, were sitting around the Canadien office when they heard the news on a radio broadcast. About 10 minutes later Richard came in. He had just been discharged from hospital. According to Ferguson this is what followed:

Richard asked, "Is the ruling out yet?"

Irvin was silent for a few seconds, then said quietly, "Be prepared for a shock, Rocket. You're out for the season—including the Stanley Cup playoffs."

Richard didn't believe it. "You're kidding—now tell me the truth."

Irvin said, "Sorry. That's the way it is, Rocket. No kidding."

Richard shrugged his shoulders, said good night and walked off to his car. Nobody spoke. A few seconds later Lach said, "There goes the greatest of them all."

Richard later told me that the decision came as a great shock. "I didn't expect it to be so severe. I had always been in the playoffs before. I was so disappointed I didn't know whether I would stay in Montreal or not. My first impulse was to go to Florida. But I changed my mind. I wanted to watch my team play. I didn't want the fans to get the idea that I was no longer interested just because I was suspended."

No sports decision ever hit the Montreal public with such impact. It seemed to strike at the very heart and soul of the city. Upon first hearing of the suspension a French-speaking employee in the *Gazette* composing room broke down and cried. A bus driver became so upset by the news that he ignored a flashing railway-level-crossing signal and almost killed his passengers. The French station CKAC invited listeners to phone in their opinions: 97 per cent said that although some punishment for Richard was justified the suspension for the playoffs was too severe. The switchboard became so jammed, the station had to appeal to listeners to stop calling. The sports departments of the newspapers were so besieged by the phone calls and visitors that some of the writers had to go home to get their work done.

There were portents of what was to happen on the night of March 17 in the phone calls received by Campbell. Many of them were taken by Campbell's secretary, Phyllis King, an attractive, willowy blonde in her early 30s. "They were nearly all abusive and they seemed to grow worse as the day wore on," says Miss King. One of the first callers said, "Tell Campbell I'm an undertaker and he'll be needing me in a few days." Still another announced, "I'm no crank but I'm going to blow your place up." Many of the callers were so angry they could hardly talk. There were dozens of crying women on the phone. A 40-year-old secretary from Toronto ran up a $20 long-distance phone bill pleading with Campbell to call off the suspension.

The strong racial feelings engendered by the decision should have sounded an ominous warning. These were reflected in hundreds of letters that Campbell received. One of them said, "If Richard's name was Richardson you would have given a different verdict." From Verdun: "You're just another Englishman jealous of the French, who are much better than you."

There's abundant evidence that Richard holds a special place in the heart of French Canada. Perhaps ancient nationalist feelings would not have been as important a factor in causing the riot had people in positions of authority urged acceptance of Campbell's decision in the interest of law and order. Such mollifying statements were not forthcoming in sufficient number to influence public opinion. On the contrary, many prominent people added fuel to the fire. Mayor Jean Drapeau issued a statement castigating Campbell. "It would not be necessary to give too many such decisions to kill hockey in Montreal," he said.

The Montreal press, both English and French, reinforced the fans' feeling that Campbell had victimized them. *Le Devoir* called the punishment "unjust and too severe." One French weekly published a crude cartoon of Campbell's head on a platter, dripping blood, with the caption: "This is how we would like to see him." The English press followed a similar line, although somewhat more temperate in tone. Dink Carroll said "it was a harsh judgment" in the *Gazette*, while Baz O'Meara in the *Star* found the decision "tough and unexpectedly severe."

On March 17 at 11:30 a.m. came the first sign that Montreal fans would not be content to limit their protests to angry words. A dozen young men showed up at the Forum where Canadiens were scheduled to play Detroit that night. They bore signs saying *"Vive Richard"* and *"A Bas Campbell."* At 1:30 about 20 young men arrived, apparently college students. They carried signs, one with a picture of a pig with Campbell's name on it; another had a picture of a pear which is the French equivalent of knucklehead. The police felt they weren't doing any harm and allowed them to march up and down. At about 3:30 another group of men between the ages of 18 and 35 arrived.

An air of excitement and anticipation hung over the city. Newspapers and radio stations headlined every new development. The crucial question now was: Would Campbell dare show himself in public at the game that night? When Campbell announced that he would definitely attend, excitement reached a fever pitch. At four o'clock, station CKVL dispatched a mobile sound unit to the Shell gas station across the road from the Forum and set up a direct line to its transmitter. "We were almost certain that there was going to be trouble," says Marcel Beauregard, feature editor of CKVL. "It was in the air." It was at about this time, too, according to a Montreal newspaper report, that an attempt was made to buy up a number of tickets near Campbell for the express purpose of tormenting him.

Why did Campbell decide to go to the game? As he saw it, he would be hanged either way. If he failed to go, he would be branded as a coward. "I never seriously considered not going to the game," he later said. "I'm a season ticketholder and a regular attendant and I have a right to go. I felt that the police could protect me. I didn't consult them and they didn't advise me not to attend."

Mayor Drapeau offers a different version. Campbell, he says, phoned the police during the afternoon to announce his attendance and ask for protection. A highly placed officer suggested that he stay away. Richard, the other central figure, was undecided about going until the last minute. His wife finally made up his mind for him. "She told me that she was going so I decided to go along too," he says.

The activity outside the Forum mounted steadily as the hour of the game approached. Bands of demonstrators moved up and down with signs saying "Unfair to French Canadians." At about 6:30 a number of panel trucks circled around Atwater Park, across from the Forum, a few times and discharged a number of young men in black leather windbreakers bearing white insignia. Their windbreakers had special significance for the police. They were the garb of youthful motorcyclists who had been involved in disorders on previous occasions. Other groups kept arriving steadily. By 8:30, when the game started, there were probably about 600 demonstrators. The Forum loudspeaker announced that all seats were now sold. A picketer shouted back, "We don't want seats. We want Campbell!" The cry was taken up and repeated endlessly with savage intensity.

A few minutes after the Canadien–Detroit game started, Richard slipped into the Forum unnoticed and took a seat near the goal judge's cage at the south end of the rink. He gazed intently at the ice, a look of distress on his face: the Canadiens were playing sloppy hockey. At the 11th minute of the first period Detroit scored a second goal and the Canadiens saw their hopes of a league championship go up in smoke. It was at this minute that Clarence Campbell entered the arena. He couldn't have chosen a worse time.

As soon as Campbell sat down the crowd recognized him and pandemonium broke loose. They shifted their attention from the game to Campbell and set up a deafening roar "Shoo Campbell, Shoo Campbell"... "*Va-t'en, Va-t'en.*" "The people didn't care if we got licked 100–1 that night," says Dick Irvin. "They were only interested in Campbell. Evidently our players were too because they paid no attention their hockey." In the remaining nine minutes of the first period, Detroit was able to score another two goals, making the score 4–1. The next 40 minutes were to be sheer torture for Campbell. Vegetables, eggs, tomatoes, rubbers, bottles and programs rained down on him. They were from the $1.50 seats and standing section far above. Campbell was wearing a dark-green fedora and a dark-grey suit. They were soon smudged by oranges, eggs and tomatoes. At one point Campbell's hat was knocked off by a heavy flying object and an orange hit him square in the back.

Campbell's ordeal was shared by his neighbors. Jimmy Orlando, an ex-hockey player who sat below Campbell was struck by a potato. Campbell's friends who shared his row—Audrey King, Hilda Hawkes, Mr. and Mrs. Cooper Smeaton and Dr. and Mrs. Jack Gerrie, were struck and splattered. A city hall employee who customarily sits near Campbell became alarmed by the violence. "Go home... Please go home," he pleaded with Campbell.

But Campbell stood his ground. He was tight lipped but occasionally managed to smile. He tried to carry on his usual practice of making notes on the refereeing in a black notebook, but had to abandon it as the hail of peanuts, pigs' feet and programs continued. Each time he got up to brush the debris from his clothes, the clamor grew louder. Whenever the Detroit team scored the crowd's temper rose and the shower of objects on Campbell thickened. From his rinkside seat, Richard occasionally turned to see what was happening. "This is a disgrace," he said to physiotherapist Bill Head who was sitting beside him.

The first period ended. Ordinarily, Campbell spends the intermissions in the referees' room. Tonight he decided to remain in his seat, believing that this would cause less excitement. His friends in the same row did likewise. A woman going by leaned over and whispered in Campbell's ear, "I'm ashamed. I want to apologize for the crowd." She was close to tears. About a minute later, one André Robinson, a young man of 26 who resembles Marlon Brando, confronted Campbell. Without uttering a word he squashed two large tomatoes against Campbell's chest and rubbed them in. As he fled down the stairs Campbell kept pointing at him, signalling the two policeman to arrest him. At that moment, Frank Teskey, of the *Toronto Star*, aimed his camera for a shot. A grapefruit came whizzing down and knocked the camera out of his hand. Now hordes of people came rushing down from the seats above, surrounding Campbell's box. The ill feeling against Campbell was growing more intense by the second and there was nobody to help him.

Where were the police? On hockey nights the Forum is responsible for maintaining order inside the arena; the Montreal police department, outside. Because of the special circumstances on March 17 the police stationed two of their constables near Campbell's box. Frank Selke, manager of the Canadiens, employed eight plainclothesmen for similar duty, but they had to be rushed to guard the entrances against the demonstrators outside. Ordinarily, the Forum employs 350 ushers, 12 policemen and 24 firemen; for the Detroit game they added an extra 15 police—regular constables who were off duty. Ordinarily, the police have 25 men outside the Forum; on this night they had double that number to start with. But at 9:11, when Campbell was being surrounded by a hostile mob, none of them were there to protect him. At that critical moment he was delivered by the explosion of a tear-gas bomb 25 feet away. As the thick fumes fanned upward and outward, the crowd immediately forgot Campbell and began fighting their way to the fresh air outside.

Who threw the bomb? This question has never been answered. There is no evidence that the thrower intended to befriend Campbell but that's what he may have done. Chief of Detectives George Allain later observed, "The bomb-thrower protected Campbell's life by releasing it at precisely the right moment." The bomb, a type not on sale to the public, landed on a wet rubber mat on the aisle adjacent to the ice surface. The people nearby, of course, didn't know what it was. Some thought that

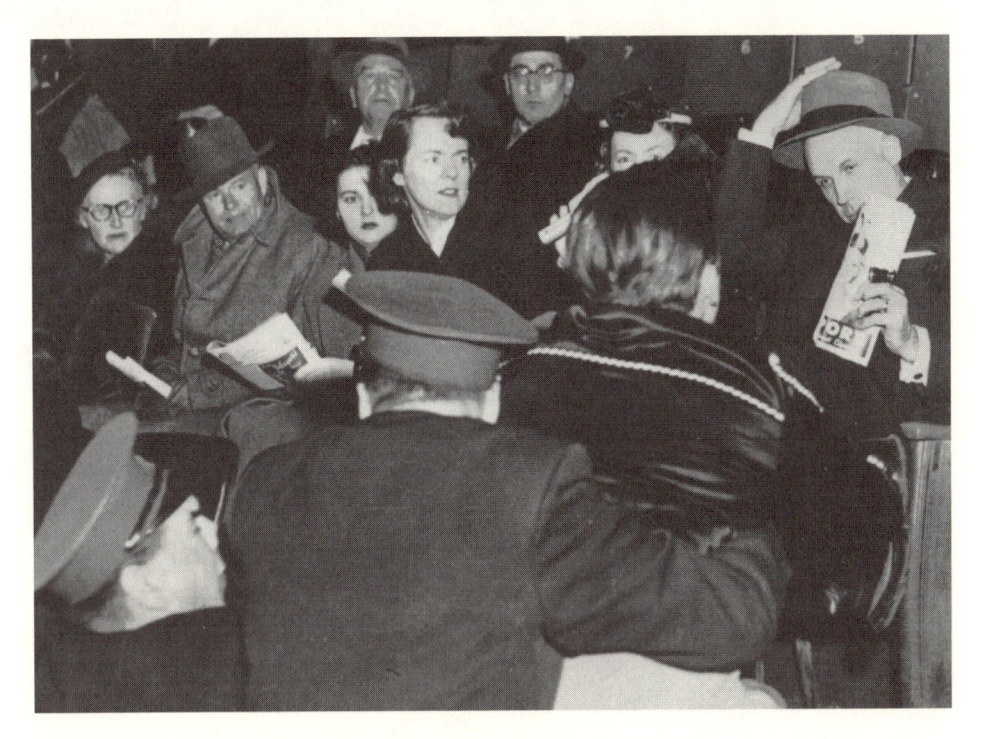

Clarence Campbell (upper right) under attack in the Forum after suspending Richard.

the ammonia pipes had sprung a leak; others that a fire had broken out in the basement. Within a few seconds they were coughing and choking as the fumes clogged their eyes, throats, stomachs and lungs. To protect themselves as they hurried out they wrapped coats around their faces. Women were screaming. Somebody yelled "Fire!" A middle-aged man got stuck in one of the turnstiles in the lobby and was shouting to be released but nobody could hear him above the din. A pregnant woman fought her way to the fresh air outside and had to be taken to hospital. At the height of the exodus, with tears streaming from everybody's eyes, the organist high in the loft began playing "My Heart Cries For You."

Panic was averted by the fast work of police and firemen. When Tom Leggett, director of police, saw the bomb go off he immediately assigned his men, who were outside the Forum, to keep all exits open and to keep the crowd moving out. Jim Hunter, the superintendent of the building, hurriedly switched on his 13 powerful fans to suck the fumes out of the building. Campbell made his way to the first-aid centre 50 feet away under the stands. Richard had also made his way to the first-aid centre but had never come face to face with Campbell because he was in a different room. He was aghast at what had happened. "This is terrible, awful," he said. "People might have been killed."

In the next 10 minutes the outcome of the Montreal-Detroit hockey game was to be decided. Armand Paré, head of the Montreal fire department, was unwilling to have the game continue. He felt that the temper of the crowd was such that there was real danger of panic and fire. Campbell sent the following note to Jack Adams, the Detroit general manager, after conferring with Selke: "The game has been forfeited to Detroit. You are entitled to take your team on its way anytime now. Selke agrees as the fire department has ordered this building closed."

Back in the Detroit dressing room, manager Jack Adams was in an angry mood. News of the forfeiture seemed to intensify it. "What's happened tonight makes me sick and ashamed," he said. He then turned to a group of newspapermen. "I blame you fellows for what's happened. You've turned Richard into an idol, a man whose suspension can turn hockey fans into shrieking idiots. Now hear this: Richard is no hero! He let his team down, he let hockey down, he let the public down. Richard makes me ashamed to be connected with this game."

Until the bomb exploded, the demonstration outside the Forum was neither destructive nor out of control. The explosion, however, signalled a change of mood. When thousands of excited, frightened fans poured outside and joined the demonstrators it seemed to unleash an ugly mob spirit which ended in a shameful episode of physical violence, vandalism and looting.

In a mob riot only a small core of people are required to initiate violence. They act as a catalyst on the crowd. Other people are carried away by the excitement and drawn into their activities. In the Richard riot, the core of violence was made up of bands of teen-agers and young adults. There were probably about 500 or 600 of them. Like packs of wolves, they moved up and down in front of the Forum, shrieking wildly and inflaming the crowd. They took rubbers off the feet of spectators and threw them at the police. There was soon a high pile of rubbers in front of the Forum. They attacked a side door of the building and tore it off its hinges. They hurled chunks of ice and empty bottles, smashing windows. Dissatisfied with this ammunition, they marched off to where a new hospital was being built half a block away and returned with chunks of brick and concrete.

The police had cleared a wide space directly in front of the Forum, pushing the crowd back to the park across the road. As soon as the rioters discharged their ammunition they sought shelter in the crowd. "It was dangerous to rush into the crowd to get them," says Chief Leggett. "It was full of women and children—some of them in carriages, some in arms. It was slippery. Had we used too much force, many people might have been trampled."

It is doubtful whether most of the troublemakers were hockey fans. Inspector William Minogue arrested a husky man in a black-and-red mackinaw. He identified himself as a lumberjack from Chalk River, Ont. "You must love Richard," said Minogue. A blank expression came over his face: "Richard? Who's he?"

Across the street CKVL broadcasters were giving the Montreal public a dramatic blow-by-blow description of the riot: "The bomb has gone off! . . . There goes another window! . . . The police are rushing the crowd! . . ." This marathon broadcast and others attracted thousands more people to the Forum.

By 11 p.m. the crowd numbered at least 10,000. It was too big for the police and the Forum was now virtually in a state of siege. It was unsafe to wander in the vicinity of the windows. Don Smith, manager of the box office, ordered Violet Trahan and Peggy Nibbs, the Forum telephone operators, to close down the switchboard and leave. Before abandoning the office himself he began to shove everything portable into the vault. As he was emptying the cash register a small rock came hurtling through the window, narrowly missing him and landing in the $10 compartment of the drawer. Eddie Quinn, a wrestling promoter whose office is on the east side of the Forum, invited a friend in for a chat. "Nobody will bother us here," he said. "Everybody knows I'm a Richard fan." He was referring to the fact that he employs Richard to referee wrestling matches during the summer. A few seconds later a large rock demolished his office window.

Frank Selke was sitting out the riot in the directors' room along with other club officials and newsmen. He ordered the steward to make up a large batch of sandwiches and coffee. "Looks like we're going to be here for a while," he said. Campbell remained in the first-aid centre. The trampling and shouting of the crowd and the shattering of glass were ominously audible. Everyone was tense. Did the crowd know where Campbell was? Would they attempt a raid to capture him? Later Campbell said, "I was never seriously afraid of being lynched. As a referee I learned something about mobs. They're cowards."

By about 11:15 p.m. the back entrance of the Forum was fairly quiet. Gaston Bettez, the Canadien trainer, drove Richard's car up to the door and hastily loaded Richard and his wife into it. "When I got home I listened to the riot on the radio," says Richard. "I felt badly. Once I felt like going downtown and telling the people over a loudspeaker to stop their nonsense. But it wouldn't have done any good. They would have carried me around on their shoulders. It's nice to have people behind you but not the way they did on the night of the Detroit game." The phone rang all night in the Richard home saying that Campbell got what he deserved. It was answered by the housekeeper. Richard himself retired at 4 a.m. and slept in next morning.

At 11:30 Jim Hunter, the Forum building superintendent, entered the first-aid centre and announced, "I think it's safe to go home now, Mr. Campbell." Leggett concurred. There was some discussion as to whether it would be safe for Campbell to spend the night alone at his home. Billy Wray, an undertaker and friend, was insisting that Campbell be his guest for the evening. Someone else suggested that he check into a hotel under an assumed name. Campbell refused both suggestions. Led by Hunter and a husky policeman, Campbell and Miss King made their way to the back of the building where Hunter's dark blue 1951 Ford was waiting inside. The policeman sat in front with the driver; Campbell and Miss King sat in the back.

Campbell, who lives four miles from the Forum, was dropped off first. As soon as he got home he phoned his father in Edmonton to say that he was safe. Although his phone is unlisted it started to ring incessantly. Most of the callers were abusive and spoke in broken English. He lifted the phone off the hook and went to bed about one o'clock. "I had a fine night's sleep," he said. He got up at his usual hour of 7:30.

By midnight the frenzy of the rioters outside the Forum became almost demoniacal. They were unaware of Campbell's departure. They attacked a newsstand at the southwest corner of Ste-Catherine and Closse Streets, sprinkled it with oil from a small stove they found inside and set it afire. Within a few minutes it was a pile of smoldering ashes. It was a wanton and tragic act. The stand belonged to Auguste Belanger, the 56-year-old father of four children. After a considerable struggle he had only recently managed to set himself up in business. "Why did they have to do such a thing to me?" he sobbed.

The rioters now turned their attention to the firms that rented space on the ground floor of the Forum, facing Ste-Catherine Street. They heaved rocks through the plate-glass windows of the Royal Bank of Canada. The supervisor and three salesgirls of a United Cigar Store had to barricade themselves in the stock room to escape injury. Patrick Maloney, proprietor of a jewelry store, took refuge in the small windowless room where he repairs watches. His windows and stock were demolished by chunks of rock, metal and bottles. Many objects were stolen, including a $490 diamond ring. Maloney passed the time brewing coffee. Occasionally, he would step into the store and pick up a full bottle of beer or pop that had been hurled in and drink it. Debris came flying through the windows of the York Tavern. Benny Parent, the manager, ordered that the building be evacuated. The police continued the hard task of arresting the rioters. Whenever they had a full load of them, the patrol wagon would rush off to the police station with its siren wailing. A young doctor from the hospital across from the Forum stepped outside for a minute to see what was going on; before he knew what was happening he was on his way to the police station in a wagon. A little old lady with fire in her eyes approached Chief Leggett. "Let's start getting tough with them," she said, "I'm with you."

The little old lady was not the only person offering advice to the director of police. Dozens of people urged him to use more forceful methods against the demonstrators. Had he wished to do so the means were at hand. Each constable was armed with a stick and a revolver; a police car stood by with a supply of tear-gas bombs; the firemen had a high-pressure water hose ready. But Leggett withheld the order to use any of these strong-arm methods. "It might have led to panic and hysteria—and that's when people get killed," he said. As it was, not a single person was seriously injured.

By midnight some people had left, but even more had arrived, drawn by the radio broadcasts. Finally, Pierre DesMarais, chief of Montreal's executive committee, appealed to the radio stations to stop broadcasting news of the trouble. He reached Marcel Beauregard, who was at the scene of the riot. "It would help the police if you went off the air," said DesMarais. Beauregard checked with his boss, Jack Tietolman, the proprietor of CKVL, who agreed. CKVL finally went off the air after more than seven hours of on-the-spot broadcasting. The other stations did likewise.

By one o'clock the crowd had thinned out. About 40 policemen, linked arm to arm, formed a solid chain across Ste-Catherine Street. They started moving slowly eastward, taking the crowd along with them. They felt that at last the riot was on the wane. But they were wrong. Ahead of them, hidden from view by hundreds of people, groups of demonstrators began smashing store windows and stealing their contents. A heavy safety-zone lantern was hurled through the window of the International Music store; instruments were smashed and looted. The mob noticed a picture of Richard and the Canadiens in the window of Adolph Stegmeier's photographic studio. To get at it, they hurled a 20-pound block of ice they found on the road at the window. Before they could reach in and seize the photograph their way was barred by tenants who occupied apartments above the studio. Signs at Red Cross headquarters were torn down. Costly plate-glass windows at Ogilvy's department store were shattered. When Gilles Rouleau, owner of a florist shop, heard the crowd approaching, he locked his doors, doused his lights and waited. The rioters passed him by. He noticed that the vandals were teen-agers but that they were being egged on by older people, many of whom appeared to be drunk.

In the 15 blocks along Ste-Catherine Street, east of the Forum, 50 stores were damaged and looted. The stolen goods included kimonos, men's pants, dresses, highchair pads, shoes, bracelets, cameras and assorted jewelry. At first it was believed that $100,000 worth of goods (including windows) had been damaged and stolen. Revised estimates scaled the amount down to $30,000 or less.

The police now sent out special patrols to find the vandals and recover the loot. They arrested one man who was carrying an armful of alarm clocks. By searching restaurants along Ste-Catherine Street they were able to pick up three other young men in possession of stolen goods. Only a few items of the pillaged goods were ever recovered. "Most of the stolen objects were mass-produced small items not easy to identify," says Chief Detective George Allain, "and there were no clues to follow." A few days after the riot A. Jeffries, proprietor of a photo-supply store, received a parcel in the mail containing a camera worth $100 that had been stolen from him. An unsigned note said, "My conscience has been bothering me ever since I took it from your window."

By 3 a.m. the last rock had been hurled, the last window had been smashed and the last blood-curdling shriek of "Kill Campbell!" had been uttered. The fury of the mob had spent itself. By the end of the riot the police had picked up 70 people and delivered them to No. 10 police station. Twenty-five were juveniles (under 18) and were driven home to their parents. The remainder were transferred to the cells at police headquarters on Gosford Street. They talked hockey for an hour or so, then stretched out and went to sleep. At seven in the morning a guard came in and announced (wrongly) that Campbell had resigned. The arrested men roused themselves, cheered, jumped up and down and broke out in a song. Addressing the offenders in municipal court the next morning, Judge Emmett J. McManamy intended his words to go far beyond his courtroom. "Last night's riot," he said, "brings home to the people of Montreal a terrible lesson of the narrow margin between order and disorder. It must never happen again."

The mood of most Montrealers following the riot was a mixture of shame and regret. It was well summed up by the terse opening sentence in Dink Carroll's column in the *Gazette* on March 18; "I am ashamed of my city." Others, like Mayor Jean Drapeau, were less remorseful. Drapeau issued a statement which, on the surface, seemed to absolve the public of all responsibility for the outbreak. It came about, he said, because of "provocation caused by Campbell's presence."

Campbell showed up at his office the next morning at the usual hour of 8:30. He refused a police offer of bodyguards. Newsmen were asking him for a statement. He said that he had no intention of resigning, as had been frequently suggested. Richard was still asleep when reporters knocked on the door of his home at eight o'clock. It was answered by his six-year-old son who said, "I hope you didn't come to talk to him about hockey." When the reporters returned later, Richard was attired in a white T-shirt and a pair of slacks. His face was lined with fatigue. "This certainly isn't the time for me to say anything," he said. "It might start something again." By three o'clock he changed his mind. He showed up in Frank Selke's office and said that he wanted to make a public statement. Selke said he could see no objection. At seven o'clock, seated in front of a battery of microphones, he made the following short speech in French:

Because I always try so hard to win and had my troubles in Boston, I was suspended. At playoff time it hurts not be in the game with the boys. However I want to do what is good for the people of Montreal and the team. So that no further harm will be done, I would like to ask everyone to get behind the team and to help the boys win from the Rangers and Detroit. I will take my punishment and come back next year to help the club and younger players to win the cup.

As he repeated the speech in English, Richard appeared restless and upset. He rubbed his eyes, tugged at his tie and scratched his left ear. His words seemed to have a settling effect on the city. The question of his suspension was laid aside, at least for the time being. Mayor Drapeau and other leaders followed Richard with strong pleas for law and order. There was to be no further violence for the remainder of the season, despite the fact that the Canadiens lost the championship.

Freelance writer Sidney Katz was a Maclean's *staff editor and writer from 1950 to 1965. He wrote widely on health and behavioral issues and was the first writer in North America to explain from personal experience the effects of taking the drug* LSD.

STARS OF THE ORIGINAL SIX

Is Jean Beliveau the Best Ever?

Trent Frayne

March 3, 1956—Jean Beliveau, a bland and bashful centre for the Montreal Canadiens, is a unique figure in the history of hockey. He has glided serenely through a career in which cities, hockey magnates and even politicians have engaged in push-and-pull struggles for his services, and he has been virtually a one-man industry paying off the mortgage on a multi-million-dollar rink. Now only 24 years old and one of the highest-paid hockey players in history, Beliveau has emerged from this seething caldron to a cool pedestal completely devoid of controversy: modern hockey authorities, who agree on almost nothing, believe he is the most gifted player of all time, and potentially the greatest. A few savants, such as Lynn Patrick, the general manager of the Boston Bruins, are convinced already. "No question about it," Patrick says flatly, "he's the finest player I've ever seen."

Older and possibly more meditative heads await the test of time and toss in occasional riders based on the fact that Beliveau has not yet completed three seasons in the National Hockey League and therefore cannot possibly be compared with, say, Eddie Shore, Howie Morenz or Beliveau's teammate, Maurice Richard. Art Ross, who built hockey in Boston starting in 1924 and who retired last year as vice-president of the Bruins, calls Beliveau the greatest young player he ever saw, and it was Ross who took young Eddie Shore to Boston. Conn Smythe, the president of the Toronto Maple Leafs, says that if Beliveau goes along at his present clip for another seven or eight years he'll be the greatest ever.

In fact Smythe, a Toronto loyalist who rarely tosses garlands of love beyond his native city borders, employs Montreal's Beliveau as his end-all illustration in a running war he's conducted in recent years with people who feel modern hockey has deteriorated. "Beliveau is the greatest thing that could have happened to the modern game," cries Smythe, in the manner of a man who has just found his missing laundry ticket. "They say there's no room left for stick handling and brains and technique.

When has there ever been a better stick handler? Who has ever shown more savvy? Who ever got a shot away faster?

"And where did this kid come from?" he shouts triumphantly. "He came from the helter-skelter modern game! Helter-skelter my eye!"

This notable lack of argument in a controversial business is one of the more remarkable aspects of Beliveau's position in hockey today, but he wasn't always clear of controversy. Hot battles swirled around him before he reached the NHL: in fact, two prominent hockey executives fought so strenuously to gain his services as a junior that they have few kind words for one another to this day. They are Frank Selke, the managing director of the Canadiens, and Frank Byrne, who was the owner of the Quebec Citadels of the now-defunct Quebec Junior Hockey League. To keep him in Quebec City when he graduated from junior ranks, men close to Premier Maurice Duplessis became involved, and it was widely believed in Quebec that the licence to operate a tavern in the Montreal Forum—a big money maker for the Canadian Arena Co., which operates the Forum and the NHL Canadiens—would be revoked if Beliveau were enticed to Montreal by the Canadiens. He stayed in Quebec City for two seasons where record crowds flocked to worship him and spend money that helped pay for the lavish new Coliseum, a bowl devoid of posts that seats 10,338 people, and frequently bettered that total with standees during Beliveau's stay.

In Beliveau's first year with the Quebec Aces of the Quebec Senior Hockey League, the team drew 281,000 fans in a city of 225,000 people. In his second year, which was the 1952–53 season, they drew a whopping 386,334 fans in 30 scheduled and six playoff games, one of them totalling 13,791 paid. In the three years since Beliveau departed, the Aces drew 255,000 two years ago, and only 103,000 last season. According to coach and general manager George (Punch) Imlach, they won't reach 100,000 by the end of the current season. "As long as we had Beliveau the people knew they were watching the best in the world," says Imlach. "They refuse to settle for less now."

Hockey men in all camps strive to find new ways of applauding Beliveau. Imlach, who coached Beliveau for two years with the Quebec Aces where Jean was the world's highest-paid pseudo-amateur at $20,000 a season, came up with this remarkable appraisal: "He'll never reach his potential ability because the National Hockey League isn't good enough to bring it out." Hap Day, the general manager of the Toronto Maple Leafs, was asked recently if there were any known way of stopping Beliveau. He said crisply; "Of course there is. But it isn't legal."

Jean Beliveau lifting the Cup after defeating Chicago in the finals, May 3, 1965.

Beliveau is truly an arresting figure. He stands six feet three and, by dieting carefully, he can keep his weight at 205 pounds. He has handsome, sharply defined features, with crisp light-brown hair and a warm smile. He views the furor that has centred on him for the last seven years in a detached, occasionally self-conscious manner, explaining that in Quebec City the people made a fuss over all the hockey players, and that in Montreal—well, in Montreal everybody feels a great deal of pride in the Canadiens, don't they? In Quebec City merchants gave him suits and dinner and even an automobile, and in Montreal he earns a basic salary of $20,000 a year on a five-year contract. This, with a year-round public relations job with Molson's Brewery at $10,000 a year, and the bonuses he can earn in hockey gives him an income of close to $40,000 a year. It is doubtful if hockey fame has ever brought any other player as much. Selke has said that, because of the eminence of Maurice (Rocket) Richard, no player on the Canadiens would ever receive a higher salary, but it's unlikely that Richard makes as much as Beliveau off the ice.

With all of this, Beliveau is a remarkably unaffected and actually modest young man. "I think the fans overdo it too much," he says solemnly in deep throated, accented English. "It helps so much to be on a good team." This statement falls into the department of which came first, the egg or the hen. It is true that the Canadiens were a good team before Beliveau joined them, but they have become a great team since. The Beliveau magic seems to rub off on those who play beside him. Last season his linemates, Bernie Geoffrion and Bert Olmstead, who had been better than average players before hooking up with Jean, blossomed spectacularly; Geoffrion's 38 goals tied the output of Richard at the top of the goals list, and Olmstead led the league by a wide margin in assists with 48.

Curiously, the average spectator has to watch Beliveau play several games before he begins to appreciate what makes him so good. "That's because Jean makes the game look easy," explains Dick Irvin, the coach of the Chicago Black Hawks, who served in the same capacity with the Canadiens during Beliveau's first two seasons in the NHL. "You've got to look close to appreciate his finesse."

Over a couple of performances though, it begins to sink in. At first because of his size, he does not appear to be a fast skater. He has a long, fine, powerful stride that is misleading, and he gets a shot away with a smoothness of motion that fools the layman. One night in Toronto he let one go right after cruising across the blue line. No player obstructed goaler Harry Lumley's view, so the customers were surprised to see the puck bulge the back of the net. A few of them booed Lumley. "He has the hardest shot in the league," said Lumley afterward with defiance. "In fact, he shot one after that goal that was even harder. It missed the net, but I heard it whack the backboards while I was still moving for it."

Even Beliveau's teammates worship at the shrine, and Doug Harvey and Dollard St. Laurent, a Canadien defence pair, occasionally stand at the blue line during a game and shout unbelievingly to one another when they see some new fact of Beliveau's technique. "There ought to be two leagues," St. Laurent told Vince Lunny, sports editor of the *Montreal Herald*, one night after a game, "one for the pros and one for Beliveau."

No one is quite sure how Le Gros Bill got so good. He inherited neither his size nor his dedication to hockey from his family. His father, Arthur Beliveau, is of average size and has no athletic background; his mother, the former Laurette Dube, had no interest in sports as a girl and then was too busy raising her family of eight to acquire one after her marriage. Jean, born Aug. 31, 1931, in Three Rivers, is the eldest of five sons and two daughters. Ten years ago a third daughter, then five, was struck by a car and died in hospital.

When Jean was 16 he began attracting outside attention and two groups, the Quebec Citadels and the Montreal Canadiens, tried to sign him. The family had moved from Three Rivers to Victoriaville, in Quebec's eastern townships about 100 miles from Montreal, where Arthur Beliveau got a job with the Shawinigan Water and Power Company (he's still there, now a foreman). There was no junior hockey in Victoriaville, but Jean hung around the rink every day after school and played with any team that needed an extra man. One evening Frank Byrne, the owner of the Quebec Citadels juniors, got a telephone call from Lucien Duchene, a former Citadel goaler who was then playing for the Victoriaville seniors. "I want you to come right down," Duchene told Byrne. "There's a kid here, about 16, who practised with us today and he damn near knocked my head off with a shot. He's big and he's all bone."

About the same time Frank Selke, managing director of the Canadiens, had become interested in Beliveau when the coach of the Victoriaville team, Rollie Hebert, recommended him. Selke made a trip to Victoriaville in an attempt to sign Beliveau. He discovered no one in the family spoke English, so on a succeeding trip he took Montreal defenceman Butch Bouchard with him as an interpreter. They were informed by Beliveau's father, according to Selke, that "hockey players are bums." This sentiment apparently was based on the fact that Arthur Beliveau believed his son was spending too much time around the Victoriaville rink which, he felt, was populated by ne'er-do-wells. Frank Byrne helped dispel this blanket indictment of hockey players in a meeting with the senior Beliveau, pointing out that he would see that Jean roomed with a family in Quebec just like his own, that he would be paid a good salary for playing hockey (there are reports, which Byrne declines to confirm, that the Citadels paid Beliveau $7,500 to play for Quebec) and that he could either work or go to school. Byrne's offer was accepted and in the fall of 1949 Beliveau moved to Quebec City.

Selke, meanwhile, put Beliveau's name on a Canadien negotiation list, thereby preventing other NHL teams from grabbing him. "I could have outbid Quebec and got him as a junior," says Selke, "but I refused to pay all the junior players what I'd have had to pay him, and I don't think it would have been fair to the other players." Selke must have decided that the best thing for sport in Quebec was to leave Beliveau at the capital because the young man collected $20,000 a year, helping to pay off the mortgage on the new Coliseum for the next two seasons. Actually, he earned more than the $1,000 a week he received for 20 weeks of the hockey season. He got $2,500 as a public relations representative of the Laval Dairy. When Beliveau's father learned the denominations of the bills his hockey-playing son could command, he was quickly able to convince himself that not all hockey players were bums. In lining up outside jobs, Beliveau was helped by a widely known Quebec City sportsman, Emile Couture, who had watched and admired the young player's ability at Victoriaville. "He was so shy," Couture recalls, "he didn't like to say anything for himself."

Even today he has retained that reserve, sitting quietly in a hotel lobby when the Canadiens are on the road and solemnly signing autograph books if youngsters recognize him, or reading a magazine or a pocketbook. On trains, when the players congregate in the smoking room at the end of their sleeper to play hearts, he is the quietest player in the room. The English-speaking players on the club call him John; the French-speaking players give his name the soft accented Jean. For years he has been called Jean Marc Beliveau in the newspapers, but he has, in fact, no middle name, and has no idea where the Marc originated.

Jean mixes his French and English among the players but speaks only French to his pretty blond wife of three years, the former Elise Couture (no relation to sportsman Emile Couture) of Quebec City. She speaks English fluently. Their exchanges in French are a carryover from the days of their courtship in Quebec City where, as Beliveau puts it, "nobody speaks English." The Beliveaus have no children. They recently moved into a six-room house in Longueuil, a Montreal suburb, where they spend most of their evenings quietly, watching television when Beliveau isn't making a rather self-conscious speech or presenting a trophy on behalf of Molson's. He travels all over Quebec for the firm during the summer, umpiring ball games, making presentations or attending banquets for the brewery, a tall, reserved, slow-striding figure. He samples the products only occasionally during the summer and rarely during the winter.

As yet he has no long-range business plans. "I am only 24," he says. "Rocket Richard is maybe 10 years older, and what a great hockey player. I would like to go on for some years and I will if there are no injuries." He frowns when he speaks of injuries, as though they preoccupied him. "The injuries," he says, "you never know about them." He has invested his money liberally in Canada savings bonds.

And he steadily has been becoming a better hockey player. "It's something new every game," says linemate Bert Olmstead. "He has such remarkable reflexes, can so quickly take a pass in front of the net and fire the puck hard and accurately. He has the same sense of direction as the Rocket, and is big and strong in front of that net, hard for the defencemen to knock down." He's getting tougher in a tough game too. Through his first two seasons he took knocks and digs without retaliation, feeling they were part of hockey, but this year he has been striking back and drawing more penalties for it. In 70 games last season he had 58 minutes in the penalty box. This year, after just 40 games, he had already been penalized 100 minutes. "I used to wonder why Rocket Richard would blow up when other players chopped at him," he remarked recently, "but I am beginning to understand."

His new attitude pleases his employers, who feel that it has given him a greater respect by lesser players who used to take advantage of him. Kenny Reardon, assistant managing director of the Canadiens, was asked recently if there were anything about Beliveau that bothered him. "Just one thing," he replied. "How'd you like to have the job of signing him when his five-year contract runs out?"

In that 1955–56 season, the star of Jean Beliveau eclipsed that of Maurice Richard to become the premier player on the Canadiens. He won the Hart Trophy as the league's most valuable player and led the Habs in scoring during their run to winning the Stanley Cup. Beliveau won the MVP award a second time in the 1963–64 season, but perhaps his greatest feat is playing on 10 Cup-winning teams. Beliveau retired in 1971, but didn't leave the game. For 22 more years he served as official spokesman for the Canadiens until stepping down in 1993. Beliveau still lives in suburban Longueuil where, in his trademark quiet and classy way, he runs a charitable foundation for children.

Nobody's Too Big for Ted Lindsay

Trent Frayne

October, 1957—Straight ahead is the only direction Ted Lindsay has ever travelled in 13 years in the National Hockey League. As a snarling, mocking, richly talented performer for the Detroit Red Wings from 1944 until he was traded to the Chicago Black Hawks last summer, he recognized no detours in becoming the highest-scoring leftwinger of all time, and one of the stormiest. Lean and scarred and built like a middleweight boxer, he has taken on defencemen who outweigh him by 50 pounds, and while they've cut him up and knocked him down they've never changed his mind. He has publicly charged the president of the NHL, Clarence Campbell, with prejudice. He has fought on the ice with his own teammates and off it with fans, policemen and even his long-time employer, general manager Jack Adams. They stopped speaking to each other two years ago. For 13 years Ted Lindsay has never backed down from anyone and now, this fall, in addition to moving to a new challenge with the lowly Hawks, he is taking on the largest order of them all—the men who run the league.

He'll do this as president of the National Hockey League Players' Association, a union formed by the ice-bound serfs in awesome secrecy during a three-month period last winter, with Lindsay as one of its principal instigators and organizers. When its existence was announced by Lindsay at a press conference in New York last February, the club owners and league executives expressed an astonishment matched only by that of most hockey fans. The sudden materialization of a players' union was unexpected in itself; still more remarkable was the materialization as the players' spokesman and president, their archenemy during working hours, the little hellion Lindsay. Lindsay's announcement on the formation of the players' united front was made with studied understatement. "We have organized to promote and protect the best interests of the players," he said. "We don't intend to start a revolution. We aren't displeased or discontented about a single thing."

But no owner was reassured by these seemingly innocuous words. Conn Smythe, of Toronto, was so moved by the idea of a union that he called his own team's representative, Jimmy Thomson, "a traitor and a Quisling," according to Thomson. Thomson, who joined the Leafs in 1945 and was with them for 12 seasons, then had his contract dispatched by Smythe to the farm club in Rochester, N.Y. Six months later, Thomson was sold to Chicago. Smythe speaks cautiously in public about the union, as do all the owners who, after their initial gasps of surprise, have adopted a wait-and-see attitude. Adams, for example, said nothing publicly about Lindsay's leading role in formation of the union, but Detroit sports writers were predicting as far back as March that it was the final incident in his disenchantment with Lindsay and that he would be traded to Chicago. The trade finally was announced last July 23.

There was a day when Adams loved Terrible Ted as a son. "Lindsay?" he beamed in 1952. "He's my kind of hockey player." Later, explaining why he had appointed him captain of the Red Wings, he said, "Lindsay is captain because Lindsay is a fighter and a leader. He's a player who never quits himself and can stir his team up in the dressing room and on the ice." But two years ago, possibly because the maturing Lindsay was beginning to show a lively individuality in discussions with Adams, the passions faded. Independence of thought is not, Lindsay had concluded, a characteristic that is encouraged by NHL executives. "They don't think we have minds of our own," Lindsay says of the moguls. "They treat us like we were little babies."

Whatever the reason, Adams removed the captain's mantle from Lindsay's shoulders, and then the two stopped speaking to each other. Through last season, while the player was enjoying his greatest year in a Red Wings suit, Adams charged him in the newspapers with "complacency." Once undismayed by the number of penalties incurred annually by his tiger, Adams observed balefully of Lindsay that "a man can't score from the penalty box." By the time the season ended, one in which Lindsay compiled his own all-time high of 85 scoring points and was named for an unprecedented eighth time as the NHL's all-star leftwinger, the breach was complete. Adams announced that his one-time "untouchable"—his own word for a player who will not be sold or traded—was available for trade. Lindsay told newspapermen that if he was traded he'd quit hockey.

At first he was adamant in his decision to retire. Then two things changed his mind. "The Chicago club gave me an opportunity that I can't afford to pass up," he says. This followed what Lindsay calls "derogatory statements" by Adams about him

Ted Lindsay (right) with linemate Gordie Howe.

and his family. He doesn't want to expand on the subject. "I'm not going to get into a name-calling exchange with Adams," he says. "I want the whole thing to blow over. I'm not sore at Adams. I pity a man like that."

Opposition from the game's executives is not likely to faze Lindsay in the committee rooms because he's been overcoming opposition, some of it unbelievably violent, ever since he broke into the league. Early in his career, he got involved with Butch Bouchard, a Montreal defenceman who is six to eight inches taller and 50 pounds heavier. Bouchard swung his stick as Lindsay started to skate away and he ducked his head before he realized that Bouchard's stick was swung low. Instead of hitting him on the thigh or the hip, it caught him across the temple. He went to hospital with a concussion and was under observation for four days. He says now it was an accident. "I shouldn't have ducked."

At other times in his tempestuous career Lindsay suffered a fractured cheek bone, two shoulder separations, so many broken noses that he has lost count, two broken hands, and assorted other lumps, sprains and bruises. He estimates that he carries the imprint of 270 stitches, so many of them in his face that his nickname around the league is Little Scarface.

He's dished out his share of hemstitching, too. Bill Ezinicki, a solid rock of a right winger for Boston in 1951, was cooling people out with impassive violence after two straight seasons with Toronto as the league's penalty leader. Lindsay and Ezinicki exchanged a few brisk taps with their sticks during a lull in the play and then their tempers burst and they began wood-chopping each other. Then they threw down their sticks and gloves and the carnage was incredible. Ezinicki needed 11 stitches to close a stick cut from eyebrow to hairline. He raised four stitches on the side of his head. He needed four more on the inside of his mouth, and he had one tooth broken off. Lindsay required only one stitch but, not altogether unexpectedly, needed treatment for a scarred and bruised right hand.

Just last February Lindsay became involved in a tangle with Jerry Toppazzini, of Boston, in which Toppazzini's face was so battered that he refused to let photographers take his picture in the hospital. "I don't want my family to see me looking like this," he mumbled through swollen lips. Sixteen stitches were required to close cuts above his right eye, across his nose, which was broken, and around his mouth. Lindsay insists the injuries were accidentally inflicted. "It was the kind of play that happens dozens of time a season," he says. "we didn't see each other until the last possible second. Then I threw up my hands to protect myself. Somehow my stick hit his face." Toppazzini, visited by Lindsay in hospital, bears out this version. "It was entirely an accident," he says. "I told Ted that. It could have been him."

Lindsay, who confesses that he hates anybody on the other team once a game starts, has even fought a teammate. That was a rookie named Red Eye Hay who was playing against Ted in an intra-squad exhibition game in Sault Ste. Marie, Ont., in 1953. Lindsay says he took exception to the manner in which Hay was "throwing his weight around against one of our kids," so the two of them went at it. Afterward, in the penalty box, a fan began badgering Lindsay and another fight ensued. Lindsay fell down a flight of stairs and when a policeman grabbed him, Lindsay started swinging at the arm of the law, too.

He says no man can last in the NHL who backs away from a fight. "The first thing they find out in this business is if you can take it," he says. "A little guy has to have plenty of self-confidence, maybe even seem cocky. I had the idea that I should beat up every player I tangled with, and I'm still not convinced it wasn't a good idea. What are you going to do when some guy starts giving it to you—skate away? You wouldn't last five games."

Lindsay has lasted 13 years at this point, and no other performer in hockey history has so successfully mixed so much skullduggery with so much skill. Lindsay, who has scored 321 goals, is now fourth in the all-time scoring list behind Richard, Gordie Howe, of Detroit, and Nels Stewart, a former great who scored 323 goals in 15 seasons. They are the only players in hockey history to score more than 300 goals; indeed, no one else has scored more than 270.

His skill and his combativeness, his scars, his visit to Toppazzini after that crash, and his refusal to back away from a fight—all these things are keys to the character of the volcanic Lindsay, an unexpectedly calm, personable and even gentle person away from the battle pits. Being a comparatively small man of five feet eight and weighing between 163 and 168 pounds, he has the small man's compulsion to prove he belongs. He claims he hasn't started more than half the brawls he has been embroiled in, an appraisal that in the words of veteran defenceman Jim Thomson, "is maybe just a little too high."

"He's sneaky," says Thomson. "You've got to keep your eyes open all the time or he'll cut your heart out. He can be the friendly fellow off the ice, but when they drop that puck, look out. He has to win." Put differently, it could be said that Lindsay just can't stand losing. His wife, a beautiful black-haired blue-eyed Detroit girl, says he can't even stand to lose a game of cards. They play gin rummy and cribbage occasionally, and she says it just isn't worth it to win. "He gets pouty," she smiles.

Lindsay has carried that insatiable will to win through his hockey career. He was so determined to prove his worth when manager Jack Adams made him captain of the Red Wings that he set an all-time NHL record for penalties in a single game—30 minutes. That was against Toronto on Oct. 12, 1952, when he roamed all over the ice to stand up for his teammates. He even rushed to the aid of Gordie Howe, who is four inches taller and 30 pounds heavier and a man who has never needed help in a fight. Howe was enjoying a routine little scrap with Ted Kennedy, of the Toronto Maple Leafs, when Lindsay charged across the ice to take over Howe's role and earn himself a major penalty.

Fans in out-of-town rinks often become inflamed by Lindsay's provocative side, his fights with the home-town players and, of course, his ability to put the puck in the home net. Consequently, he is one of the most often booed players in the game, a fact that causes him no concern whatever. "As long as the fans don't boo you at home you don't have to worry," he says. "If they boo you on the road you must be doing something to help your own club. As for other players, I'd like them all to be my friends—off the ice."

This terrible-tempered Mr. Bang of the ice lanes is a softie around the house. His wife, Pat, recalls that he always got up in the middle of the night when their youngsters Blake, now three, and the little girl Lynn, now two, were months-old babies crying in the night. "He'd change them and soothe them," Pat says, "and even now he still brings me my orange juice in bed. And I used to hate him!" That was prior to 1952 when Pat occasionally went to games in the Detroit Olympia. She was a Red Wings fan all right, but she recalls that "he irritated me on the ice." They met through a mutual friend. "I found, as so many people have, that he's a real Jekyll-Hyde kind of person," she relates. "I found him delightful."

The Lindsays live in Birmingham, a residential suburb of Detroit. Their L-shaped, grey-brick house overlooks the Oakland Hills Country Club's golf course and has nine bedrooms and three bathrooms, with a green slate floor and Tennessee ledgerock fireplace in the recreation room. They drive two cars, a Ford station wagon and an Oldsmobile hardtop convertible. Such baubles of splendor were not part of the Lindsay menage in Renfrew, Ont., back on July 29, 1925, when the ninth and, as it turned out, last child was born to Mr. and Mrs. Bert Lindsay. Bert Lindsay, who had played hockey in Victoria and Renfrew with men like Lester Patrick, Cyclone Taylor and Newsy Lalonde, worked for a trucking firm. When it failed in 1933, he went to Kirkland Lake in the gold-mining area of northern Ontario and got a job as manager of the rink. He moved his six boys and three girls north, including the baby who had been christened Robert Blake Lindsay. The Blake was in honor of a favorite uncle, Blake Johnston, nicknamed Ted, and thus little Robert Blake Lindsay became Ted, too. Later the boy grew weary of explaining that Ted was a nickname and added Theodore to his list of Christian names.

Lindsay got his first pair of skates when he was nine, given to him by a neighbor named Mrs. Brady. Even before he learned to skate he acquired the first in his long list of injuries. He was out one day on an open-air rink in 30-degree-below-zero weather with his hands stuffed in his pockets, trying to bring the reluctant skates into line. The severe cold caused a long crack in the ice, which the unsteady boy was unable to avoid. He fell face down, his hands still pinned in his pockets, and broke off two front teeth.

Fearing his mother would forbid his skating excursions, he didn't mention the broken teeth and perfected a method of smiling, when necessary, without moving his upper lip from his teeth. But after three weeks, the teeth became infected and he had to have three removed, and a permanent plate installed. He was small as a boy and so learned early to use guile and pugnacity to keep even with the bigger kids. He played hockey for the Holy Name school, won a couple of all-Ontario championships, and then turned down offers from the Galt and St. Catharines junior teams because they couldn't guarantee he'd be able to keep up his schooling. He entered St. Michael's school in Toronto.

Except for an injury, he'd probably have become a member of the Toronto Maple Leafs. A fan recommended "a kid playing the wing for St. Mike's" to Leaf coach Hap Day, who asked the team's assistant manager, Frank Selke, now managing director of the Canadiens, to take a look. But Lindsay had been speared in the calf by a skate point and was hospitalized for two weeks. When Selke watched St. Mike's he saw a wingman named Joe Sadler make several good moves and assumed that this was the player in whom Day was interested. When Lindsay returned to St. Mike's lineup, he was spotted by the late Carson Cooper, Detroit's chief scout, who followed him for a couple of games. When he saw Lindsay win two fights and score a goal he put his name on the Detroit list.

In the spring, with the Oshawa Generals in the Memorial Cup finals, coach Charlie Conacher selected Lindsay as a replacement for an injured player and Lindsay helped the Generals win the national junior championship in 1944. Conacher, former star of the Maple Leafs and later coach of the Chicago Black Hawks, has never changed his high opinion of Lindsay. Not long ago he named him the greatest left winger he'd ever seen. "He's like Ted Williams," says Conacher. "He can do everything, does it with a flourish, and has a mind of his own."

Certainly, Lindsay has never been a conformist, from the instant he jumped straight to the Red Wings from St. Mike's as a 19-year-old until the February day in 1957 when he announced that the players had formed an association, with himself as president. He feels that one incident illustrating the need for a union is the case of Jim Thomson, who was shipped off to the minors by his outspoken employer, Conn Smythe, and was on the minor-league roster all summer until his sale in August to Chicago. "It doesn't seem fair that after 12 years in the big leagues a player can be shipped off like that," he says. "There ought to be greater recognition of a man who has proven himself. He ought to become a free agent and be allowed to make a deal for himself."

The players also feel the owners could contribute more to the players' pension fund than the administrative costs they now bear. As of now, fund money comes from the players, each of whom contributes $900 a season, from a 25-cent surtax imposed on tickets for playoff games, and from two-thirds of the annual all-star game's gate receipts. No money from television networks goes to the fund. Last season the Columbia Broadcasting System paid the clubs $100,000 for permission to carry 10 games across the United States. This year the American network will carry 21 games, reportedly at an increased fee that might mean $300,000 or more. Lindsay feels a portion of this money might well be allocated to the pension fund.

It isn't the snarling stick-flicking Linsday who talks of these things, a scarred 32-year-old veteran of a hundred hockey wars. It's the other Lindsay, a calm young business executive, neatly dressed and controlled. This is the Lindsay who is a partner in two firms in Detroit supplying automotive accessories to the vast automobile industry. An executive who does business with him predicts "he's going places—he's $100,000-a-year material if I ever saw it." This Lindsay declines to talk publicly about his fallout with general manager Jack Adams, beyond terming it "a conflict in personalities."

Such earthy diplomacy couched in such lofty terms helps explain why his fellow players elected Lindsay their first president even while fingering the scars he'd inflicted. As one of them observed cheerfully, "It's nice to have the little rat on our side for a change." It would appear, then, that this Lindsay—the one with the velvet glove—will prove quite as formidable as the other—the one who climbed to the top carrying a big stick and never backed down from anyone.

Lindsay spent three seasons in Chicago before hanging up his blades in 1960. But he came out of retirement to don his old red-and-white Detroit jersey for the 1964 season at age 39. Following his playing days, Lindsay became a successful businessman in Detroit and ran his own plastics manufacturing company. During the late '70s, he was briefly hired as general manager of the Wings. Lindsay, now semi-retired, has continued to fight for fairness for NHL players and has been vocal during the on-going legal proceedings surrounding pension money for hockey veterans.

The Awful Ups and Downs of Terry Sawchuk

Trent Frayne

December 19, 1959—Of all the stormy and troubled occupations of man, none is filled with more ups and downs than that of the goalkeeper for a professional hockey team. The mere physical nature of the job compels its tenant to hurl himself, legs and arms asprawl, to a concrete-hard sheet of ice as many as 30 times in a 60-minute game, then spring erect in the next split second in the uncertain hope that a steel-hard rubber disc is not about to clunk him on the head at a speed of 120 miles an hour.

Emotionally and psychologically, the big-league goaler faces even greater and more perilous shifts of fortune. His single mistake can cost his teammates the victory that represents thousands of dollars in playoff money, a charge that can never be made so strongly against the forward who misses an open net or the defenceman who misses a check. These mistakes can be amended; a goalkeeper's never can. He either stops the puck or the red light goes on.

Of all the great members of the craft, none has ever suffered more ups and downs than Terry Sawchuk, the masterful and complicated young man who guards the padded cell for the Detroit Red Wings. Sawchuk's activities over the last 10 years have been remarkably unpredictable, even in so unpredictable a business. Indeed, since the day he broke in, it's been impossible to guess what's going to happen next to Sawchuk, a moody man of exuberant peaks and mute hollows, whose name has crowded into the headlines, for one reason or another, ever since he became a professional hockey player in November of 1947 at the age of 17. Injuries, domestic crises, illness, accidents, five medical operations, illogical trades and the abnormal tensions of his pressure-cooker occupation have plagued him. His playing weight has vacillated from a high of 228 to a low of 162—a spread of 66 pounds on a five-foot-ten frame—and by his own estimate he has picked up 250 stitches in his face alone, three of them in his right eyeball.

Through all the turmoil he has remained one of the game's great performers. Indeed, one objective authority, Frank Boucher, who started an NHL career as player in 1926 and concluded it 29 years later as general manager of the New York Rangers, says without equivocation that in all that time he never saw Sawchuk's equal. Last year, playing doggedly for the league's worst team, Sawchuk was named to the NHL's second all-star team, recognition rarely achieved by the goalkeeper of a last-place club.

Even insiders in hockey are often surprised by the things that happen to Sawchuk. Four years ago, pads deep in praise after he'd won his third Vezina Trophy in four seasons and had helped the Wings to the Stanley Cup, Terry was acquired by Boston to the undiluted astonishment of—of all people—Boston's own general manager, Lynn Patrick. "Oh, we'd been negotiating a trade with Detroit over several players, all right, and they knew we wanted a goalkeeper," Patrick says now. "But no goaler's name had been mentioned, and we thought it would be Glenn Hall, Edmonton's man in the Western League who was owned by Detroit. In our wildest dreams we didn't think we could pry Sawchuk loose. When we learned that the mysterious goalkeeper of our negotiations was Terry we were dumbfounded."

Detroit's general manager, the ostentatious veteran Jack Adams, apparently decided that Hall, though only two years younger than Sawchuk, was a better long-range bet, a decision he was to rue when he and Hall stopped speaking for a season. Hall was eventually sold to Chicago. Sawchuk simply flabbergasted the hockey world halfway through his second season with Boston. In spite of a virus blood ailment called infectious mononucleosis that hospitalized him for two weeks, he was so successful with the Bruins, whom he'd squired to first place, that he was named on the NHL's mid-season all-star team. He greeted this news a few hours later by announcing abruptly that he was through with hockey. In a hare-and-hounds act that confounded pursuing Boston reporters, he boarded a train for his home in Detroit. There, his physician announced, "Mr. Sawchuk is on the verge of a complete nervous breakdown."

In the wake of *that*, Sawchuk turned up in the Detroit cage the following season, again to the surprise of Boston's Lynn Patrick. "I must say I was startled when I heard that Jack Adams was interested in getting him back," Patrick said recently. "We were satisfied with Don Simmons, who replaced Terry when he left us. Terry just wasn't happy in Boston. When he'd see Jimmy Skinner (then the Detroit coach) he'd call to him, 'When are you going to get me back?' I found he constantly needed assurance that he was great."

Sawchuk scoffs at reports and innuendos that he bolted the Bruins because of homesickness. He and his wife, Pat, and their three children (the reserved and soft-voiced Mrs. Sawchuk, a Detroit girl, is expecting a fourth child in January) live in a ranch-style house on one acre in Union Lake, a suburb 35 miles from downtown Detroit, and the family stayed there during Terry's time with the Bruins. "Sure, I missed them, but not that much," he says. "I mean, I appreciated that hockey was my living, and I told the Bruins when I was recovering from mononucleosis that I'd be back when I was better. Hell, I left home when I was a kid of 15. I've been on my own for a long time."

While Sawchuk insists that moving back to his home had nothing to do with his recovery, doctors accustomed to the never-never land between physical and emotional disability cannot be so sure. In any case, Sawchuk did have the symptoms of mononucleosis—enlargement of the lymph nodes in his neck, armpits and groin—and a heavy feeling of fatigue.

"I lost 20 pounds in two weeks," he recalls. "I was tired all the time and sometimes in the third period I wondered if I'd be able to finish the game."

Once, driving home with his wife after Boston had played a game in the Detroit Olympia, he stopped his car for a sandwich and found he couldn't get out of it. "I just couldn't move my legs," he says. "They felt like lead."

He stayed close to home, first resting and relaxing, later playing golf at a municipal course operated by his father-in-law, Ed Morey. Soon he was playing 27 holes a day. "By midsummer I was feeling as well as I ever had in my life," he says now. "When I heard I'd been traded back to Detroit I won't deny I was glad to be playing at home, but I still would have gone back to the Bruins if they hadn't traded me."

The Sawchuks live a quiet suburban life in Union Lake, the centre of their existence being their television set during the hockey season, and golf course during the summer. Pat likes golf and plays it when she can with Terry, but because the children are still small, her opportunities are limited. When the two of them can slip away, though, late in the evening, they like to spend an hour or so sitting quietly in her father's lounge, wearing informal clothes, sipping beer and chatting with the hockey fans who recognize the Red Wing goalkeeper.

Sawchuk, who will turn 30 on December 28, talks earnestly and in an excited flow

Terry Sawchuck in net with the Detroit Red Wings.

of words, shifting quickly and often in his chair. His wife, Pat, says this is his usual manner, except on the day of a game, or after a defeat. "I never say a word to him on the day he's playing," she smiles. "He's like an old bear. He blows up fast, but he gets over it just as fast. The kids used to bother him but, you know, Terry left home so early that he didn't know what home life was like. It made him too independent."

Sawchuk agrees with this last appraisal. "As for the other thing, the way I am on the day of a game, well, I do worry about every game. The crazy thing is, though, that when I'm actually on the ice I don't worry at all; it's only before the game or between periods that I really brood. Another thing, as soon as I go into the net I bend down and take a sideways peek at the goal posts. If they look close I know I'm gonna have a good night. Some nights those damn posts look a mile away."

In action, Sawchuk is one of the most acrobatic of all goalkeepers. Someone once wrote that he doesn't move so much as he explodes into a kind of desperate epileptic action, down the glove, up the arm, over the stick, up the leg pad—all in such incredibly swift succession that he resembles a human pinwheel. He plays a whole game in a kind of pent-up tension, shouting at his teammates, crouching, straightening, his pale face drawn and tense. His style likely accounts for the great number of facial cuts he accrues but the possibility that he might be cut never occurs to him and he has no fear. Once, playing for Omaha in a game in Houston, he got a stick in the eye and doctors feared he might lose the eye. He watched the operation through an arrangement of mirrors as the eyeball was laid on his cheek and three stitches were taken in it.

From the day he broke in, he has had a happy exuberance when things are going well. When he was 17 and playing goal for the Windsor junior Spitfires, Detroit boss Jack Adams called him across the river to the Detroit Olympia, gave him $2,000 to sign a professional contract and told him he was flying out immediately to join the Red Wing farm club at Omaha, Neb. Before departing, Sawchuk sped back to a Windsor bank where foreign exchange then favored American funds and turned his money into about 2,100 one-dollar bills. He carried the neatly packaged stacks to his room, closed the door and hurled them against the wall, scattering the rug with a green cascade of bills. He wallowed around in them, grinning and chuckling, a chubby adolescent who'd never held one-twentieth as much money before.

He weighed 175 when he departed for Omaha, and when he returned to his home in Winnipeg in the spring his parents met him at the station but they didn't recognize him. He'd added 35 pounds. He figured 210 was his playing weight for a couple of years, and he held that weight in the off-season by playing baseball for the Elmwood Giants in the Mandak League, comprised of teams from Manitoba and North Dakota. He led the league in hitting .376 and received letters from the St. Louis Cardinals and the Pittsburgh Pirates, suggesting trials. He decided to stick to hockey, playing ball only to retain his condition, and discovered when the season ended that his weight had climbed to 228.

Jack Adams, the Detroit leader, was horrified when he saw Sawchuk at training camp and ordered him onto a strict diet. When he got down to about 200 he went off the diet but he continued to lose weight. By the time he'd become ill in Boston he was playing at 162 pounds. Now, eating what he likes when he likes and indulging in occasional bottles of beer, he has worked back up to 175. He has no idea what his best playing weight might be.

The loss of weight may be traceable to his highly strung nervous system, or to the physical and mental problems that have beset him. Two years ago he received an emotional shock when Pat, his wife, sued him for divorce. When he heard of it, Jack Adams says, he "broke down, cried and sobbed." Then he and Pat talked over their difficulties and were immediately reconciled. "We worked it all out," Pat says, dismissing the subject, "everything is wonderful with us now."

Even an off-season motor accident has contributed to Sawchuk's trials and tribulations. He was driving home from a golf course when a tie-rod broke in the car's steering. The car crashed into a tree, and the steering wheel crushed his chest. In an ensuing operation his lung was collapsed to relieve the pressure.

Sawchuk has also had an emergency appendectomy and three operations on his right arm, which is two inches shorter than his left because of a boyhood football injury. During his first three seasons in the NHL, the arm—which he can't straighten—bothered him a lot, and each summer he had some chips removed. He estimates he's had 60 chips taken out, 22 of which he keeps in a small jar at home.

Things never were easy for Sawchuk as a child, which may explain why he has been able to take adversity in stride in his maturity. His dad, Louis, was a tinsmith in the East Kildonan suburb of Winnipeg when Terry was born at the beginning of the Depression in 1929. His brother Mike played goal at school so, as Terry says, "the pads were always around the house and I fell into them." Terry was 10 when Mike died of a heart ailment at 17. Another brother, Roger, died of pneumonia when he was a year old.

When Terry was 13 and 14 he worked in a farm-implement company's foundry, and for a sheet-metal company installing canopies over giant ovens in bakeries. He took his money home to his mother, who allowed him a quarter a week. While he was working Sawchuk was usually able to find time for hockey. He was a kid of only 12 when Bob Kinnear, a Winnipeg scout for Detroit, got him onto a midget team sponsored by the Red Wings. As a 15-year-old he played junior for the Winnipeg Rangers and was so promising that Detroit decided to transfer him to eastern Canada with the Red Wing-sponsored team at Galt, Ont., in the Junior OHA. Terry remembers that he packed two pairs of pants and a red flannel jacket into a cardboard suitcase for the train trip east. His mother gave him a $10 bill—"one of the few she ever had"—to buy essentials until he'd settled in Galt.

"There was a crap game in the smoker," he says, "and after a long battle with my conscience I decided to get in. After an hour I'd won a hundred bucks, and I crouched there with it sweating in my hand, wanting to quit while I was ahead but being afraid to because I had most of the money. Finally, there was only one guy left who I hadn't cleaned out, and we rolled. He won it all, except the 10 bucks I'd kept back."

He played a year at Galt, earning $20 a week. "Well, actually, I got eight dollars a week," he clarifies. "The other $12 went straight to the landlady. I remember seeing a pair of shoes in a store window that I wanted desperately. They were 12 bucks. I faithfully gave the guy two dollars a week for six weeks, staring in the window every day at the shoes that would soon be mine. Finally, I made the last payment, put on my new shoes and walked proudly out of the store. I discovered walking down the street that I didn't like them and I never wore them again."

Which, of course, wasn't surprising. Terry Sawchuk is a very unpredictable fellow.

Sawchuk played four more years for Detroit before being traded to the Toronto Maple Leafs in 1964, where he helped win his fourth Stanley Cup in 1967. A four-time winner of the Vezina Trophy, Sawchuk still holds more NHL records than any other goaltender, including most wins, most shutouts and most games played. Terry Sawchuk, then a member of the New York Rangers, died in a New York City hospital in 1970 while trying to recover from internal injuries sustained in an off-season fight with a teammate he was sharing a house with.

Viva Mahovlich!

Peter Gzowski

February 25, 1961—Hockey has been called a game for brutes and Canadians. It is also a game for heroes. Every decade of its history has belonged to one man, perhaps two—Morenz, Conacher, Richard, Howe, a few others. They were, or are, hockey's equivalent of what bullfight aficionados call the *torero del era*—which translates as the man the non-brute (and often the non-Canadian) customers pay to see.

This year, the era of Richard is over. The era of Howe is ending. (Howe still dominates any game he's in, but he has slowed down; he is now only a very good hockey player.) And this year, a young man named Frank Mahovlich is making an honest, exciting and, it appears now, a worthy bid to claim the new era for his own.

Mahovlich, 23, weighs 200, stands six one, has miner's hands, fullback's legs, dancer's hips, stevedore's shoulders and a sleepy, Slavic face. He is handsome, even with his hockey player's false teeth out. He is single, Catholic, the eldest and devoted son of an immigrant goldminer from the Porcupine in Northern Ontario. He plays left wing for the Toronto Maple Leafs. In the first two-thirds of this National Hockey League season he scored more goals than any other Maple Leaf ever did in a full one. He is the newest contender to break hockey's equivalent of the four-minute mile: to score more than 50 goals in one season. He scored 52 goals in his last year as an amateur, the year he turned 19. In four years as a pro, he has never scored fewer than 18 and in his first three years he scored nearly twice as many as Gordie Howe did in his first three.

But there are other players whose form charts are impressive. The chart does not explain why small boys breathe Mahovlich's name with the same awe they use for that of marshal Matt Dillon. Or why grown men force their wives to watch the Maple Leafs on television and bellow at them to look at number 27 (which is, appropriately, just three times the number worn by both Howe and Richard). Or why, when Frank was 14, the Chicago Black Hawks offered his father a fruit farm if he would move to

Frank Mahovlich in action at Maple Leaf Gardens.

the Niagara Peninsula so his son could play for their junior team in St. Catharines, Ont. Or why Maple Leaf Gardens crackles with excitement every time Mahovlich carries the puck as much as 10 feet—the way it seldom has since Ted Kennedy, the "heart of the Leafs," retired. Or why, even though he is not captain, Mahovlich usually (after the goalie) leads the Leafs onto the ice. Or why there are louder cheers when he gets an assist than when almost any other Leaf gets a goal. Or why a bellboy approached Mahovlich in the lobby of a hotel in Maurice Richard's Montreal and asked in a French accent for the autograph of the "greatest hockey player of 1960 and '61."

What *does* explain these things? Why *is* Mahovlich so apparently the heir to Richard's throne?

First, you'd have to say his style, the way he skates. There are other excellent skaters in the NHL—Henri Richard, certainly, and Bobby Hull. Mahovlich himself says that Carl Brewer, a *defenceman* with the Leafs, is faster. But no one else is so elegant, so electric, so furious, so fluid. Other skaters stride, he swoops. They glide, he soars. They sprint, he explodes. Head down, shoulder up, legs churning, one hand on his stick, Mahovlich looks like the Super Continental coming through Saskatchewan, and he is almost as powerful and as hard to knock down.

And there are the goals. There is, after all, nothing quite like a goal. Mahovlich can spot an opportunity to score the way Billy the Kid could spot a slow draw. Then he circles like an eagle, pounces like a panther, strikes with the accuracy of a king cobra. In one game in Boston this winter, he took five shots and scored four goals. He has been scoring one of every four the Leafs get.

And, like all other real champions, Mahovlich is lucky. Of his first 40 goals this season, there were at least four that, because of empty nets or perfect passes or defensive lapses, Mazo de la Roche could have scored. But the most distinctive quality about Mahovlich is his laziness. He is like the little girl who had the little curl: when he is good he is very, very good and when he is bad he stinks up the place. He is so lazy that his laziness takes on a sort of heroism. No one but a great star *could* be that lazy. *He* calls it "positional hockey," but it looks from the stands as if, while his teammates are battling heroically to get the puck out of their own end, Mahovlich is preparing to take a nap at centre ice. This drives the customers berserk. The result is that when Mahovlich is on the ice he is either being roundly cheered or lustily booed (one lady in the east blues boos him *all* the time, on principle) but he is always being watched.

Mahovlich's arrival as a superstar has wrought some changes in him. As a hockey player, he is facing great adversity—usually in the shape of an elbow, a grasping arm, a subtly lifted knee, a deftly jabbed hockey stick—as the enemy tries to stop him, block him, slow him down. The enemy also tries to detonate his temper. For one angry moment in Montreal last month he stood snarling like a bear cornered by hounds. He gets a lot of penalties, but he hasn't really exploded yet. He is changing off the ice too. The crowds of autograph seekers, almost a novelty to him until this year but now with him like outriders wherever he goes, are beginning to bore him. But he is still, appealingly, somehow pleased with being Frank Mahovlich, boy celebrity, though that pleasure is almost hidden behind the casual and casually profane air of the pro athlete. He does not confess readily that he is now doing what he once dreamed of. In his team, his emergence as a mature star has wrought an important change—the Leafs are once again in the running for first place in the National League.

For hockey and for the NHL, Mahovlich came exactly when he was needed. In spite of the *toreros* of the most recent era, big-time hockey has been degenerating more and more into a game of violence, of mass shoot-it-into-the-corner-and-scramble attack, and more and more away from the contest of grace and excitement and even, sometimes, beauty that it can be. Mahovlich, and the all-too-few others almost like him, may yet do something about that. Olé!

Frank Mahovlich fell two goals short of potting 50 that year and never did reach "hockey's equivalent of the four-minute mile." He remained an important contributor in Toronto and played well during their Cup season in 1967, but it wasn't until he was traded to Detroit the following year that he found his scoring touch again. He also played with Montreal, helping the Canadiens win two Stanley Cups to add to the four he won with the Leafs. He finished his career in 1978 with the Birmingham Bulls of the World Hockey Association. On June 15, 1998, Mahovlich was sworn in as a member of the Canadian Senate, after being appointed to the Upper House by Prime Minister Jean Chrétien.

Bobby Hull: Hockey Hero

Trent Frayne

January 22, 1966—When Bobby Hull is in his own living room, you don't get the picture that here is the Golden Jet of the Chicago Black Hawks, the most dashing and attractive player in hockey. On the ice, who can miss him? He is beautifully right for his game. When Hull swoops to his left, his right leg crossing high, his motion is as fluid as a bird's in flight. When he breaks into full stride and shoots the puck in a black blur, he brings a sudden expectant "*oh-h-h-h*" from the great crowds that falls to a hush if he misses the net or explodes in a roar if he scores.

Hull is hard to miss, even off the ice. In television commercials he's a dimpled pitchman for hair tonic, rubbing his blond head with Vitalis and advising you to try it, too. In magazine advertisements, he models swimsuits and sweaters and socks. In four-color displays for practically suitless swimsuits, there he is in Hawaii on the sands of Waikiki, his tawny pelt glistening in muscles piled on muscles, grinning down on a doll wearing a delicious dispersement of skin. Or, back on television, there he is being interviewed after firing three goals against the Toronto Maple Leafs, telling interviewer Ward Cornell with a nice warm gratifying smile and a nice warm rewarding touch of humility that it was fine to score those three goals, all right, but the thing that really matters this year, Ward, is that the *Hawks* finish on *top*.

Good grief, the millions wonder, watching and reading, is the guy for real? Well, yes . . . but you've got to hold onto the thought hard if you drop into his Chicago home and see the game's most flamboyant figure wandering around in his socks, his unbuttoned white shirt trailing outside his pants; or occasionally burying one of his three young sons deep against his chest or playfully piling him into the pillows of a couch; or exchanging barbs with his wife, Joanne.

Bobby Hull and Joanne and their boys—Bobby, who is four, Blake, three, and Brett, a year and a half—live in a surprisingly modest three-bedroom bungalow in a working-man's suburb of Chicago called Addison. They own the house but live there only during the hockey season. Joanne is a slim, frank, outspoken girl, blue-eyed and freckled, with short auburn hair. She was an ice-show skater and met Hull six years ago when the show played Chicago. The boys, whom she calls "my mutts," are an enormously energetic handful, built along their father's burly lines, all with light-blue eyes and great thatches of hair so blond as to be almost platinum. When they're indoors they roam across the living room's royal-blue rug like balls of prairie thistle in a high wind, yelling, crying, laughing, slugging one another, standing parade-ground still for admonition, tearing off, wailing, giggling; in short, boys. Joanne, with the help of a quiet bespectacled girl named Sheila Bourette, who lives year-round with the Hulls, battles gamely to maintain law and order with her mutts, running the motherly gamut from cajolery to a high-pitched shriek, kissing them, belting them, fawning on them, hauling them apart by the hair, slumping to a couch at the end of a day when the three sweet-faced boys are bathed, have peered, scrubbed and angelic and pyjama-clad, at *Lassie* and *Walt Disney* on the color television set in the living room, and have been bedded down and hugged and kissed goodnight. Or *good night*!

The living room, the focal point of the day's action, is unpretentious and comfortable. There are two abstract paintings, both done by Joanne's brother Jim McKay, a university student in California where Joanne was born. The only photograph on the walls is a recent one of the three boys: baby Brett is chewing on the lace of a skate and he's wearing a hockey helmet bearing his dad's number, 9. Blake and Bobby are standing over him in skates under their long pants, wearing Black Hawk sweaters and holding sawed-off hockey sticks. Below the picture is a small table on which stand five trophies and a single photograph. It is not hard to conclude that this corner in this room represents the distillation, the very essence, of Bobby Hull's existence.

One of the trophies is a miniature of the Stanley Cup, which the Hawks won in the spring of 1961, and another is a framed scroll for something called the Chicago Festival of Leadership, declaring him "Chicago's Leading Athlete For 1962." The other three are bronze plaques, two from the NHL as the Hart Trophy and Lady Byng Trophy winner last season—the Hart goes to the league's most valuable player, the Lady Byng to the one who best combines sportsmanship and ability—and one from *Sport* magazine naming him "Top Performer In Hockey 1962."

These are the memorabilia you expect of the most glamorous hockey player of his time; what you're not prepared for is the single framed photograph, a color picture of a brown-and-white bull, a shaggy low-slung blank-faced hulk which Hull matter-of-factly reveals "is a Hereford, a *Hardean* Hereford, H-a-r-d-e-a-n. It is

Bobby Hull on the farm.

named for Hardy and Jean Schroeder, who developed the breed. This one weighs 2,200 pounds; he's a two-year-old. The man who owned him before I got him refused an offer of $75,000."

Hull's passion for purebred cattle is as vital a part of his life as the kids in the picture and the bric-a-brac underneath. Four years ago he bought a 600-acre farm near the little eastern Ontario community of Demorestville, not far from Belleville in the area of the Bay of Quinte where he was born and raised, the oldest boy in a family of eleven, with four older and three younger sisters, and three younger brothers. The sire of this vast close-knit brood, heavy-set shambling Robert, now 56, was a mill foreman at the Canada Cement plant at Point Anne while they were growing up in a sand-colored, two-storey, stuccoed house provided by the company. Bobby, who is called Robert by the family, was a mere 14 when he left home to play hockey for a Hawk-sponsored Junior B team at Hespeler, Ont., and he's been away every winter since. His mother, a doting, serene woman, recalls that when he first left home he was extremely homesick, so in her daily letters she rarely mentioned the family but wrote only of trivia. He told her when he got home briefly between games, "Gee, Mom, keep those letters coming with nothing in them."

It was to these familiar surroundings that Hull returned after every hockey season, even after he and Joanne were married. For their first summer they bought a beautiful sprawling four-bedroom home on the shore of the bay, to which they return each spring when hockey ends. Their farm is four miles away. Hull and his 21-year-old brother Dennis, now in his second year with the Hawks, stocked it with a 160 Hereford cattle. They have seven bulls in the herd, which Bobby estimates are worth $120,000. His prime interest in cattle is in their breeding, the search for new and productive bloodlines. "This is likely the best herd in Canada," he says, "and I'd argue it's the best in the world."

Recently he was considering buying more property near Oshawa, Ont., 220 acres on which he would put half his herd, and he discussed the purchase idly one afternoon with Joanne. "It's a pile of money," he said, frowning. "They want $150,000 for it."

"I keep telling you, it's because you're Bobby Hull," Joanne said. "Tell them you don't want it; they'll come down."

"Oh, Joanne," he said in some exasperation, "people aren't like that."

"The hell they aren't," she muttered.

Joanne turned to me. "Bob doesn't think anybody would ever try to take him," she said. "He's too... what? Modest? He really does downgrade himself. It's the difference in our upbringing, I think. Bob's dad's way of being an admiring father was to tear him down a little. My family was always praising me. So I give him that; I praise him. For example, I honestly feel he's worth $100,000 to hockey..."

"Oh, Joanne, for Pete's sake..."

"You are," she said, frowning at him.

"But he wouldn't tell Mr. Norris that," she went on. Mr. Norris is James D. Norris, the millionaire owner of the Black Hawks with whom Hull signed a three-year contract last October. "He and Mr. Norris get along but he wouldn't ask for $100,000. That story from Hawaii last summer, about Bob wanting $100,00 a year? That wasn't for real. Oh, he might have muttered something about $100,000 being a nice round number, but he doesn't *really* think he's worth it. He wouldn't actually ask Mr. Norris."

Hull doesn't say what he did ask Norris for, but on a question of whether his income, including advertising contracts, television appearances and other sidelines, reaches $100,000 a year, he paused for a moment, and then nodded. "You could say that and be close," he said impassively.

His mood was calm, and I asked him if it usually is when he's at home. "Yes, I guess so," he said, pondering. "Nothing really bothers me."

"If he doesn't score any goals, he's unbearable," interjected Joanne. "He's not fit to live with. And he knows he can't be talked to the day of a game. He just won't admit it."

"Joanne, you imagine things."

"Oh, Bob, nobody dares speak to you on a day of a game. You're impossible to talk to."

"Well, you bug me." Suddenly, he grinned at her.

"Yes, I know, dear," she said, smiling, "but you'll admit I bug you most on days of a game."

She crossed to him and sat on his knee. "You didn't even kiss me hello at the airport," she said. "I almost was coming for your autograph."

He laughed. The Hawks had arrived at Chicago's O'Hare Field from a five-day road trip that day, an hour and 20 minutes late. Joanne had gone to meet her husband, taking the two oldest boys and leaving little Brett home with Sheila. A couple of hundred fans had gone out to meet the plane, too, and had waited the extra hour and a half. When Hull stepped through the arrival gate with the rest of the players, mobs of people surged toward him. The other players made their way anonymously, or at least unhindered, through the crowds. But Hull was circled by a surging throng. Youngsters flung all shapes of paper and cards at him for his autograph, and a dozen or so men and women popped flash cameras at him, shouting and shoving to clear paths for their pictures. One woman asked him to hold her little girl in his arms while she blazed her flash gun. Joanne laughed and called to him, "How does it feel, Bob?" He smiled, and Joanne explained, "He wants a little girl," she said. "Hey, where are my mutts?"

They were in the midst of the crowd, on either side of their father, holding onto his knees, staring up at him as he signed the endless stream of papers, two solemn little eggs in blue Levis and faded yellow T-shirts, impassively waiting for their dad.

Hull stood there for 18 minutes by the clock, writing his name over and over, fixing a smile as now and then a flash bulb exploded. I said to Joanne at length, "Doesn't he get sick of it?"

"He feels if they're interested enough to keep staying, he'll keep signing," she said.

At the airport exit a few of the Hawks stood looking for transportation, and Hull joined them, inquiring if they had rides. He called to a fan he recognized and asked him to give two of the players a lift, and he told two others, Doug Jarrett and rookie Kenny Hodge, to come with him. They, Joanne, the two boys and I jammed into Hull's week-old Plymouth; it had been given to him, he said, by a car dealer who wanted Bobby Hull to be known, or at least seen, as a Plymouth driver. Hull also has a Dodge station wagon, which a dealer had given him last year, and an Oldsmobile convertible.

He had barely cleared the front door at home when he was out of his shoes, coat, tie and had opened his shirt. He's a man who likes familiar things around him and is uneasy in strange surroundings. When the swimsuit makers flew him to Hawaii last summer for photographs, they invited him to stay for two weeks of business and pleasure. Hull's segment of the shooting was finished in five days, and he hurried home to his farm. When sports-clothes pictures were made last winter in California, he stayed one day, returned home for one day, and went back the next for a TV commitment. "I come home from everywhere in a hurry," he says. "I don't like big hotels or fancy dining rooms—I'm uneasy in them."

He feels most relaxed holding a hockey stick or wrestling a calf. In the spring he fixes fences on the farm, reseeds the meadows, plants corn and oats and hay, drives tractors, plows and combines, working with his brother Dennis, his brother-in-law Bill Messer, and a friend, Ralph Richards. In addition to the grazing pastures, he has 75 acres of corn and 75 acres of oats, and he takes off 10,000 bales of hay. Bobby tattoos calves, indenting the ears with pincers and applying indelible ink. He supervises the breeding of the cattle, and watches his kids romp. He drives the four miles from his summer home on the bay to the farm by 7:30 every morning, and returns in the early evening. His sister Maxine, who lives with her husband, Bill Messer, on the farm year-round, feeds the youngsters and the men at noon.

Through the winters, *Le Comet Blond*, as they call the Golden Jet in Montreal, works thoughtfully on his game. To some it appears he paces himself, even loafs, sometimes. "No," he argues, "it isn't loafing; it's experience. You don't waste energy. You pick your spots and you go when you know you have the edge. It's an instinct. You get so that you can anticipate when you should outrace or outbody or outmanoeuvre. You sense your opening and you react. There's a lot in knowing what you yourself can do. If you see an opening, something tells you if you can make it or not make it. And being in shape is the most important thing. If your legs aren't going fluently, nothing ever gets co-ordinated."

Hull never talks of outslugging an opponent and he'd just as soon forget last spring's semifinal against Detroit in which he massaged the Red Wings the way a bulldozer explores stumps. The Hawk brain trust had urged Hull to throw his weight around, advising their Lady Byng winner that he never would have picked up two serious knee injuries late last season if he'd played tougher hockey. He was injured, he was told, because in playing what he calls "pamby" he'd been a sitting duck for board checks that wrenched his knees. By the time the Hawks reached Montreal for the final round against the Canadiens, enough of the sophisticated addicts in the Forum had been exposed through television to Hull's rampage to boo him roundly. This shook him, for Hull is a man who wants to be liked. "It hurt my feelings to get booed in Montreal," he says. "It had never happened there. This year, I'm playing my own game—outmanoeuvring them."

And, by coincidence or otherwise, in playing a comparatively "pamby" game earlier this season Hull went out of action again with a knee injury incurred in the Hawks' 12th game. The blow that sidelined him came after he'd started the season at a scoring rate never before known in hockey. He'd scored 15 goals in his first 11 games, a rate of about 100 goals for the season. (In 1962 he scored 50, and he and Rocket Richard and Boom Boom Geoffrion are the only NHL players who've ever hit that figure.)

Hull's chances of reaching a lonesome pinnacle appear to depend on the soundness of his knees. There's no question he has all of the other requirements. An unusual accolade was given him not long ago by Al Laney, a thoughtful New York hockey observer who has been covering the game for the *Herald Tribune* since 1926. "The plain fact is that any time Hull gets a shot," Laney wrote, "it is a potential goal. He is the most spectacular player in the game and he may be the greatest from this point of view that hockey has ever known, in spite of the fabulous Rocket Richard and Gordie Howe. Hull is a popular figure with the crowds, too, even when he is murdering the home team. There never has been a faster skater or one with stronger leg action. It is very likely that Hull fires the puck faster than any man who ever played the game."

Hull wants to be on the ice every day to skate and to shoot. Using a stick with a pronounced hook in the blade, a model introduced by teammate Stan Mikita, Hull works on the accuracy of his shooting from long distances and odd angles. The stick has enabled him to add a shot to his repertoire in the fashion of baseball pitchers adding a new pitch, and in Hull's case this shot makes the puck behave like a knuckleball, with an unpredictable flutter. "If you don't quite catch all of the puck as you let it go, it'll rise or drop suddenly, depending on the spin," he notes. "Drawing it toward you as you let it go sets up a different spin that produces a curve."

These refinements have not gone entirely unnoticed by Johnny Bower, the Toronto goalkeeper. "He needs another shot like I need a hole in the head—which I may get," Bower observes dryly. "I used to be able to figure him out, but this year he's been shooting from all over the place and more accurately. In the past he used to come in over the blue line and let go with a telegram. Now he's using radar, or something. This guy has everything—speed, power, drive and a murderous shot. Lead me from him."

Bower, who is 41 going on 46 or so, is apt to be gone from the NHL scene before Hull takes his leave—but not by that much. "Playing is not forever," Hull says. "I've got no scoring records in mind, no record number of years I want to play. I'm a country boy at heart. I'll have nine years in after this year. If I played 15, which would be six more, I'd be 32 or 33. That might be enough."

Bobby Hull scored 54 goals that year, becoming the first player to ever count more than 50 in one season. He would score more than 50 goals five times in his NHL career and four more while playing for the Winnipeg Jets in the World Hockey Association. The Golden Jet was an essential ingredient in the success of the upstart WHA during its six-year existence following his signing to Winnipeg in 1972 for a then unheard of $2 million over five years. His life off the ice has been nearly as troubled as his life on the ice has been heroic. He suffered through a widely publicized divorce from his wife, Joanne, during the late '70s and in the early '80s was involved in a car accident which paralyzed the mother of one of his children. Hull now owns a farm and lives near Belleville, Ont.

The New Eddie Shack

Susan Dexter

February 5, 1966—One of the more endearing characteristics of a 28-year-old hockey player named Eddie Shack is that when he sets out to congratulate a teammate on scoring a goal, fans can never be certain whether he'll shake the fellow's hand or knock him down. On one occasion early this season the "new, reformed" Shack charged down the ice to give linemate Brit Selby a pat on the back, forgot to stop, and bowled him over. And Shack's inadvertent but bruising bodycheck aggravated an injury to Selby's ankle which sidelined the high-scoring rookie for the next three games.

This sort of misguided exuberance and unpredictability has been known to infuriate coaches—though it never fails to delight the fans. In fact, a lot of Toronto Maple Leaf partisans wouldn't mind their team being in the National Hockey League cellar, just as long as a left winger named Shack was getting a lot of ice-time. "He's like a big airedale on skates," says one regular patron of Maple Leaf Gardens. "He's too strong to skate smoothly," says Ed Sweeney, who played for a couple of years on a line with Shack in the junior leagues. "When Shack makes a goof, the fans cheer," says Leaf coach Punch Imlach, mystified. Coach Eddie Bush recalls the days when Shack was playing for him at Guelph in the junior-league Ontario Hockey Association and working part-time as a coal-truck driver. "Even with his overalls on, he was exciting... When Shack starts to skate, the crowd screams and the ice just flies—chipped right out."

Shack's only problem in the major league has been that his coaches, and particularly his current coach, Punch (George) Imlach, have not been impressed with ice chips—they've wanted goals. Even his most devoted followers can't agree why the "old" Shack didn't get more. Some say his reactions are slow; others insist they're quick—but wrong. One thing is sure: his goals have been as rare as drunks at a temperance party—that is, unpredictably enough, until this year.

Now Punch Imlach is not known as an admirer of Shack's shenanigans, and he felt, after last season, that Shack should be playing less to the crowd and more for the bench. For after winning the Stanley Cup in three successive years, the Leafs last season were knocked out in the semifinals. Now all Imlach's players were going to have to deliver—in goals. So when Punch took a look at Shack's dismal record of five goals in 67 games last year, he decided to send him down to the Leaf's minor-league team at Rochester, N.Y. (Another reason for Punch's decision—some say the determining factor—was that gate receipts were down in Rochester, and the Leaf management wanted a crowd-pleaser, namely Shack, to pull them up.)

To many fans, this looked like high treason, and such slogans as "Bring Shack back" began to gain currency at the Gardens. But, oddly, though the Maple Leaf management was braced for a deluge of abuse, only a trickle came through the mail. There were fans, though, who thought the sports writers were too easy on Punch, for they had the forbearance not to remind Imlach that his nickname—earned after he took a concussive bodycheck in amateur hockey about 30 years ago—was originally "Punchy." Anybody nicknamed Punchy was hardly in a moral position to put down Unsteady Eddie.

Then, as if in a vindication of Shack partisans, the Leafs wilted in their first seven games of the season, winning two, losing four and tying one. For while Shack was pining away in Rochester and doing nothing in particular to distinguish himself, the rest of the Leafs weren't earning any accolades for their NHL performances. So Punch relented, and back came Shack.

This time it was—again unpredictably—a new Shack. Now he was the quiet modest interview subject who shrugged off his accomplishments as though they were preordained. He was the bashing but bashful hero who kept out of the penalty box enough to become the Leaf's number-two scorer, with 14 goals in his first 22 games (Bob Pulford led, with 15 goals in 29 games). Eddie was a chastened man. He wasn't trespassing on other players' territory, he wasn't creating traffic jams in front of his own net, he wasn't terrorizing his own teammates, and he wasn't careering into the boards all by himself. No, sir, Shack was all business. In practice, he was no longer drilling the puck as he once had—so hard that he would sometimes sting and bruise the hands of goaltenders Johnny Bower and Terry Sawchuk.

The charisma of Shack (both old and new) is something that baffles many hockey professionals and at least some hockey fans. For though Shack has a good build and a powerful shot, his resemblance to such superstars as Gordie Howe and Bobby Hull

Eddie Shack in action.

ends right there. But to his fans, Shack is not just a hockey player, but . . . well, an experience, a windmill of a skater, a living, panting study in artless inefficiency and jagged action, all arms and legs and elbows and bucking and jumping, a bowlegged straining case of desperate singlemindedness. Shack is often so determined to get to the other end of the rink, he just bulls through opposition players (and even his own teammates) if they get in his way. In Eddie Shack's rather limited vocabulary, there's no such word as finesse. On other occasions, when he has lost the puck, he'll skate around for a minute or two, looking forlorn and a little betrayed, as though he can't quite figure out what happened. And Shack, when he sets his mind to it, can probably look more forlorn than anyone else in the NHL, with his widely spaced, startled-fawn eyes and his great penguin nose. Shack has one of the biggest noses in professional hockey, but he always breathes through his mouth. When the play is on the other side of the ice, his mouth hangs open at half mast. And once he gets the puck, the pressure goes up and the mouth goes down, down, down, until it looks something like a gaping elevator shaft.

For someone who takes hockey seriously, the kind who can shout, "Stick to the point, Shack," and know that he's talking hockey, not criticizing conversation, the new Shack was just great. But for someone like me, the emergence of Eddie Shack, Conventional Hockey Player, was, to say the least, disillusioning. The old Eddie was so delightfully illicit—I mean, even people who hated hockey and didn't know what the game was about could get a kick out of the old, buffooning Shack. But still, there are enough glimpses of the old Shack to nurture our hopes that he'll have a relapse, that this responsible-young-hockey-player switch can be turned off. And maybe we'll see more glimpses of the Shack that was; maybe we'll again be treated to the kind of Shack who once humiliated a rival player by grabbing him up in his two hands and whacking him with his head. (There are times, though, when the new Shack is somewhat appealing. In fact, recently he literally knocked out two New York Rangers at the same time, and did it with such cunning that the referee and the announcer attributed the knockout to a collision between the two—Shack wasn't even suspected of the crime.)

Certainly, there are some players among the Leafs who aren't convinced that the new Shack is here to stay. At a recent game in Toronto, as the crowd cheered when Shack took the puck, his linemate Bob Pulford eloquently raised one glove and protectively covered his head as though afraid Shack would shoot at him. Such fears are kept alive partly by some of the old stories about Shack. In one, Bert Olmstead had nimbly avoided a check by an opposing defenceman, only to be knocked to the ice by Shack. Olmstead, in apparent fury, picked himself up, grabbed Shack's sweater and demanded, "What color is it, Eddie?" Shack allowed as how it was blue. "That's right," Olmstead shouted. "Stay away from blue, Eddie, stay away from blue!" The very fact that such elementary instruction has ever been necessary is one reason why most Leafs display little enthusiasm for Shack—old or new.

With fans, of course, it's a different story. A psychologist who has given thought to the Shack mystique believes he is a natural hero of the working class. He says that working men identify with Shack because he makes such splendid, larger-than-life mistakes, and because he's always in trouble with the boss. That makes for sympathy. Further, working-class fans admire a man who can deliver a good belt in the chops, and Eddie has a reputation for coming across with a few. And, they say, his lack of education may help make him a popular folk hero with the lunch-pail crowd.

For somehow, Shack managed to go to school in Sudbury, Ont., until he was 15 without learning how to read and write. Yet he has his own philosophy on his lack of education, and a characteristic way of phrasing it: "It's not because I'm stupid," he says, "... As long as I know what my hands ... have to do (I can look after my wife and two children). You know, I mean, a guy could be the most educated fellow (but) if he doesn't know how to do things, he's not accomplishing nothing." Other teams sometimes get on Shack's back about his slow intellectual development. On one famous occasion a couple of years ago, Shack took constant abuse from a rival team and its coach. According to legend, the players were shouting that Shack was so stupid he didn't even know how to spell. Then Shack scored one of his few goals. As the red goal light flashed on, he skated serenely over to the opposition bench. Leaning over, he told his tormentors, "s-c-o-r-e. That spells score."

Being the new Shack has advantages. As long as he remains a high scorer, Shack doesn't have to act as the team's policeman, bodying opposing players and provoking fights. "Before it was just check, check, check," he says, "and I don't like hurting anyone like that. But I had to do something to earn my pay."

If hockey hadn't worked out, Shack wouldn't have been a policeman, he would have been a butcher. As a boy in Sudbury, he took a job in a grocery store and worked his way into the meat department. "I always worked hard and always ate well. That makes you strong. I worked as a butcher. I worked hard there lifting hind quarters of beef, halves of bacon and lamb and boxes." His wrists today look large and swollen, not through injury, but simply because he has developed wrist muscles the size of hard-boiled eggs.

Of course, they didn't develop just from hoisting hind quarters of beef. Shack has been playing hockey since he was a kid of six, back in Sudbury. His route to the majors was through Guelph, Ont., the New York Rangers farm team. The Rangers moved him up to their own lineup in 1958, and for most players the promotion would have been the happiest move of their careers. For Shack it was almost a disaster. First he broke a leg and spent a substantial part of the season recovering. Then he put in two more seasons with the Rangers, all of them unhappy. In all two years he managed only 16 goals. And in those days you didn't have to watch closely to know when Shack was going onto the ice—you could tell by the Bronx cheers.

It is only since 1960, when the Leafs took him over in a trade, that Shack even showed signs of becoming what he is today: a second-rate player who is nevertheless a press agent's dream. Now it's a natural supposition that Shack deliberately cultivates the awkward and backward side of his personality in order to register publicly as the character in the Leaf lineup. And you might assume that he's still acting out this role, when you ask him, as I did, what he has that gives him that appeal for the crowd, and he replies, "There's something I do that gets them. I don't know what it is myself. It just comes naturally. You can't do anything if there's no reaction—it's just like a movie star. It's there now, so you can leave things the way they are. You don't try to quiet them down or anything—they're paying a good dollar, and if they're enjoying it that's fine, 'cause I enjoy playin'."

But after you've really studied him, close at hand, you find yourself hanging a new adjective on clumsy, homely, awkward, lovable old Eddie Shack. And that word, believe it or not, is sincere.

Eddie Shack, who scored a career-high 63 points that season, is certainly one of the best-loved players ever to play in the National Hockey League. Nicknamed "The Entertainer," Shack played on six different teams during his 17-year career, including two stints in Toronto. Retiring in 1975, Shack still lives in the Toronto area where he continues to parlay his popularity into endorsements and a number of successful business ventures which have ranged from Christmas trees to donut stores.

Susan Dexter was a staff writer at Maclean's *from 1965 to 1967.*

THE TURBULENT SEVENTIES

Who Is Bobby Orr?

Trent Frayne

February 20, 1965—It's lamentably true that the 1960s have seemed like forever for the lowly Boston Bruins of the National Hockey League, but the fact is that the '60s may one day be regarded as their most significant decade. It was in the '60s, you see, that the Bruins discovered Bobby Orr.

Briefly, Bobby Orr is the finest professional-hockey prospect in Canada today, and Boston owns title to his services. Bobby Orr possesses the potential to become the finest offensive defenceman since Doug Harvey, the former nonpareil of the Canadiens. Bobby Orr is a swift powerful skater with instant acceleration, instinctive anticipation, a quick accurate shot, remarkable composure, an unrelenting ambition, a solemn dedication, humility, modesty, and a fondness for his parents and his brothers and sisters that often turns his eyes moist. Put simply, Bobby Orr is too good to be true. But there he is.

A crew-cut, blue-eyed, well-adjusted, polite, medium-sized boy of 16, he is now playing his third full season of junior hockey for the Oshawa Generals. Last season, when he was 15, Orr was the unanimous choice of the Ontario Hockey Association Junior A's eight coaches as all-star defenceman on the first team. The year before, when he was 14, he was named to the second all-star team in competition with players who were crowding 20. Last year, in addition, he set a goal-scoring record for defencemen in the Junior A circuit, the top junior league in the country, with 30 goals in the 56-game schedule. He is eligible for another four seasons of junior play but, things being what they are with the limping Bruins, it appears almost certain that he will leap right into their lineup the instant he turns 18—the league's legal minimum—which will fall on the night of March 20, 1966. "He amazes me every time I see him," says the beleaguered general manager of the beleaguered Bruins, Lynn Patrick. "The way he can anticipate what's going to happen is sometimes uncanny; you know, sensing where the puck is going to be and moving there even before the puck does. I never saw a more promising player."

"Have you ever considered that the game of hockey is unique?" asks Wren Blair, a brisk and vigorous young veteran of numerous hockey jobs, who as a key man in the Bruin organization was one of the first who saw and finally signed young Orr over the importunities of numerous other NHL team representatives. "A good hockey player can play all games well, but few stars of another sport can play hockey at all. Can you imagine Mickey Mantle or Cassius Clay or Arnold Palmer or Johnny Unitas able to make even a school hockey team? Yet Gordie Howe used to work out regularly with the Detroit Tigers, and when Jim Norris promoted all the big fights and owned the Red Wings he'd look at Howe stripped down in the dressing room and he'd say, 'Gordie, with a build like that you could be the heavyweight champion of the world.' Any number of hockey players can hit a golf ball as far as most pros; in fact, a lot of them are pros in the off-season. The point is, every hockey player must have the attributes of the top athletes in any game, except he must then add the encumbrance of skates. We grow up taking these things for granted in Canada, but the truth is that hockey is the most difficult of all games to master."

Accordingly, an outstanding star at 16 has no guarantee that he will continue to develop and be still outstanding in five years when he is in against the Hulls and the Hortons and the other one-in-a-hundred survivors of the junior leagues. Thus, at this stage in Bobby Orr's development, the Bruins cannot allow themselves to be more than unusually hopeful that the fates have equipped Orr with an intangible urge to rise with fire in his eyes after some hulking oaf of an NHL defenceman has flattened him. And they must await nature's whim on whether his present slender five-foot-nine and 166 pounds spread up and out in maturity.

There are, of course, controllable elements that contribute, and the Bruins, like every other major-league team, seek endlessly to nurture these—such things as the fundamentals of shooting and passing and positional play and backchecking and even physical condition and discipline. Then, equally important as Wren Blair sees it, are factors to be avoided or, at least, placed into proper perspective—publicity, back-slappers, and what Blair calls "the cause of the greatest casualty list of them all—girls." He snorts, "They bug hockey players. They hang around the dressing room door after a game, waiting for the players to come out, hoping for a pickup. They'd like nothing better than to hook a guy, especially in junior where these kids are as big with the teen-age crowd as the Beatles.

"Hockey players are Canada's glamor boys. They get a kind of Hollywood adulation, particularly in the small- and medium-sized towns where junior hockey flourishes. In

Bobby Orr in his Oshawa Generals dressing room.

the smaller papers they get more space than Mike Pearson, particularly young Orr who, because of his extreme youth, has been getting incredible publicity for three years now. I mean, imagine playing Junior A hockey at 14—that alone is enough to attract wide attention. So I've drummed it into him over and over that it's his responsibility to be level-headed enough to handle it."

Orr smiled wanly when I asked him if the publicity bothered him. "I try not to read about myself," he said quietly. "So many people have told me not to get a swelled head that I'm scared to read the stuff." Blair, one of whose duties with the Bruins is that of general manager of the Oshawa Generals, a Bruin-sponsored team, warns Orr and the other Generals to take back-slappers in stride. "You'd be surprised how many hero-worshippers there are," says Blair. "Even in big businesses in big cities there are guys who pander to some athletes just to be seen in their company. They wine and dine a good athlete, waiting to be seen by their friends with a celebrity. Sure, it's a free ride for the athlete, but he'll wind up a lush if he doesn't learn to handle fair-weather friends."

Blair, an outspoken, profane, dedicated hockey man who was general manager of the Whitby Dunlops when they defeated the Russians to win the world's championship at Oslo in 1958, feels that discipline is the best antidote for young players' non-athletic hazards. With the Generals, there is a 10:30 curfew; nine o'clock on nights before games. The team's coach, Jim Cherry, makes spot-check telephone calls to the boarding houses where Oshawa players live. If a boy isn't home he must call the coach when he does arrive, and he's reprimanded on his first offence. If he's not home the second time, a letter is written to his parents, explaining that he has been breaking team rules. On the third offence the player is suspended by the team and sent home. Bobby Orr missed the curfew call early in December, the first time he'd been guilty, and recalls with a wry grin that he was "tongue-lashed."

The curfew grows even tighter during school examinations. "There'll be no practices until after the exams," Blair told the players prior to the Christmas exams. "We expect you guys will be on top of those books, so the curfew will be nine o'clock every night until they're over." The Bruins pay tuition to the board of education for all their players, buy their books, pay their room-and-board and give them $10 a week spending money. In addition—although they retain "amateur" status—the players are paid up to $60 a week for hockey. Blair points out that that's only for the senior players, the top 19-year-olds. The average is about $50 a week, and those who don't attend school are permitted to find jobs.

Blair had to use all his persuasiveness in convincing Orr's parents that even at 14 their son was not too young to leave home and play junior hockey in the Bruin organization. Bobby is the third of five children of Doug and Arva Orr, who live in Parry Sound, 140 miles north of Toronto, with their other four children—two girls, Pat and Penny, who are 19 and 13, and two boys, Ron and Doug, 18 and 10. Doug the dad is a lean, tall, crew-cut, gregarious, sports-loving man of 39, born and bred in Parry Sound and a hockey player there in his youth. His forthright wife has a strong will, a level eye, a plain-spoken pride in her brood. It's virtually impossible to curb her when she's watching Bobby play hockey. "I try to let on I'm not with her," says Bobby's sister Pat, with a smile. "Let's says she's unrestrained." Arva doesn't like sitting with her husband at hockey games. "He sits me down too often," she explains.

Doug's married sister, Marg Atherton, is equally unfettered. Once, at a game in St. Catharines, a home-town player, Chuck Kelly, got in a fight with Bobby near Marg's seat. "You brute!" cried Marg, reaching toward Kelly and actually planting a punch on his forehead. "Don't you dare hit Bobby!"

Doug Orr works for Canadian Industries Limited, packing high explosives five days a week and viewing the Generals on car trips to Junior A towns on weekends. Ten-year-old Dougie, a devoted Toronto Leaf fan, is dismayed by Bobby's affiliation with Boston. "I'll cheer for Toronto until Bobby turns pro," he says gravely, "and then I guess I'll switch." He is not alone in wondering why Bobby selected the battered Bruins, but the player himself, even at 14 when he made the decision, showed a precocious business sense. "They need players," he noted to his dad. In other words, the top clubs are well stocked; the road to a regular berth is longer.

The Bruin saga in signing Orr began when the boy was 12. He was playing for the Parry Sound bantams who travelled to Gananoque, near Kingston, for a provincial playoff. This was the spring of 1960 and Blair, general manager and coach of the professional Kingston Frontenacs, had just joined the Bruins. He'd been watching a couple of Gananoque kids and he invited Lynn Patrick to give his appraisal of them in the games against Parry Sound. Toward the end of the first period, he turned to Patrick. "Do you see what I see?" he asked.

"I see what you see," said Patrick. "Who is he?"

"You got me."

Blair moved off to inquire. "That number 2 is named Bobby Orr, reported Blair. "Nobody's sponsoring him." What this meant was that no professional team held sponsorship rights in the Parry Sound area. So no pro team had a claim on the players.

I asked Blair recently what he'd seen in this 12-year-old youngster that set him apart. "Oh nothing much," he replied. "He was only skating rings around everybody on the ice, he had the puck all the time, and he played the whole game save a two-minute penalty."

For two years Blair haunted Parry Sound, visiting with the Orrs at every opportunity. When the Kingston Frontenacs were travelling, he always arranged a stop for a meal at Parry Sound and dropped in at the Orrs' big, comfortably old stucco house to advance the advantages of Boston. To enhance Bruin prestige in Parry Sound, the NHL club paid $1,000 a year for three years toward minor hockey there. In the autumn of 1962, when Bobby was 14, Blair persuaded the boy's parents to let him attend a Boston junior tryout camp at Niagara Falls. By now he was old enough that Blair feared another NHL club would induce his parents to let him move to a town whose team it sponsored. "We had about 70 players at the Niagara Falls camp," Blair recalls, "and the kid was a stickout. My wife, Elma, and I drove immediately to Parry Sound to convince the Orrs that Bobby ought to move to Oshawa and sign a Junior A card with the Generals. Then we'd have him, and my worries would be over."

The Orrs were reluctant. All through a Saturday evening Blair talked to Bobby's father, but though Doug was beginning to bend, he wouldn't break. Through Sunday Blair cajoled and implored. "Mr. Blair, he's just too young" said Mrs. Orr. "Next year. I promise you, he'll go. But not yet."

"I'll find a fine family for him to live with in Oshawa," countered Blair. "He'll get the best of care. If he stays here another year he'll just deteriorate as a hockey player. He's too good for these boys. He'll just learn bad habits."

And then Blair had an inspiration. "Just let him come on a four-game trial basis," he suggested. "You come with him. See the school. See the folks he'll live with. Watch him play. If you're not convinced after four games, we'll forget it."

So they went.

After four games, and some relatively modest financial arrangements, the Orrs agreed, with the stipulation that instead of moving to Oshawa, Bobby would commute. And so he did. Two or three nights a week and on Sunday afternoons, the Orrs or friends of the family drove Bobby 150 miles south for the games and 150 miles more after them, through snowstorms sometimes, and sleet and rain. "Imagine," marvels Blair now, "The kid never once practised with the club and he made the second all-star team."

When he was 15, Bobby moved to Oshawa, where he now lives in a red-brick modern bungalow with Mr. and Mrs. Jack Wild. He scored three goals in the second-last game of the 56-game schedule for a total of 30 goals, which beat the old record established by Jacques Laperriere, now of the Montreal Canadiens, when Laperriere was 19. And he attained a 71.3 per cent average in passing grade nine. He kept in frequent telephone touch with the family and sometimes hitchhiked from Oshawa to Parry Sound to visit.

Meantime, in the off season Bobby does what he can to improve his NHL chances. He works on barbells twice a day for 45 minutes, and carries a set of handgrips with him which he squeezes by the hour to strengthen his big wrists and forearms. He runs twice around the harbor every day—two miles per trip. He picks up what money he can, too. When he was 13 he was a bellboy at a dollar a day at the Belvedere Hotel, which has since burned down, and earned $500 in tips. When he was 14, after the hotel burned, he got $10 a month from the school board for being the caretaker's helper after school, cleaning out furnaces and shinnying up and down narrow flues to clean them. At 15, he spent the summer working in his uncle's butcher shop for $25 a week and all the steaks he could eat. Last summer he made $35 a week as a clerk in Adams Men's Wear. "He lost money on that deal," says sister Pat. "He poured all his money on his back. What a Beau Brummell!"

Through all of these years, in most waking hours and some of the sleeping ones, too, he's dreamed of playing for the Bruins. He's dreaming of that moment now, and so is sister Pat and his mother and his father. And so is Wren Blair, who's brought him along to this point, and so is Lynn Patrick, who has suffered through the Sixties with the Bruins and could stand a little sunshine.

"That's apt to be a big night," Patrick noted not long ago, "that night of March 20, 1966."

And then Lynn Patrick said it all. "We'll see," he mused. "We'll see."

As it turned out, Bobby Orr played his first NHL game in the following season. But before that moment he was involved in something equally dramatic. Orr shocked Boston management by arriving for contract negotiations with a lawyer who immediately declared that Orr would not wear a Bruins jersey until he received a deal equal to his ability. It was viewed as an outrageous demand, especially since Orr had never played a game in the NHL. Orr's representative, Alan Eagleson, eventually helped secure a two-year $150,000 contract for the defenceman. The deal created shock waves across the league—both because of its size and the involvement of a player-agent—and helped to consolidate the importance of the NHL Players' Association and Eagleson's place at its top. Bobby Orr won the Calder Trophy as the league's top rookie his first year and was on his way to becoming one of the greatest players ever.

The Dead-End Kid who Wants to Be a Superstar

Stan Fischler

November, 1969—The National Hockey League is facing its own kind of sexual revolution, led by an irreverent, 23-year-old centre with the Boston Bruins named Derek Michael Sanderson. Sporting bell-bottom sideburns and razor-cut hair, the 176-pound Sanderson is determined to "do his own thing" in the face of the hockey Establishment, probably the most conservative in major-league sports. His avowed projects for 1970 include:

>   Wearing and selling hockey's first white skates.
>   Opening a hip men's boutique in partnership with his friend, Cleveland Indians' Ken Harrelson.
>   Becoming a partner in the Boston branch of Joe Namath's Bachelors III restaurant in downtown Boston, next door to the Playboy Club.
>   Keeping his status as fashion plate and unofficial clothing consultant to the Boston Bruins.
>   Settling a few grudges on a list that includes Bob Baun, Gordie Howe and Noel Picard.

Although no threat to William F. Buckley in debate, Sanderson says what he thinks, often not the kind of thing the NHL would encourage: "Give me 10 of the best-looking women in the city and I'll play for nothing... almost," or, "The square hockey world could use a change, and I'm the guy to change it," or, "I've never said a thing I'm sorry for in all my life."

All of which has led to the inevitable comparison with Joe Namath, the quarterback of the New York Jets, who led his team to an upset win over the Baltimore Colts in the Super Bowl. Even Sanderson's teammates call him Little Joe.

Although he received a great deal of attention last season, particularly in the playoffs, Sanderson had not caught up to the star billing of teammates Bobby Orr and Phil Esposito. "There are three things you need to make money in professional sports," he says. "One is talent. The second is points. The third is color. Orr had the talent. Esposito had the points. The only thing left for me was the color."

Sanderson started being colorful as soon as he arrived at the Bruins' training camp last season. While most of the hopefuls showed up with the regulation quarter-inch NHL haircut, Sanderson had cultivated a prodigious set of Ponderosa sideburns. "When Milt Schmidt (the Bruin's general manager) saw them, he was sick," says Sanderson. "He said, 'Cut those things off!' I said to him straight, 'Don't worry about how I cut my hair. How I play hockey is all you got to worry about.'"

That wasn't the end of the problems. A few weeks later Sanderson showed up for an exhibition game with a wardrobe straight out of *Mod Squad*. Schmidt laid down the law. "Straight shirt and tie, kid," he said. "What do you think you're doing?" Sanderson patiently pointed out that bell-bottoms, Nehru jackets and turtle-necks were very much *de rigeur* in the best of places. Schmidt was persuaded, reluctantly, and soon Ted Green, Gerry Cheevers, Phil Esposito and Bobby Orr all joined the Sanderson fashion parade.

"Orr used to have a brushcut," says Sanderson, "and I told him, 'Bobby, the brushcut, forget it. It makes you look like a kid of 16.' So then I got him to a hair stylist. Now his hair is longer and it looks better, right? I told him to grow sideburns, too, but he's got no beard, so he can't grow the sideburns." (Orr is one of the youngest players in the NHL.)

Sanderson's fashion consulting branched out to include shirts and ties. "Take Johnny McKenzie," he says. "He used to wear a Christmas tie and socks to match. So I told him, that don't go. He tells me to get him a shirt and tie. So I go out and bring them back for him and tell him to give me the dough—37 bucks for a shirt and tie. He was sick. But I told him, 'You want a little class, kid, it'll cost you a few bucks.'"

Class means a lot to Sanderson, and he is ready to spend whatever it takes to meet its obvious demands. He owns not one car, but two—a Cadillac Eldorado and a Mustang Shelby. He dines out regularly and with style at such places as the graceful Hawthorne-by-the-Sea, overlooking the Atlantic at Swampscott, near Boston. "I like a class evening," he says. "I'm not in the pizza-and-beer kick. I like a nice quiet dinner. A little candlelight, a little wine."

For after-dinner there is, of course, The Apartment, Sanderson's home in suburban Boston. It's split-level, with beamed ceilings giving a sort of Spanish air to the place (even the kitchen is beamed.) There's a sunken living room, with wall-to-wall lime-green shag rug; in front of a cork wall there's a six-stool bar; one other wall is entirely mirrored. Up the stairs on the next level is the bedroom, with an eight-foot circular bed and an ankle-deep, wall-to-wall, white-fur rug. One wall is mirrored.

The day I talked to Sanderson he looked like a hip Clint Eastwood, his dark sideburns arched above a frilly yellow shirt cut to the navel, setting off cream-colored hip-huggers. He poured a gin-and-tonic for me, a Coke for himself (he's not much of a drinker). Settling himself comfortably, he answered the obvious question. "You want to know what kind of girl I like?" he said, reflectively. "The girl has to be feminine, but she has to have a head on her shoulders and know what she's doing. My whole theory is that a woman can interest you with her body, but she can hold you with her mind, right? I like a girl who is really good-looking, feminine. Sensitive and soft. The type of girl who can fit into a dinner at the Waldorf or a draft beer down at the beach. Very few girls can do that. And she has to be the kind of girl who can make a man feel like a man."

Sanderson walked across the room and pushed open a long sliding door. Inside, the closet was jammed. "I got the shirts, the Edwardian suits, the boots," he said, "and since I got the classy suits and the sideburns, the success I've had with women this year over last year has been phenomenal."

Marriage? "Let's put it this way: I'm not fighting love. If it comes my way, I'll take it. But right now I'm not looking for it."

According to many of the men who run hockey, sex and ice don't mix. Once, when his Springfield, Mass., hockey club was suffering through a slump, owner Eddie Shore ordered all his players to abstain from sexual activity. There is no question that Sanderson could never have played for the disciplinarian Shore.

"Don't get me wrong," says Sanderson. "My theory is: 'Everything in moderation.' If I'm going to be with a broad the night before a game, I'll take her to dinner at eight o'clock, get home at nine, be with her until midnight, then go to sleep. For me, I know I've got to have my rest, right? I plan everything I do with the game in mind, right? That's the most important thing—it's my whole life."

Derek Sanderson with unidentified friend.

Such careful planning resulted in Sanderson's superb playoff performances last spring against the Toronto Maple Leafs and the Montreal Canadiens. A few weeks before the playoffs, he decided it was a good idea to play house for a while. "I said to myself, 'Okay, what kind of broads do I have surrounding me?' Then I said, 'All right, this one is a good cook, good looking.' She had me eating breakfast every morning, right? I lived with her, stayed home all the time—got plenty of rest. But after the season, it was over. After all, variety is the spice of life, right?"

Sanderson's father, a pleasant man in his mid-40s, is a production foreman for a General Motors subsidiary in St. Catharines, Ont. There was never a question in Harold Sanderson's mind but that his son would make it in the NHL. "I'll tell you," says Harold, "he was a helluva good son. When that boy was 10 years old, I said to his mother, 'He's something special—he's sure-fire NHL calibre.' I could tell then because he had so much desire. The only thing I ever said to him was, 'Don't take any nonsense from anybody.' And he never did. The kid never looked back."

When Derek was three, Harold had him balancing on skates on the living room carpet. At five, he was on the ice, and by seven he was turning both ways and doing stops and starts. "Dad changed his hours at the Kimberly-Clark plant, where he then worked, to a four-to-12 night shift so he could see me in the daytime. My father never made that much money—$40, $50 take-home from his mechanic's pay. When I was nine, he gave me $50 hockey gloves. I got Taks, the best skates, as soon as my feet were big enough. Every Christmas I got a brand-new pair of skates—no problem. That's what my Christmas consisted of—no toys, nothing!—just hockey equipment. A lot of fathers push, but he didn't push me. He just encouraged me and said, 'I'll see ya out there today,' and he'd be out there."

At 17, Derek quit high school. Harold Sanderson was not overjoyed about his son's decision, but he didn't interfere. "You're man enough to make the decisions for yourself," he told Derek, "but remember, there are three things in your life—a social life, an educational life and a career in hockey. To make it in one of those three, you're going to have to sacrifice one of the others." Sanderson sacrificed school.

By this time, the Sanderson image—a dead-end kid on skates—was capturing headlines across Canada. Once, during a game in the Ontario Hockey Association Junior A League, a fan tossed hot coffee in Sanderson's face. After a Memorial Cup game in Edmonton, six men jumped him and beat him up. To this day, some Edmontonians insist that Sanderson deserved the beating as payment for his treatment of home-town defenceman Bob Falkenburg. Falkenburg, who was taller and considerably heavier than Sanderson, pestered him into a fight and Sanderson knocked him out. "Then," Sanderson recalls, "I figured I had to bring it to a head. I went over to their bench and said, 'Okay, who's next?' Nobody made a move."

Another time, while playing for the OHA Junior A All-Stars, he nearly ignited an international incident by jabbing a member of the Czech National Team in the stomach with the butt-end of his stick. Sanderson claims that the Czech spat at him several times. In any event, Sanderson enjoyed the publicity. "I said to myself, 'Publicity out of a fight—not bad. Keep fighting, kid.' In the remainder of my junior career, I ended up with 46 fights."

But when he arrived at the NHL, his Boston teammates warned him that the league policemen would take a dim view of his decorum. Boston *Record American* columnist D. Leo Monahan warned him in print not to go out of his way to antagonize Gordie

Howe, "probably the strongest—and meanest—man playing professional hockey." Sanderson was not impressed and even went so far as to pick a battle with Howe. "One theory I go on," he says, "I don't care who he is; his face will bleed just like mine, right? That stick is a great equalizer. I've cut people so often I can't remember who or when. So has Howe."

Sanderson's penchant for class has led him to challenge the best fighters in the league. During his rookie year, he fought Orland Kurtenbach, Ted Harris, and Terry Harper, as well as Howe. When teammate Ted Green congratulated him at the end of the 1967–68 season, Sanderson mistakenly thought Green was praising his scoring ability. "No," said Green, "I'm shaking your hand just because you got that body of yours through this league. When I saw you in training camp I didn't believe you could do it. I thought you were going to get killed."

Sanderson refuses to wear a helmet for protection. "A helmet would turn me right off," he says. "My whole theory on helmets is that if you're going to wear one you've got to be conscious of injury because it's an added piece of equipment, and if you're conscious of injury in this game, get out of it. The second you worry about it, you're going to get hurt bad."

Sanderson's father was against helmets and it was Harold who toughened Derek up when he was only nine. His head had been cut for two stitches and he bled profusely. Derek had never seen blood before and he was sick. But Harold urged him to return to the ice. "Later, I started to get proud of stitches. Dad used to cut out the stitches and put 'em in a little box. He saved my first hundred."

There was a knock on the door. It was Bob Woolf, Sanderson's attorney, a Boston lawyer who also represents Boston's Green and Esposito. Woolf is a sort of father-away-from-home for Sanderson. He gives him a weekly allowance, holds power of attorney for him and advises him on business deals. "This guy," said Sanderson, "handles every move I make—aside from women."

Sanderson told Woolf he had just received an engraved gold invitation to the Boston Debutantes' Ball. "I'd rather not have you go," said Woolf, wincing, "unless you improve your manners. I've got to train you how to say 'please' and 'thank you.' I think you ought to go to charm school first."

A few months ago, Woolf accompanied Sanderson to the formal Press Photographers' Ball. Woolf thought it would be a good time to teach Sanderson a chapter or two from Emily Post. They arranged a contest: Sanderson would get one point for "thank you" and two points for "you're welcome." But he would be penalized for every miss. By the end of the evening, Sanderson had lost, 11–8. "I came up in a dead-end neighborhood," Sanderson explains. "I came up where you scratched and fought all your life. It was dog-eat-dog. If you wanted a cigarette, you'd say, 'Gimme a weed,' and that was it. You didn't say, 'May I please have a cigarette?'"

The Bruins management, who couldn't care less about Sanderson's etiquette, took a dim view when they learned he not only planned to wear white hockey skates, but would market a "Derek Sanderson White Skate." "The Bruins don't see eye to eye with me on the skates," said Sanderson in a moment of rare understatement. "They're a little stuffy; they figure it's 'Americanizing' the game, and that the players, who are nearly all Canadians, might take offense."

Manager Schmidt tried to reason with Sanderson. "Listen," said Schmidt, "you've got two things to face if you're planning to wear white skates: First of all, they're going to try to run at you till you're silly. Every tough guy, every fringe player, is going to take a run at you because you're trying to be a big shot with the white skates. Second, you've never looked down at your feet and seen white skates. You'll be taking a faceoff and look down and when you see white skates you might get sick."

Sanderson considered the objections—and then advised the factory to construct the white skates as planned. He is not perturbed about the prospects of opposing players running at him: if they do they will have to absorb about four feet of lumber in their solar plexus before reaching him. Like Namath, Sanderson is regarded with hostility by many of his opponents. In part, the anger is due to behavior that is bizarre by hockey's square standards. In part, it's because of Sanderson's candor. Minutes after the Canadiens had defeated Boston in the Stanley Cup semifinal last April, a reporter put a question to Sanderson, expecting a gracious tribute to the champions. "They (the Canadiens) don't have the team, the defence, the talent or the guts," said Sanderson. Reminded of the observation several months later, he said he meant every word of it then and means every word of it now.

He has an irreverence that will put down an opponent without hesitation. Talking about the playoffs, he was reminded of a fight he had with Montreal's Dick Duff. "He's the only guy under 200 pounds I've ever fought," he said, shaking his head. "I was amazed that the guy threw a punch at me, right? I mean, it was no contest. There's just no way he's going to win, right?"

Sanderson the fighter is not equalled by Sanderson the hockey player, and he knows it. Though he won the Calder Trophy as Rookie of the Year in 1967–68 and scored a respectable 26 goals and 22 assists last year, he believes he's four years away from his peak. "The thing I haven't gotten yet, but may get this season, is the opportunity to kill penalties and work the power play. And I can do both. But Harry (Sinden, the coach) has a whole theory of his that he's not going to break me in too fast. But you don't get an all-star rating unless you're on the power play. You just gotta take those things in stride. I'm not gonna bitch. As long as we keep on winning. Phil Esposito is putting money in my pocket."

The money could have been more substantial in the first two NHL years, but ex-Bruin Manager Hap Emms induced him to sign a contract he considered far below his worth. But at last season's playoffs, the Bruins sweetened the pot, and with Woolf's advice his income should reach $50,000 by 1970.

He hasn't forgotten who made it all possible. "I bought Dad a boat," he reveals. "I bought him a motor (car), bought him a color TV. He wanted to see me in color."

Sanderson offered me a fresh gin-and-tonic, then pulled out another cigarette. "I know what I'm doing," he said. "I know what this life is all about. I know exactly what it takes. I know where everybody's at. I mind my own business. You want to do your thing, you do it. It won't affect me as long as I'm happy, right? I climb into my own little corner of the world and let every other flaky idiot do what he wants to do. As long as I'm doing what I'm doing. I'm getting ahead and I'm not hurting any of my friends, right?"

Anything you say, Little Joe.

During the 1975–76 season, Sanderson scored 24 goals and became one of the best penalty killers in the league. Later, Sanderson symbolized how free-agent signings would come to change the game when in 1972 he signed a $2.5 million, five-year contract with the Philadelphia Blazers of the WHA. But unhappy in the WHA, he would play only seven games before returning to the Bruins. Sanderson played 13 years in the NHL, but for nearly half of those he was drinking heavily. He skated for six different teams in his final six years and was forced to leave the game in 1978. His downward spiral ended when he found himself living in New York City's Central Park. That incident, the loss of his hockey career and nearly all his money prompted Sanderson to finally stop drinking. Since the early '80s, he has worked as a Boston hockey broadcaster as well as doing public relations work and speaking to children about the perils of drug and alchohol abuse.

Stan Fischler is an American sports writer and broadcaster who has many hockey books to his credit, including biographies of Gordie Howe and Derek Sanderson. Fischler wrote regularily about hockey for Maclean's *in the 1960s and '70s.*

Dr. Jekyll and Mr. Hull

Jack Batten

March, 1973—Bobby Hull felt lousy. He was sitting slack and tired against the rich grey upholstery in the backseat of Ben Hatskin's black Lincoln Continental. Hatskin, president of the Winnipeg Jets and Hull's boss, was behind the steering wheel, guiding the car with one nonchalant hand through the brilliant cold winter noon in downtown Winnipeg. The Continental moved silently except for the noise Hull made clearing his throat of all that damned phlegm. "Doesn't that sound rotten?" he apologized. "I dunno what's wrong. I got the runs in Boston and I been no good ever since."

The morning Hull had put in hadn't come as any relief to his condition. He'd been up at a quarter to eight, time only for half a cup of coffee. Then he'd driven to CKRC for a phone-in radio show, to the Winnipeg Arena for a light team drill before the game that night against the Los Angeles Sharks, then to a photographer's studio to choose the color pictures for a special one-dollar Bobby Hull program.

"Arrrrgrahhhh," he gargled in the back seat.

Hatskin wheeled the Continental into the driveway of the Fort Garry Hotel. He stopped a few feet from a no-parking sign and told the doorman to keep an eye on the car. Handshakers ringed around Hull in the hotel lobby, businessmen who showed him big grins and admiring deference. There was another emotion at work, too, something like gratitude. "Thanks for coming to Winnipeg, Bobby," one man said. The businessmen belonged to the Kiwanis Club, and Hull was a head-table guest at their luncheon meeting. They escorted him into the hotel's ballroom, a cavernous room done in French Provincial trimmings and gold-painted chandeliers. The turnout, the president mentioned, was the biggest of the year. Waitresses served mushroom soup and veal cutlets. Someone read into a microphone the names of members on the mend in hospital. The president handed out cigars to three men celebrating birthdays, called for a round of applause for the member who'd sold the most Kiwanis apples, and introduced the head table. Hull drew the noisiest hand.

Hatskin, also a head-table guest, introduced as "the fella that had the guts to bring us major league hockey when the monopoly that runs the NHL deprived us of top hockey and gave it to Atlanta and Long Island," came second in applause.

The luncheon's advertised speakers took their turns at the microphone, three Kiwanians, including the Lieutenant-Governor, who reminisced for 15 minutes each about their trip to Moscow during the Canada-Russia hockey series. The three finished and the president asked Hull for a few words. He hadn't expected to speak, and for a moment, as he stood up, he looked touchingly vulnerable. He's a surprisingly short man, not more than five feet 10, but he radiates muscle. His smile, projecting honest charm but with a touch of satire to it that takes away the saccharin, is his best expression. The upper half of his face is dented with the blows of 20 hockey years; there are scars around the eyes and breaks down the nose. He's a no-sell advertisement for hair transplants; his haven't taken, and he combs the few remaining blond strands from left to right over the crown of his head.

The moment of vulnerability passed in a hurry. Hull talked for 15 minutes. He was relaxed, funny and frank, neither a dumb jock nor a smart-ass jock. He told the audience that Harry Sinden had phoned him in August to say he was on Team Canada but that the NHL owners later overruled Sinden. He sank a shaft into Al Eagleson, whom Hull clearly doesn't like, referring to him as a Judas character. He said Team Canada might not have won the series "if they hadn't crippled Kharmalov who always controlled the play when he was out there." And he ended, dramatically timed, on a ringing climax: "You people have been overdue for pro hockey for too damn long, and I'm proud to be a part of the Jets." The Kiwanians rose and cheered.

Out in the hotel driveway, two cars waited, the Lieutenant-Governor's with a chauffeur behind the wheel and Hatskin's Continental with the doorman keeping an eye on it. Hull leaned into the backseat upholstery, tired again. He wore a tight, wistful little smile. "Y'know," he said, "when the Russian team came to Winnipeg, all their players asked for me. They had their pictures taken with me and we had some good long talks about how to play the game." Pause. "I'm told I was the only Canadian player the Russians wanted to meet that way." Pause. "I would have liked to've played in the series."

Hatskin spoke from the front seat: "Those were big men in the community at the lunch today, Bob."

"Sure were."

"That's who we need on our side."

"Gotcha."

Hatskin drove the Continental into the parking lot outside the Winnipeg Arena where the Jets have their offices. Hull switched to his own car to drive home for a sleep before the game against Los Angeles. He was carrying two cakes he'd bought at the luncheon, proceeds to a Kiwanis kids' charity. The Kiwanians had cheered him for that, too.

The two men who organized the WHA, Gary Davidson, a lawyer from Santa Ana, Calif., and Dennis Murphy, a marketing executive from Fullerton, Calif., warmed up for the job by starting the American Basketball Association. The two lost money on the ABA. They recouped with the WHA. They sold the first 10 franchises in the league for $25,000 each, then split the $250,000 as a kind of finder's fee.

"Hockey has fallen into the hands of non-hockey people," says Mark Mulvoy, who writes about hockey for *Sports Illustrated* and who says he's the only writer, maybe the only person, to see games in every WHA and every NHL city. "It's the money men who call the shots, not the sportsman type of guy, the Conn Smythe type we used to have. Not local people either in a lot of cases. Just investors looking for a property." But in one way or another, the WHA staggered into business with 12 teams. "Except nobody took us seriously," says Hatskin. "Not till we signed Bobby."

Hatskin worked out the deal with Hull: $1 million out front, another million in Hull's bank account by December 1, 1972, a third million over the next 10 years for services as left winger, coach and, not the least, public relations man. "So," Hatskin explains, "at the next owners' meeting I told them the whole league was gonna benefit—right?—and everyone should throw in for the front million dollars." Which is why a huge blowup of the Hull payment hanging in the Jets offices shows the crucial cheque to be drawn on the account of WHA Properties Limited.

(Hull, incidentally, didn't bank the entire bonanza, even after taxes. Some went to pay off money advanced to him years earlier by the late James Norris of the Chicago Black Hawks, Hull's old team. Hull considered it something less than a loan. Arthur Wirtz, present Chicago owner, called it a loan. Wirtz won. Hull also paid out for an attractive 15-room house, priced around $200,000, complete with indoor swimming pool, on a large corner lot in the Tuxedo area of Winnipeg. "I'll tell you what sort of district Tuxedo is," says Don Wittman, a Winnipeg TV personality and a neighbor of Hull's. "The NDP doesn't bother to run candidates out there.")

With Hull signed and the first WHA pucks dropped, the new league presented two questions. How would it affect the NHL? Would the WHA itself survive?

To the first, Alan Eagleson, speaking as the NHL Players' Association boss, has the answer: "I'd say in the first year the WHA plus normal inflation has cost the NHL $5 million in increased salaries. Bill Harris, the number-one draft choice from the Toronto Marlboro Juniors, wouldn't have got $250,000 for his first two years out of the New York Islanders if the WHA hadn't been bidding for him too. In 1971–72, players' salaries made up 24 per cent to 28 per cent of the NHL's gross receipts. Now it's 40 per cent to 45 per cent. And take the average salary increase for individual players—it was about 15 per cent in 1971–72, more like 35 per cent this year."

But will the WHA last?

"Last?" says Ben Hatskin. "Why else spend millions on Bobby Hull?"

Five thousand, one hundred and five people showed up for the Jets game against Los Angeles on the night, a Tuesday, of the Kiwanis luncheon. The 5,105 cheered when Hull came out for the pregame warm-up. They cheered when he appeared for his first shift and for his first slapshot (it missed the L.A. net, cracked against the glass and rebounded all the way to centre). They cheered louder for the announcement of Hull's assist on Winnipeg's third goal than they did for the announcement of the goal scorer, Chris Bordeleau. They blew their minds when Hull himself scored the sixth Winnipeg goal, a hard shot, not a slap, from close in off a lovely sweeping move around Los Angeles' right defenceman. They even cheered when a nervous man from the Selkirk Steelers team presented Hull with a steel puck for, so the nervous man said, Hull's promotion of junior hockey. Our Bobby: 5,105 minds thinking as one.

The game was a laugher, 8–0 Jets. The level of play was often closer to senior amateur than to NHL professional. And most of the evening's entertainment value came in those moments when Hull powered his slapshots, when Hull wheeled at his own blue line and headed up ice waiting for the pass that he and everyone else in the building knew was coming his way, when Hull swept in on the Los Angeles goal in that characteristic move of his, guiding the puck in the curve of his stick with one hand, holding off the checkers with the other. No player anywhere, you thought at those moments, can lift a hockey crowd the way Bobby Hull can.

When Ben Hatskin sits at his desk, he sits very very still. Nothing moves, not his smallish, direct eyes, not the large, handsome, impassive head, not the hefty body. He is a very composed man. His clothes are without a flaw, black suit, white shirt, black tie, polished boots. He reminds you of an important Don in The Godfather.

Bobby Hull as a Jet.

Hatskin has made his money in various things: jukeboxes, a nightclub or two, corrugated cardboard.

Hatskin doesn't have big big money, and when he took on the Jets franchise—he's always been sports-minded—he brought in his friend from the Winnipeg Jewish community, Dave Simkin, for 50 per cent. (Simkin died in early December, and his share remains in his estate at this writing.) Hatskin's brother Rubin came in for another 15 per cent. Hatskin's share is only 35 per cent, but he calls the shots. The Hull caper was all his.

"I'd say Bobby has meant at least 1,500 more tickets for every game he's played," Hatskin says. "He's also brought in a different class of people. At first, when the courts wouldn't let him on the ice, we had mostly kids coming to the games. Now we got all classes. You have to remember that, in comparison to the big NHL cities, Winnipeg isn't the richest place in the world. A hockey ticket's a big investment for a working guy out here even if he has been dying to get pro hockey in his own city for a long, long time."

Hatskin shaves dollars where he can. He tried to talk the provincial government out of its entertainment tax in order to hold ticket prices at five and six dollars. No dice; prices, with tax, are $5.50 for blues, $6.60 for reds. The government helped out, though, by buying 550 season tickets, which it uses, in the words of Ron Lyon of the Jets front office, "for people who normally wouldn't see a game—unemployed fellas, people in hospital and Indians."

Lyon also concedes that, with the Jets, "there've been disappointments in some areas." For instance? "We thought the rink'd be jammed the first few times Hull played—it holds 11,300 with standing room—but the crowds were only around 7,000. We thought season tickets would move faster, but they were just at 2,000 at the beginning of the season. It's a psychological thing—people in Winnipeg think $254 is a lot for a season ticket. But they have to realize they're getting 39 games for that. So what we're trying to do is build the Jets like the Saskatchewan Roughriders in football, a community thing in other words, and we're starting to get that. There's busloads of fans coming in from Kenora and Brandon and the Dakotas and from Thompson up north. We're working at it." Or, as Ben Hatskin likes to say, "You gotta put up a front even if there's nuthin' in the bank."

On the morning after the Winnipeg-Los Angeles game, Vincent Price, the actor, and Karen Magnussen, the skater, took the same plane from Winnipeg to Edmonton that the Jets travelled on. But the passengers in the waiting room and on the plane had eyes only for Bobby Hull. Hull gave Price a glad hand as he passed him boarding the plane, nothing condescending but it let Price know who the real celebrity was that morning. On the bus from the Edmonton airport into the city, the driver asked Hull to arrange tickets for the night's game between the Jets and the Alberta Oilers, "a treat for my nephews, Bob." No problem, Hull said. He reached his room in the new and sleek Chateau Lacombe, and a line formed to interview him, an American magazine writer, an Edmonton newspaper reporter, two radio men trailing tape recorders. Hull shaped something fresh for each questioner, mini-scoops all around.

To Ken Nicolson, host of a coach's talk show on CJOB, Winnipeg, aired before the broadcast of each Jet game; "Ken, I don't think it's quite fair to charge Edmonton fans

WHA prices in an arena like the one they have in the city right now." To John Bohonos, host of a chitcat show, *Johnny-On-The-Spot*, on CJCA, Edmonton: "No, John, I don't think all that money's changed me. I never think about it except for the security for my family. The thing about moving to Winnipeg is that life goes at a slower, easier tempo than in Chicago."

After the last tape recorder had left, Hull splashed some water on his face, loosened his tie and contemplated his role in the WHA: "The guys you deal with, the WHA owners I mean, have a different attitude than in the NHL. Talking to Ben Hatskin isn't like talking to Sam Pollock in Montreal. Ben isn't hard and regimented like that. In Chicago, gawd, in Chicago, they wouldn't give you the sweat off their ass. NHL people don't care about anything, about how they treat the players, as long as they make a lot of money. But I could have stayed with the Black Hawks and not worried about money or about missing part of the season like I've just done. Life would have been much simpler for me. But, hell, the WHA is something that's been needed. It's made room for more guys to play and make a living, and it brought entertainment to people who used to be able to only get big-league hockey on TV.

"What was stupid about the NHL, looking back, is that whenever I'd go into an expansion city, the other team'd always send out some fast kid to check me all night. 'So-and-so held Hull scoreless'—how many times did I read that in the papers. But that's senseless. The people who come out to the games want to see me score goals. That's why they pay their money. Then what happens is that the other team makes sure I don't even get a chance to score. All right, the team's coach is paid to win games, but what's the sense of winning if you're gonna drive fans away and kill the franchise anyway? I hope they don't go in for that in the WHA."

Bill Hunter, the general manager of the Alberta Oilers, is the man who got the Alberta franchise off the ground. He hustled the backing money, some of it from Canadian Cablesystems (who own a big chunk of Famous Players), and he signed the players. But, yes, he grants that the franchise has its problems. Yes, the arena is too small, just under 6,000 capacity. Yes, the Oil Kings junior team is tough competition because it's firmly entrenched with Edmonton fans. And, yes, the crowds haven't been that big so far, about 3,640 average. Still, Hunter's full of fight and confidence. There'll be a new arena any year now, and, no fear, the fans will come around.

Hunter was at his wheeling-dealing happiest on the afternoon of Hull's arrival in Edmonton. He had the season's first sellout on his hands. The phone rang. Hunter answered. Damn. The fire chief wouldn't let him sell standing-room tickets. The phone rang again. It was Hull asking for some tickets (ah ha, the bus driver and his nephews). Hunter put the tickets in an envelope and handed it to a messenger. "Hey," he said to the messenger, "make sure Hull pays for these. He's got more money than us."

When Hull skated onto the ice in the Edmonton Gardens, he suggested the great old champion putting his flash and brilliance on display in the tank town. The arena is almost as old as the century. Horse shows used to be its main business, and its thick cold air still holds whiffs of hay and urine and horsemen's whiskey. For hockey games, not more than half the seats offer clear views of the entire ice surface. Pillars insist on getting in the way. But on this night everyone in the Palace spotted Hull's first step off the bench, and a great emotional roar shook the building, as if the people inside were announcing to themselves that, with Bobby Hull there, they'd joined the big leagues. Hull drew another cheer, almost a ritual response, with his first slapshot, and at 18:45 of the opening period he spooked the Alberta goalie, Jack Norris, to the game's first score. The Jets' Bordeleau was ripping in on Norris from the right side, Hull from the left. Bordeleau carried the puck. Norris looked for the inevitable pass to Hull. Bordeleau shot instead: 1–0 for the Jets.

Then Alberta's Val Fonteyne, ex-Detroit Red Wing and a tireless skater, took over for the night. He hung four or five feet off Hull's trail through the rest the game, checking, dogging, bugging him. The crowd held silent through much of the second period. "What the hell's there for them to yell about?" a man said in the press box. "Hull's not doin' a thing." They cheered near the end of the period when Fonteyne let a shot go from inside the Winnipeg blue line and tied the score.

Halfway through the third period, Alberta's Jim Harrison broke away and Hull, the last man back, tripped him. Penalty. Hull went off and Alberta scored: 2–1. A few minutes later Hull zoomed a slapshot that hit Fonteyne's leg. He limped off. But it was too late for Winnipeg, and Alberta scored at 18:57. Hull was on the ice at the time. 3–1. Game over.

A couple of dozen kids waited with their parents outside the Winnipeg dressing room. Hull gave them autographs and smiles. He patted a little girl on the head and asked if anybody still needed a scrap of paper signed. He smiled some more. But later when he heard how an announcer on CBXT-TV led off the sportscast—"Val Fonteyne did a masterful job of holding Bobby Hull tonight as the Alberta Oilers…"—he said one cranky word. "Crap," he said.

Three weeks and five days after the Jets game in Edmonton, Bobby Hull was sitting early in the afternoon, a Monday, in an elegant private dining room off the mezzanine floor of the Hotel Sonesta in Cambridge, Mass. The Jets players had finished a team meal before the game that night against the New England Whalers. A hotel assistant manager arrived in the dining room, smiling, rubbing his palms. How, he wondered, was the meal, Mr. Hull?

"No hell."

The assistant manager's smile dropped away at the edges, the palm-rubbing accelerated. Hull: "Those eight-ounce steaks were four-ounces meat, four-ounces fat. Too, ah, petite for growing boys"—Hull took his turn at smiling—"I know you're gonna fix that next time we come through town." The assistant manager retreated.

Hull looked healthy. It had something to do with the skin under his eyes, not so purple and loose as a month earlier. "My blood count was down was what it was," he said, fiddling with his coffee cup. "Now I'm taking iron pills. I told everybody I wouldn't get really going until close to the New Year. It was like that the year I had to hold out in Chicago the first 14 games. Took me two months to warm up."

At that point in the season, there in the Sonesta, Hull had visited every WHA city at least once, and, sitting over his coffee, he didn't mind toting up the league's strengths and weaknesses.

"Ottawa. Civil servants aren't sports fans. The owners'll have to find another spot for the franchise. Los Angeles. The fans are okay but you must have a winning team out there. L.A. only turns up for a winner. Quebec. There's a lot of good people behind the franchise. The government's behind it, too, and the fans know the game. Strong. Chicago. They'll have to build a new arena in a well-lit area out in the suburbs. Then the fans won't be nervous about going out at night. Houston. The fans need an education job on hockey, then things'll be solid. Minnesota. Good franchise, even better when their new big hockey centre opens. Edmonton. They could do a better job. The fans could do a better job. These are Canadians who understand the game and they've been waiting so long for big-league hockey. But they're not backing the team and I don't get it.

"The one sour point I've noticed around the league is that too many players in too many franchises aren't selling the game. You should do everything to get people into the buildings. I told some of the young players in Houston they should go out and sign autographs in appliance stores and shopping plazas, be seen, talk to fans, talk to the kids and tell them to bring their parents to the games. You gotta work at it, but some of the guys drawing big money from this league aren't moving their asses."

The game that night, Jets vs. Whalers, started at 7 p.m., the only way, according to Howard Baldwin, to beat the telecasts of ABC's Monday night football game. Baldwin was right: by 7 p.m., 9,119 people were waiting in the ancient and ramshackle Garden. New England was in first place in the WHA's Eastern Division, Winnipeg led in the Western Division, and the game seemed to promise something special. It delivered on the promise—the hockey, especially in the third period, was superior and exciting.

In many ways, the style of play reminded you of the early days of the former American Football League before it merged, successfully, with the National League—it was full of dash and eagerness and the old college try. The Whalers didn't put a specific man on Hull, but they gang-checked him relentlessly. Three times in the third period, Hull was crashed to the ice, once into a goal post. He didn't score all night, though he set up one Winnipeg goal with a masterful bit of feinting and passing. New England won, 4–3. One of the Boston University grads scored the tying goal, a Boston College grad got the winner. And the fans went home happy, happy with the win, happy with the local guys' private triumphs, happy with the bodying of Hull.

"Know what this is all about?" Hull said after the game. "Know what we're in? What the league is?"

"What?"

"Show business."

Then Hull packed up his gear, getting ready for the trip to, let's see, Philadelphia next, two games with the Blazers. Taking the show on the road.

Bobby Hull finished fifth in scoring in the league's first season, scoring 51 goals. Winnipeg finished atop their division that year, but lost the Avco Cup, the WHA championship, to the New England Whalers. But the Jets went on to win titles in 1976 and 1979. In 1972, the same year the WHA began operations, the NHL expanded to 16 teams, and the resulting bidding war for players drove salaries into the stratosphere. In 1979, the Winnipeg Jets—with Hull still an active player in his last season—along with WHA franchises in Hartford, Quebec, and Edmonton were absorbed into the NHL. In 1996, Winnipeggers lost their professional hockey team when it moved to Phoenix.

Jack Batten is the author of 30 books including several on the Toronto Maple Leafs. He worked as a staff writer at Maclean's *from 1963 to 1965 and was a regular contributor for the next decade.*

Coaching Scared

Trent Frayne

November, 1974—Fred Shero has been dealing with fear in many forms all his life and his handling of it has turned him into a revolutionary kind of hockey coach. It has rocketed him and the muscles he masterminds, the ungentlemanly Flyers of Philadelphia, from nowhere to the Stanley Cup in three years. It has brought him from an unknown worrywart at 45 to international recognition stretching all the way to Russia at 49. It has made him the highest-paid thinker in the history of hockey. Standing behind the bench of the most turbulent and at the same time the most disciplined team in the game just now, Freddie Shero displays all the emotion of a guy viewing a march-past of soldiers. Occasionally he'll move both hands to the frames of a pair of trendy silver-rimmed sunsensors or he'll bend to talk quietly to a Flyer player on the bench. He appears calmly in command. Who'd ever suspect, looking at him, that he's a guy who firmly believes the sky is falling?

When he was a kid in school he used to dream he was going to fail. So he worked twice as hard and always passed with honors. When he played the game (he was in the NHL briefly with the Rangers) he kept dreading the day when he'd be washed up. So he studied hockey the way stockbrokers study the market tables, figuring a coaching job might open. Then, in 13 years as a minor-league coach, he was afraid he'd never get a shot at running an NHL club so he studied some more, tried new things, devised crazy schemes to take the boredom out of practices for the players. In his last seven years down there, he finished first five times, second once, third once. That record got him his break with the Flyers.

Yet when he finally arrived in 1971 he wasted a year, afraid the things that had worked for him were too unsophisticated for the big league, even a watered-down big league and even with an inept bunch like the Flyers. He missed the playoffs, had the guts to kiss goodbye to his awestruck ways and brought in the deep-think that had won for him in the hinterland. In the next two years, Freddie Shero turned the Flyers into the most talked about bumper-bangers in the game, the Mad Squad, the Broad Street Bullies, all that. And in the high excitement last spring when they won everything, beat the old-line Rangers, out-big-badded the big bad Bruins, he stood there like a guy watching a cortege roll by.

Even now, with the Stanley Cup and a fat and reassuring $100,000 contract for each of the next three years as concrete evidences of his worth, there's still this Mr. Doom-and-Gloom. I talked to him one day at Allan Stanley's hockey school in the Kawartha Lakes district of eastern Ontario where he worked with kids for two weeks in August. "There must be something more to life than hockey," he said then, his lean face sombre. "I look around and I see brainy men, people I went to school with, contributing to society in important ways. A friend of mine is a chest surgeon on the west coast and another is a defence attorney. I was smarter than they were in school and look what they've done and what I'm doing. I feel maybe I could have been the same thing, and I wonder sometimes what the hell I'm doing in hockey." Typically, struggling to counter his doubts, what he's done is return to an extension course in law at Chicago's La Salle University to guard against whatever disasters may lurk ahead.

But fear is also a tool of the hockey trade that Shero knows how to turn to advantage, and it has played a big part in the success of the ferocious Flyers. His team is the most penalized in hockey history, combative, tough, belligerent and loaded with eager fighters. Shero denies he's ever instructed a player to pick a fight but he knows the Bullies scare the hell out of a lot of teams just by showing up. His man Dave Schultz has become a folk hero because of the countless times he's mugged somebody. Shero is aware of Schultz's impact and, if he's never spelled it out in specific terms, there's no question Schultz has caught the message. "Intimidation is a big part of the game," Shero says. "A lot of guys would be better off if they'd fight but they're afraid. If there's skating room, they look just great and they score a lot of goals against the easy teams. But when things get tight, in the tough games, they freeze. There are guys who rush into corners determined to come out with the puck. On the other hand, there are guys who always make sure they're late arriving in the corners. We don't have any of that second kind."

Shero has been given a lot of credit as the thinking man's coach since he turned his pumpkins into champions because, except for goaltender Bernie Parent and centre Bobby Clarke, his roster is remarkably bereft of Hall of Fame candidates. Though largely anonymous outside Philadelphia, the rest play an aggressive organized style, staying in position, forechecking in an orderly rather than haphazard way, covering their checks, keeping their goal mouth uncluttered, passing the puck accurately; in short, executing the fundamentals of the game with a minimum of error. The patient Shero has instilled in them the discipline to perform these basic tasks, and he overlays the fundamental concepts with often inspired and occasionally heretical innovations.

Consider, for instance, two of the most widely accepted and broadly employed facets of the game: the slapshot and the tactic of shooting the puck from the centre red line into the opposing team's zone. On the Flyers, they're not allowed. Well, "not allowed" is a little heavy; on the Flyers, very little is not allowed. But they are discouraged. "The slapshot is ridiculous," Shero says. "Once a guy makes up his mind to shoot he can't change it; if somebody gets into better position, it's too late. Winding up takes time, too, so the shot's often blocked or deflected. Also, who can control it?"

He abhors the idea of shooting the puck in. "All you're doing is giving it away," he says. "Why should you give the other team the puck?" But once he did condone giving away the puck; in fact, it was his own idea, and it was an inspired one. Last spring, before the Boston final, he and his right arm Mike Nykoluk, the assistant coach, were struggling for strategy that would nullify the effectiveness of Bobby Orr and Phil Esposito. They spent hours analyzing films of their games with the Bruins and of the Team Canada-Russia series. "We're a hitting team but we've always made the mistake of treating Orr and Esposito as untouchables. So they'd been killing us all season, especially Orr. The referees think that Orr is God. He's not God. We had to stop treating him like God. I remember when Howe and Rocket Richard and Bobby Hull were in this league, they had to earn their way. Everybody went after them, but nobody goes after Orr."

So Shero instructed his players to *give* the puck to Orr, to dump it into the corner on his side of the rink, forcing him to go back and retrieve it. Then, instead of one man going in to check Orr, Shero had his forwards swing in front of the net, forcing Orr behind it, compelling him to pick his way toward centre in slow curving routes with one or the other of the forwards always getting a little piece of him. "The idea was to make Orr work harder than he normally has to work, to tire him if we could." And of course the tactic worked.

Against Esposito and his towering linemates Wayne Cashman and Ken Hodge, physically the most powerful line in the game, Shero refused to send out a purely checking line to try to contain them. "We'd sometimes make three line changes against their single shift." Shero had another reason for not assigning a designated checker to hawk Esposito. "When you break up your lines or shuffle them to contain one man, you're playing in fear," he says. "You're providing an out for not winning. The hell with that."

A surprising thing about Shero, nobody knocks him. That's practically unheard of in hockey, where even Stanley Cup coaches are put down as dumb-bells lucky enough to be assigned to geniuses. But with Shero it's all hearts and flowers. He levels with the press, never ducks a question, always returns calls, and the minions respond positively to this. Rival coaches understandably are able to contain their enthusiasm but they give him marks. "He didn't make any mistakes," Punch Imlach, Buffalo Sabres' general manager, says of Shero's work in the playoffs. "That guy in the goal turned the Flyers around last year," says Chicago's Billy Reay of Bernie Parent, "and Shero did the rest." Rival players admire him. "He was the difference against us," says Phil Esposito. "He won the Stanley Cup for them."

And his own players have only respect. "I think our success is Freddie," says Bobby Clarke, the team captain. "He brought in his kind of players. And we play his system." Parent's praise was mute but it had flourish. The goaltender won a car from a magazine as the outstanding player of the playoffs. He gave it to Shero.

Even the Russians were eager for words from him. He enrolled along with 99 other coaches and hockey students in a sports course at Montreal's Loyola College that involved a three-week visit to the Soviet Union to study physical education. But when they arrived the Russians prevailed upon Shero to give three lectures. One was on Philadelphia's system, another was on the styles of all NHL clubs, and the third was on what Shero had learned from the first four games of the 1972 Canada-Russia series. He even held impromptu midnight seminars for the Canadians. He'd crawl around on his hands and knees in the hotel room shifting Russian beer bottles on the carpet to explain his system.

"We've accomplished very little in our game in the last 30 years; in fact, we've gone back," he says. "The only thing we've improved is our skating and that's only because kids are bigger and stronger these days. But our shooting is not half as good. The Bentleys could thread a needle; hell, everybody could. But now everything's that damned slap-shot. We can't stickhandle as well, we can't pass the puck as well, we can't manipulate it with our feet as well, and mostly it's because the centre red line has made everybody lazy."

Shero is the only NHL coach who has taken the Russians seriously. The truth is, he has taken them seriously since 1960. Then, coaching in St. Paul, Minn., he watched a team of touring Soviet teen-agers coached by the now universally renowned Anatoli Tarasov and was amazed by the things the kids could do. In 1972 when the Russians landed at Montreal Shero watched them in every workout; his peers not only avoided the Russian practices, most of them even avoided Montreal. He has incorporated

Tarasov's innovations into Flyer practices. He has three-on-two drills in which the forwards manipulate three pucks, passing and receiving them as they skate ("It makes them think"). He has defencemen play forward and forwards play defence so each will appreciate the other's problems. He puts wingmen on their wrong sides and centres on the wings so each will learn to make and take passes better. "

One day in Philadelphia I asked Shero about the reluctance of coaches to share ideas or to adopt the better elements of Russian hockey. "A lot of them are afraid for their jobs," he said. "They don't want management to think they don't know it all." It was a hot day and he was driving into town from a rink in Villanova on the western outskirts where he'd been supervising youngsters at a hockey school. He spent his whole summer, apart from the three weeks in Russia, at hockey schools. "Everybody thought I was nuts when I brought in Mike Nykoluk as an assistant coach," he said, tooling the car Parent had given him. "That's ridiculous; if he can take my job, okay. I just want his help. I'm the only coach in the NHL who has four eyes. The rest have only two because they're afraid to tell the boss they need help. And *that's* ridiculous."

In Winnipeg, where Shero grew up, people who knew him remember him as studious, quiet, a loner. "He was a tough kid but he didn't show it much," says Bill Mosienko, a fellow Winnipegger and former Chicago Black Hawk star. "If somebody tried to push him around, look out." There were 12 Shero kids but four died in infancy. Their parents came to Canada from Russia in 1910. The family name was Schirach. When Alex Schirach enlisted in the Canadian army in 1915 he simplified the name to Shera but his naturalization papers spelled it Shero, so Alex stuck to Shero. Freddie's brother Vic is the only member of the family still living in Winnipeg. Vic remembers that their father, a carpenter, could fix anything—wiring, plumbing, he could even sew. They had a huge garden. They rented a large vacant lot from the city for a dollar and raised all the vegetables the family could eat through the long Manitoba winter.

Fred's father took him out of school every year in May to help him with his carpentry. One summer Freddie built a two-storey frame-and-stucco home on Pritchard Avenue for his parents not far from their old place. The house is still there, 1172 Pritchard. Vic Shero and his wife live in Winnipeg's eastern suburbs now. Thinking back, he remembers a musical household on Pritchard. The family couldn't afford music lessons but they learned to play the mandolin or guitar or violin from instruction books. "Fred played the violin," Vic recalls. "He was a very quiet boy. He stuck to himself. He read a lot and he was awfully good in sports. That's where he let himself out, I guess. He played quarterback for the Isaac Newton school football team, the city champions one year; he played hockey and soccer and baseball, and he could box, too."

Fred went away to play hockey with the old New York Rovers, a Ranger farm club, in October of 1943 before he turned 18, lured by the Rovers offer of $60 a week. Then he joined the Royal Canadian Navy. When the war ended he returned to the Rovers, but he was convinced he'd never amount to anything if he didn't broaden his education. He used a veterans' grant to enroll in summer school at the University of Manitoba and took extension courses when he went away to play hockey. He got two years toward a BA that way. Studying history and English he was turned on by Dostoyevsky and Shakespeare and read them voraciously.

The Rangers took him into the NHL as a defenceman in 1947, but a back injury ended his big-league career two and a half years later. He had a crushed disc in his vertebrae, which he had refused to reveal for fear he'd lose his place on the roster. He went back to the minors in 1950 but finally he couldn't handle the pain, and he turned to Frank Selke, then the managing director of the Canadiens, who hired him to run a farm club at Shawinigan Falls, Que. There, he met his black-haired vivacious wife, Mariette, and they spent the next 15 years in Shawinigan, St. Paul, Buffalo and Omaha, Neb. They have two sons, Jean-Paul and Rejean, who now call themselves John and Ray. "They were born in Shawinigan," says Shero. "I figured they'd be raised there."

Instead, home for the Sheros is now Cherry Hill, across the Delaware River from Philadelphia in New Jersey. Chances are they'd be there forever if Fred could shake the notion that events will yet overcome him. When Flyer chairman Ed Snider presented his record contract, he wanted to make it for five years. Shero turned down an extra $200,000 and insisted it be for only three.

Why?

"Well," says the most revolutionary coach in hockey, fingering a new Fu Manchu moustache, "a coach has to be under pressure. It makes him work harder. Who knows what could happen in five years?"

Of course. A guy might get the notion he's made it.

Fred Shero coached the Flyers from 1971 until 1978 and led them to Stanley Cup victories in 1974 and 1975. In 1978, he left Philadelphia to serve as coach and general manager of the New York Rangers, retiring in 1981. Shero was the first NHL coach to hire a full-time assistant and his .612 winning percentage makes him one of the most successful coaches of all time. Shero died of cancer in 1990. He was 65.

Good-Time Harold

Roy MacSkimming

September, 1975—The grimy yellow-brick fortress of Maple Leaf Gardens, squatting hugely on its city block in midtown Toronto like something the glaciers left behind, contains one NHL regulation-size hockey rink, 16,316 seats painted gold, red, blue, green and grey (most of them upholstered), dressing rooms, refreshment stands and ticket wickets, and a sporting goods store. It also contains (and this isn't the least bit apparent from inside or out) an indulgently furnished apartment. There's a bedroom with Wedgwood-blue broadloom, twin beds with gold-trimmed blue spreads and matching canopy. The bathroom comes equipped with sauna, the kitchen with the latest appliances. There's a sitting room for sitting, and a much larger office for working. In spite of its spaciousness the office manages to seem cluttered because of all the memorabilia festooning its wood-panelled walls—walls that slide back to reveal a small library (raunchy paperbacks) and a four-tiered bar.

The occupant of this office-apartment doesn't drink himself. He prefers the hard candies, mints and chocolates that fill bowls placed strategically around the room, or the bottles of Fresca and Tab that crowd his refrigerator. He is 67-year-old Harold E. Ballard, and he was able to have these opulent quarters built for himself in Maple Leaf Gardens because he owns the joint (now valued at $30 million) or at least 85 per cent of it, which means he also owns the Gardens' best-known asset, the Toronto Maple Leafs hockey club.

Since his wife, Dorothy, died in 1969, Ballard has spent less time in the winter at his suburban Etobicoke home, the home that figured so prominently in his 1972 fraud-and-theft trial because he'd had it remodelled with Gardens' money, and more time in his office-apartment or on the road with the Leafs. The man who slept alone for a year in a narrow dormitory room in Millhaven minimum security centre now has 16,000 people over for an evening's hockey, or 18,000 for a rock concert. The crowds scream just a few steps from his pillow.

On my way up the escalator to Ballard's office I passed Johnny Bower going down. Bower, whose shy, poker-faced heroics I'd observed for years when he was the Leafs' goalie, is a team scout now. I wondered what he'd think of Alice Cooper, the ghoulish American rock band, which would be filling the Gardens the following week, performing just about where Bower used to play nets.

Deep bulldog creases run down either side of Ballard's mouth. He's more given to thoughtful eye-crinkling smiles than the guffaws and barks and bombast I'd been led to expect. At that first meeting he was dressed like a summer tourist in a short-sleeved navy-blue shirt, a white tie with big blue polka dots, teal-blue slacks and sporty two-tone shoes. It wasn't a costume calculated to distract attention from his formidable girth, but that's typical of the man: he hides very little, leaves himself wide open all the time. Such vulnerability isn't a hazard to him, it seems, because he has the total self-acceptance of a rhinoceros, albeit a rather appealing one, with a hide to match.

Harold Ballard appealing? That capitalist ex-con, symbol of the greedy grasping tycoon?

But symbols aren't people, and Ballard is as complicated and paradoxical as anyone else. He has reformed in at least one respect: having embarked on that most North American penance, the diet, he has lost 40 pounds. But he still doesn't look remotely like the 19-year-old who set Canadian speed-skating records for 220, 440 and 880 yards ("I set those records because everyone else in the races fell down," he explained), which gives you an idea of how fat he was before the diet. All the Frescas and Tabs are sugar-free now. "I used to drink 20 of those things a day," Ballard said, waving a paw toward a Coke. "It was nothing for me to eat a couple of pounds of ice cream in one day either. Anybody with a five-pound box of chocolates had to look out, he might get his arm snapped off."

Somehow, all his excess weight has never slowed Ballard down. A typical itinerary for him this past hockey season goes as follows: In New York Sunday night for a Leaf game; a meeting with a players' agent and a New York radio interview the next morning; a flying trip with Leaf vice-president King Clancy to take in the races in Philadelphia that afternoon; back to New York and out to Denver Tuesday morning, to look over player prospects from the Denver Spurs; to Las Vegas for pleasure that evening; in Oakland Wednesday for a Leaf game, followed by a flight on the Red-Eye Special at midnight, arriving in Chicago at 5 a.m. and thence to Toronto by seven.

All this reinforces the image of Ballard as a self-aggrandizing opportunist, a 67-year-old Anglo-Saxon Duddy Kravitz. Indeed, when I was in his office he took a phone call from his boyhood friend Red Foster of Foster Advertising about the advertising contract that was up for renewal for the famous Maple Leafs calendar that hangs in practically every barber and smoke shop in Ontario. Ballard told Foster, "I don't care if Export 'A' has had the calendar for 30 years, I want a hundred thousand for it this time and if they won't pay it, someone else will."

But a few minutes after Foster's call, another tip of the Ballard paradox surfaced. King Clancy came into the office with a worried look—Clancy always has a worried look on his face—for what I was sure would be an urgent Leaf consultation from which I'd be excused. Clancy said, "Eddie Shack's downstairs and he wants to know what you think of his dune buggy."

"I think it looks terrific," said Ballard.

"But he wants to be sure you've seen it," Clancy emphasized, frowning.

"Tell him sure I've seen it, and it looks great, just great, just great," Ballard rumbled patiently. Clancy nodded, frowned some more, and hurried off on his mission. Ballard directed a smile at me which had more of the Buddha about it than the leer of a Duddy Kravitz, "I had Eddie's dune buggy painted for him."

Paternalism, certainly, but then Ballard didn't have to do that small kindness for Shack, who didn't even get into uniform for the Leafs' playoff games. Just as Ballard didn't have to give the Gardens ice, free of charge, to the Tiny Tyke Tournament, proceeds to the Society for Crippled Children, for which he has worked as a fund raiser for years; just as he didn't have to employ a couple of ex-fellow-Millhaven inmates at the Gardens along their road to rehabilitation.

On the other hand, just to keep the man in perspective, he can exercise his power in petty ways too. When he acquired personal control of the Gardens in 1972, he behaved vindictively toward Tom Smythe, son of his deceased partner Stafford Smythe and then manager of the Marlboro team. "Whether young Smythe keeps his job depends on how good a job he does," Ballard told the *Toronto Star*. "Let's say I hope I could be impressed by some good crowds and a Memorial Cup championship." The Smythe family had just failed in its attempt to block Ballard's takeover of the Gardens.

"The worst thing that ever happened to me was my wife's death," Ballard said. A large color photograph of Dorothy Ballard hangs in its frame on the wall behind his head. She appears to have been a friendly, gently smiling lady in late middle age, standing in the sun on their cottage balcony with the blue of Georgian Bay behind her. People will tell you that her graces were the perfect foil for Ballard's jovial

Harold Ballard in his Maple Leaf Gardens office, 1985.

vulgarity. "It was after she died that I really brought this place alive," he said. "There used to be a lot of dark nights around here."

First in a three-way partnership with Stafford Smythe (Gardens founder Conn Smythe's son) and John Bassett (former publisher of the *Toronto Telegram*, former owner of the Toronto Argonauts, present CFTO-TV boss) and then as majority owner, Ballard has been responsible for the secularization of the Gardens from a hockey cathedral, which it was in Conn Smythe's day, to a year-round entertainment palace. It's said that of all Ballard's department heads, attractions manager Peter Larsen has the most freedom: Ballard may have no use for rock music (he likes Dixieland) but he has a great appreciation of profit statements. And yet Conn Smythe told me, "Harold Ballard has done more legwork for hockey than any living soul: He and I may disagree on the ethics of certain things, but I certainly don't disagree with his results."

Ballard is hardly a parvenu in the House that Smythe Built; he joined the Leaf organization in the '30s, after organizing and managing the National Sea Fleas, which won the world hockey championship in 1932. He became responsible for the Marlboro teams, both seniors and juniors. Stafford Smythe played under Ballard before the war and later became his close friend; Smythe coached the junior Marlies while Ballard managed them, and they won two Memorial Cups. Later still, they called themselves "The Gold-Dust Twins."

They joined forces with Bassett to buy out Smythe Sr. in 1961. Those were profitable years for Gardens shareholders, and the Leafs did well too, winning three consecutive Stanley Cups under Punch Imlach between 1962 and 1964. Smythe and Ballard purchased Bassett's shares in September, 1971, for about $6 million, and then in February, 1972, several weeks after Stafford's death from a bleeding ulcer, Ballard came up with another $7.5 million, borrowed from the Toronto-Dominion Bank, to buy Stafford's stock from the family. This chagrined the Smythes mightily, but the money covered Stafford's considerable debts.

Ballard hasn't always had this kind of borrowing power. His father was a machinist who made the leap to the upper middle class by building up the Ballard Skate Company, eventually sold to the Star Skate Company of Dartmouth, N.S. Ballard started his own business, Harold E. Ballard Limited, in 1930, supplying machinery to Toronto's garment industry. He closed the business last year, long after it had given him the financial resources to buy into the Gardens organization. "I always had dreams of owning an NHL club," Ballard told me. "Even when I was operating the Sea Fleas and we were the Marlboros' archenemy, I owned some Maple Leaf Gardens stock. Whenever I had a few dollars I'd buy some. I could see the future and tell the way hockey was going. You didn't have to be a Rhodes Scholar to know it would be a winner some day."

He never misses a Leaf game, or a Marlboro game if he can help it. "I like to formulate my own opinions about players. All the decisions about personnel are mine in the end. Of course I want to listen to the scouts and King Clancy and (coach) Red Kelly and (general manager) Jim Gregory. The more conversation the better, and if I agree with their point of view I'll go along with it." But doesn't that tend to erode the authority and self-confidence of the coach and general manager? "It's my money," he grunted. There's no appeal, apparently, from the prerogatives of capital.

Leafs fans (and there are many of them) who feel that Ballard's one-man control has damaged the team may be delighted to know that he's willing to sell it. But he'd never sell the Gardens: that's where the big profits are. Ballard talked expansively about the giant sports complex he wants to build not far from the Gardens. He envisions it as including a hockey arena holding 25,000 spectators, a football and baseball stadium (for the major-league baseball franchise he hopes to bring to Toronto) and convention facilities, and it reveals him as a Toronto version of Jean Drapeau. But he'd still hold on to Maple Leaf Gardens. "The Gardens could be turned into anything: a parking garage, a storage warehouse, a refrigeration plant—there's lots of people around looking for refrigeration—or we could make ice cubes to sell to all the bars around here, after all we've got the ice-making machines. Can you imagine how much ice the Royal York uses in one day? Hell, there's no reason why the Gardens couldn't be an important trade centre, you can spit to here from any of the major hotels..."

I remarked that it would be sad to see the Gardens go that way. "Oh I suppose so," Ballard said across the 35 years separating our ages, "but time marches on. You can't stand still." That last, familiar statement, so beloved of developers and Rotarians, is typical of Ballard's old-fashioned boosterism. But as much as he'd like to be remembered as the man who brought major-league baseball to Toronto, or raised hundreds of thousands of dollars for crippled kids and the mentally retarded, or made his shareholders rich, Harold E. Ballard will be remembered by many as the plutocrat who went to prison.

On Oct. 20, 1972, Ballard was sentenced in Ontario county court to three years for fraud and three years for theft, the terms to run concurrently. It was the culmination of a six-week trial and a dogged three-year investigation by federal tax investigators and, later, Metro fraud squads into the way Ballard and Stafford Smythe had run the Gardens. Smythe, who was 15 years younger than Ballard, had died before the trial began. He had been charged with fraud and theft involving Gardens operations, amounting to some $395,000. Ballard's conviction was on 47 counts involving a total of nearly $205,000.

The fraud related to the use of Gardens money to pay for Ballard's personal expenses, from such glaringly large items as house and cottage renovations to picayune ones such as motorbikes for his sons and limousine service at his daughter's wedding. The theft indictment concerned cheques that Ballard and Smythe had diverted to a private bank account, although they were intended for the Marlboro hockey club owned by the Gardens. During the trial, Crown prosecutor Clay Powell charged that Ballard had used Maple Leaf Gardens, a publicly traded company, "as a private banking source" in perpetrating frauds from 1965 to 1968. In his final judgment, County Court Judge Harry Deyman of Peterborough found "a clear pattern of fraud" throughout the evidence. Rejecting the defence argument (by prestigious Toronto counsel J.J. Robinette) that Ballard had not known of the misuse of Gardens funds, Judge Deyman stated: "The problem is, did Mr. Ballard know that this was occurring and was he party to it? In my view, the evidence is not open to any other rational conclusion but that he was."

Ballard served one year of his sentence before being paroled from Millhaven. He insists now that he has paid his debt to society and the Gardens—he made complete restitution of the money before entering the penitentiary—and the case is closed and he doesn't see why people want to re-hash it, and he's right, in a way: except for two things. One, he should know that somebody who has made himself so visible, who loves and thrives on publicity, must take the bad publicity with the good—and there has been plenty of good. Second, and more important, there is something truly extraordinary about Ballard's trial and prison saga, namely that he went through a prolonged public humiliation and punishment (a year is a precious long time at the end of your life) that would have broken most other men, and came out the other end bloody but unbowed and, if anything, more indomitable than before.

It's precisely this, of course, that upsets people. Similarly, Ballard's notorious jocular remarks about how comfortable and well-fed he was at Millhaven and how he couldn't wait to get back, made to the press while he was out on a three-day pass, caused a public furor. Politicians and others demanded that he be sent to a real prison, with cell bars and searchlights and bread and water, to teach him a lesson. There is a conviction among people close to Ballard that he was scooped up in a net really intended for Stafford, and that Stafford had been singled out by the authorities because of the tremendous animosity he aroused in so many people. But even Ballard doesn't deny doing the things he was charged with. "Sure I had the Gardens pay for repairs to my house. I didn't know it was being done at first, that it was a system Stafford had introduced, but in the end I knew. But what I did is in the general run of business activities. I didn't fight it at the trial because I knew they wanted to make an example of me. So I did what I thought they wanted me to do, and went to jail."

And it wasn't, in fact, such a terrible experience compared to the embarrassment of the trial publicity. "The prison officials were very kind to me. I wasn't treated as a very hard-nosed criminal. I was able to keep in touch with the Gardens by phone every day, and Clancy came down once or twice a week. There wasn't a day went by when some friend or newspaper guy didn't come down. I was never lonely."

All of which makes it easier to understand how Ballard's psyche survived the experience. On top of that, he insists he felt no guilt in prison: a moral blind spot certainly, an unforgivable arrogance. And on top of that, he had a job: he was kept busy looking after the inventory of prison supplies. He had an office, and a desk, and ledger books to keep. Not among the photographs on Ballard's office walls are some color snapshots taken while he was in Millhaven. Harold operating a front loader, smiling. Harold in the warehouse wearing a yellow hard hat, smiling. Harold at his desk, just like at the Gardens, smiling. The interior of Harold's "cell," a tiny but decent bedroom, decorated with the portrait of Dorothy that now hangs in his office. Even in prison, Harold was a boss.

Ballard keeps these snapshots in a black binder, which also contains letters he prizes, accolades from such people as former partner John Bassett (for whom he helped to make $7 million) and Toronto police chief Harold Adamson and fellow-owners of NHL teams, each letter preserved in clear plastic. Twice he hauled the binder out, thrust it under my nose and read some of the letters aloud to me, his index finger running along under the lines, his powerful voice quavering slightly, not reading every word with precision, as if he'd never taken the trouble to read properly or perhaps because he'd memorized the letters from so many repetitions and wasn't really reading at all.

For the first time in my presence he looked his age, an old man anxiously justifying his life through the words of others. For a moment too he seemed to belie Conn Smythe's description of him as "a reincarnation of the old pirates—the buccaneers who went where they wanted and boarded other ships and took what they could get, knowing full well the penalty was death." It's an overly romantic description, no doubt. Ballard once called Smythe "a miserable old bastard" in print.

But Ballard has had at least two genuine scrapes with death, both during the '30s. One occurred when he became friendly with a stunt pilot at the Canadian National Exhibition and went up with him "to do a few flips." They didn't gain enough altitude (Ballard's extra weight?) and hit the top branches of a tree at the edge of a farmer's field. Both men were hurled out of the open cockpit. Ballard soared through the air like a bird and landed in a haystack—unharmed. The pilot had an ear torn off, his jaw broken and was almost killed. Ever since, Ballard has said, he's felt as if he's living on borrowed time. He still loves to fly.

In the other incident, Ballard and two friends, Red Foster and speedboat racer Jimmy Rogers, were capsized by a high wave when sailing in Toronto harbor, and Rogers was drowned. After being rescued, Ballard went back out and dragged for the body until he found it. In the meantime it had gone over the radio that Ballard had drowned too, and a reporter arrived at the Ballard Sr. household for a photograph. "Father," Ballard's mother called, "Harold's been drowned."

"Oh, no, he hasn't," Ballard's father replied, "just tell them to keep looking for him. He'll be there."

Harold Ballard continued to run the Maple Leaf organization with an iron grip until his death in 1990. The Leafs, always one of the league's best franchises, became one of the worst during his tenure. In the 1980s, they never had a .500 season. But when Ballard died at 86, his estate was worth an estimated $50 million.

Roy MacSkimming is a writer and consultant who was a contributor to Maclean's *in the mid-'70s. He has written books on the 1972 Canada-Russia series and Gordie Howe.*

A Farewell to Greatness

Robert Miller

February 21, 1977—Late last month, in what was probably his last appearance as a professional hockey player, Bobby Orr was able to play only two shifts against the inept Vancouver Canucks. Power plays, of course. During the second, the puck skipped past him at the Vancouver blue line. Instinctively, he started to whirl and give chase. But he couldn't do it. Even a routine pivot was beyond the wounded knee. Orr winced, limped to the Chicago bench and sat, with buried heart, watching the game sputter along to a weary draw. The world's greatest hockey player—and who, really, can argue the point?—was through. Even Orr thought so. Washed up and perhaps even permanently crippled at the age of 28. "I can't go on like this," he said a day or so later, before leaving for Florida and writing off yet another National Hockey League season. No, Bobby. You can't. Neither can we.

It has been said far too often: Bobby Orr on one leg is better than most hockey players on two. Maybe he is. Certainly he is better box office. But Bobby Orr was never just a hockey player. He was a virtuoso, an original, possibly a genius—and he had been those things since boyhood, skating his way from the ponds of Parry Sound, Ont., to the great arenas of the continent. Glenn Gould can probably play a brilliant one-handed piano. Rudolf Nureyev can certainly dance a mean boogie. But would they? Should they? Why should Bobby Orr try to play one-legged hockey? Why should anyone—fan, owner, coach, teammate—demand it of him? Let him go now, away from the pain and the spotlight. Let him leave with his dignity and his millions. He has earned them. Let him leave us with the memories, with the knowledge that when we watched him we were watching a man/boy play our game at a level we had never realized it could reach.

Canadians have always made too much of hockey—and not enough. It is, as a friend of mine often says, our third official language. Well, Bobby Orr gave it a grammar and a new accent. He changed hockey, and our perception of it, in a way that no individual

Bobby Orr as a Hockey Night in Canada *commentator, 1977.*

performer had ever changed a team sport before. The Russians, perplexed, called him a halfback, borrowing a football term to explain Orr's innovative approach. How else to explain a defenceman who won scoring championships? Ever practical, though, the Russians did not attempt to play in the "Boo-bie Orr" manner. They left that to the less gifted North American pros. The Russians knew what we all knew: there was only one Number 4. Anyway, when translated into Russian, Canada's third official language became ideologically correct: a collective pastime, played impersonally, impassively, efficiently. Orr, a capitalist, played it all by himself, even though he always let his teammates share in the fun, the exuberance, the rewards of the game. He made them better than they were, richer than they dreamed. In the good years, he absolutely dominated. There was nothing he couldn't do with a puck, a stick and a pair of skates. His fellow pros paid him the ultimate compliment: they never took their eyes off him when he was on the ice. Later, in their own practices, they would try to copy the things he did. The most talented would master some of Orr's moves. Orr would simply invent new ones that rendered the old ones obsolete, and take the game on to a higher level.

When he left Boston, home of the GOD BLESS ORR COUNTRY bumper sticker, Mayor Kevin White was able to say without blushing: "Bobby Orr has been to Boston the equivalent of a great natural or historic resource, like Paul Revere's horse or the Bunker Hill monument." When he signed with the Black Hawks for $3 million (not one cent of which he has accepted, because he doesn't feel he has earned it), the *New York Times* made him the subject of its "Man in the News" column, where normally statesmen and tycoons are profiled. Although the press in Canada faithfully chronicled his exploits, his agonies and his wretched medical luck, a strange resentment seemed to lurk between the lines. A Toronto newspaper poll coughed up his name as one of the world's biggest bores. How typically Canadian.

We have too few heroes in this country, just as the Americans have too many. We have a habit of chipping away at our heroes, digging for flaws, hauling them down and, finally, enjoying their humiliation. Orr deserves better, but could be pardoned for doubting he'll get it. He has heard the boobirds of Maple Leaf Gardens. He has seen the anticipatory glint in the vulture's eye every time the knee went. He has read the injudicious (and, until now, premature) obituaries. Denis Potvin, an excellent defenceman whose talent nearly matches his ego, has even dared to disparage Orr's work in the Canada Cup series last fall. Overpraised, grumped Potvin, who complained that his own efforts had been simultaneously under-appreciated. Wrong. I remember Orr, bad leg and all, taking on the world at half speed and still showing everyone, Potvin included, how it's done, how our game is played. Orr has endured it all—the boos, the bloodlust, the jealousy and the pain—without complaining, just as he has accepted the cheers and the honors and the fame and the money without gloating.

But how frustrating the past few seasons must have been. How infuriating for the body not to be able to obey the brain's commands. How depressing to watch lesser talents flash by, doing their best but not quite doing it right. How satisfying it would be to come back, just one more time, healthy, and win a scoring title or a Stanley Cup. It would be in Orr's nature to try. Al MacNeil, one of the four Team Canada coaches last fall, says he has never seen an athlete with as positive a mental attitude. "The guy is just fantastic, that's all."

Orr and his friend-lawyer-agent-big-brother Alan Eagleson insist that no final decision on Orr's future has been made: the doctors and the knee will decide next summer. Hockey fans everywhere, to say nothing of beleaguered franchise owners, naturally hope a medical miracle will occur. But if there is to be no miracle, if there is only to be a half-speed Orr, a one-legged wonder, then I hope the player and his agent will agree to leave well enough alone. The fans don't owe Orr anything but respect; he has always given them his very best. Orr doesn't owe the fans anything either, except maybe the right to remember the way he played our game. No one wants to see Orr tagged a has-been. Let him surrender his mantle to Potvin or, more likely, Larry Robinson or Borje Salming. But don't let one of them tear it off his shoulders as he tries to hobble by.

Bobby Orr played only 20 games that season and six more the following year, before deciding to retire after 12 seasons. Although he was only 30 when he left hockey, his achievements are legendary: three-time league MVP; named best defenceman eight times; two scoring titles; and twice winner of the Conn Smythe Trophy as best performer during the playoffs. Following his retirement Orr was named a special assistant to NHL president John Ziegler, but resigned two years later saying he was little more than a figurehead. He has become a successful Boston-area businessman and pitchman, and still remains active in hockey as a consultant.

A Flower for All Seasons

Roy MacGregor

I retired in 1971, the same year Guy arrived and he came to me and asked me what I thought about him taking my sweater number. "If you want it, take it," I told him. "But don't you think you already have enough on you? Why don't you pick another number and make it famous yourself?" —Jean Beliveau

October 16, 1978—The new smell of Quebec is known by its trade mark: No. 10. The odor may be appropriately described as flowery as it rises this fall out of pre-shave, after-shave, cologne, deodorant and the true savior of Christmas, soap-on-a-rope. The same number can be found pushing automobiles, skates, sticks and yogurt. No. 10 surfaces on the binders, pencil cases and exercise books the children carry to school. Even the company is called Number 10 Promotions Inc., and the president—for those without programs—is Guy Lafleur. The company he keeps as a hockey player, however, has narrowed down year by year until today there is only himself.

It is Lafleur's enormous gift that makes him special, certainly not his walk—the steps too long—nor his face: greaser soft, it is more the look of someone who should be topping up your battery. The eyes, however: brown and shimmering, they seem to ransack the immediate area about him. Not in fear—though that was once the case when undercover detectives took every step he took—but in simple anticipation. Everywhere, even in the USSR where customs agents asked for his autograph, they know the man who, like Bambi's skunk, is proud to be called "Flower." Crossing de Maisonneuve Boulevard, the eyes intercept a sultry woman who steps sideways just long enough to kiss Lafleur on the lips. Out of a hydro manhole two workmen rise and call his name. A woman brings her son forward for a laying on of his hands. Those who don't want just to touch would like to give. A man promises a new suit, a girl a present. An unnamed European country this summer offered a butler, a housekeeper, a villa on the water, a new luxury car and a hockey lord's ransom, all tax-free. To collect it, he only had to change his sweater.

The man an entire province prayed for when Jean Beliveau moved on has arrived at his full bloom. It is hardly possible to believe today that those same hands that ruffle children as if their imaginations were crops he himself had planted, once struggled to put down his desperate feelings in poetry. It is harder still to realize these same friendly eyes could have spilled tears over the red, white and blue *les Canadiens-*colored chesterfield in Jean Beliveau's office as Lafleur sat crying over whatever it was that had gone so wrong with his promised life.

But eyes can also weep for joy. And Antoine Viau, who has waited much of his life for this moment, is dampening slightly as he stands watching his beloved Canadiens skate and shoot and actually breathe. The Montreal Forum is empty of fans, but Guy Lafleur—who an hour earlier has said "What good is money when you play and lose?"—is skating with Stanley Cup intentions during a $25-per-man pre-season scrimmage. His wispy hair matted with the cream cake his teammates have used to celebrate his 27th birthday, Lafleur commands his magic to turn a 4–2 deficit into victory. In the dying minutes he scores, sets up the tying goal, then single-handedly wins the game in overtime with a phantom shot from the point. He has served notice against the best hockey team in the world, his own, that Lafleur is ready for the new season. For Antoine Viau, who sweeps floors nights at the American-owned IBM plant, the state of *les Canadiens* is, in many ways, the state of his own well-being. The team and Lafleur are an unspoken vindication. "Ah, Lafleur," Viau says, courteously speaking English to the reporter who helped him sneak in, "Lafleur... Lafleur... I love it!"

Guy Lafleur is more symbol than human to a great many Québécois. "There is," says Jerry Petrie, Lafleur's agent, "probably more pressure on him to perform from the people in this province than there is on René Lévesque." We may be, as Irving Layton has said, "a dull people enamored of childish games," but Layton is certainly not speaking for those to whom hockey is a far more mature passion than politics. For them, Lafleur occupies the highest office in the land.

"I think over the last five years Lafleur has proved himself to be the finest player in North America," says Alan Eagleson. "Guy is the true throwback," says Ken Dryden, the Canadiens' goaltender. "I look out sometimes and see the St. Lawrence skater, not the player, and it is a beautiful thing to behold." Pierre Larouche, who came to Montreal from Pittsburgh last year, says he actually used to cheer for Lafleur

Guy Lafleur, leading Montreal Canadiens scorer, 1977.

when their teams played: "They'd be ahead 6–1 and I'd be on the bench wishing he'd score more, just so I could watch and see how it is done." The last to recognize this special status has probably been Lafleur himself. In Moscow this summer he was asked by the head of hockey and the director of all Soviet sports to pick his own world all-star team and when he came to right wing he blushed deeply and said "Me!"— quickly covering his embarrassment with a laugh that implied it was merely his own little joke, but the Soviet officials gravely nodded in total agreement.

"The Flower is a very strange person," says Lafleur's linemate and good friend Steve Shutt. It is not for any obvious idiosyncrasy such as his superstitious tap of the goal netting to start each game and period; what is truly odd, in Shutt's evaluation, is that Lafleur is "the farthest thing from an athlete you'd ever want to see off the ice." A loyal consumer of Molson's ale (the brewery owns his team) and a chain smoker who two weeks ago switched to a pipe—Lafleur does little more than work out with suntan oil in the off-season. "He shows up at camp, puts on his skates and it's the first time he's been on them since the playoffs," says Larry Robinson of the Canadiens. "And the frightening thing is he just flies by everybody immediately." For people like Jean Beliveau, who even in retirement runs two to three miles a day, it is a continuing mystery how Lafleur—who hasn't attended an optional practice in years—remains so fit. "The most amazing thing about him is his physical resistance," says Beliveau.

"It's because he's so hyper," says Shutt. "He winds himself up like a coil." The bad nerves are a mixed blessing: what Lafleur gains in reflex and metabolism he gives up in what it does to his mental fitness. Before particularly important games he has been discovered in the dressing room at three o'clock in the afternoon—his equipment on, his skates tightened—fully five hours before game time. By the time the puck drops he is strained, which partially explains his periodic slumps in critical games. Before the pipe came along he tried to smoke out the devils inside, and there have been games, one teammate says, when he would begin chain-smoking hours before a game and continue through the intermissions.

The best solution, he has discovered, is to rinse the mind completely of all hockey thought. He spends the jittery pregame hours reading car magazines, clipping from architectural books for the dream-home file he keeps, or taking bubble baths. On the road he and his roommate, Shutt, fight over the television, Shutt constantly looking for sports events and Lafleur's bad nerves making any contest, even tennis, an unbearable agony. He is at his happiest watching reruns of *The Three Stooges*.

Lafleur likes to keep things simple. His priorities always place the team and the game first, and either his fans or family second. Only once, when the team was in a rare slump, has Lafleur deliberately tried to inspire by anything but his own standard of play. He moved from his locker to the play blackboard near the showers, picked up the chalk, thought a moment, and then scribbled, "A winner never quits and a quitter never wins." He then moved back to his locker where he sat staring up at the approving, legendary faces of les Canadiens of past years, and he read again the lines of the poet John McRae that are stencilled just below the ceiling: "To you from failing hands we throw the torch; be yours to hold it high."

"I may never be able to play like him," Lafleur once said of Beliveau. "But I'd like to be the man he is." It is a hero worship that has been both inspiration and salvation to Guy Lafleur. Twenty years ago in the Ottawa River town of Thurso, Que., Lafleur's parents found him sleeping in his new hockey equipment, and though the dream of that night has long since faded it is not unlikely that Jean Beliveau threaded a breakaway pass to his new young winger, and that the roar of the Forum crowd for Lafleur's goal sounds yet in whatever dimension wishes retire to.

As Beliveau had before him, Lafleur left the small town for Quebec City and their resulting glory was comparable. As an "amateur" junior, Lafleur made close to $20,000 a year, drove a free Buick and dressed in the finest "gift" clothes. He wore No. 4, Beliveau's signature in Montreal, and Lafleur made sure he kept a poster of his idol taped to the wall beside his locker. In Lafleur's final year—when he scored an astonishing 130 goals—it was arranged that the sensation would come to Montreal. By rights, as the best amateur in the country, he should have gone to the last-place California Golden Seals, but a celebrated sleight of hand by Montreal's general manager Sam Pollock saw the Canadiens come up with Lafleur.

It was accepted that Lafleur was carrying Beliveau's torch even before the 1971–72 season began. Ken Dryden remembers an exhibition game against the Boston Bruins when he overheard Phil Esposito growl to his linemates, "Which one is Lafleur?" The season before, Esposito had scored a record 76 goals, but there was obvious concern in his voice. So much was Guy Lafleur on people's minds—despite never having played a single professional game—that a manufacturer was rushing production to get a Lafleur-endorsed table-hockey game out in time for Christmas. Its main competition, naturally, would be the Phil Esposito game.

By the third winter, however, the Lafleur game was off the market. Not only had the rookie award gone to his teammate Ken Dryden, but the word around the league was that Lafleur was "yellow." The junior promise had become a professional deceit. "He'd been somewhat of a bust, you might say," says Steve Shutt. "My legs were in Montreal," Lafleur says, "but my heart was in Quebec City. My mind wasn't on hockey." With the press constantly demanding what was wrong, Lafleur took to hiding in his Montreal apartment and writing depressing poetry about the meaninglessness of life and unfairness of death—a melancholia that still surfaces from time to time—and his game deteriorated even further. To give him confidence the Canadiens countered a $465,000 (over three years) lure from the Quebec Nordiques of the WHA with a new contract for Lafleur—$1 million over 10 years, fully guaranteed. He responded with his worst season of all: 21 goals.

The unhappy sessions in Jean Beliveau's office weren't providing a solution either. It took a gamble by Beliveau in the spring of 1974 to provide the remedy. Beliveau let it be known that he was less than pleased with the performance of his heir, and he castigated Lafleur for not working hard enough. The effect, at first devastating, became "a wake-up" for Lafleur and he emerged from his sulk by announcing "I'll show the bastards." When training camp opened, he discarded his yellow stigma with his helmet and the new Guy Lafleur suddenly and aggressively emerged as Beliveau reincarnate. A broken finger probably cost him the scoring championship that year, but he has held the title for the three years since. The legendary team that in the past revered such names as "Battleship," "Boom Boom," and "Rocket" found itself following the "Flower," but as Pierre Larouche says, "He's as gentle as a flower, but plays like Superman. In Quebec, hockey is a religion, and Lafleur is the new god."

In the four years since the rebirth, there have been times when Lafleur has found himself in his office in Pointe-Claire looking at the tiny skates with the red laces that now keep the door open, the same skates he began on, and poring over the two massive albums, one a foot thick, that are offered to his glory. "It is like a dream to me," he says at these times. "Even now it is like a dream."

There have, however, been darker sides that are not pasted in any album but linger anyway. And this has led him to wonder rather than gloat. In April of 1976, the Montreal police were investigating the holdup of a Brinks truck when they stumbled on a plot to kidnap Lafleur before the playoffs began and hold him for a rumored $250,000 ransom. He will never forget what it was like when Jean Beliveau told him. "I was at home and the phone rang," Lafleur recalls, the memory sending his fingers searching for cigarettes. "It was Jean and he said he wanted to see me. I said OK, tomorrow. He said no, right now, and he'd come over because we couldn't talk about it over the phone. I hung up and my wife said 'What was that?' I didn't know what to say—I thought I'd been *traded*. Then Jean arrived with two big guys and they're cops and they tell me I have two choices. I can go to Miami and the club would pay for it and make excuses for me, or I can stay. I said I just wanted to play hockey."

For a full month Lafleur lived in sight of two detectives. His wife, Lise, and eight-month-old son, Martin, stayed for a while in a hotel and then with her parents in Quebec City. The Lafleurs had a home in the country at that time—a renovated 200-year-old farmhouse at the end of a long, dark drive, and his nerves, never reliable, erupted. A squirrel would drumroll across the roof and Lafleur would scramble for cover. Night after night he couldn't sleep and once knelt shaking by the windowsill as a large black car pulled part way up the driveway and sat idling. All he could make out were the glows of four cigarettes, rising, burning brightly, then falling. After a torturous hour the car left, but the reality of the threat stayed. Lafleur's play disintegrated and when the fans and press squeezed him for answers he had to fight to keep it from pouring out.

The very next year he made up for that small lapse by winning the Conn Smythe Trophy as the most valuable player during the playoffs. But there was a new threat to deal with. One of the Boston Bruin players, John Wensink, whose hockey talent is to Lafleur's what punk rock is to Beethoven, proudly announced: "If I get on the ice, Lafleur will not come out alive." Lafleur survived, of course. Wensink, who has trouble catching his own wind, had to make do with Lafleur's as the Canadiens star flew by and led his team to its record 20th Stanley Cup. But the incident had its effect on Lafleur. "It's supposed to be a sport," he says of his beloved game, "not butchery."

It is such things as this that cause Lafleur to measure just what it is all worth. Even a simple vacation with his family must now be spent in the south of France, so badly have the adoring fans crippled his freedom in Canada. He turned up at a charity baseball game this summer but was forced to give up in the third inning when the worshippers insisted on running out and playing the field with him. He is now paid—thanks to the team renegotiating his 10-year-contract—approximately $200,000 a year, a sum that is vast only until it is recognized that Lafleur's salary would not place him in the top 20 of professional hockey. His present contract depresses him to the point where he refers to it as an "iron collar" and is currently pressing the Canadiens for yet another renegotiation.

There are times when he rises in the dead of night and goes into his son Martin's room and crawls in beside the boy. Martin is only three and though he has seen firsthand what it means to be Guy Lafleur—the fawning attacks at shopping malls, the crowds that wait in the streets—he has already announced to his father that he, too, will be a great hockey player one day. Lafleur, who saw his own youth pummelled by fame, is concerned. "I tell him to sit down and relax," he says. "I know he'd have even more pressure on him than I had. And that... ? Well." He shrugs and can say no more.

Guy Lafleur is the only Canadiens player ever to win the scoring title three consecutive years. Lafleur scored 50 goals or more six times in his career and was named the NHL's top player in 1977 and 1978. Lafleur retired from the Canadiens in 1984, but four years later, just after he was inducted into the hockey Hall of Fame, he signed with the New York Rangers, and finally ended his career at age 39 in 1991 with the Quebec Nordiques. Lafleur has since pursued varied business interests and has recently returned to the Canadiens organization as a goodwill ambassador.

Roy MacGregor was an editor at Maclean's *from 1973 to 1975 and a senior writer from 1978 to 1982. Until recently a sports columnist at the* Ottawa Citizen, *MacGregor has won numerous awards and is the author of 14 books, including eight on hockey.*

King of the Kings

Roy MacGregor

March 24, 1980—Before it is over, the death toll will reach 27. But on this, the first of 10 days of California downpour, the rain is but a small annoyance, lightly chording on the clover-shaped pool. A dark, stubby man with the build of a Chubb vault stands beneath the eaves of his $400,000 home and scowls toward the mist lingering over his neighbor's corral. He stops talking, grabs his head and bends over double, the rain turning the 18-stitch cut over his left eye into a black caterpillar. Yet it is neither injury nor weather that bothers Marcel Dionne; it is the future. "I have got to think positive," he says in a rising voice. *"Pos-i-tive!"*

For four hours he has sat working over a few cans of Coors beer and the past. He has touched on the sacrifice—the marriage breakup his parents once faked, the baby his Aunt Denise lost—all tied to the young Marcel's hockey. He has traced himself from Quebec's Drummondville through Ontario's St. Catharines, from Detroit to Los Angeles, once running from his own demanding family, once from his own damning mouth. In awe, he has spoken of Guy Lafleur, first the boy and now the man, and whom, boy and man, Dionne has "been chasing since he was 10 years old," in the words of his own best friend, Mickey Redmond. Only this past weekend, with Dionne a distant 16 points ahead of Montreal's Lafleur in the National Hockey League scoring race, has that 18-year chase seemed won. And with that accomplishment may come another: with agent Alan Eagleson demanding a $500,000-per-year-*plus* contract from the Los Angeles Kings, Marcel Dionne is about to become the best-paid performer in the sport's history.

North on Crenshaw Boulevard, up and just off the San Diego Freeway, Jerry Buss walks his fingers around the rim of a second rum and Coke. Buss's jeans, Texas boots and open-necked cranberry shirt say nothing of the more than $500 million that has grown from the $83.33 a month he and a friend each began setting aside in the summer of 1958. A year ago, perhaps sensing that the sexiest thing about real estate was his rising profit curve, Buss masterminded a $67.5-million deal to buy the Los Angeles Kings hockey team, the Lakers basketball team, the Los Angeles Forum and a 13,000-acre ranch from Californian-Canadian Jack Kent Cooke. And so, on May 29, 1979, at the age of 46, Buss capped an American dream, which began in Wyoming as the son of a divorced waitress, by driving to pick up the keys to the Forum in a Rolls-Royce Camargue.

This particular Jerry Buss night, like most others, has its visible assurances—new friend Gordon Lightfoot in to share a drink, a satin-eyed, raven-haired comfort waiting to go home with him—but Buss is a man whose confidence needs few external trappings. "If you can learn medicine in four years," he says in a soft, sure voice, "you should be able to learn hockey in four years." Having known the joys of indulgence, Jerry Buss does not believe in denial. For his sweet tooth he has stocked his office with jelly beans and lollipops. For his ego he has filled a large, black picture album with scores of the women he has known. For his ambition he has locked into a vision of the Stanley Cup. And though he may tower over his star by six inches, he has come to recognize that this particular dream lies more within the reach of Marcel Dionne than himself.

"Look," he says, tapping a cigarette tight, "you either subscribe to the crazy world we live in or you don't. I do. I have seen people get up on a stage, shuffle their feet, and get $100,000 a week. If you can get people to pay to see you, then I don't think we should interfere with that process... So Marcel Dionne is worth whatever he can get from me."

"In what sport," the KLAC Los Angeles sportscaster asks as a leadoff to his noon report, "is the Stanley Cup symbolic of over-all supremacy?" Cut to commercial while laid-back listeners throughout the state mull over the possibilities... African exploration?... tool manufacturing?... making love to Mrs. Roper?... "The answer," the sportscaster shouts incredulously on return, "is HOCKEY!"

In this city ice comes crushed for margaritas. It is a sports city that nail-bites over the Rams and Dodgers and Lakers coming *second*, not the Kings standing *11th*, a city where a Marcel Dionne—who came for money and escape more than hockey potential—is lost among the Garveys and Jabbars, who in turn lose out to Paul Newman's cars and Johnny Carson's tennis. "You couldn't get recognized here if you were Bobby Orr," says actor Larry D. Mann, a Canadian who attends all the Kings' home games.

"Have *something* good tonight," the Forum's All-American Salted Peanut-seller shouts as he mounts the stairs during a listless Kings' game against the Washington Capitals. "At least peanuts ain't so hard to swallow as this!" Down on the ice Marcel Dionne is doing what comes naturally—"dancing with the puck," his linemate Charlie Simmer calls it—but to no avail. His delicate, perfect setup is to a defenceman who simply cannot complete the obvious. A Trudeau shrug and Dionne skates off the ice, thinking to himself what he later puts into words. "What do we have?" he asks in his living room. "You see what we have. It's *terrible*!"

But that is the team, not Marcel Dionne. His is a career poorly served by mere statistics. When he was awarded the Lester B. Pearson trophy last year as hockey's most valuable player, the significance was that this award is voted on by peers, not sports writers. And it may reflect his outspokenness and daring as much as his ability. Still, for most of this season the talk has been about Los Angeles' Triple Crown Line of Dionne, Simmer and Dave Taylor. But for mid-season knee injuries to Simmer and Taylor the Dionne-led line probably would have become the highest scoring line in hockey's history. Even so, Dionne's 126 points with nine games remaining may have established him as the premier player of the game. Dionne even brags he could score 200 points if only he played for a decent team, but he also claims, unconvincingly, that this is not what matters most to him. "He's always saying how phoney those awards are, the trophies, the all-star teams," says Dave Taylor. "But I'd bet on him wanting to win it badly."

Victory, should it come, would finally stop its nearly two decades of teasing. In 1971, their first year as professionals, Lafleur was drafted first, Dionne second; and Dionne's phenomenal first year (a record 77 points compared to Lafleur's meagre 64) was soured when Montreal goaltender Ken Dryden won rookie of the year honors. Until this year, Marcel Dionne was known for but a single first—the five-year, $1.5-million contract he signed with Los Angeles in June of 1975.

"Marcel Dionne can be our Moses," Jack Kent Cooke announced on that occasion. "Marcel Dionne is no Moses," retorted Ned Harkness, the Detroit Red Wing manager who had just lost Dionne. "The only tablets he should bring down are Aspirin tablets because with him around, Cooke and the Kings are going to need plenty of them."

But now it is 1980 and the game of hockey is beginning to emerge from a prolonged mid-life crisis. In the year since the North American game discovered it could no longer get it up for the Soviets, merger between the NHL and the World

Marcel Dionne,
King of the Kings, 1980.

Hockey Association has come about and the gutted house is showing signs of falling back in order. Though 10 of the new league's 21 teams are projected to lose money this year, attendance is up five per cent thanks to sell-out crowds in such new NHL cities as Edmonton. Because of the Soviet example, the guerrilla hockey of the 1970s may be forced to switch to a creative hockey for the '80s. And as for the sport's main bugaboo, violence, an outcry against it is just now beginning to come from a few of the truly talented players, led by Marcel Dionne and echoed by the likes of Guy Lafleur, Phil Esposito and Mike Bossy. "If I had my way," says Dionne, who now serves as vice-president of the NHL Players' Association, "we would have a full debate on violence."

But Jerry Buss is naturally less concerned with the violence than he is with financial loss. "Other people think in words," he likes to say. "I think in numbers." That being so, he might well consider the following points: his Kings will lose him $900,000 this year; attendance at the Forum hockey games has declined steadily since Dionne's arrival five years ago; and Dionne is currently looking for a new five-year contract in the area of $3 million.

But J.B., as he likes to be called, is hardly a fool. He does, after all, have a PhD in physical chemistry and his idea of fun is to play Monopoly from memory. If he heard Team Canada's Dr. Derek Mackesey say that, over the past few years, "Marcel Dionne has been the heart and soul of the teams we have sent to Europe," Buss would acknowledge that this is also true of Dionne in Los Angeles, where his popularity and respect have finally risen to match his ability. The headaches have not come from Dionne, as Harkness predicted, but from those who are supposed to help him. Buss would also acknowledge the truth of what Marcel Dionne has to say about his own team, though he would be well advised to grit his teeth while listening.

"I can't do everything," Dionne said one afternoon. "My hockey's suffering. When you have a lot of people who are inferior and they don't think like you do, then a lot of people suffer. They look for leadership but it isn't going to come, because there's not enough people to back it up." Buss believes he can remedy that in a mere four years. "I'm a quick study," he says. His remarkable real estate success was not by accident, but the result of careful computer programming applied to property and land. Having at one time mathematically determined how many footsteps would wear out a carpet, he may be on the verge of discovering how many head fakes will bring him the Stanley Cup.

Should Buss have any thoughts about reducing Marcel Dionne to an equation, however, he may as well forget them. Marcel Dionne is not merely a hockey player, but also an idea, one that was originally created by a huge family back in Drummondville, and is protected and prodded by that family even today. What computer could measure the grey stucco, 17-room house at 89 13th Avenue, l'Epicerie Dionne in the front, the large kitchen behind packed with many of his 13 uncles, each with a personal touch of advice for *Le p'tit Marcel?* And what of those late Saturday evenings, the big men sitting seriously, their territories traced in empty "quart" Molson's bottles, the sound of sliding coins rising up toward the boy's bedroom where he lay awake knowing that in the morning he would have the price of a new hockey stick? How could a computer be fed the letter from *Les Canadiens* that arrived there when Marcel was barely in peewee hockey, telling his parents to take special care of him because Senator Molson and the *organization* were watching? Or how Marcel would skate about the rink after a victory, the fans reaching down to touch him, and how, when he undressed, he would find dollar bills stuffed in his gloves?

And who but Marcel Dionne himself will ever understand why he not once dared to dream of playing in the NHL, knowing that dream would be ridiculed each time he had trouble reaching over the boards to sign autographs, or when his uncles whispered in the kitchen, thinking him asleep? *He was too small.* It made the pressure even worse. "Hockey... hockey... hockey... hockey," he says, his voice dropping to a tense whisper. "I was going *nuts.*"

When faraway St. Catharines Black Hawks wooed him at 17, he jumped from the Quebec to the Ontario junior league. And when outraged home-town fans threatened court action—to keep him *where he belongs*—his parents, on a lawyer's advice, fabricated a ploy to make it seem as if they were separating. His mother, Laurette, brother and three sisters ended up in totally foreign St. Catharines, expenses to be met by the delighted new team.

He calls that his moment of truth. He began putting on weight, his playing blossomed and after four months his mother and sisters returned to the icy stares of Drummondville. The darling of Drummondville became the darling of St. Catharines, spoiled and worshipped. Two successive junior scoring titles followed, climaxing in 1971 when St. Catharines met Quebec Remparts to decide the best junior team in Canada. More accurately, the best junior player in Canada, for Quebec's star was none other than his old nemesis, Guy Lafleur. Sadly, the series turned to such violence—Dionne was savaged as a "traitor" in the Quebec press, his family had garbage thrown at them and his Aunt Denise miscarried shortly after a near riot in Quebec—that St. Catharines refused to complete the series and Quebec won by default.

Incredibly, this was not to be Marcel Dionne's low point. He was billed as "the next Gordie Howe" from the moment he arrived in Detroit, but his four years there are remembered more for the tears and anger and open fights with management than they are for his hockey. Small talk to a Detroit *Free Press* reporter about his two Dobermans and the baseball bat he carried in his car ended up as the next day's headlines: DIONNE CAN'T WAIT TO QUIT. With his dislike of the city and the team in print, Dionne was advised not to dress that night for a game against Minnesota, but he refused, sitting sobbing as he dressed and then, finally, standing up and, in a cracking voice, telling his teammates: "I'm sorry. I get confused. I make mistakes." Then he went out and scored two goals, leading the team to victory.

Leaving Detroit was less a problem than where to go. Montreal wanted him. And Toronto. "You bring that young man out here," Edmonton's Wild Bill Hunter told Eagleson associate Bill Watters, "and we'll put his name on the licence plates: Alberta—home of Marcel Dionne." Los Angeles, however, offered both the best money and the farthest escape. "It was the easiest way to go," Dionne says. With the accusations trailing him—"He can rip a team apart," Johnny Wilson, one coach offered—he came to a team that had just had its best season, standing fourth over all, and was offering defensive, disciplined hockey under coach Bobby Pulford. He was suspect from the beginning. Pulford hadn't even been told about Cooke's deal and was so distraught at first sight of his stocky little star that he assigned him immediately to the team's "Fat Squad," forced him to skate extra laps at practice with plastic sheets wrapped around his swollen stomach. But this time Dionne did not walk out on practice, as he had done in Detroit. And instead of sulking, as he might once have done, he worked and listened. "Pully thought I was a zipper-head," Dionne now says. "If he could've made me crawl, he would have. I wouldn't crawl. I respect him for what he did because after a while he knew I was not what he had heard."

Pulford discovered, as so many others have, that the tallest part of Dionne is his pride. "I don't want to kiss anyone's ass," he had decided just before turning professional and, though he has certainly suffered for his refreshing frankness, hockey's own belated maturing over recent years has meant that Detroit's "big baby" is now seen as Los Angeles's leader and highly articulate spokesman—without Dionne himself having changed much. He once said, "There seems to be a tiny part of me I can't control." But his railing against archaic management and gang-warfare hockey has in truth been extremely calculated. "If I had to do it again," he says, "I'd do it. And I'd tell you why—because I know I can play for any team in this league." Before Dionne, the outspoken hockey player was a rarity—Ted Lindsay in the '50s, Bobby Hull to a lesser extent later—but today, with Darryl Sittler fighting management in Toronto and Guy Lafleur attacking lazy, wealthy hockey players in Montreal, the cures for the ill health of hockey are coming, as it should, from the game's healthier cells. "I had to say to hell with it," says Dionne. "If that's what hockey's all about, I'll say it. It depends on how much guts you have and how much you believe in yourself."

This game is over, thankfully. Washington has come from behind to win 4–2, the contest as interesting as seeing which brand of paper towel will give away first under the faucet. Dionne, the singular example of grace and caring among so many of those he contemptuously refers to as "slackers," dresses quickly and alone in a far corner of the dressing room. His teammates know better than to speak to him following a loss, as do the local reporters. Hair still dripping from the shower, he buttons up his jacket and walks away from the disgrace, momentarily pausing in the clutch of Jerry Buss and Gordon Lightfoot. A quick handshake and Dionne leaves, silently.

Outside, in the accelerating rain, he climbs into his Mercedes and pulls away, the weight of his anger falling on the gas pedal. It is a time for avoiding thought. There is little concern for making more than $500,000 a year or even for one day being as well-known in Los Angeles as Lightfoot, as Buss has promised he one day will be.

Playing for the Kings, there is little to be gained by contemplating the game of hockey, where failure is beyond a single man's prevention. Better instead to think of baseball, a sport he loves better, and how he treasures those suspended moments in the batter's box because "when you're up there you're only one man, alone—nobody can help you."

He knows that it is nearing midnight. With the time difference it will shortly be morning in Drummondville, and the radio in the big house on 13th Avenue will report that the home-town wonder managed but a single assist in the loss, and he knows that it will not be enough. "They want me to win the scoring title so badly," he will say next afternoon. "*More* than I want it."

But he will also know that words are not necessarily truth. "If I was not Marcel Dionne and he was not Guy Lafleur," he will say slowly, "maybe then it wouldn't matter so much." Then he will say, "But..." And after that, nothing.

Marcel Dionne won the scoring title that year, but it would be the first and last time. Wayne Gretzky and Mario Lemieux would dominate the points award until Dionne left the sport in 1989. As good as Dionne was, the Kings of that era will be better remembered for their gold and purple uniforms than for an abundance of talent. Despite the many failings of his team, Dionne was finally able to overshadow Guy Lafleur in one regard: he still sits in third place behind Gretzky and Gordie Howe in total career points with 1,771, while Lafleur is 15th. Dionne now lives in western New York state where he runs a sports marketing company.

Hockey Goes Global

Team Canada in War and Peace

Jack Ludwig

December, 1972—Say you wanted to do it all as a film script. Who would believe you? Who would believe that a country harbored a grand illusion that it was mighty in only one thing, hockey; that in order for this might to remain supreme it had to destroy the pretender following in its wake? Canadians, men and women, held to the credo that hockey was *our game*. When the Soviet Union and Czechoslovakia started winning in international competition and in the Olympics, no Canadian had any doubt that we could absolutely demolish the opposition if we would only put our best hockey players together on one team and not the 10th-raters classed as "amateurs" who had been wearing Canada's colors in recent sad international hockey years.

We knew that five, six or seven hundred "better" players were made ineligible by international ice hockey rules. Top among these were, of course, the 100 or so "very best" playing in the NHL. These guys, we knew, could whip the pretenders any day of the week: we wanted a series between the USSR and a team of NHL stars not to prove anything to ourselves. *Our convictions required no proofs*. We wanted that contest only as a means of teaching the usurpers what hockey was really all about.

Most of us thought the match would never come off. That fools in international federations and fools in the NHL would never find a way to make this match happen. Suddenly, however, the NHL and the NHL Players' Association and Hockey Canada put together this Team Canada; just as suddenly the confrontation devoutly to be wished was *here*. We couldn't wait to see the USSR wiped out on the ice.

That was the script we turned out to see shot on September 2, 1972, in Montreal. We saw another script unfold. We saw Canada lose 7–3. We watched an entire nation plunge into the depths of a terrible doubt: if we weren't the country that could do it all in hockey, who were we? If our illusion about ourselves on the ice was so palpably false, what was there that we could cling to as true?

Some observers tried to find working alibis: cop-outs abounded. We'd been outfoxed, or, to shift animals, the Soviets had been playing possum when our scouts weaseled their way into the USSR. *They* played together more. *They* played together longer. We were just an itsy-bitsy country and they were so-o-o-o-o-o big. Their winters are longer, I, a Winnipegger, had to hear!

Yet, when the new Soviet-scripted script began to unfold, it, too, was full of surprises. By game four, in Vancouver, which Team Canada lost 5–3 and might have lost 8–3 or 9–3, the Canadian myth hung by a hair: by game five, the first played in Moscow, in which Team Canada blew a three-goal lead and ended up losing 5–4, Canada's situation seemed hopeless. A once mighty hockey nation acted as if it had been castrated. But then, out of a seemingly hopeless situation, down in the series three games to one, with one game tied, Team Canada regenerated itself, and regenerated this nation. Three games in a row we won—each one with Toronto's Paul Henderson scoring the winning goal. From the slough of despond—call it the Moscow River—a cartoonish Jackie Canuck emerged drenched and dripping, put his hat back on at a cocky angle, and walked off into the European sunset!

Oh how the unmighty had risen!

Canadians in Moscow shot champagne corks into the night air. Gallons of the sweet bubbly foamed over glasses in salute to the team—and *us*! Our nation was restored. The myth still hung by that thin hair. Our manhood, our macho, our national selves were, even if pounded a bit, still intact. Drunk or sober, show a Canadian in Moscow even a lapel flag and he was just as likely as not to break right into *O Canada*. When Paul Henderson scored what proved to be the winning goal in game eight, Canadians in Moscow went wild, but Canadians at home went even wilder. People in offices jigged a dance not seen in the country since the Second World War ended. Cars stopped on the 401 in the middle of the rush hour. *O Canada* was sung here and there and again and again and again. The Team Canada players who had been bums and bushers and lushes and louts now were only heroes, and Canadians were the baskers in victory's heroic lights.

But all the questions raised by the series yet remained. Was hockey still our thing the way we thought it was before this series began? Were our players getting all the help they required in order to make the most of their talents?

We wanted simple answers to the questions raised by the heroic Canadian turnaround: the fans in Moscow wanted to be told their flags and cheering were the cause of it all. Mystics sought a more profound cause, something to do with Canadian will and the triumph of the indomitable Canadian soul. How else could a team come back when down so low and *win*?

I suggest a partial answer. I suggest that hidden behind the Show Biz shoot-it-in-and-chase-it hockey played by the NHL was the natural hockey talent Team Canada players didn't always have to use in that NHL. I suggest that in the days that followed that 7–3 Montreal loss, each and every one of the players painfully dredged up his memories of hockey past: that someone like Phil Esposito, who in the past years had become a crease-parker waiting for a Wayne Cashman or Kenny Hodge to get the puck to him, turned himself back into a brilliant all-round hockey player who, in spite of the fantastic speed of the USSR men, forechecked with them and backchecked with them and did his own digging in the corners: that Paul Henderson, almost instantly recognizing the challenge in the actual play of the USSR, rather than the silly reports about their failures, pitched his performance at the high level set by Valeriy Kharlamov and Aleksandr Yakushev, driving himself relentlessly from shift to shift in ways nobody had seen him perform either as a Detroit or a Toronto NHLer: that Pat Stapleton and Bill White—as well as Gary Bergman and Guy Lapointe—joined the injured Serge Savard in changing their style of play so that they once again were defencemen with some commitment to keeping the play away from their goalkeeper: that, in short, the Team Canada players went to school to the USSR team, that they learned and adapted and did this by giving up the bad habits picked up in the lazy years of NHL Show Biz.

And thus the Canadian identity crisis passed with only a long "Whew!" On the brink of a national wipe-out, the team gave up its carousing heavy-drinking John Wayne image and, like the Soviet team, *played hockey*. It withstood the turmoil caused by someone like Vic Hadfield quitting the team, and going back to the United States, which paid his tab year after year. That Rich Martin and Gil Perreault and Jocelyn Guèvremont went back too was no help to Team Canada's spirit or practice. Both Harry Sinden, Canada's coach, and Jean Beliveau told me they were shocked by Hadfield's action.

To start at the beginning, though, is to remind us all what it was we felt as the first game neared. We didn't feel any apprehension at all, I suggest, only a great excitement because a wished-for event was finally coming to pass. Almost nobody I knew entertained the slightest notion that Team Canada could lose a game, let alone the series. It was going to be the greatest *exhibition* of good hockey ever seen—this was our expectation as the first game in Montreal approached.

Paul Henderson after scoring the winning goal, September 28, 1972.

On Saturday, Sept. 2, 1972, a very warm day in Montreal, I sat sunning on the lawn of some friends in Westmount, talking hockey. Before six on a sultry evening this Montrealer, as much of a hockey nut as I am, and I were eating dinner at Moishe's, and talking hockey. All around us hockey was the only subject at every table. Everyone this night was some kind of hockey nut.

Shortly after Team Canada's training camp opened in Toronto I began watching the players work out in that familiar kibitz-loaf-spurt style that goes with being an NHLer. One of the firmer assumptions still alive in those late August days was that anybody good enough to make the NHL didn't need further coaching. We assumed, too, that the USSR guys, with their "shoddy skates" (as NHLers and hockey writers referred to those things carrying the Soviet players in a blur around the Forum) and crummy sticks and lousy pads and gloves and helmets were born losers. Canada wept a little for the poverty of these guys, and rushed to deliver some real equipment to them so that the contrast between pro and have-not would not be too blatant. The Soviet players, in contrast to Team Canada, carried their own equipment, or came to the rink already dressed. After practice, one of their first-stringers would actually gather pucks up in a green plastic pail! It was as if some intermediate team from Neepawa had blundered into an NHL enclosure, oblivious of the fate waiting inside the "bullring."

Their coach, Vsevolod Bobrov, carried a hockey stick in practice, and looked much like the coach of a university team—terribly erect though, in great shape, balding a little, a man with obvious class. He was the only USSR hockey player ever to receive the Order of Lenin—no small recognition in that country. He and his assistant, Boris Kulagin, had lovely titles like "Honoured Coach" and "Honoured Sports Master" of the USSR. When asked about his team, Bobrov was modest: when asked about Team Canada, he seemed, like his players, in awe. Many of his players had a dream fulfilled—not just to play against NHL "stars" but to see Bobby Orr in the flesh, and, if lucky enough, get Bobby's autograph.

So, finally, it was here. We filed into the Forum like small kids anxious to get first crack at Santa Claus. Team Canada came out on the ice in their dazzling bright red uniforms with a huge white sunburst maple leaf disappearing down their fronts. The fans cheered loudest for the Montreal Canadiens on the team—building up to "high" for Yvan Cournoyer, a little restrained for Pete Mahovlich and Guy Lapointe, then "higher" for Frank Mahovlich, and deafeningly "highest" for Ken Dryden. Everyone was in a good mood. Even Prime Minister Trudeau, walking the red carpet to where the ceremonial puck was to be dropped, got a hand.

Almost as soon as Mr. Trudeau got back to his seat, after the national anthem was sung, silently in French, and falteringly in English, Team Canada did exactly what we all expected. Gary Bergman got the puck to Frank Mahovlich who passed it onto Phil Esposito's stick and poof—Canada was leading, 1–0, and only 30 seconds had passed. At that rate of scoring Canada would win 120–0.

But when at 1:03 Paul Henderson was called for tripping, the USSR team began to look *formidable*. Twice they got off shots that Dryden had to be good on. They didn't score, but something was quite evident. In races for the puck, they won. When a Team Canada player and a USSR player banged together the Soviet guy barely budged and the Team Canada man frequently bounced back. Ron Ellis went charging into a Soviet player whose head was seemingly down, hit what felt like a concrete pillar, and himself went down. At 6:32, however, Henderson caught USSR goaler Vladislav Tretiak nodding, and banged home a pass from Bobby Clarke. This made it 2–0. At that rate, Team Canada could only win by 10–0, a sudden drastic drop. Five minutes later, the USSR did the impossible—they put a puck past Ken Dryden.

At 11:40, a big stoop-shouldered hard-skating left winger, Aleksandr Yakushev, took a pass from Vladimir Shadrin and set up Evgeni Zimin: Dryden was *beaten*. His defence was nowhere. His forwards were being outskated, outhustled and outgunned.

A pall settled over the Forum. Team Canada so obviously lacked spark. Even explosive Yvan Cournoyer looked slow. At 17:19 Aleksandr Ragulin tripped Brad Park. Team Canada coach Harry Sinden sent out Park, Seiling and the highest-scoring line in NHL history, Ratelle, Hadfield, Gilbert. Gilbert clumsily fanned on the puck, Boris Mikhailov shot into the clear, passed to Vladimir Petrov and, unbelievably, the score was *tied*.

We could not believe what we were seeing. The USSR had more cool, better puck control, better recovery. Their goalie, when tested, showed incredible skill and command. *Tretiak*. The man, we realized, was young enough to be playing *junior* hockey in Canada!

The crowd sat in silence: when the organist tried to get the usual NHL response to a fight, or go Canada go, the cheers were chokingly unenthusiastic. Almost no sound and even less fury. In front of TV sets fans watched in horror. Not only Canadians but Americans who believed, with us, that Team Canada was the greatest because the NHL was the greatest: hadn't Gerry Eskenazi, hockey reporter for the astute *New York Times*, said, "The NHL will slaughter them in eight straight"?

With less than three minutes to go in the second period the predicted "slaughter" began, but the victim was Team Canada: number 17, someone called Valeriy Kharlamov, stickhandled his way around the all-star defence as if he were playing against peewees, scored, and the USSR *was in the lead*! All of Team Canada looked terrible. Errant passes went skimming over the ice. Suddenly, "big leaguers" who couldn't catch up with a USSR guy tried, instead, to trip him or hack at him. Chippy bush play—from NHLers!

At 9:46 of the second period the Montreal crowd actually booed Team Canada—

for icing the puck. By 10:18, when the USSR went ahead 4–2 on an incredibly fast wrist-shot release by that same Kharlamov, he was the man Montreal applauded. Kharlamov, and goalie Tretiak. At 17:50 of this same period Montreal's organist played "I'm Dreaming Of A White Christmas." A guy near the press box said, "Man, this makes the Stanley Cup pure sh——."

What was evident, by then, was not only the USSR's superb physical condition but its equally superb preparation: Bobrov and Kulagin said they had looked at films of 1971 and 1972 Stanley Cup play. They had obviously seen a lot. They came in on Dryden believing he could be *stickhandled around*, made to drop to the ice. A man his height—six feet four—had to have trouble handling low off-the-ice shots on his glove side.

The Montreal crowd came to life only once in the dreaded third period: when Bobby Clarke, assisted by Ron Ellis and Paul Henderson, scored. Team Canada looked alive and almost well. But at 13:32, Boris Mikhailov broke in on Dryden, drew him to one side, and lifted a backhand past him. It all looked so easy. Less than a minute later Evgeni Zimin took advantage of a Brad Park goof to make the score 6–3. With five minutes left the same people who had been dying to get into the Forum couldn't wait to get out. They were spared, as Dryden wasn't, Yakushev's backhand score and the mock cheers for Dryden that followed. They didn't hear the boos another Canadien, Guy Lapointe, got for what the crowd thought was a cheap shot at a Soviet player. Phil Esposito was booed for the same kind of chintzy play. At the buzzer Team Canada, led by Esposito, charged off the ice. Only three men—Ken Dryden, who had given up *seven* goals, Red Berenson, and Peter Mahovlich—stayed around to congratulate the winners. Team Canada had not been told to line up to shake hands, Harry Sinden told me. Doug Fisher of Hockey Canada said it certainly had: the Montreal crowd took the omission to be willful. Its heroes had let the country down, so people said, even in deportment.

Montreal's *Sunday Express* headlined the national disbelief in letters big and black enough to announce the start of World War III — WE LOST. A headline in *Dimanche-Matin* said, LE CANADA ECRASE 7–3: "*écrasé*"—crushed, overwhelmed, humiliated. The loss on September 2 raised doubts about even our national purpose.

Hundreds of thousands of people who "live" hockey all season long went into shock with that 7–3 loss. In Toronto on September 4, Team Canada turned things around 4–1, but nobody was convinced. In Winnipeg Team Canada carried a 4–2 lead half way through the second period, only to have the Soviet "university line," three men of 21, Lebedev, Bodunov, Anisin, combine to tie it up. And the doubts began all over again.

But what almost destroyed Team Canada was the 5–3 loss in Vancouver. The USSR made that one look so easy. Many of us believed they had actually "laid off" when they could have scored three or four more goals in the third period. In that game Bill Goldsworthy was hit with two deserved penalties for essentially meaningless muscling: two *identical* power-play goals quickly followed. And booing. The booing stepped up later in the second period when an easygoing clean player like Frank Mahovlich held goalie Tretiak so he couldn't get back to his nets. The booing became loud and bitter at the end of the second period. The Vancouver fans didn't mind the team losing as much as they clearly objected to a classy player like Frank Mahovlich doing something unworthy.

It was this booing that embittered quite a few Team Canada players, Phil Esposito most prominent among them. Nobody could have booed Phil for his own play since game one. In Toronto, Winnipeg, Vancouver he became the take-over guy who cooled his side, getting bigger and bigger with each game. Esposito was truly a giant in those Canadian games, he and Paul Henderson—who also got better and better and, for my money, was the outstanding player in the total range of eight games. Nobody wanted to boo Tony Esposito either; or even Ken Dryden, who, after two games, had the incredible goals-against average of six!

What had happened was, truly, in the eyes of hockey nuts, a national disaster: places like Dieppe and Dunkirk turned up in accounts of the Montreal and Vancouver games. Rumors of dissension sprang up. The benched New York Rangers were as unhappy with Team Canada as Canada was, obviously, unhappy with those Rangers.

But lo! in Edmonton, Toronto, Montreal a great band of hockey nuts was gathering for a flag-displaying invasion of Moscow. Decked out with red maple leafs on their hats, sweat shirts, waving mammoth flags, their lapels covered with flag pins, Canada's hockey pilgrims hit Moscow with tons of Kleenex, toilet tissue, instant coffee and booze. Women were even more fanatic than men. Americans from Boston, Detroit, Chicago, New York—all old-established NHL towns—joined other Americans from "new" NHL cities like Philadelphia and Minneapolis and even Los Angeles to infiltrate the Canadian invaders converging on Moscow. Red-eyed, impossible to surfeit alcoholically, the hockey nuts staggered into Moscow, hot to go, with cheers busting in their throats, and a million unsung *O Canada*s too.

The Canadian team, an Air Canada hostess who had worked one of their two planes told me, carried more booze with them than she had ever seen before in her life. They were a wonderful bunch of guys, she added, "except for one or two." I wondered how much stuff the men would have brought with them had they been leading, as we once thought they would be, the USSR by four games to none. Once in Moscow the players stayed more or less to themselves, working out at the Dvoretz Sporta—Sports Palace—every day for a couple of hours, then taking short walks around the Intourist Hotel which was quite close to the Kremlin, the Bolshoi Theatre, and GUM, Moscow's large department store.

Only Ken Dryden, of all the people on the team I knew about, ventured out on his own. He was also one of the few people on the team who, with his wife, looked forward excitedly to seeing Plisyetskaya dance in her own ballet, *Anna Karenina*. That took place on the eve of the all-important eighth game. In the dressing room, after practice that morning, I asked a bunch of players who was going. "We have to go, Phil?" asked brother Tony Esposito. "We can always leave at half time," Phil reassured him.

A number of the players wouldn't be caught dead at a "fag" thing like the ballet—even though their wives or girl friends were dying to attend the famous Bolshoi. Those who went went, in large part, reluctantly. I sat near Frank Mahovlich and his wife: at the first intermission he raised his eyebrows to ask me if this was it, I shook my head. Ron Ellis, who was on the other side of me, never did come back after intermission one. At the second break Frank asked, "Is that it?" Again I had to tell him *no*. He stayed to the end—which was a lot more than could be said for his teammates. That night I asked Harry Sinden what his players would do if it were established that ballet exercises were the precisely right muscle-builders for a guy getting ready to play hockey: "Don't be silly," he said.

Yet, from what I had learned in my tour of the editorial offices of Soviet Physical Culture and Sport, and the Army Club (with Ken Dryden), and the Institute for Physical Culture and Sport (again, with Dryden), I was convinced that were someone to tell the USSR players that ballet was what they *needed* they would turn to it—without fear that by doing so they were surrendering their "tough guy" athletic manhood.

Most Canadians were struck by the clean streets in Moscow and it's true that the tourist areas were remarkably clean. But far more interesting were the old slum areas of Moscow the authorities didn't want people to visit. Here the streets were narrow, humped, filled with litter among other signs of human presence frowned upon by the commissars. The houses were wooden, askew, battered, winter-harried, something like the western Canadian slum areas immigrants settled in years ago.

Moscow teemed with extraordinary human beings, and choked on secret police and finks you couldn't move two steps without bumping into. Resentment against this kind of terrorism made some Muscovites welcome Team Canada with a political significance none of us had foreseen: in the halls of hotels, on the streets, even in the rink itself, people who knew they weren't being observed—on staircases, say, or passing in the top-floor press corridors—would flex a thumb-up salute with one hand, and say "Kanada, da," or "Feel Esposeeto," referring not to Phil as a player only, but as a counterforce.

The correspondents stationed in Moscow saw the series far differently from the way North American observers watched it. For them every action, from a challenge to the referee to any other rejection of absolute authority, was a showpiece Soviet citizens were witnessing for perhaps the first time. Most Muscovites were genuinely shocked by the antics of Esposito or Gary Bergman or Rod Gilbert in the penalty box: others, quite political in their orientation, took the act to mean far more than what our guys intended it to mean. A choke sign was somehow a semaphor of freedom: someone giving a cop the finger or the arm wasn't being a boor but a political hero.

Pravda, reporting on the first game in Moscow (game five in the series), began with a wry observation that anyone who wondered how strong the roof was at the rink now knew it was pretty strong if the incredible cheering of the Canadians hadn't lifted it off. *Pravda*—and *Izvestia*, and *Trud*, and *Soviet Sport*, and *Football*—could be expansive after this game. The USSR, pouring five goals in on Tony Esposito in the last period, had overcome a 3–0 and 4–1 lead to win 5–4 and go up in the series three games to one, with one tie.

At the end of the game Tony Esposito slammed his stick down on the ice as brother Phil rushed over to console him. "There's no way we lost that game," Rod Gilbert told me, "we gave it away." On the press bus later that night I encountered Jean Beliveau. "I wondered," he said, "when I was vacationing in Germany, how we could lose that one in Montreal. Now I know. We collapsed. We just fell apart in the last 10 minutes."

Those questions that had been raised not about Team Canada but about the USSR were with me when I got up the next morning. I decided to go to see the editorial minds of the publishing house Soviet Physical Culture and Sport and talk with them about USSR sports philosophy. A man from the Tass Agency, who spoke English very well, joined in our talks. From these people I learned that the hockey program was only one of a vast and complicated assortment of programs calculated to keep the population in top physical condition—and the USSR teams internationally competitive. The put-down line in our talks came later: "We have our eyes," an editor said to me without blinking, "not on this interesting match but on the international world championships to be played in March."

Next day Dryden and I decided to head out to the Army Club, that great Moscow sports complex that delivered a dozen players to the Soviet team—including Tretiak. Dryden had the usual Moscow difficulty picking up a cab so while waiting for him I decided to see what was happening in sports other than hockey. It was 2:30 in the afternoon as I started to walk through the Army Club's sporting facilities. In one of the largest buildings I found a dozen children doing gymnastics with an astonishing ease and almost balletlike grace. They stayed with no exercise overly long, but moved effortlessly from one motion to another. They all seemed most anxious to do what they were doing, and had great rapport with their instructors, most of whom were Olympics participants of fairly recent date. In the swimming pool building I saw children learning how to dive, and swim, with tremendous emphasis on form. It was almost as if each sport had been subjected to sophisticated systems analysis which then prescribed exactly what the muscles should be able to do in order to facilitate, say, freestyle swimming, or the butterfly, or the breaststroke.

What was even more impressive was what the boys were doing outside. Kids between eight and 10 were practising slapshots against a kind of handball wall. The purpose of the exercise, as far as I could see, was to keep the ball moving, and not trap it with the stick but rather smack at it and set up a rebound or ricochet someone else would have to deal with. I found Dryden and together we walked over to where those eight- and nine- and 10-year-olds were continuing their workout. They had put down their sticks and, arms linked, back to back, were taking turns pulling each other up on their respective backs, holding for a count of three, then smoothly settling the boy's feet down so he in turn could pick his partner up on *his* back. Then they unlinked arms, and took turns carrying each other, walking first, and then running. All this time Coach Brezhnev kept up a steady good-humored chatter, always calling the boys by their first names, hurrying them along.

When the carrying-and-running was over—in about two minutes—the boys picked up their sticks and began to stick handle rubber balls through a medicine-ball slalom obstacle course that their coach had set up. When all the kids were through the slalom course they turned immediately to stick handling the ball all over the play area, trying, again, to stay out of each other's way, and keep the ball moving with the same darting, thrusting, pullback motion we had seen on the ice with Valeriy Kharlamov. Gary Bergman had told me most NHL forwards, if they're good, have one move they can put on a defenceman: the rare player has *two* moves—which almost nobody can handle. Kharlamov, Bergman said, put *three* moves on him. As I watched these kids go through their routines, I could understand that.

I asked Dryden if anything like this went on at hockey camps such as small boys attend in Canada during the summers. He assured me *no*. I asked him if peewee coaches had any such routines to teach the fundamental skills to young kids—again he said *no*, not as far as he knew.

Before the final game I spoke to Arkady Tchernishev, coach of the Moscow Dynamos and assistant to Anatoli Tarasov during the USSR's best years in Olympic and international competition. He told me a couple of things I think Canada should know: that these boys we had been watching were strictly forbidden to body check until they were a certain size—and age, usually close to 16. The emphasis on stick handling and skating continued through the first seven or eight years of a boy's hockey beginnings. Ninety-nine per cent of the kids in the Soviet Union—unlike the ones we had seen at the Army Club—skated *only* on outdoor rinks the whole of their playing lives. Apart from the Dvoretz Sporta where the Team Canada-USSR series was being played, and the Army rink we had seen, the only other artificial surface at that moment was strictly for figure skaters. Dynamo was building its own rink with an artificial ice plant—but did not have those facilities right now.

So next day, Tuesday, September 26, when game seven was coming up and Tony Esposito, not Dryden, would be in goal, I picked Dryden up at the Intourist and we took a long taxi ride out to the academic institution behind all the coaching and training going on in the Soviet Union, the *Institute* of Physical Culture and Sport—by this time I understood the significance of the "and" in its title. It poured this day and Dryden was without a raincoat—his having been pinched in Sweden. We found ourselves in an old villa in an advanced state of decay. From the entry on Kasakova Street we ran through a series of arches and then made our way into the old building. Entering, we found ourselves—astonishingly!—in an anatomy lab: at both ends of this long narrow room hideous plaster statue imitations of Greek poses presided: the walls held specimens of human bone, and detailed diagrams of the muscle structure of all parts of the body, including the face. After gawking, we decided to investigate further, opened a door onto a room lined with specimens of tissue and organs. In that room we found our first student, a young man named Andrei who knew as much English as I knew Russian. It took us no time at all to realize we both needed help.

Soon faculty members of the institute came out to greet us: in my faltering Russian I introduced them to Dryden and explained that I myself was a writer anxious to understand what this institution was all about. In a few minutes Dryden and I found ourselves seated across from six or seven institute faculty members and a very pretty young lady who was to be our interpreter. Before we could get properly under way, the chief of the Hockey Department, a man in his early 60s, at most five feet six, stared at Dryden: "You are too tall," he said.

Dryden laughed. "We," the man continued, "would never let someone your height try to become a goalie."

"There are disadvantages," Dryden said, "but there are advantages too—my reach. I can cover a lot of goal."

"Never," the little man said. "The disadvantages are much bigger than the advantages."

From this conference we learned that the institute was one mammoth phys-ed department to which Soviet stars in all sports came to study coaching. The ordinary course of events would take five years to complete, but someone engaged in Olympic competition or international hockey, say, could stretch that out. The institute offered a regular university degree and was the highest form of education for aspiring coaches. In order to coach, men had to learn all about the body, about what the body could do and what it should not be expected to do. A coach was a master of physical culture as well as a strategist and tactician: he would no more think of sending under-conditioned athletes into a contest than he would try to drive a car without filling its tank with fuel.

When we told the institute people what it was we did in Canada they couldn't believe that coaches would leave *the body* and its conditioning completely to *trainers*. Our coaches of the young, to them, were either pretty dumb, or worse, incompetent.

On any level, the most important day was Thursday, September 28—when Canada took it all. That game, as everyone knows, was a wild one. In the first period J.P. Parisé, objecting to a penalty, charged the referee, and was kicked out, which made Sinden explode and send a chair skidding across the ice. Later there was the incredible sight of Alan Eagleson, held by the Soviet cops like a New Year baby in a stork's bill, being rescued by an armored division of Team Canada's padded finest, led by Pete Mahovlich, six feet eight on skates, and all of him swinging; released, Eagleson gave the cops an unplanned full-arm and single-finger salute television cameras have recorded for posterity. To show they were still the toughest force in the building, they rushed reserves in on the double.

Those reserves were standing shoulder to shoulder when, with only 34 seconds left in the game tied 5–5, Paul Henderson took a Phil Esposito pass and banged home the winning goal. Every Canadian flag in the rink was out and waving: people who had been drunk with despair at the end of the second period when Team Canada was behind, 5–3, found victory a transforming lift. The moment the light went on for that goal Ken Dryden took off for the fastest length a goalie ever skated, ending with him draped around Paul Henderson who was being pounded by players, coaches, Team Canada officials, all of them suddenly on the ice and whooping. The countdown of the final 12 seconds was the loudest sounds the Soviets had heard that night—even louder than the blasting *O Canada* that roared out of Canadian throats—and American throats too (they were provided the words to *O Canada* on small orange cards), as well as from a few furtive Russian throats (the singers reading from a transliterated text!). "I don' care how we won, we won!" a Calgarian roared in vodka-ese.

His was probably the majority view. I have little doubt that his was the majority Team Canada view. After all, now women and men could stand in the streets and shout, "We're Number One, we're Number One" in another American imported catchphrase, and that upraised forefinger would get its message across to any Muscovite. Now it was assumed Canada's primacy in hockey had been clearly demonstrated—and in what dramatic terms! *Oh what a great day this was to be a Canadian!* An entire nation rose from the barroom floor and rocketed up over the moon. It was in many ways touching, the people gathered at the Intourist Hotel to cheer each and every Team Canada player and his wife or fiancée back into the hotel after the victory party at Hotel Metropole down the street. Let anyone in Moscow say "O" and the whole of *O Canada* was sure to follow. It was a great comeback, and a fantastic victory. And should have no "buts."

As I think of it all—and celebrate the great players who really came through in that final game—Henderson, Phil Esposito, Dryden, Pat Stapleton, Bill White and—for his one and only good hockey night—Brad Park: when I remember the look on Yvan Cournoyer's face when he scored the tying goal—the team was full of hockey at that brilliant end. Yet, as I think of it all, I come back to those kids at the Army Club and wonder if we have the stature to learn anything from what we experienced that September. Whether it isn't time for a real double take that shows us we've been deluding ourselves and hoaxing our hockey players—no, all our young people engaged in athletics.

What's needed now, I suggest, is a revolution. The revolution will turn its attention to helping boys who want to play hockey build the muscles and the skills needed to play hockey *best*. The NHL will have to rethink its training camp programs: the NHL will have to get itself some *coaches* and people who want to coach in hockey will have to use their imaginations, and their intelligence, and open hockey up to new possibilities. Unless that happens this great Moscow triumph could only be a final epitaph: it would make a mockery of Team Canada's achievement if the final word on Canadian hockey became:

Their greatest victory was also their last.

Best known as a writer of short stories and novels, Jack Ludwig was a contributing editor at Maclean's during 1973 and 1974. He wrote two non-fiction books on hockey including one on the 1972 Summit series.

The Deck Was Stacked

Michael Posner

October 4, 1976—Of all conclusions now being drawn from last month's Canada Cup, the least persuasive is that Canada once again reigns supreme in hockey. Anybody naive or chauvinistic enough to believe that Rogatien Vachon, Bobby Orr or Darryl Sittler have rescued the great Canadian game from all those barbarous imitators in Europe deserves a week in Murmansk with Alan Eagleson. Second prize is two weeks.

Admittedly, Team Canada won the first legitimate world cup of hockey—and with it the dubious privilege of instant sanctification by the Canadian media. But they played all their games in Canadian arenas, before heavily partisan crowds, on smaller ice surfaces inhospitable to the free-skating European style. Their schedule gave them two easy games (against Finland and the United States) before facing the heavyweight Swedes, Russians and Czechs. They were close to families, suffered none of the gastric surprises of a foreign diet and could read in at least one official language the daily hallelujahs of the sporting press. Given those edges, the only wonder would have been their losing.

It should also be remembered that the Soviets did not send their best possible squad; that the Czechs got inconsistent goaltending (good as he was, Vladimir "Godzilla" Dzurilla too often played like the B-club goaltender he is back in Brno); that the Swedes were ill-prepared to play 60 minutes of hockey; that the Americans used one end of their sticks better than the other, producing an impressive number of stitches but not too many goals; and that the flying Finns left their horsepower in Helsinki.

Those quibbles aside, it's only fair to add that the team put together by Montreal Canadiens general manager Samuel Pollock represented the best collection of talent ever seen in Canada; that they beat some pretty fair hockey teams; and that, in doing so, they provided the finest display of hockey Canadians are likely to see for some time. And there's the rub: in the wake of this tournament, too many people are only too acutely aware that the game poet Al Purdy once called "the Canadian specific"

Bobby Orr anchoring Team Canada, September, 1976.

has become the Canadian soporific, Saturday night's cure for insomnia. Worse, the Stanley Cup—that annual rite of spring (it used to be winter, but most NHL owners weren't back from Florida and needed some diversion in May) becomes a minor-league trophy. Can Les Habs hold off the vengeful Flyers? Can Bobby Orr resurrect the moribund Black Hawks? Does anyone care? The only question that can matter now is when Team Canada will again meet the Russians and the Czechs. Eagleson has seen the future, and it is not the Colorado Rockies.

More positively, the series may have altered the North American concept of coaching. The Western press once made a great joke of the Soviet coaching system, as convivial as the Kremlin, but not as easy to penetrate. How could any team with four coaches succeed? Wasn't it amusing to see two or three guys simultaneously directing traffic behind the bench? Apparently not. In fact, it was so clearly unamusing that the Team Canada brain trust itself elected the four-coach system. And though Scotty Bowman and Bobby Kromm were plainly the men in charge, it was

Don Cherry—consigned to watch Team Canada from the stands—who noticed the Czech goalkeepers coming out too far and committing themselves too soon. "If you can fake the shot and keep going, you can beat them," he said. That observation, delivered to the dressing room before the overtime period with the Czechs, remained in Darryl Sittler's memory long enough for him to fake a shot at the blue line, skate wide and put the winning goal behind a "committed" Dzurilla.

Finally, the Canada Cup provided an opportunity for some great hockey players to show off their remarkable skills, for Rogie Vachon (stop), Dennis Potvin (hit), Gilbert Perreault (skate), and Bobby Clarke (check) to do what they do as well as or better than anyone else in the world. But no one was more impressive than Bobby Orr, crippled knee notwithstanding. Viewed from the top of the arena, hockey is a game of geometry, a kind of high-speed chess. From the top it is possible to see not only the million things a player may do with the puck in any situation, but the one thing he should do. Nine times out of 10, Orr does that one thing—as if he too could see the flow of play from the top. His shot is wicked, his passing crisp, his control of the game awesome. But his instinct for knowing precisely what to do with the puck, and the exact moment to do it, surpasses understanding. He is a genuine marvel. It's nice to know that Canada won the tournament, but it's a hell of a lot nicer to know that Bobby Orr is still able to perform as the game's supreme craftsman.

Darryl Sittler's overtime goal in Montreal gave Team Canada a two-game sweep in the best of three playoff final against the world champion Czech team.

Michael Posner was a senior editor and writer at Maclean's *for ten years ending in 1985. He has worked at several Canadian magazines and newspapers and has written books on politics and the arts.*

Exploding the Myth

Hal Quinn

February 26, 1979—As the teams warmed up for the third and decisive game of the Challenge Cup the second weekend in February, the National Hockey League All-Stars blasted randomly bouncing pucks at a goaltender who had just stepped onto the ice. Youngsters hung over the boards screaming for some little acknowledgement from their demigod heroes. At the other end of the rink, the red-sweatered Soviet National Team sprinted from blue line to goal line and the team's captain flipped pucks to alternate corners of the net as the goaltender gradually flexed and stretched. The white jerseys swarmed in, two against a defenceman, slapping passes that drifted into the corner boards, managing one shot in three against the goalie. The red sweaters, meanwhile, flew in a figure eight, first to their backhand, then to their forehand, dancing the goalie from left to right.

With New York's Madison Square Garden's ice glistening, thousands of partisans roaring and millions of fans around the world fixed to their television sets, the crucible of Canada's unofficial national sport was unveiled. Moments after the contest began, Bryan Trottier rubbed his leather glove in the face of Alexander Skvortsov, Lanny McDonald menaced Helmut Balderis with the butt end of his stick and Don Marcotte slammed Valeri Vasilyev into the boards. When the final buzzer mercifully sounded with the Soviets ahead 6–0, Ed Snider, owner of the NHL's Philadelphia Flyers, called it a monstrosity, "the worst disgrace in hockey history."

If ever there was a touchstone of national pride, a focal point of unanimity that transcended language and distance among Canadians, it was hockey. Since the late 1800s, it has been called our own, an island of superiority unique, unchallenged, undefended. It was.

Arrogant rowdies had condescended to waltz and elbow their way past the weak-ankled, timid pretenders of mid-century, as the nation smirked. But when the international crown was usurped by *their* amateurs, when our redefined idealists couldn't win it back, there was always the National Hockey League—executor of the true jewels of the sport. They were finally uncased in the third quarter of the century and defeated the Soviets only by feverish emotion and last-minute miracles. A weaker Soviet assault was turned back in 1976, but only just.

This time, this "Series of the Century," this three-game Challenge Cup of 1979 was to be different. This time the $200,000-a-year pearls were to be in peak physical condition at their mid-season, play on their size of ice surface, with their fans and their officials in two games. And it *was* different. On Feb. 11, the touchstone exploded on foreign soil, the NHL myth disintegrated and the crown travelled 5,000 miles to the east, probably never to return.

The teams faced each other amid the most grandiose blare the NHL could muster and New York and the American media have ever ignored. For two periods of the first game, Canadian fantasies, hoarded over the last two decades, were given some substance. From then on, the vapors evaporated in the Soviet swirl and the NHL and its disciples were left with the truth. During the 180 minutes of play, the Soviets dominated for 140, outscored the NHL 13–8 and held them scoreless for the final 94 minutes and 54 seconds while scoring nine times.

All the elbows, high sticks, crosschecks, boardings, punches, threats and body slams rang hollow as Soviet captain Boris Mikhailov laughed in their faces and the Soviets, as a team, displayed pure hockey skills demonstrated only by individuals in the history of North American hockey.

With eight months to prepare, the NHL introduced the All-Stars to each other three days before Game 1. The league packaged the event with the hope of attracting a much-needed U.S. television contract and making money for the players' association pension fund. They succeeded only in proving that a team isn't formed in a week, that U.S. television isn't interested and likely never will be and that international hockey makes money ($3 million gross with more than $1 million expenses). The humiliating defeat at the hands of the Soviets demonstrated that the entire project was ill-advised but, more important, that the NHL style of play is poverty-stricken, that the highly paid and once hero-worshiped stars of the league are light-years behind the Soviets in physical conditioning and that the fundamental skills of skating, puck handling and passing have eroded in the NHL just as they have been honed to excellence by the Soviets.

NHL Hall of Famer Jean Beliveau stood in the runway under Madison Square Garden as the shell-shocked All-Stars solemnly trooped past. Beliveau shook his head. "Astounding. The Soviets are in such terrific shape and are such beautiful skaters. You know, the greatest difference between the NHL now and my day is the mobility of the defencemen. Now their defencemen are much faster and more mobile than ours. They have shown us that hockey is a game of speed and we have never had a team as fast as theirs. We must regroup and examine what we have lost."

Before the Challenge Cup, Fred Shero, coach of the New York Rangers, had said, "I don't use any of their training techniques over here. We don't do any dry-land work. Oh, we tried it in Philadelphia with the Flyers. You can get away with it in training camp because some of the players may not have signed contracts and they want to impress you. But after that, they complain."

A white-faced Borje Salming likened the waves of red sweaters pouring over the blue line to playing the Montreal Canadiens, but added: "The Soviets are faster." All-Star and Canadien Coach Scotty Bowman agreed that "sometimes we look like that, but we couldn't play a whole game at that pace."

Excuses, tumbled forth since the last Canadian team won a world title in 1961, no longer worked. The Soviet superiority was too dramatic, its skills (like Helmut Balderis breaking over the blue line, teasing the defence by dropping the puck into his skates, then kicking it back onto his stick—at full speed) were too evident. Minor, intermediate, junior and college coaches, rudely shocked out of their complacency, now searched for tangible results from the millions of federal dollars poured into the sport in the last decade.

After acknowledging the Soviets' diplomatic post-series comments that the NHL could ice 10 quality teams to their one, and as the shock and anguish swept from coast to coast, even washing up on the floor of the House of Commons, the NHL governors returned to business as usual, putting thoughts of hockey skills in the back of their minds and almost looking forward to facing red ink rather than sweaters.

From a six-team professional league and self-proclaimed global supremacy, major North American pro hockey, as played by Canadians and a handful of Swedes and Americans, has devolved to 17 teams and decided international inferiority. The World Hockey Association has contracted faster than it expanded and the NHL has merged two teams while barely holding its position as a sport of regional interest. "Just take a look at a place like Washington," says Alan Eagleson, executive director of the NHL Players' Association. "Not a bad hockey club, with a turnaround in attendance, and the owner is probably going to lose $1 million to $1.5 million this year. Colorado draws 5,000 a game and has to blow $2 million. St. Louis used to draw

18,000—now it's getting 6,000 and 7,000. I have to think that the owners must wonder whether they should go it again next year."

The Boston Bruins general manager, Harry Sinden, says there are not enough talented hockey players for more than 16 or 18 teams: "Once you lower the skill level below major-league, how can you sell it? How low can you let it go?" As Eagleson points out, the St. Louis Blues used to beat Montreal and Toronto the odd time but "now they're just trying to keep the score down. I would like to see the NHL contract to maybe 14 or 12 teams and then grow in a proper manner. Right now we have three or four franchises that must be wondering—fans, players and owners alike—what they're doing in the NHL."

Sonny Werblin, the man who made the American Football League by signing Joe Namath and who brought the Swedish connection, Anders Hedberg and Ulf Nilsson, to the New York Rangers, agrees that the NHL's problems stem from the top. "They either lack awareness of merchandising or just don't know how to do it." As for the NHL's latest PR coup of inviting embarrassment at the hands of the Soviets, he would rather not comment. "Any league does better with more frequent competition between division rivals. The way the league is set up, natural and regional rivals come to town about three times a year. Fans don't have a chance to identify with the teams.

"The greatest names in hockey—Orr, Howe, Lafleur—aren't known throughout the States. The top players on the Rangers are faceless in New York. It's a question of merchandising, of going out and selling the product."

The NHL, in the wake of the Soviet conquest, must now face the mirror and the echo of half-empty arenas as the Rockies, Caps, Blues, Canucks, North Stars et al come to town. The veil has been lifted from the league's Dorian Gray and those who pay the tariff, and the networks don't like the picture. The Challenge Cup was a hard but necessary lesson and one the league invited. The message is clear and directed at Canadian hockey's power brokers and czars from house leagues to Parliament Hill. This is not its first coming and it has been ignored before. But at least, as all-star defenceman Serge Savard hoped after the Soviet series, "It will be a lesson to the NHL owners to get back and develop hockey players instead of developing goons."

Like Leon Spinks, set up then put in his place by Muhammad Ali, the NHL players want another shot at their tarnished crown. Alan Eagleson is demanding that the Canadian Amateur Hockey Association be barred from international negotiations to allow him to organize a Canada Cup series in September. The weight of potential revenue from a rematch, a "Thrilla in Taranta," makes it almost inevitable. Down and bloodied, the players want another chance to fly heart and emotion in the face of discipline and superior craftsmanship.

The people will come, whatever the price, because Canadians still love hockey, because the NHL and WHA regular season and championships are now more meaningless than ever and because they are starved for well-played hockey. But if games with the Soviets, Czechs, Swedes and Finns are ever to become more than profit makers, if the government or concerned Canadians value hockey supremacy, then our entire approach to the game must be reworked. We must take helmet in hand and learn from the Soviets, introduce their training and style to our youngest players and—perhaps a generation from now—we may legitimately challenge for their cup.

The 1979 Challenge Cup Series featured three games played in New York City during a break in the regular NHL season. The NHL All-Stars won the first game 4–2, but dropped the following games 5–4 and 6–0.

Freelancer Hal Quinn was a writer and editor at Maclean's *from 1978 to 1993.*

Greatest Show on Ice

Hal Quinn

September 28, 1987—The towel around his neck was soaked with perspiration and champagne. From the ceiling in the Team Canada dressing room, spray from shaken Labatt's beer cans dripped steadily, pausing only briefly on his brow before joining the stream of sweat running off his chin into his saturated jersey. Minutes earlier Mario Lemieux had snapped a perfect shot—his 11th goal of the Canada Cup tournament—past Soviet goaltender Sergei Mylnikov. That goal, with one minute and 26 seconds remaining in the third period of the final game of the tournament, proved to be the exquisitely fine difference between the world's two best hockey teams in three of the greatest hockey games ever played. Amid the bedlam that followed Canada's 6–5 victory over the Soviet Union in the decisive third game, Pittsburgh Penguin Lemieux reflected for a moment and said: "All the players in this room have to go back to their NHL teams, and they are not 'the best teams in the world.' We have to realize that and start all over again."

But as quickly as the Canadian NHL stars staked their claim to world hockey supremacy, their reign ended. Even as champagne corks ricocheted around their dressing room at Hamilton's Copps Coliseum, the realization set in that the team—together for 44 days in August and September—would never be together again. They had survived a 6–5 overtime loss to the Soviets in Game 1, after recovering from a three-goal deficit. They had lost the lead twice in Game 2, before winning 6–5 in the second overtime period in perhaps the single best hockey game ever played.

And in the final game, they had stormed back, after trailing 3–0, to lead, tie and then win the Cup on Lemieux's goal. Said Edmonton Oiler left winger Glenn Anderson, who recovered from a knee injury in training camp to play a key role in the Canadian triumph: "This is a better feeling than winning the Stanley Cup, but it's sad too. You don't know how good these people are until you play with them. The individuals became a team, and it will be sad to see them leave."

Wayne Gretzky jumping on Mario Lemieux after Lemieux's winning goal in the 1987 Canada Cup.

The 1987 team was unique. It was a group of NHL superstars who, at head coach Mike Keenan's direction, accepted supporting roles to the world's best player—Wayne Gretzky, who led all tournament scorers with three goals and 18 assists in nine games. They were also playing in the shadow of 21-year-old Lemieux, potentially the game's best scorer, who in addition to his 11 goals collected seven assists. Said Keenan, after pairing wits with Soviet coach Viktor Tikhonov—line-change for line-change—for more than 215 minutes of the swiftly paced hockey: "When you make a team like this, with thoroughbreds, you don't have the balanced personnel you would have on an NHL team. We had to establish roles for players who had never had those roles before."

Among those accepting unfamiliar roles harassing the skilled Soviet attackers was centre Dale Hawerchuk, who has averaged more than 100 points in the past four NHL seasons with the Winnipeg Jets. The group also included St. Louis Blues Doug Gilmour, who scored 42 goals last season, and Mark Messier, who collected 107 points in the regular season before helping the Oilers win the Stanley Cup. Said Hawerchuk, who scored Canada's fifth goal in the final game, assisted on the fourth and won the faceoff that set up the winner: "Something about falling behind brought out the best in this team." Added Gilmour, who earned more playing time as the tournament progressed: "Just being involved with this calibre of players is scary." Said Messier: "The offence of both teams was so tremendous that the defence couldn't shut everybody down. Three 6–5 games, it's just unbelievable." The Soviets, at least their assistant coach and spokesman Igor Dmitriev, believed it. Declared Dmitriev: "With 17,000 Canadians in the arena hoping for them and with a Canadian referee [Don Koharski], they could not lose."

The undisputed star of Team Canada and the tournament, Gretzky, has said he would like to finish his professional career with another similar series. Said Canada Cup chairman Alan Eagleson: "If Wayne wants an eight-game series with the Soviets in 1990, we will do it. The game of hockey owes it to him." Until then, hockey fans will savor the memories of watching three of the best games ever played.

Henderson Scores!: Recalling 1972

James Deacon

September 29, 1997—Settling into a chair in a quiet corner of Maple Leaf Gardens' famed private club, the Hot Stove Lounge, Paul Henderson takes a moment to look around. The decor in the upstairs room—as dated as the Leafs' glory days—is dominated by an alarmingly bright mural, a rainbow of colors not found anywhere in nature. "This place is the same as it was when I first played here in the late '60s," Henderson says cheerfully. He hasn't changed much, either. Dapper in a blue blazer, crisp blue shirt and grey flannels, the 54-year-old Henderson still plays recreational hockey regularly, works out three times a week and proudly reports he hasn't gained a pound since his playing days. And the years seem to melt away entirely when he talks about scoring the most famous goal in the history of his sport—the one that, on Sept. 28, 1972, gave Canada its come-from-behind victory over the Soviet Union in the so-called Summit Series. "All I remember right after that is that I was hugging Yvan Cournoyer so hard," he says, clutching his chest to illustrate the point. "It's a good thing he was so strong because I might have hurt someone else."

Henderson, Cournoyer and the first-ever Team Canada did not celebrate alone. Approximately three out of every four Canadians were glued to their TVs and radios for that final game from Moscow. Employers experienced an epidemic of midday absenteeism. Schools interrupted classes so that students and teachers could watch. And rare are people who cannot recall where they were when Henderson scored. Toronto communications consultant Katherine Van de Mark, now 40, remembers her Grade 10 physics teacher—"the only male teacher in an all-girls school"—bringing a TV into their classroom so they could watch the eighth game. When Henderson broke the 5–5 tie by snapping his own rebound past goaltender Vladislav Tretiak with 34 seconds remaining, Van de Mark and her classmates did what 15 million other Canadians did at exactly the same moment. "We all went completely nuts," she says.

Talk about therapy for the national psyche. For a country perennially searching for an identity, Henderson's goal did more than reaffirm that the birthplace of Joliette, Morenz, Howe and Beliveau was still the best hockey nation on earth. That one spine-tingling victory was somehow a symbol of what it meant to be Canadian. The fans who hugged and hollered and jumped up and down identified with the character of the players—their flexibility in adapting to the Soviets' baffling, unfamiliar style of play. And they took pride in a team that did not give up when all seemed lost—that had one win, three losses and a tie going into the final three games in Moscow. It was to Canadians what Neil Armstrong walking on the moon was to Americans—one giant (if low-tech) step for the men in white (the Soviets wore their home reds). "I am more recognized today than I was in 1972," Henderson says. "People are always stopping me for autographs and to talk about the goal."

The event had an even greater impact on the sport itself. The National Hockey League, operated like an Old Boys' Club, had smugly assumed that it was God's gift to the game—until the Soviets unleashed their swirling, five-man attack. They emphatically demonstrated to NHL general managers and coaches that they needed to rethink their strict positional style of play, and that Canada did not have a corner on the talent market.

And the overwhelming fan reaction sent hockey on an international breakaway. To satisfy the suddenly ravenous appetite for multi-nation competitions that allowed the use of professionals, officials organized the six-country Canada Cup in 1976 that, four Cups later, begat the World Cup of Hockey in 1996. That, in turn, was a dry run for next February's Winter Games in Nagano, Japan, where, for the first time, all of the world's best professionals are eligible to compete for Olympic gold. "What's happening is the globalization of hockey," says Bob Goodenow, head of the NHL Players' Association. "It's the natural evolution of interest in a great game."

It was a minor miracle that Canada versus the Soviet Union occurred at all. The first discussions between the various governing bodies took place in Stockholm in 1969, and there were innumerable diplomatic hurdles, not to mention the objections of NHL team owners. Adding to the potential fireworks was the confrontation between Soviet bureaucrats and Alan Eagleson, the then-players' association boss who spearheaded the Canadian delegation. Tired of watching Canada's amateur entries get humiliated by the amateur-in-name-only Soviets at international tournaments, Eagleson barged into the negotiations with all the subtlety of Wayne Cashman crashing the boards.

Paul Henderson in Maple Leaf Gardens, September, 1997.

"The Soviets had proved they had the best amateurs in the world and we were the best professionals," he explains. "So I took the position that we should play our best against their best."

It was three years before a deal was finally struck, and the result was more than just a hockey tournament. "It was during the Cold War, remember," says Rod Seiling, a Team Canada defenceman. "It was Us versus Them." Even then, the Canadians were not prepared. Many of them arrived at training camp that August out of shape and overconfident. "I saw those guys at a banquet before the series, and some of them were 10, maybe 15 lb. overweight," says CBC analyst Don Cherry, who was then coaching the minor-league Rochester Americans. "They didn't take it very seriously at all." The players soon learned their folly. After falling behind 2–0 early in Game 1, the supremely fit Soviets—led by their brilliant winger, Valeriy Kharlamov—skated rings around their hosts in Montreal and swept to a stunning 7–3 triumph.

After four games at home, Team Canada had only one victory and a tie, and appeared in disarray. But desperation is the mother of improvement. Coach Harry Sinden whipped his troops into shape during a 10-day layover in Sweden prior to the four Moscow games and, despite losing Game 5, the Canadians battled back to take the final three contests. The victory, says Eagleson, ranks "Number 1" in his career. "Nothing else comes close, at least professionally," he says. Eagleson, who is ostracized from the game and faces criminal charges of fraud and embezzlement, has boxes full of souvenirs from 1972. "If I ever have a memorabilia sale," he jokes, "I'll be able to pay some bills."

Ironically, some analysts now say the victory did North American hockey a disservice. Had they lost, the theory goes, NHL and Canadian officials would have been quicker to adopt Soviet-style development programs that included year-round practices and dry-land training. Ken Dryden, the starting goaltender in the final game, agrees to an extent, but says he certainly did not mind at the time. "Personally, I'm glad Paul scored," the now-president of the Leafs says with a chuckle. "It's one thing to learn a lesson, and it's another to be hammered over the head with it. And that's what our experience would have been had we lost."

Slowly at first, NHL teams opened their doors to European players and even to their training methods. The melding of styles, however, was not complete until the fall of communism released dozens of top players from Eastern Bloc nations. Detroit owed its Stanley Cup victory last June in part to the stellar play of its five Russians. And as a further symbol of how things change, three of those Russian Red Wings took the Stanley Cup to Moscow last summer.

Currently, more than 20 per cent of NHL players come from Europe, and to some, that is too many, too soon. CBC's Cherry, of course, regards all imports with suspicion. "I don't like a lot of things they brought over," he says of the European players, rhyming off helmets, visors and even rink-board advertising as examples of the scourge. "And they take dives," he adds. "I mean, [former Philadelphia Flyer] Billy Barber was good, but these guys are like Tom Mix." Yet, even Cherry admits there are benefits for the NHL. The influx of new players helped the league avoid a dilution in talent when it added five expansion teams in the early 1990s. As well, he says, younger Europeans who are just joining the NHL seem prepared for a tougher style. "I see a lot more of them coming over now," he says, "and you can't tell the difference between them and the Canadians."

Some Russian officials have complained that the loss of stars to North America diminishes interest in domestic leagues. But NHL commissioner Gary Bettman suggests the opposite is true. "In the last five years," he says, "the 'A' leagues in Europe have grown by 20 per cent in terms of the number of teams, and major-junior hockey in Canada has grown 23 per cent." And it would be difficult now to stem the flow of talent to North America. There is both the lure—the average annual NHL salary is more than $1 million—and the opportunity—four expansion teams are scheduled to join the league by 2000. They will have to find players somewhere.

From his 47th-floor office in New York City, Bettman can see a world of possibilities springing from the NHL presence at the Olympics. The tournament is expected to build interest in NHL products and TV programming, not just domestically but also in Europe and the Pacific Rim. More importantly, Bettman says, the Olympics offer a chance to create new fans and encourage more kids to take up the game, thus adding to the talent base. "It's an opportunity because more people worldwide will be exposed to this game and our players than ever before," he says.

That exposure is why NHL owners are willing to suspend the coming season for 17 days in February. Along with national pride, it is why millionaire players are willing to compete for expenses only. And it is why Bettman and Goodenow set aside their labor differences to work with the International Ice Hockey Federation, the International Olympic Committee and a dozen other organizations for the common good. If nothing else, Bettman says, the event is certain to be an artistic success. "You are taking the best hockey players in the world and asking them to play for their countries," he says. "So the competition will take care of itself."

The veterans of 1972 say they had no idea at the time how profound an effect the series would someday have on hockey. "I never imagined that, 25 years later, all the best players in the world would play in one league," Dryden says. Few could fathom the impact on themselves, either. Henderson's 18-year pro career was solid but unspectacular—he is not in the Hockey Hall of Fame. But supporters argue that he should be, pointing out that he scored the winning goals in the three final games of the groundbreaking '72 series. "I never, ever dreamed of being the hero," he says. "I would have been happy just to sit on the bench and open and close the door for the guys." Since retiring from hockey in 1984, though, Henderson has drawn on the experience of 1972 and his resulting high profile in his work as a Christian missionary. "I think the opportunities it has given me, in terms of giving back, are the best part of it," he says. "I am probably more satisfied with what I have achieved since 1972 than what I did before, but it will never go away. The day I die, the stories will say I was the guy who scored the goal in 1972."

Along with the joy, he remembers sheer exhaustion. "My tank was empty, physically, emotionally, every way there was," he says. "I sat in the dressing room for about 45 minutes and I couldn't even get my skates off." Early the next morning, he and the others had to board a plane for Prague for an exhibition game, and as soon as they returned home, they had to report to their regular teams' training camps. For Henderson, that meant rejoining the then-miserable Leafs under their meddling owner, Harold Ballard. "What irritates me to this day is I never really got a chance to celebrate," he says.

As if to compensate, Henderson, Seiling and another '72 alumnus, Ron Ellis, formed a non-profit group to organize events honoring this week's 25th anniversary. They include a private dinner in Toronto for the players, a golf tournament and a fund-raising inter-squad game at Maple Leaf Gardens on the anniversary itself. For the players, it will be a chance to renew an old but strong bond. And across the country, the occasion will likely spark a flood of reminiscences—people recalling where they were, who they were with and, perhaps, what it feels like to be Canadian.

James Deacon, sports editor at Maclean's, *joined the magazine as an associate editor in 1990.*

The Russians Remember

Malcolm Gray

September 29, 1997—The broad face, above a powerful frame now softened by a slight paunch, still draws brief flickers of recognition in Moscow. Aleksandr Ragulin was a rock-like presence on the blue line for the Soviet national hockey team 25 years ago, and even now he cannot park his car—an ordinary blue Lada—in the centre of the city without encountering fans who want to recall the Super Series. That's what Russians call the first eight-game encounter for the 1972 Canada Cup, which pitted the best Canadian players of the National Hockey League against a Soviet team that was professional in all but name. To the relief of a country whose national identity seemed to be on the line, Canada scraped through to victory when winger Paul Henderson scored in the last minute of the final game in Moscow. "There were 36 seconds left actually," recalls Ragulin, handing out a correction as crisp as the checks he delivered during his playing days (though he is, as it happens, two seconds off). "Perhaps some good came from our losing. If we had won, then no one in Canada would want to remember our names."

The memories live on in both countries, for all the tumultuous changes. The Soviet Union, of course, has disappeared, taking with it the Cold War chill that helped turn a simple hockey series into an epic clash of competing ideologies. Gone, too, is the Big Red Machine, the state-supported juggernaut; Russian teams are still strong internationally, but they no longer strike fear into opponents' hearts. Meanwhile, Russian stars like Pavel Bure and Sergei Fedorov collect multimillion-dollar salaries in the National Hockey League, stripping domestic leagues of top talent and leaving behind an often-violent struggle for power and money in organized hockey. Ragulin remains philosophical: "It doesn't bother me that we were the pioneers, that the 1972 series paved the way for Russian players of today to play abroad," he says. "I could have played in the NHL, and competing against the best would have made me an even stronger player. But I never thought about

Igor Larianov brings the Stanley Cup to Moscow's Red Square, August, 1997.

leaving. That would have meant defecting and that would have made me a traitor to my country."

Time has also taken its toll on the Russian veterans of that '72 series. Boris Kulagin and Vsevolod Bobrov, the legendary coaches, are dead. So are three members of the 28-man roster, including star winger Valeriy Kharlamov, who was killed in a 1980 car accident. Those who remain are greyer, a step slower and carrying a bit more weight than during their playing days. Some have struggled to adjust to a rapidly changing society and are bitter about their lot. But others have prospered—most notably Vladislav Tretiak, the agile goaltender who allowed Henderson's winning goal but has smoothly managed the change from athlete to businessman amid Russia's transition from communism to capitalism. Tretiak is a Russian representative for Montreal-based Bombardier Inc., has done regular training-camp stints as a goaltending coach with the NHL's Chicago Blackhawks—and even helped promote the Canadian Mint's silver dollar commemorating the 25th anniversary of Henderson's heroics.

Like Tretiak, Ragulin and many other former players have strong ties to a game that elevated them to the most privileged levels of a supposedly classless society. Rags, as he was nicknamed by Canadian sports writers, is 56 now. As one of the so-called hockey soldiers who, with Moscow's mighty Central Army squad, usually formed the core of Soviet national teams, Ragulin draws a colonel's pension. With a small salary from his current post as president of a veteran hockey players' association, he has a monthly income of only about $400. He also has vivid recollections of the 1972 series. His personal highlight was the Soviets' surprise 7–3 win in the opening game in Montreal. "It was actually easier for us to play abroad," says Ragulin. "Without pressure from our fans we could concentrate on the games themselves. When we returned to Moscow, all of us thought that we were going to win the series on our own soil."

Ragulin has photographs that show him squaring off against Canadian team captain Phil Esposito. Despite later revelations that the Soviet government had indeed studded most of the buildings in central Moscow with listening devices, Ragulin believes the authorities probably did not eavesdrop on Team Canada, as Esposito and others have alleged. "Ah, Phil," Ragulin says. "We are good friends now. But I think he was mistaken about our government bugging Canadians' hotel rooms. No one was interested in their secrets. After all, they were hockey players, not spies." As he speaks, he runs a finger along a scar under his right eye, a permanent souvenir from the series. "That was a present from Esposito's stick," he adds.

Unlike Ragulin, the shine of the '72 series has been overshadowed for winger Aleksandr Yakushev by a crushing, personal loss. With seven goals and four assists, the tall, well-built Yakushev was among the leading scorers in the series. After his 17-year playing career ended in 1980, Yakushev had well-paying coaching jobs in Austria and Switzerland for four years before homesickness pulled him back to Moscow. But in 1994, Katya, his 21-year-old daughter, left the family apartment to go for a walk and did not return. Police retrieved her body from the Moscow River 72 days later but have never solved her murder. "What do I have to live for?" one of his former teammates recalls him saying. Now, after three years in an apartment where he is constantly reminded of his daughter, Yakushev and his wife, Tatiana, are moving to new quarters in another district.

Life has been tough on Evgeni Mishakov, as well. The former winger, who won five world and two Olympic championship medals during his 12-year pro playing career, lives in a two-room Moscow apartment. He has a monthly army pension of just over $100, and a limp caused by hockey injuries. "It's hard getting by these days,"

Mishakov says. "My health is not good and I can't afford proper medical treatment. I have to say that I preferred life under the old system."

Mishakov's life still revolves around the rink at Central Army's storied Ice Palace arena in Moscow. There he has access to an office as the coach of Zvezdy Rossii, or Stars of Russia, a club of veteran players who have seen a schedule of 30 exhibition games annually—and the small income it brought—dwindle to only four or five. The office is tucked away on a shabby fourth-floor corridor accessible only by stairs because the elevator is out of order. The door bears a plaque dedicated to the memory of coach Bobrov, and inside there is a good view of the rink where Victor Kuzkin, another '72 alumnus, was on this day leading Central Army players through a scrimmage.

Mishakov is one of scores of rink rats who each day line the boards at practice sessions at the Red Army rink, killing time. He has strong feelings about the Russians stars now skating in North America. "I think Russians who are playing in the NHL should donate a small percentage of their salaries to help the veterans who paved the way for them," he says. "Either that or they should participate in charity games for older players who are hard up."

Kuzkin well remembers the emotional roller coaster of the '72 series, from the euphoria of that opening victory to the crushing emptiness of the last-game loss. But as an assistant coach of the current Red Army squad, he has little time to dwell on the old days. "I have a good life, a nice apartment and a wife and daughter whom I love," he says. "I could use more money, but who couldn't." Besides the drain of top talent to teams abroad, he blames the disappearance of government subsidies and the closing of state-supported hockey schools for the rapid decline of the Russian game.

For Valeriy Vasiliev, a defenceman on the '72 team, the biggest crime may be the government's treatment of former Soviet stars who had not adjusted well to the disappearance of the old union. "They were pioneers in the development of the international style of hockey that is played now," he says. "But now the government neglects them—some are in poor health and some have become alcoholics. For those, drinking is a way out, a means for them to forget."

Vasiliev, on the other hand, lives in a prestigious district of southern Moscow. There, from the windows of an airy and well-appointed 10th-floor flat that he now owns, he can look across the street to the apartment occupied by his neighbor and former teammate, Tretiak. Vasiliev bears the marks of his hockey days: a crooked nose that was broken three times and a scar above one eyebrow—a souvenir of a high stick during a 1974 exhibition game in Winnipeg. And he will never forget the game that got away, those momentous final seconds: Henderson cutting in on goal; defenceman Gennadiy Tsigankov moving to block him; Vasiliev skating over to deliver a partial check; Henderson falling to the ice and shooting towards the net; the puck arcing over Tretiak's outstretched arm; the red light flashing on. "We knew that it was over then," said Vasiliev. "There was some time left, but some of the Canadian players told me afterwards that they would have done anything to ensure their win."

But Vasiliev is not obsessed with that series. Business—he is about to open a new bar—and time spent coaching hockey in a town near Moscow keep him rooted in the present. When asked where his trophies are, he rummages through a closet before unearthing a nondescript black plastic briefcase. Inside, in a tangle of colored ribbons, lies a glittering array of championship prizes, including two Olympic golds. "Even Olympic gold medals are not really made of gold," Vasiliev says quietly. For anyone who contested—or even watched—the 1972 series, Vasiliev has a simple message: it was a classic matchup that led to changes and improvements in hockey. But while he likes visiting the past, he has no desire to live there.

Veteran journalist Malcolm Gray is the Maclean's *Moscow correspondent. He started at the magazine in 1982 as its Vancouver bureau chief.*

Hockey Meltdown

Bruce Wallace

March 2, 1998—The 1998 Olympic gold-medal hockey game had plenty in common with all those gold-medal games of the 1960s and '70s, except this time the Russians and the Czechs wore Nike. After all the hype and great expectations, a team of hustling but lead-handed Canadians was reduced to the supporting cast in what may qualify as the greatest hockey tournament ever staged. European teams swept the medals. Canada played gamely but unsuccessfully for bronze. Just like the bad old days when they sent the amateurs.

Instead, the glory went to players like Pavel Bure, the Russian rocketeer with a sweet scoring touch, and Dominik Hasek, the Czech goaltender built like a slab of the old Berlin Wall—with Cold War-era impenetrability. The ultimate Czech victory was the reality check for all those fans who somehow imagined Olympic hockey was going to be a North American demonstration sport, pitting Canada against the United States. There were, as cautious Canadian players had warned the unconvinced all along, many dream teams in Nagano.

But prescience does not take away the sting. "The loss is devastating, the worst feeling in the world," Wayne Gretzky said in a near-whisper after dropping the semifinal, 2–1, to the Czech Republic in a dramatic, ratchet-up-the-tension Olympic twist called the shootout. The Canadians were so crushed that they failed to regroup for the next day's bronze-medal game against Finland. The Finns won 3–2 in a game played in a funereal atmosphere at Nagano's Big Hat arena, where the normally boisterous crowd seemed to sense that polite, sympathetic clapping was more suitable for a consolation game. "Sure it would have been nice to go home with a medal," said Theo Fleury, leaving the Canadian dressing room for the last time, a day earlier than expected. "But we came here to win."

That is the conundrum now facing Canadian hockey: in a sport where international parity exists among half a dozen (if not more) elite teams, Canadian players and fans remain conditioned to expect only gold from those who wear the Maple Leaf. Canada's women's team tasted similar pressure when it fell 3–1 to the Americans in the final of the first-ever Olympic women's hockey tournament. Even the players seemed to regard the silver medals around their necks as symbols of failure. "We have a silver medal, but the fact is we lost the game," said Cassie Campbell, part of a Canadian team that dissolved into inconsolable sobs after losing. "It doesn't feel like we won anything." Only the next day did Campbell recover slightly, getting a new perspective from two-time silver medallist, speed-skater Susan Auch, who stopped her in the athlete's village to tell her: "You know, Cassie, a silver medal is a great thing."

It may yet take some time before Canada's best get accustomed to playing for a place in the medals. But the excitement and drama of the men's tournament suggests that the Winter Olympics and the world's top players may now be embarking on a beautiful friendship. The games on Nagano's big ice were marvellous entertainment. Skills flourished, free from the threat of thuggery without any shortage of the jarring body-thwacking that the NHL offers. "I don't think you're going to find a guy who didn't like it," said a gracious Joe Nieuwendyk. "It's been one of the greatest hockey experiences of my career. And a gold medal might have rated even higher than a Stanley Cup."

Nieuwendyk spoke with his hair still wet from the postgame shower, and the Olympic glow may very well fade once the annual spring chase for the Stanley Cup begins. But NHL executives seemed upbeat about their Olympic moment, too. The league will decide next year whether to free its best players from mid-season duty to play in the 2002 Salt Lake City Games, a likely scenario given that those Olympics will be more conducive to American prime time than Japan's other-side-of-the-globe time difference allowed.

There were still a few forced smiles among NHL brass over the American team's clunker of a performance, however. The U.S. men never gelled, never seemed to concentrate on hockey. "I can't look in a guy's eyes and tell if he's more focused than me," sneered Brett Hull when asked if the Canadians were better prepared, showing more snap in his quotes than in his shot. The irritable Americans complained about the bigger ice, the officiating, and how the hockey gods had fingered them alone to face hot goalies. "We got a raw deal," said forward Doug Weight after losing to Canada, 4–1, in the round-robin part of the tournament and insisting that Canada's second goal should have been disallowed for having a man in the crease.

Coach Ron Wilson tried to motivate his players by showing clips from the frat movie *Animal House* before the quarter-final against the Czechs. His team went out with a whimper. The *Animal House* lessons came in handy later at the Olympic Village, though, when a few players snapped some of the wooden Japanese furniture in their rooms and covered the walls with fire-repellent foam. "I know it doesn't look good on paper," said Wilson after his team was chased by the Czechs. It did not look good on or off the ice.

The Canadians, by contrast, could at least take home a consolation ribbon for good behavior. They revelled in mixing with other athletes in the village, removing any skepticism that hockey millionaires could get into the Olympic spirit. "I think our team has handled everything with class," said forward Rob Zamuner. "Every one of us represented our country very well."

The Canadians can also claim North American bragging rights after their convincing win over the Americans in a much-anticipated rematch of the 1996 World Cup final. Hasek's fine play in beating the United States kept the Canadians and Americans from meeting again. "We're going to fire a lot of rubber and go to the net," said captain Eric Lindros when asked how his team would solve Hasek. But Steve Yzerman was more circumspect. "Everybody's tried pretty much everything with Hasek," he said with a shrug. "You just go in and shoot where he isn't."

Once the game began, it took 58 minutes and 57 seconds before Trevor Linden finally ricocheted a shot at the Czech goal where Hasek wasn't, tying the score at 1. Ten minutes of overtime resolved nothing, bringing on the shootout: five players from each team in an Olympic version of a street hockey showdown. After Robert Reichel scored on the Czech's first shot, Hasek stoned five consecutive Canadian shooters (none of them Gretzky, providing fodder for years of barstool arguments). "It's obviously very exciting, but I didn't care much for it before and I care for it less now," said Yzerman of the shootout. The Czechs, meanwhile, will probably put one of Hasek's saves on a national stamp.

The Canadian women's loss was just as heartbreaking. In the most important women's hockey game to date, a team that had won all four world championships came up flat. Their freewheeling third period was not enough to overcome a swifter—on this night—American squad. And just as men's team general manager Bobby Clarke had taken heat for his selection of players, women's coach Shannon Miller endured sniping for the handling of hers. Most attacks focused on the way she prepared her team for the Olympics, suggesting players were too high-strung and tight under her guidance.

Shedding tears after losing the gold medal hockey game at the Nagano Olympics, February 17, 1998.

Opponents like U.S. captain Cammi Granato certainly thought the Canadians were tense. "They had all the pressure of holding off a team that has finally caught up to them in talent," said Granato. American coach Ben Smith handles his team in a fatherly manner, says Granato. He tells parables before a game. Canada's Miller, on the other hand, likes to keep her team in "the bubble," isolated from distractions like family, then "motivate the hell out of them" at the last minute, she says. The last minute for the Canadians came before a desperate third period when the team—down by a goal—watched video clips of their finest moments to the tune of "Simply the Best." The move provoked sneers from critics. "It worked," retorted Miller, whose team went on to play their best period of hockey. "Yeah," said assistant coach Daniele Sauvageau wryly. "Maybe we should have played the video earlier."

Miller's players defended her to the hilt, suggesting that male hockey writers just don't like the women's game. But in the aftermath, the Canadians looked like crash survivors. Tears flowed freely hours after the game at a reception for players and their families. They talked of the importance of the Olympic journey, but it was still too soon to forget the dashed expectations.

"You'll wake up tomorrow and feel dead, completely drained," Clarke told a group of the women, as they all sucked on cigars. "But in two or three days, you'll come back." Perhaps when the players and the nation come out of their funk, they will take a little pride in the way the world has embraced Canada's game.

The Czech Republic beat Russia in the gold-medal game, 1–0.

The Great One

The Best in the World

Peter Gzowski

January 25, 1988—You can play it over and over in your mind's eye, and it is still just as pretty as it was last September.

With a minute and a half left on the clock, the Canadians line up for what could be the final faceoff of the series. They are deep in their own end, tied 5–5, and the crowd in Copps Coliseum in Hamilton is throbbing. Gretzky coasts into the red circle, but, when the Russians send out their faceoff specialist, he gives way to Dale Hawerchuk of the Winnipeg Jets and takes up a position on the far reaches of the right wing, like a sleeper in the old football play. The other Canadian skaters—Paul Coffey on the left, Hawerchuk, Larry Murphy and Mario Lemieux—are strung out in a single rank. The Russians are set three and two.

Hawerchuk wins the faceoff. Lemieux pounces from his position on the right and slaps the puck outward and toward the boards at the left. Meantime, Gretzky has left his sleeper's position and crossed the ice. As Lemieux lifts his eyes, he sees the familiar 99 ahead of the play, sprinting along the boards. He shovels the puck forward. Gretzky scoops it up in full flight and heads across centre.

Now Larry Murphy breaks clear on Gretzky's right. As they cross the blue line, they are two on one against a retreating Soviet defenceman. For an instant it looks as if the moment has passed—as if the rush has been diffused and the Soviets, flying back into their own zone, will have a chance to regroup. Gretzky veers left, still carrying the puck. The defenceman, now sure Murphy's momentum has carried him past the point where he can receive a pass, flings himself to the right.

And now comes the moment of magic. Gretzky gently wafts the puck into what at first appears to be the open ice behind the play. But only at first. Suddenly, there is Mario Lemieux, now in full control of his body and skating at full steam into the Soviet zone. The puck clicks neatly onto his stick. He glides, aims, cocks the trigger and fires a classically perfect wrist shot into the top right corner of the net, shooting, as the scouting reports have suggested, high on Sergei Mylnikov's glove side. From faceoff to the glow of the goal judge's light, four seconds have elapsed. The Canadians, for the time being at least, are back on top of the hockey world.

In the winter Wayne Gretzky turned three—he was born in January of 1961—his father, Walter, made a rink in their backyard in Brantford, Ont. All through Wayne's childhood, the rink was a passion for both of them. In the daytime, the boy would skate on it and play hockey with the sticks Walter used to shave down for him. In the evenings, they would work together on the drills Walter had worked out. Wayne skated through networks of tin cans and practiced leaping over sticks. Walter would water the rink every night using a lawn sprinkler, until the year his wife, Phyllis, refused to go to the hardware store to buy a replacement for the one that had broken. "They will think I'm crazy," Phyllis said, "buying a lawn sprinkler in February."

Wayne started in organized hockey when he was six, and Walter was his first coach. Walter had his own drills there too. He would shoot the puck into a corner, for instance, and tell the kids to chase it. When they chugged doggedly into the corner, he would yell "No, no." "Wait for it to come round," he would say. "Don't go where it is—go where it's going to be. Anticipate, anticipate." Watching Gretzky appear so quickly in front of Lemieux last fall, you could think about that.

The year Wayne turned eight, he scored 104 goals in 40 games. When he was 10 and stood four feet four, he scored 378 in 68 games. I met him when he was 14. He had scored 988 goals by then. He came into *This Country in the Morning*, the CBC Radio program I was hosting at the time. He was already, if you remember, quite a celebrity. Much later I came to know a couple of young men who had played against him, and they told me that they thought he was a little spoiled, set apart. But I liked him. He knew he was good, all right, but to my eye, at least, it hadn't gone to his head. He was polite and rather serious. He had a kind of buck-toothed look, partly from the three teeth that had had to be pegged into his mouth to replace those he'd broken on the hockey rink. I remember asking him if he thought he'd ever make $100,000 a year playing hockey, and he just laughed.

In the summer of 1980 I decided to write a book about hockey. Although I hadn't figured out what shape to impose on it, I was toying with the idea of following one NHL team through a season. I called Wayne, who was just coming into his own as the dominant player of his time—he had tied with Marcel Dionne for the scoring leadership the season before—and we arranged to play golf. He suggested that I choose the

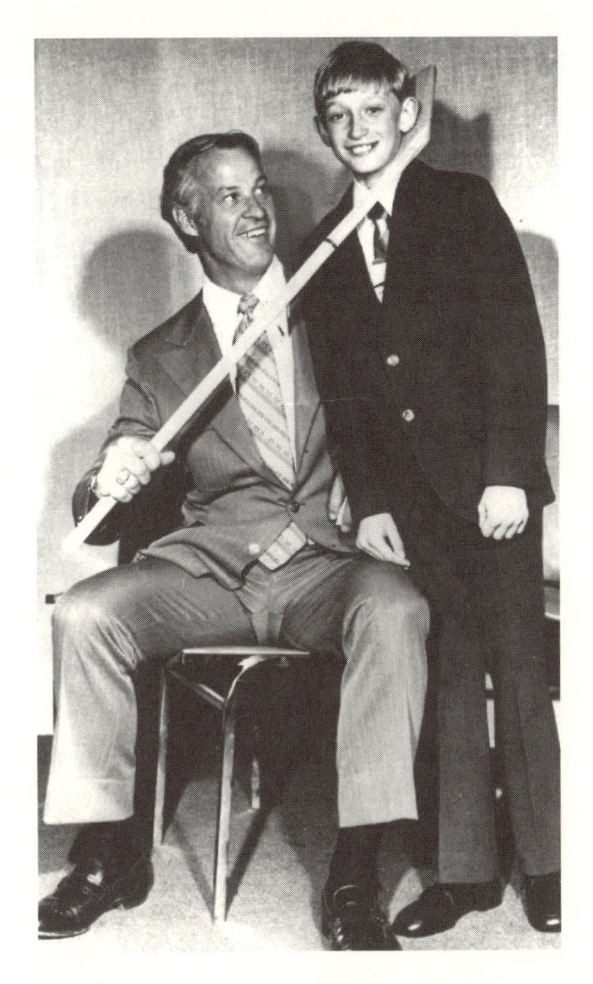

As a boy with Gordie Howe.

Edmonton Oilers. The result was what I called *The Game of Our Lives*. But most people who mention my treatise on hockey just describe it as "your book about Gretzky."

I know why, of course. He is hockey now. Although virtually every age of the game has had its pre-eminent players—Morenz, Richard, Howe, Hull, Orr—no one has ever transcended it as he has. An American magazine that once used to treat hockey with little more seriousness than steeplechasing has called him the "greatest athlete in the world." A newspaper piece I read last weekend on the news of his engagement made reference to Charles and Di. The little kid from Brantford is now the biggest star we have.

We spent a lot of time together in the season I followed the Oilers and, I'd like to think, became friends. Even then, though, it was hard to get time alone with him, away from the groupies and other hangers-on. I used to wonder at his patience.

Everyone he talked to—including me, of course—wanted something from him; as best he could, he tried to give it.

He was always most comfortable talking hockey. He didn't read much about anything else, and, on the rare evenings he had to watch television, he was happy with *The Love Boat*. But on the game, he was an encyclopedia—and nearly always serious. Though our relationship was an easy one, involving much banter, I could never tease him about his occasional lapses on the ice: the missed breakaways or the lost faceoffs. His face would turn red, as I am sure you have seen it after a referee's call against him or after his team goes down a goal.

At one point in the season I left the team and spent some time among academics, trying to figure out what gifts Wayne had that so set him apart from all the other boys who had started playing as he had and who at least seemed to have similar physical gifts. When I returned with the theory I eventually expounded in the book, which involved a lot of phrases like "short- and long-term memory" and "chunks of information," and drew analogies from everything from chess to jazz piano, he understood it instantly, and used to enjoy going over tapes of his goals with me and showing how it applied. I thought of those days again, too, when I contemplated his pass to Lemieux, for essentially my theory holds that where lesser players see the positions of other individuals in a game, Wayne sees situations. In reaction to any particular pattern of play, he simply summons up one of the chunks of information he has stored in his long-term memory, without having to go through the process of rational thought—having taken the pass from Lemieux behind him, he knew without thinking where Lemieux would next emerge.

I don't see him much these days. The television where I live shows too many less interesting teams than the Oilers, and, with the hockey book behind me, I have returned to broadcasting and other interests. When I do call him, I am embarrassed to say, it is almost always because I, too, want something from him—an interview for the radio, an appearance at some event. When he can, still, he accommodates me, and it impresses me, as much now as it did in 1974, how little he has let his fame go to his head.

The "Royal" Wedding

Mark Nichols

July 25, 1988—The crowd along Edmonton's Jasper Avenue began gathering in the morning and, by late afternoon, it had swollen to nearly 10,000 people. Sidewalk vendors hawked "Wayne and Janet" balloons and peddled hotdogs, popcorn and ice cream to the good-humored crowd in the warm, sunny weather. There were flurries of excitement as limousines deposited celebrity guests at the doors of St. Joseph's Basilica. Then, there was a restless 40-minute wait as Edmonton's—and perhaps Canada's—wedding of the century unfolded inside the massive Roman Catholic cathedral. Finally, at 4:30 p.m. on July 16, Wayne and Janet Gretzky emerged from the basilica and descended the fern-draped church steps between two ranks of Edmonton city firefighters in red coats and white-topped hats. "We love you, Wayne," someone shouted as the couple kissed, and kissed again, and again, for the photographers. Declared Brenda Savella-Smith, an Edmonton graphic designer who was in the crowd: "In England, they have the royal family. In the United States, it's Hollywood. But we have to make our own heroes in Canada."

In the hectic days before the wedding, the Edmonton Oilers' star centre deplored newspaper comparisons between his marriage and the nuptials of British royalty. But, in the end, after all the hype and the hoopla—and some cheap shots against the modest young Canadian who is the world's greatest hockey player and his American movie-actress bride—it was an elegant and even regal event. The bride wore a dress that surpassed the wildest rumors—a shimmering creation of French-made Duchess satin sewn with tiny pearls and glass beads and trailing a 15-foot-long train. And in that moment when the couple—both blond and both 27—stood on the basilica steps before plunging into the first chapter of their life together, they performed the traditional royal function of embodying the fears and joys of every citizen. Like any other man, Gretzky looked relieved. And his new wife, the former Janet Jones of Los Angeles, looked joyful.

Inside the 25-year-old basilica, Gretzky, known for his masterful composure on the ice, appeared nervous as the Roman Catholic pastor, Rev. Michael McCaffery, and Rev. John Munro, a retired Anglican minister from Gretzky's native Brantford, Ont., jointly conducted the marriage service. The Great One stood rigidly through much of the service, while Jones, relaxed and radiant, frequently reached for the groom's hand and smiled at him reassuringly. The couple's vows to one another included promises "to love and cherish... and to be faithful to you alone." Declared Munro later: "I have a feeling their faith in marriage is going to take hold. Father McCaffery and I declared them married together."

There were some incongruous touches to the otherwise glittering wedding. As a convoy of stretched Cadillac and Lincoln limousines drove up and dropped off guests at the basilica, hockey legend Gordie Howe, Gretzky's boyhood idol, and his wife, Colleen, arrived in a dilapidated taxicab. Joked Howe: "It's a grand day. It will be a happy marriage if only he can learn to play hockey." Dave Semenko, the bruising ex–Toronto Maple Leaf and former Oilers teammate of Gretzky's, attended the wedding dressed in light blue trousers and a dark blue jacket and wearing no socks.

It was probably the most publicized wedding ever performed in Canada—and no marriage has generated greater interest among Canadians since that of then-Prime Minister Pierre Trudeau and Margaret Sinclair in 1971. Unlike the Trudeaus' Vancouver wedding—which was only revealed to the world after it had taken place—plans for the Gretzky-Jones marriage were announced in January, allowing six months for public interest to reach fever pitch.

It was an opulent affair, that may have cost as much as $250,000. The nave of the basilica, which was patterned on the Gothic style and boasts 60 stained-glass windows, was decked with masses of fresh champagne-colored roses and plate-sized white Casa Blanca lilies. The bride walked down the aisle to the strains of her favorite song, "Somewhere in Time," played by a 15-piece string and woodwind ensemble from the Edmonton Symphony Orchestra. And her gown alone—made by Los Angeles designer Pari Malek—reportedly cost more than $40,000. On her left hand, the bride wore the three-carat diamond engagement ring—estimated to have cost at least $125,000—which Gretzky gave her last January. During the ceremony, Gretzky placed another diamond-studded double band of gold on her finger. When the couple next visits the bride's Los Angeles apartment, the $250,000 tan-and-cream-colored Corniche Rolls-Royce that Gretzky gave Jones as a wedding present will be waiting. Her gift to him: a simple kiss.

With bride, Janet Jones, July 16, 1988.

In the days leading up to the wedding, Gretzky maintained his aplomb in the face of relentless questioning by reporters. After picking up his fiancée at the Westin Hotel on Thursday—she had arrived earlier by air from Los Angeles with nine boxes containing the wedding dresses for herself and her eight bridesmaids—Gretzky was pressed to disclose how much the wedding arrangements cost. He refused, telling reporters that the scale of the wedding had been "blown out of proportion." Added Gretzky: "I hope people aren't disappointed because they are expecting 10 Rolls-Royces or anything like that, because it isn't going to happen." In a separate interview, an *Edmonton Journal* reporter asked Gretzky how he felt about Jones's earlier involvements with such celebrities as tennis star Vitas Gerulaitis and television actor Bruce Willis. Said Gretzky: "I think that her life is her life and what she did before she met me is none of my business."

The 22-member wedding party included Gretzky's best man, former Edmonton Oilers goalie Ed Mio, Gretzky's three younger brothers, Brent, Keith and Glen, Oilers Mark Messier and Kevin Lowe and former Oilers defenceman Paul Coffey, who is now with the Pittsburgh Penguins. Looking on were Gretzky's parents, Walter and Phyllis, and his sister, Kim, was one of the bridesmaids—along with former *Playboy* playmate Tracy Vaccaro. On Jones's side of the aisle were her mother, Jean, her brother, Johnny—who gave away the bride—and her sister, Jeanette, the matron of honor (her father died of cancer in 1978).

Among the more than 600 invited guests who attended the ceremony and a reception later at Edmonton's Westin Hotel: hockey czar Alan Eagleson, NHL president John Ziegler, flamboyant sports broadcaster Don Cherry and Los Angeles-based Canadian television star Alan Thicke of the TV sit-com hit *Growing Pains*. They were joined by hockey legend Howe, Vladislav Tretiak, the retired Soviet goalkeeping star, Alberta Premier Don Getty and his wife, Margaret, Edmonton Mayor Laurence Decore and Edmonton Oilers owner Peter Pocklington. One notable absentee: Prime Minister Brian Mulroney, who was invited, but who sent his regrets because of an inner cabinet meeting at Meech Lake, near Ottawa.

Tretiak, who arrived by air from Moscow with his wife, Tatanaya, a few hours before the wedding, gave the Gretzkys a traditional Russian wedding present known as a podnos—an oval silver tray embossed with a flower pattern. In Russia, the tray is traditionally used to collect cash gifts from wedding guests for newlyweds. Said Tretiak: "Wayne's wedding is big news for Russian hockey fans. People are always interested in the lives of stars."

During the wedding ceremony, Denise Gendron, a friend of the bride, and Brent Gretzky read verses from the Old Testament's *Song of Songs*. Later, at a dinner in the Westin, the Gretzkys and their guests—in honor of the Gretzky family's Polish background—dined on traditional Polish dishes, including perogies and cabbage rolls, as well as a California-style breast of capon with peaches and Madeira sauce and, for dessert, a chocolate cup filled with chocolate mousse. Later, with their honeymoon plans still unknown, the couple retired for the night to the hotel's 20th-floor Crown suite, which has a fireplace, its own library and a king-sized bed. The suite has been used in the past by Queen Elizabeth II and her husband, the Duke of Edinburgh, and by Prince Charles and Diana, the Princess of Wales.

The day of ceremony and celebration ended weeks of preparation that created controversy in Edmonton, where resentments surfaced over the apparent extravagance of the wedding—and over the marriage of two Protestants in a Roman Catholic church. Still, much of the prenuptial attention was friendly. Signs heralding the wedding appeared on buildings near the basilica. The cheery, ecumenical message displayed by Teddy's pub and delicatessen, next door to the church on Jasper Avenue, read "Mazel Tov [Hebrew for 'Congratulations'], Wayne and Janet."

As well, recurring criticism of Gretzky's decision to marry a woman who posed semi-nude in the March, 1987, issue of *Playboy* magazine surfaced in the days leading up to the wedding. Declared one indignant letter writer to the *Sun*: What I can't figure out is why he chose to marry a *Playboy* bunny when he could have the pick of the crop. Who knows, maybe Hugh Hefner will be strutting through the cathedral." But although invited, *Playboy* publisher Hefner sent his regrets and did not attend the wedding.

Despite such carping—and the onslaught of reporters representing more than 100 North American and several offshore news organizations—Gretzky and his bride conducted themselves throughout their hectic wedding day with poise and dignity. They were cementing a link that began to form back in 1980, when Gretzky and his future wife met, briefly, on a Los Angeles television show. Jones was then a regular performer on the syndicated television program *Dance Fever*, and Gretzky, the brilliant young star of the Edmonton Oilers, appeared as a guest judge of the contestants. But it was not until last June, when they ran into each other at a Los Angeles basketball game, that a casual acquaintanceship blossomed into a full-scale love affair.

Gretzky's eventful springtime meeting with Jones occurred during a period of crisis in his life. He now acknowledges that he was unhappy about the pressures of his career—and an eight-year-old relationship with Edmonton singer Vicki Moss, which was coming to an end. During that troubled period, Gretzky found in Jones a woman whose life, in many respects, paralleled his own. Both are the product of conventional upbringings in large, closely knit families. Both were passionately fond of sports as children—and both were thrust into high-stress lives as professional performers while still in their teens.

The Missouri native, who was born 16 days before Gretzky, grew up in Bridgeton, a middle-class suburb of St. Louis, where her father, Robert, was vice-president of an airport equipment firm. The sixth of seven children, Jones at first was a tomboy who loved to play softball with her four older brothers. But as a teenager, she developed a passion for dancing. She launched her professional career in 1979 when she won the Miss Dance of America contest in San Francisco. Following a stint as a dancer at New York City's Radio City Music Hall, she settled in Los Angeles in 1979, working as a model and as a regular performer on *Dance Fever*.

By the time Gretzky appeared on the show, Jones was involved in her first serious relationship—with Nels Van Patten, a professional tennis player and actor, which lasted nearly five years. In 1984, she made her film debut playing the girlfriend of star Matt Dillon in the critically praised movie *The Flamingo Kid* and, in the following year, she won a part in Sir Richard Attenborough's *A Chorus Line*. She played her first starring role as a gymnast in the 1986 flop *American Anthem*.

By then, Jones had acquired a new boyfriend—Gerulaitis, the fading Brooklyn, N.Y.-born tennis star who arrived in her life after she and Van Patten broke up. A celebrated ladies' man, Gerulaitis once boasted that "if I could be as successful on the tennis court as I am off it, I would be No. 1." After the couple's two-year engagement ended last year, Jones briefly dated Willis, the brash star of ABC TV's hit private-investigator show, *Moonlighting*. Clearly, the young actress was drifting—personally and professionally. She posed for *Playboy* and had a prominent role in the rowdy sex comedy *Police Academy V*, released last spring.

Gretzky's own unrest owed much to the pressure of his astonishing career. Launched into professional hockey at the age of 17, when Vancouver entrepreneur Nelson Skalbania signed him to play with the Indianapolis Racers of the now-defunct World Hockey Association, Gretzky joined the Oilers in 1979. And since that entry into the NHL, the man fans call "The Great One" has dominated his sport as few other athletes ever have. The NHL's leading goal scorer for seven consecutive years, Gretzky led his club to four Stanley Cup victories during the past five years and was awarded the Hart Memorial Trophy as the league's most valuable player for eight consecutive seasons.

Still, by last spring, despite the estimated $3 million that he earns annually for his hockey playing and endorsements and the other material rewards of superstardom—including a two-storey penthouse apartment in Edmonton and his specially built champagne-colored Nissan 300 ZX convertible—the strain of being Canada's biggest celebrity was showing. The unrelenting pressure that he had been under since he first began playing organized hockey when he was six had started to wear him down. "I guess it finally caught up with me last year," he said recently. Gretzky began to talk of retiring and he even hinted that he might not take part in last September's Canada Cup series. He later relented and was the dominant player in the tournament as he led Team Canada to a dramatic 6–5 deciding victory over the Soviet Union in Hamilton.

At the same time, his long relationship with Moss, his live-in girlfriend, was coming to an end. Gretzky has never publicly discussed the breakup. But Moss—who moved to Los Angeles two years ago—told *Maclean's* last week that although she and Gretzky were never formally engaged, he wanted to marry her. According to Moss, 26, the breakup was a result of her decision in the spring of 1987 to stay in Los Angeles and pursue her career for another year. "Wayne was so bitter with me," said Moss. "It was a shame he could not handle it."

As it turned out, Moss played an accidental role in Gretzky's pivotal meeting with his future wife. In May, 1987, Gretzky went to see Moss in Palm Springs, Calif., where she was singing at a nightclub. Later that same day, recalled Moss—who last February married Los Angeles record producer David White—Gretzky rented a limousine so that he and his friend Thicke could go into Los Angeles to see the home-town Lakers play the Boston Celtics in a National Basketball Association championship game. "He and Jones ran into each other," said Moss. "He said he had a girl who didn't want to settle down." According to Moss, Jones then replied, "Maybe we should start going out."

They did. Gretzky said later: "From the first day, we hit it off well. It kind of hits you like a ton of bricks." The affair became public knowledge during the summer when the couple vacationed together at a southwestern Ontario cottage that was owned by Gretzky's friend Coffey. Then, in January, they announced their engagement. Declared an exultant Gretzky: "It's definite. We were meant to spend our lives together." Still, some of the reaction to Gretzky's announcement clearly caught the couple off-guard, particularly when criticism of Jones's discreetly draped poses in *Playboy* appeared in Alberta newspapers. Declared Jones: "In the beginning, the press made me out to be some kind of American playmate. I think Canadians are more conservative than Americans. Americans were complaining that I should have revealed more."

The nudity issue came up again when the Protestant couple—Gretzky is an Anglican and Jones comes from a Methodist background—decided to have their wedding in the 1,200-seat Roman Catholic basilica. That was because Edmonton's All Saints' Anglican Cathedral, Gretzky's first choice, was too small to accommodate hundreds of wedding guests. But shortly after Edmonton Archbishop Joseph MacNeil gave his approval, the Edmonton-based *Western Catholic Reporter* noted that about 40 people had contacted the weekly newspaper to protest the use of the basilica for a non-Catholic marriage. For his part, McCaffery staunchly defended the decision to hold the wedding at St. Joseph's. He added: "Wayne is a prominent member of the community. This is a gesture of hospitality and openness."

Earlier this summer, as the wedding date neared and the media intensified their coverage of the couple's activities, Gretzky and Jones retreated again to Coffey's cottage, where they were joined by Gretzky's parents. During the second half of June, they spent two weeks in the Hawaiian islands to attend the wedding of Mary-Kay Messier, the sister of Gretzky's Oilers teammate. But the extent of public interest in the wedding had clearly unnerved the couple. Said Gretzky: "If we had realized the attention it was going to get, I think we would have eloped."

As a married couple, the Gretzkys—who plan to maintain residences in Edmonton and Los Angeles—will have to deal with the pressure generated by his NHL schedule and the demands of their separate careers. Still, both husband and wife say that they are anxious to have children. Shortly after she and Gretzky became engaged, Jones remarked that her agent had chided her for not paying enough attention to her career. Said Jones: "I'm just such a lovebird, and he got frustrated because he could see me doing a lot more with my career than I have." She is also aware that she and her husband will continue to be subject to close scrutiny. Added Jones: "We both know what a fish-bowl it is—especially in Canada."

Gretzky—the sadness of a year ago now firmly behind him—has spoken of some day playing hockey with his sons, as his hero Howe did when he and his sons Mark and Marty became members of the World Hockey Association's Houston Aeros in 1973–74. Gretzky also maintains that he will retire "when I can't play anymore the way I'm capable of playing." Still, he was clearly resentful when Oilers owner Pocklington said in a radio interview last spring that his playing ability might be adversely affected by his forthcoming marriage. Said the star: "I didn't need the owner quoted as saying the same things I knew a lot of fans had been thinking." But Gretzky is known for his ability to stay cool and in control of situations on and off the ice.

By submitting to the ordeal of a luminescently public marriage, Gretzky showed that his generosity of spirit is not confined to the hockey rink. Last Friday, Oilers fan Lena Magega, a 62-year-old Edmonton dental assistant, was one of the hundreds of people who waited outside the basilica during a rehearsal for Saturday's wedding. When Gretzky emerged, she was rewarded with a kiss from her hero. "I feel like a million dollars," she said. "That is my Wayne." It was a small demonstration of The Great One's ability to give pleasure to his fellow Canadians—which is why so many of them wished the Gretzkys the best in the years to come.

Written with files from John Howse, Elaine O'Farrell and Terry Jones in Edmonton, Anne Gregor in Los Angeles and Heather Kneen in Toronto

Mark Nichols, now science and technology editor at Maclean's, *joined the magazine as national editor in 1984.*

Gretzky Inc.

James Deacon

December 5, 1994—Ducking into a Beverly Hills pasta bar, Wayne Gretzky hardly looks himself. Maybe it is the ball cap pulled low on his forehead, the uncharacteristically glum expression on his face or the fact that hockey's proverbial white knight is, from T-shirt to cowboy boots, dressed completely in black. Wearily slumping in his chair, he orders a beer and sighs: "I guess that's it." National Hockey League commissioner Gary Bettman had just rejected the players' eleventh-hour offer and locked them out, jeopardizing a season that was supposed to start the next day. Concerned about undermining hockey's budding fan interest in the U.S. Sunbelt, Gretzky views the labor impasse as about as welcome as a stick to the gut. "I just hope that people understand and the game doesn't suffer too much," he says gloomily. But his mood brightens considerably when the subject turns to hockey's long-term prospects. "I'm probably more optimistic and more determined than ever," he says. "Of all the major sports, hockey is the one most on the rise."

Such positive thinking springs easily from a man who is thoroughly enjoying himself. Gretzky is happily ensconced in the lush life of Los Angeles with his actress wife, Janet, and their three thriving children. His father, Walter, with whom he is extremely close, has recovered from a near-fatal brain aneurysm. The herniated thoracic disc in Gretzky's back that nearly cut short his career in 1992 has been consigned to memory. And at 33, he has emphatically demonstrated that reports of his athletic demise were greatly exaggerated: last spring, he scored his 802nd career goal to overtake Gordie Howe's all-time NHL record, and he won his 10th league-scoring title.

But virtually since the day he first laced a skate as a professional, Gretzky has quietly pursued a second arena of achievement—business. "It's pretty simple," he explains. "I was bored by not doing anything with my time off, and before I got married and had kids, I had a lot of time." After a comparatively slow start, his office activities have given new meaning to the term "net profits." He and his agent, Los

Angeles-based Michael Barnett, now juggle a diverse portfolio of endorsements and partnerships with companies that sell everything from hockey sticks and soft drinks to insurance and consumer electronics. His corporate partners, eager to associate with The Great One, seek bigger profits and higher market profile. In return, they pay Gretzky fees and royalties that, added to the staggering $11.6 million-per-season stipend that the Los Angeles Kings pay him for playing, push his annual income to an estimated $23.5 million. "Gretzky's legend has transcended his sport so that even mainstream American companies have been able to use him," says Jeff Jensen, who covers sports marketing for *Advertising Age*, the Chicago-based trade journal. "People know what he stands for even if they know nothing about hockey."

Gretzky has kept his business affairs mostly to himself—he hardly needs more publicity, and, besides, it is his business. But what he once jokingly referred to as "my little empire" has become difficult to ignore. He stars in major television advertising campaigns for such consumer giants as Domino's Pizza and Sharp Electronics. He is a corporate spokesman for Coca-Cola and Zurich Insurance. He has boosted the bottom-line fortunes of such smaller companies as Easton Sports and in-line skate-maker First Team Sports. His name and image are licensed on dozens of products, from trading cards and posters to T-shirts and coins. He has one restaurant in Toronto and will soon help launch a North American chain of sports-themed restaurants in an all-star partnership that includes gridiron hero Joe Montana, tennis ace Andre Agassi and basketball behemoth Shaquille O'Neal. Time Warner, the giant U.S. communications firm, has designed an interactive video game around him, and he is spearheading a plan to build privately financed, family-oriented ice rinks across North America. "We have tried to build something I can fall back on when I retire, something I can do when I finish playing hockey," he says.

In a series of recent interviews with *Maclean's*, Gretzky talked about how he and Barnett have woven a seemingly disparate group of partners into a mutually profitable web. Although neither he nor his sponsors would divulge the exact dollar details of their contracts, one thing is eminently clear: off ice as well as on, Gretzky is money in the bank. If pro sport ever had a can't-miss kid, it was young Wayne Gretzky. The Brantford, Ont., native was a certified phenomenon at age 10, when he scored 378 goals in one 69-game season as a peewee. He signed his first pro contract at only 17, and tied superstar Marcel Dionne for the most points in his rookie NHL campaign. Since then, he has won the Stanley Cup four times and respectfully but inexorably obliterated just about every league offensive record—including the supposedly untouchable milestones set by his idol, Howe. His league-wide impact has been equally impressive: his trade to Los Angeles in 1988 turned around a falling franchise and paved the way for the league to add five more Sunbelt cities.

The endorsement world took longer to conquer, partly because in sport it is not so much what you do as where you do it. Mark Messier, Gretzky's former teammate with the Oilers, won the Stanley Cup five times in Edmonton, but only became the object of marketing desire after winning the Cup last spring with the New York Rangers. Gretzky found the spotlight in Los Angeles, arriving as a bona fide star in a place that worships and rewards the species. Today, his annual endorsement earnings, estimated at about $12 million, are topped only by the gods of athletic commerce—including Michael Jordan (estimated at $40 million), basketball's ubiquitous O'Neal ($20 million) and venerable golfers Arnold Palmer and Jack Nicklaus ($20 million each). And Gretzky has done it all despite the fact that hockey, for all its recent inroads, remains a poor fourth in the U.S. sports consciousness after basketball, football and baseball. According to Brandon Steiner, president of Steiner Sports Marketing in New York City, hockey stars such as Mario Lemieux, Brett Hull and Eric Lindros simply do not yet have the profile to carry a national U.S. advertising campaign. "You put most of those guys in street clothes out on Madison Avenue," said Steiner, "and no one notices them."

Not so Gretzky. He excites advertisers not so much for the records he sets as for the manner in which he sets them. He has a style all his own—signature moves inside an opponent's blue line that give him space to shoot or to set up a teammate in the clear. He is creative, finding scoring opportunities from seeming chaos. He is a team player, whose assist totals are even more remarkable than his goal records. And he is generous, reflecting glory on teammates, past players and the greatness of the game.

Clean-living and clean-cut, he is a model citizen off the ice as well. Advertisers cringe when their walking billboards attract negative publicity: examples range from the relatively benign, such as figure skater Nancy Kerrigan's post-Olympics petulance, to the more serious—golfer John Daly's alcoholism, sprinter Ben Johnson's steroid scandals and, of course, the arrest of ex-footballer O.J. Simpson on murder charges. Gretzky, meanwhile, is unfailingly polite to both fans and reporters. He comes across as the guy next door, albeit a very famous one—an enthusiastic family man who honors his parents, his team and his small-town values. Amazingly enough, associates say, the image is accurate—Gretzky really is all those things.

But for sponsors, the most intoxicating ingredient in the Gretzky mix is the

After tying Gordie Howe's goal-scoring record, March 20, 1994.

amount of attention he generates. Even last season, playing on a team that would not make the playoffs, Gretzky was still featured on the news each night as he neared and finally surpassed Howe's goal-scoring record. As a result, his renown extends well beyond the narrow confines of the hard-core hockey crowd. He is frequently invited on talk shows and hosted NBC's *Saturday Night Live*. His presence at a Coca-Cola-sponsored kids' hockey camp last summer in Anaheim, Calif., attracted a camera crew from TV's *Entertainment Tonight*, the weeknight half-hour of Hollywood Lite. He is no longer a mere athlete, he is a full-blown celebrity. Sharp, the Japanese electronics firm, made Gretzky the spokesman for its most important consumer product, the Viewcam—without even identifying him as a hockey player in its TV ads. As it happens, Gretzky's first attempt at being a corporate spokesman was a complete bust. Nelson Skalbania, the Vancouver entrepreneur who in 1979 signed Gretzky to his first professional hockey contract—with the Indianapolis Racers of the Word Hockey Association—wanted his prized employee to dress up an otherwise drab ceremony marking Skalbania's purchase of a brewery in Prince George, B.C. Gretzky, who was then an extremely nervous flyer, jetted from Indianapolis to Prince George via Vancouver, but when he arrived, he was refused entry. The event was being staged at a bar, and Gretzky, though already a star, was only 17. He took a cab to the airport and flew back to Indiana.

In great demand to attend corporate functions or charity golf tournaments, Gretzky remembers his first off-season as a blur. "I didn't have a schedule, a datebook—anything," he recalls. "I needed someone in Edmonton to help me, to organize my life. It's hard for me to say no to people—I'm not good at it and never will be." He had met Barnett, then an Edmonton restaurateur, the year before, and they became friends during the 1979–80 season, Gretzky's first in the NHL. After discussions with his father, they struck a deal, and soon Gretzky's off-ice affairs began to take shape. His face appeared on Pro-Stars breakfast-cereal boxes, and he was featured in Canadian advertising for such products as Mr. Big chocolate bars, 7-Up and GWG Jeans. By the time Gretzky left Edmonton in 1988, his off-ice income reached an estimated high of more than $1 million per year—chump change for Michael Jordan perhaps, but big bucks by hockey standards.

Gretzky's market muscle was evident with his first endorsement, signed in 1979 with Titan hockey sticks. The then-Finnish company agreed to pay $5,000 a year for three years. "I was 18 years old, I got to travel, meet people, play in golf outings, shoot some local TV commercials—it was great," he recalls. "Great" understates the impact on Titan. As Gretzky began establishing his hall-of-fame hockey credentials, stick sales took off. By 1989, when Gretzky switched to Easton sticks, his income from Titan had climbed to $125,000 per year plus royalties on sales of specific models. During that same period, the company ceased importing its North American stock from Finland and built the world's largest stick manufacturing plant in Cowansville, Que. From a lowly No. 15 in the hockey-stick world in 1979, Titan had rocketed to No. 1 a decade later. "Wayne was responsible for us building that factory in Canada," says Bob Leeder, sales director for Titan. "He *made* Titan hockey sticks—no one in our company would dispute that."

Despite piling up points for the Oilers and profits for his sponsors, Gretzky may as well have been shovelling snow as far as many American advertisers were concerned. They understood basketball, baseball and football; they knew Magic Johnson, Reggie Jackson and Joe Montana. But although he had some U.S. contracts, Gretzky had still not broken through with mainstream America. That attitude changed when he moved south. Overnight, hockey became cool in California, and Gretzky became a hot commercial property. Kings president Bruce McNall, who has seen his own fortunes plummet and now faces four charges of defrauding banks for more than $300 million, said that even the entertainment industry took notice. "I remember having to go to a party the first night that Wayne was in L.A., and all the stars were lined up to get his autograph," McNall recalled last summer. "He was shocked and a little embarrassed, but I think it showed the level to which he was known even before he played here."

The attention was flattering, but it was not an enjoyable time for Gretzky. He was leaving Edmonton, where he had been happy, and the Oilers, one of hockey's greatest-ever teams. Even today, his voice takes on a hard edge when he talks about Oilers owner Peter Pocklington "selling me out of Edmonton." But Gretzky knows how to make the best of a bad situation—consider how many goals he has set up while being cornered behind the opposing team's net. So he decided to make the best of the trade to Los Angeles, and as a result he has become rich beyond his wildest dreams.

It is a stinking hot July day in Southern California, and the tar is bubbling up between cracks in the deserted parking lot surrounding The Pond of Anaheim. But inside, the arena is cool and alive. In the plush home of the NHL's Mighty Ducks, a scene befitting the namesake Disney movie is in full swing. On one section of the rink, weak-ankled kids career around like bumper cars, collectively trying to steal the puck away from the lone adult in their midst. They slash him, hook him and call him names. Finally, they hound him down, capture the puck and send their victim gasping to the bench in search of water. Leaning against the boards, Gretzky drags a towel across his forehead and laughs at the suggestion that he has met his match. "This stuff isn't easy," he protests. "Those kids are good."

Although he enjoys working with kids, summer shinny is strictly business for Gretzky, one of many corporate obligations on his off-season slate. Companies pay him six- and seven-figure annual fees to be their spokesman, and two of the five days he works for Coca-Cola each year are spent playing host to the kids at the Future Stars camp. Gretzky's duties vary with the company. With some, he meets with staff or speaks at sales meetings. Most use him in print and TV advertising. Others simply ask him to join key clients for a day on the golf course.

Profit and publicity are the goals and assists of the marketing game, and Gretzky delivers both. Tony Luppino, vice-president of corporate communications for Toronto-based Zurich Insurance, says that his firm started using Gretzky in its advertising in 1988 and, within three years, scored 20 per cent better in customer-awareness surveys. Every summer, thousands of kids around North America buy six-packs of

Coke and fill in ballots in hopes of winning the chance to scrimmage with Gretzky at the camp. And Stuart deGeus, national director of field marketing for Ann Arbor, Mich.-based Domino's Pizza Inc., reports that using Gretzky in advertising has given the company market prominence in Canada that outstrips its relatively small presence—180 Canadian outlets compared with 4,700 in the United States.

But Gretzky is more than a figurehead. He can, in the sales vernacular, move product, so he has several deals with smaller firms that cannot afford his usual up-front fees but offered him a percentage of profits. Industry analysts say that such royalties can push his annual stipend from a single successful firm to well over $1 million. And with Gretzky's help, some of his sponsors have been extraordinarily successful. Easton, for instance, approached him in 1989 about endorsing its aluminum-shafted stick. When the company built one to his specifications, Gretzky signed a fee-plus-royalty deal for four years (it has since been renewed). Easton, a private company based in Van Nuys, Calif., does not release financial information, but industry sources estimate that its hockey sales have increased to more than $40 million from about $14 million in five years. First Team Sports, a Minneapolis-based manufacturer of Ultra-Wheels in-line skates, signed Gretzky in 1990 and saw its skate sales climb to an estimated $95 million in 1994 from only $4 million in 1990. "We are trying to grow in Europe," says Dave Soderquist, the company's vice-chairman, "and even in places like Switzerland or Austria we can show buyers a catalogue with his picture in it and everyone knows Wayne. He opens doors in new markets."

Gretzky is extremely cautious about which hockey products he endorses. Barnett has had to turn down rich offers from skate companies because Gretzky prefers a brand—Daoust—that pays him nothing but fits perfectly. (Perfect is a relative term: Gretzky has weak ankles, so, to improve his skating, he crams his size 9s into a custom-made pair of size 6 3/4 skates.) "My profession is hockey," he explains, "and if I can't function at my best, I'm not going to be sought after in other areas."

In recent weeks, Gretzky has agreed to endorse The Official All-Star Cafe, a new restaurant chain run by Robert Earl, who founded the successful Hard Rock Café and Planet Hollywood franchises. Earl is counting on Gretzky, Montana, O'Neal and Agassi to push people out of sports bars and into full-service restaurants. And in November, Time Warner InterActive announced that Gretzky will go digital as the star of the forthcoming "Gretzky! All-Star Hockey," a home video game due out next March. Also coming in 1995 is a new athletic shoe—for street hockey—designed with Gretzky's help by Santa Monica, Calif.-based L.A. Gear.

For all he does elsewhere, the rink remains Gretzky's main place of business. It is what pays him most and what he loves best, and it is where his authority is greatest. When players' association boss Bob Goodenow wanted to add weight to an important news conference recently, he asked Gretzky to be there. When commissioner Bettman wanted to enhance the image of the league, he requested that Gretzky attend *Sports Illustrated*'s 40th anniversary TV special—Gretzky had placed 12th on the magazine's list of the most influential sports figures of the past four decades. And International Ice Hockey Federation president Rene Fasel complained that member federations had trouble fitting Gretzky's European tour into their schedules, but he complied anyway. "What can you do?" Fasel said. "He is so famous." At times, says teammate Marty McSorley, Gretzky gets too caught up in his broader responsibilities. "He can get so involved with the issues of the sport," says McSorley, "that sometimes I want to shake him and remind him that he's just a player."

When Gretzky plays for the Kings, he is paid handsomely: he is in the middle of a three-year, $34.8-million deal. At $11.6 million per year, it is the highest annual salary in team sports history. "The contract," says Barnett, "had to reflect what he had done for the Los Angeles franchise, not only on the ice but off it as well." The game, however, does more than just pay Gretzky. Despite the pressure to perform, hockey nevertheless gives him refuge from the near-constant demands of his off-ice life. "Sometimes it seems like I have been a pro all my life," he says, "but the rink was always the place where no one would bother me. That was where I was able to focus in on my own enjoyment, my hockey."

Although the economic circumstances are worlds apart, Gretzky is doing his best to bring a little Brantford to Beverly Hills. He and Janet, who met during the taping of a TV show called *Dance Fever* in 1981 and were married in 1988, moved from a somewhat isolated estate in Encino to their current house so that Paulina, 5, Ty, 4, and Trevor, 2, could grow up in a more family-oriented neighborhood. Los Angeles may at times be a dangerous place, but kids still need other kids to play with. "It's a gated community and, within that, we try to let them lead as normal a life as possible," Gretzky says. "It's not like it was for me. When I was six years old, I would get up in the morning and go to the park all day. We don't do that. The kids are never out of the sight of an adult. But it's about as normal a life as we can provide."

Amid massive homes owned by the likes of celebrities Paula Abdul and Vanna White, the Gretzky abode is comparatively discreet. The two-storey house is furnished tastefully and comfortably with antiques and overstuffed furniture, but even the contractors who repaired the damage from last year's earthquake could not mitigate the effects of children. The house is usually overrun by kids and kiddie paraphernalia. There is a steady stream of adults, too. Janet's mother has lived with them since they moved to Los Angeles, and both Janet and Wayne have had siblings stay for extended periods. Gretzky's parents visit frequently, and during training camp two Kings rookies, Jamie Storr and Matt Johnson, bunked in.

Gretzky is conservative with his personal investments, with occasional exceptions. In 1991, he split the $503,000 cost of the famous Honus Wagner baseball card with McNall—a card that, because of McNall's bankruptcy, is now up for sale. But he claims that his only major money loser was his $1-million investment in McNall's ill-fated purchase of the Toronto Argonauts in 1991. He avoids real estate and stocks, preferring steadier if less spectacular performance. "We are planning for his future," says Laurie Hunter, his full-time accountant. "He is very level-headed that way, unlike a lot of other athletes." He also watches over his business interests. Tom Bitove, whose family co-owns Gretzky's Toronto restaurant, says that Gretzky reacted coolly to news that sales in the early weeks of the operation were higher than expected. "He knew the numbers looked good, but he wasn't going to be impressed until he had seen what we had spent," Bitove says. "A lot of people think that it's just Barnett doing all the deals, but Wayne knows his way around business. He is very astute that way."

Gretzky's fiscal conservatism breaks down when it comes to family. He loves to surprise his near and dear with lavish presents: among other things, he bought a new fishing boat for his father, a Ferrari for Janet one Mother's Day and a Porsche for Paulina—the five-year-old—for when "she turns 18 or 21—I haven't decided yet." Usually, though, he is careful. "I don't like being flashy," he says. "But you still have to enjoy your success. I work really hard. I like to buy clothes, and I like to travel with my family. I just don't want to be stupid about it and send the wrong message to my kids."

Janet, who is again pursuing a performing career, steers the spotlight away from their children as best she can. "We have had a lot of offers to use our kids in things, and we have kept them out of it," she says. They made an exception with the Sharp commercial, which chronicled Ty's first-ever ice-skating adventure, but that is as far as she is willing to go. "I want him to concentrate on sports and kids and school," she says. "I don't want him to be a celebrity."

Success could go to Gretzky's head, but it would have to fight through his family to get there. His wife and father, though enormously supportive, are his reality checks. "I just try to impress upon him how fortunate he is," Walter says. "Not everyone is in his position." Nor is Gretzky likely to take his business life for granted. "I don't want to take the money and run," he says. "I get a kick when people say that their company has gone from here to there since I joined."

Still, the business that Gretzky finally retires to is probably the one he has been in all along—hockey. "I would love to be part of an ownership group, putting an entire organization together," he says. "And I would love for it to be here with the Kings." But he is not retiring just yet—he expects to play at least two more years—and that is why, beyond his worries about the effect of the lockout, Gretzky also admits to a sense of personal loss. In autumn, even in Southern California, a man who has lived by the rhythm of the rink is ready to skate. "I am at an age when I do not want to miss any time out there," he says. "I want to play." And that, for Gretzky, is the bottom line.

LEMIEUX, LINDROS & OTHER LEGENDS

Like Father, Like Son

D'Arcy Jenish

March 18, 1991—He is the National Hockey League's most unconventional superstar, a player who can dominate a game even when he is not carrying the puck and often seems to be out of step with his linemates. But despite his unorthodox style, 26-year-old Brett Hull, million-dollar right winger with the St. Louis Blues and son of hockey legend Bobby Hull, has emerged as the NHL's most prolific goal scorer. In a March 2 game against the Philadelphia Flyers, his 64th of the season, Hull scored his 70th goal of the 1990–91 campaign to become only the third player in league history, after the Los Angeles Kings' Wayne Gretzky and Pittsburgh Penguins centre Mario Lemieux, to reach that plateau in consecutive seasons. Although some hockey analysts contend that Hull is merely an opportunist with a hard, accurate shot, he maintains that his style of play bewilders and disrupts opponents. Said Hull: "I take myself right out of the play to get open. Sometimes when we're going into the other team's zone, I'm skating out of their zone."

In his own words, Hull is "the epitome of a late bloomer." He almost quit hockey altogether at the age of 18 before making a Tier 2 junior team, a level below major-junior hockey, in Penticton, B.C., where he scored 105 goals in 56 games. Hull, not a strong skater and poor defensively, failed to impress his first NHL employer, the Calgary Flames, and they traded him after only 57 games to St. Louis in March, 1988. In 1989–90, his second full season with the Blues, he scored 72 goals, a league record for right wingers. Last summer, the Blues rewarded Hull with a four-year, $8.3-million contract, which will pay him $1.4 million this season, up from $150,000 a year earlier.

With his new contract, Hull is now the third-highest-paid player in the game, behind Gretzky and Lemieux. The high salary has also meant added responsibilities. Before the season began, Blues head coach Brian Sutter told Hull that he expects him to help out captain Scott Stevens by providing extra on-ice team leadership. And Hull admits that, because of his personality, being a leader is a bigger challenge than scoring goals. "I'm so laid-back and easy-going that it's tough for me," he said. "I keep myself loose, but I have to make sure everybody else is ready to play."

Although Gretzky still dominates this year's point-scoring list, Hull has achieved several hockey milestones with his prodigious goal-scoring feats. When he scored his 50th goal of the 1989–90 season on Feb. 6, 1990, he and Bobby Hull became the only father and son ever to have reached that plateau in the NHL. This season, Hull became one of three players in league history, along with Gretzky and Lemieux, to have scored 50 goals in less than 50 games. And on March 7, Hull scored his 73rd, 74th and 75th goals of the season in a game against the Boston Bruins, breaking his own record for right wingers.

Besides blasting his way into the NHL record books, Hull has dramatically raised the profile of professional hockey in St. Louis, a midwestern American city primarily known for its major-league baseball team, the National League Cardinals. Blues president Jack Quinn said that the team currently has 12,500 season-ticket holders, an increase of 3,400 over last season, largely due to the publicity surrounding the off-season contracts signed by Hull and defenceman Stevens. Said Quinn: "Hull has made this team the city's biggest show. He is the city's biggest star right now."

With his accomplishments of the past two seasons, Hull has finally emerged from the shadow of his famous father, whom many hockey experts regard as the greatest left winger ever to play the game. But Bobby Hull's fame in Chicago and later in Winnipeg's WHA franchise brought him and his entire family painful public exposure in the late 1970s when he and his wife, Joanne, went through a bitter and controversial divorce. After 20 years of marriage and five children, Hull's estranged wife accused him of physical and mental cruelty, as well as adultery. In June, 1980, the Manitoba Court of Queen's Bench awarded Joanne Hull a total of $600,000 and custody of the children. The children—Bobby Jr., now 29, Blake, now 28, Brett, his younger brother Bart, now 22, and sister Michelle, now 20—moved to Vancouver with their mother.

The former Joanne Hull subsequently married life insurance executive Harry Robinson, and they divide their time between homes in West Vancouver and Blaine, Wash. Brett's oldest brother is vice-president of Marshall Gobuty International, a Toronto-based clothing manufacturer, while Blake Hull is living in Tampa, Fla., and attempting to qualify for the Professional Golf Association tour. Bart Hull, a running back at Boise State University in Idaho, was selected by the B.C. Lions last month in the first round of the Canadian Football League's annual amateur draft. And Michelle Hull is a third-year pre-medical student at Western Washington University in Bellingham.

Bobby and Brett Hull after Brett scored his 50th goal of the season for the St. Louis Blues, February 7, 1990.

For several years after the divorce, Brett Hull recalls, he rarely saw his father, who returned to the cattle farm he owned near Belleville in eastern Ontario. Although they now have a good relationship, Hull said that he still sees little of his father because the elder Hull spends much of the winter at a Florida resort property. But Bobby Hull attended a St. Louis Blues home game against the Toronto Maple Leafs on the night his son became a 50-goal scorer for the first time. Following the game, Bobby Hull told reporters: "I always told him he isn't a 30- or 40-goal scorer, he's a 50- or 60-goal scorer."

Despite his parents' turbulent divorce, Hull said that he retains fond memories of growing up in Winnipeg and attending Jet practices with his older brothers and their famous father. After the sessions, he said, his father would frequently sit his sons on the boards and demonstrate basic hockey skills. But Brett Hull grew up to become a markedly different player than his father. While Bobby Hull dazzled fans with rink-long rushes and intimidated goalies with a fearsome slapshot, Brett Hull rarely carries the puck out of his own end. Normally, he lags behind to watch the play develop

Like Father, Like Son 303

or races ahead to distract opposing defencemen. His primary objective is to find a patch of open ice in the offensive zone and look for a pass from a teammate.

Opposing players say that Hull is an opportunist who strikes with devastating effectiveness. Maple Leafs goalie Jeff Reese, who was in the net when Hull scored his 50th goal last season, said: "He's got one of the quickest releases in the league, and his shot is so accurate it's unbelievable. A lot of the times when he's scored on me, I thought I had him." Leaf defenceman and team captain Rob Ramage added: "He's got the gift. He's a natural scorer. He's got a great sense of anticipation, of where the net is without even looking." Philadelphia goalie Ron Hextall, who allowed Hull's 70th goal this season, said: "When he comes in on the wing, he's got an awful lot of speed. If you give him a hole, he hits it."

Hull says that he has emerged as one of the NHL's top players because of coach Sutter's patient tutoring. The 34-year-old Sutter, one of six brothers from Viking, Alta., to play in the NHL, is now in his third season behind the Blues bench. Said Hull: "He lets people do what they do best and then works on their weaknesses with videos and practice. He doesn't take a guy like me who can score and turn me into a defensive player." And Hull says that he remains perplexed over how he was handled by the Flames, who traded him even though he got 50 points in 52 games. Said Hull: "In Calgary, I wouldn't play the last 10 minutes of a period if I made a mistake. It was tough for me to learn when I was sitting on the bench."

But Hull says that he has no complaints about life in St. Louis. He lives in the affluent suburb of Warson Woods with his 26-year-old girlfriend, Allison Curran. They met six years ago in Duluth, Minn., where he was attending university on a hockey scholarship. They make their off-season home at Pike Lake, about 10 km north of Duluth. Hull plays golf every day during the summer at one, and sometimes both, of the city's private clubs. He drives a red Corvette, and two promotional vehicles, a Chevrolet Blazer and a Nissan Infiniti Q45, provided by St. Louis car dealers. And when he has spare time during the season, which does not happen very often, he stays home, unplugs the phone and tries to relax. While he may have shrugged off the expectations of being his father's son, Hull still faces the pressures he has created for himself as the NHL's top gun.

Brett Hull ended the 1991 season with 86 goals and 131 points. Only Wayne Gretzky has scored more goals in a single season, 87 in 1983–84 and 92 and 1981–82.

Lucky Lindros

Bruce Wallace

September 9, 1991—The overhead lights in Toronto's Maple Leaf Gardens have been turned off and the dim lighting that remains obscures the dinginess of one of hockey's most famous shrines. The players on Team Canada, their practice over, have all left the building on a steamy August afternoon. But 18-year-old Eric Lindros, widely considered to be the best player of his generation and the still-unscarred face of Canada's hockey future, sits in the empty stands. Hooking the legs of his six-foot five-inch, 224-lb. body over the seat in front of him, Lindros throws his head back and bellows at the rafters and the ghosts of the Gardens. "This is my barn," he shouts to the deserted arena. "I love you." Then, Lindros speaks wistfully of his future in hockey. "I don't know if I ever want to get away from Toronto," says Lindros. "Can you imagine this place if the Leafs won another Stanley Cup after all these years? The score clock would fall down and the plaster would come off the walls." His voice softens and he stares toward the ice. "Imagine," he says. "The Leafs. Alive again."

Even at 18, Eric Lindros is accustomed to making dreams come true. Without ever having played a game in the National Hockey League (NHL), he proved during Team Canada tryouts for the Canada Cup showdown that he could excel alongside the Canadian hockey elite by winning a place on the team. But while he prepared to play this month for his country against the best in the world in the Canada Cup series, Lindros found his ambitions stalled by an off-ice obstacle that not even his extraordinary size, speed or shot could overcome. His right to play in the NHL is controlled by the Quebec Nordiques, who used their first choice in the league's draft last June to pick him. But the strong-willed Lindros, who describes himself as a "rebel," says that he has no intention of playing hockey in Quebec City. "Sometimes, you have to look at the political aspect of the thing," he told *Maclean's* in the Gardens. "If things are not going well politically in a certain climate, then you have to think twice about whether you want to be there."

In a wide-ranging interview, Lindros told *Maclean's* why he was unwilling to go to Quebec City. "The people that come out of high school with the best grades go to the best universities. The people with the lower grades have fewer choices," he said. "Why should a player who comes out of junior hockey with top marks go to a city that is not his choice? I'm thinking about my family and what the pressure's going to be like on them." Lindros said that as the financial stakes in professional hockey grow, teams in some smaller Canadian cities may have trouble surviving. Said Lindros: "It's great that the Canadian teams are still here, but it's going to be tough financially for them to compete. In cities like Winnipeg, they treat hockey as a business. [But] it's going to be harder for players who want to be treated equally—financially and in other respects—to play in these places."

Lindros has signalled that he possesses grand hockey ambitions, and intends to achieve them his way. On the ice, he is a menacing presence to opponents: a marauding, extremely physical player with spectacular scoring skills and a locomotive drive to win at all costs. "You won't see me calling for an end to fighting," Lindros told *Maclean's*. "I think there is a place in the game for fighting."

But just as NHL owners salivate at the prospect of adding Lindros to the league's marquee, the confident teen-ager who has yet to play a professional game is sending shivers through the hockey establishment by refusing to play in Quebec. "Everyone has the right to work where they want to work," said Lindros. "The old way has got to change." Still, critics have expressed concern that an unrestricted campaign by players to defy the draft system and play with the team of their choice would undermine franchises in small markets, especially those in Canadian cities that include Quebec City and Winnipeg. Said Harry Neale, a hockey broadcaster and former coach with the Vancouver Canucks: "Lindros is the most extreme example of the NHL's biggest problem." Neale added that because taxes are higher in Canada than in the United States, "no player prefers to play in Canada. But if they must, the English-speaking players don't want to play in Quebec. It is a magnification of the mood of the country."

Lindros has not endeared himself to the residents of Quebec City. There, fans comforted themselves during their team's losing 1990–91 season with the knowledge that their last-place finish would give them the right to pick the most heralded junior hockey player since Mario Lemieux and, before that, Wayne Gretzky. But as far back as last May, Lindros told Nordiques president Marcel Aubut that he would not play in Quebec City. Lindros and his parents, Carl and Bonnie Lindros, insist that playing in the small, predominantly francophone market would lessen his value for off-ice endorsements. And Lindros clearly wants to establish his career with a competitive organization in a city where he might live permanently. "There is not a good fit between Eric and the Nordiques for a variety of reasons, including economically and in terms of lifestyle," said Carl Lindros, a friendly, powerfully built chartered accountant. "We warned Quebec of that before the draft in order to save them any embarrassment over trying to sign Eric."

Since then, relations between the two sides have deteriorated further. "It's an ego thing," said Eric Lindros of Aubut's refusal, so far, to trade him to another club. Despite reports in the Quebec press saying that Lindros was seeking a three-year contract that would pay him $3 million a year, Carl Lindros told *Maclean's* that "we have never made a financial demand of Quebec." Still, many Quebecers now refer sarcastically to Lindros as "the son of Bay Street." Said Albert Ladouceur, a hockey writer for the daily *Journal de Québec*: "The fans here are hurt by his attitude." And by citing political reasons for his refusal to join the Nordiques, Lindros may provoke a backlash that extends beyond the hockey world.

The Quebec furor is only the latest in a short career that has been almost as noteworthy for its turmoil as for its brilliance. Lindros has challenged hockey's ways of doing business in the past. In 1989, when the Sault Ste. Marie Greyhounds of the Ontario Hockey League (OHL) drafted him from the Toronto-based St. Michael's College Junior B team, he refused to obey the rules and move, arguing that he wanted to play hockey for a team based closer to his family's Toronto home. The league finally gave in and changed its rules to allow Lindros to be traded to the Oshawa Generals. Some NHL players have welcomed his insistence on playing hockey where he wants to and under conditions that he likes. Said Montreal Canadiens centre Brian Skrudland, who until he was cut from Team Canada was Lindros's roommate: "Eric has realized something at 18 that few of us did: that hockey is a business. And there is a lot of money in this game now."

It is almost impossible for hockey fans to remain ambivalent about Lindros. His aggressive playing style and controversial off-ice attitude have attracted intense animosity from many fans. When Lindros led his Oshawa team into Sault Ste. Marie during last spring's Junior A playoffs, fans screamed abuse and spat at him. He has been booed by Canadian fans during Team Canada exhibition games in Ottawa and Montreal. But Lindros plays with such physical ferocity and he is such a masterly goal scorer that he can win over critics, as he did with a two-goal performance in an

Eric Lindros in a 1991 Canada Cup exhibition game.

exhibition match against Team USA in Montreal on August 18. "I get pumped up," said Lindros in explaining how an arena full of hostile fans can motivate him. "I get possessed with the fear of losing."

For the London, Ont.-born Lindros, who moved to Toronto with his family when he was 10, the desire to win has been evident since he was a minor-hockey sensation. "When I was growing up, I never had a whole lot of friends because I was never into the social aspect of the game," he said. "My best friends are still the friends away from the rink." At times, his interests outside hockey have collided with the demands of the sport. As a Grade 6 student, Lindros was practising simultaneously with his peewee hockey team, which was headed for a tournament in Quebec City, and with his school band, where he played trumpet. Recalled Lindros with a disbelieving laugh: "The band teacher took me aside and said, 'Listen, where are your priorities? Are they with the band or are they in hockey?'" By the time he was in Grade 10, his music teacher had expelled him from the band.

But he never neglected hockey practices. At 13, he was practising one hour a day with the 15- and 16-year-olds on the St. Mike's team, often riding to practice on a unicycle while carrying his books and hockey equipment. "Even as a young kid, he was completely focused on hockey," said Scott McLellan, his coach at St. Mike's. "I could blast him for mistakes like older players and he never sulked and was never intimidated." And McLellan said that Lindros's parents have been unfairly criticized for their handling of their son's hockey career. "They did not interfere or push him," he said. "They simply made every concession to accommodate what Eric himself wanted."

Still, some critics say that Lindros's self-driven approach to the game turned into obstinacy when the Greyhounds drafted him. And when the OHL initially balked at changing its bylaw that prevented any team from trading its first-round draft pick for a year, Lindros simply went to play for a commercially sponsored junior team in Detroit. Seven months later, the league relented, allowing a trade to Oshawa for three players, three future draft picks and $80,000. With Lindros in the lineup, Oshawa sold out every game in its 4,200-seat arena and won the 1990 Memorial Cup, Canada's junior hockey championship. Lindros also played on Canada's last two world junior championship teams. And Lindros led the OHL in scoring last year, with 71 goals and 78 assists in 57 games.

Fans in Sault Ste. Marie never forgave Lindros. Said Greyhounds director Sherwood Bassin: "People in the Soo were offended. They felt that their families and their community had been affronted, the same as Quebec now feels." The anger spilled out in May when Lindros returned to Sault Ste. Marie during the league's playoffs. The fans taunted him by waving pacifiers and hanging signs with messages that included: "Lindros wants his mommy." To the delight of Sault Ste. Marie fans, the Greyhounds defeated Oshawa in the playoff round.

Despite his impressive credentials, some hockey commentators expressed skepticism about Lindros's lack of experience when Team Canada officials invited him to try out. Lindros dispelled the doubts by demonstrating a deft scoring touch—and by throwing body checks at some of the biggest and toughest players in the training camp, including Los Angeles Kings heavyweight Marty McSorley. He paid a price for his aggressiveness. Colliding with New York Islanders centre Brent Sutter during a scrimmage in Collingwood, Ont., Lindros sustained a mild concussion.

Just two night later, he was in uniform for his first exhibition game with Team Canada against Team USA at the Montreal Forum. The venerable arena provided an intimidating setting for his debut. Lindros, arriving early and alone for the game, walked into the wrong dressing room by mistake. Fans heckled his parents as they entered the building. In the game's early stages, boos cascaded from many of the 14,377 fans every time that Lindros stepped onto the ice.

Team Canada assistant coach Pat Burns had warned him before the game of an ugly reception. Said Burns: "The fans booed Jean Beliveau in here and I think they would boo the Lord's Prayer if they could." But Lindros seemed to be unfazed. He choked off some of the catcalls with a devastating body check on the six-foot one-inch American defenceman Craig Wolanin in the first period. Then, he scored two second-period goals and assisted on another in the third period, flashing a grin at his parents in the crowd and sweeping the Forum fans onto their feet. When he was announced as the player of the game, the ovation was as loud as the boos had been earlier.

By turning the Team Canada training camp into a personal showcase, Lindros served notice that he can already be counted as one of the NHL's best and most exciting players. "If you don't produce on the ice, then nothing is going to happen off the ice," said the Kings' Gretzky after a practice in Toronto. "Eric has talked a lot about endorsements, but those things will come with the territory. I'm not saying what he's worth, but he's going to make a lot of money."

Clearly, Lindros presents a challenge to the foundations of the NHL's established business practices. But the pressure has also taken a toll on an 18-year-old who, despite his talent and self-assuredness, is uneasy about his future. "All my friends are taking off for universities," said Lindros, who has registered for an economics course at Toronto's York University this fall. "It makes me really nervous to not know what I'll be doing." And in refusing to report to Quebec while making it known that he would be willing to play in Toronto, he runs the risk of becoming a symbol of the growing tensions between Quebec and the rest of Canada. "I'd take a pay cut to play in Canada," he said. "But why would someone take a cut to play in a place where they are not happy?" For Eric Lindros, hockey's grail may always be as difficult to grasp off the ice as on.

Team Canada won its fourth Canada Cup in five tournaments when they beat the United States in a best-of-three final. Eric Lindros had three goals and two assists during the tournament, tying him for fifth in scoring among his teammates. Lindros never did sign with the Quebec Nordiques and spent the 1991–92 season splitting his playing time among the

Oshawa Generals, the Canadian national team and Canada's Olympic hockey team, where he won a silver medal. When the Nordiques finally agreed to trade Lindros, both the New York Rangers and the Philadelphia Flyers believed they had secured his services. An arbitrator was called in and the Flyers were awarded the righs to Lindros for six players and $15 million (U.S.).

Bruce Wallace is Maclean's *Ottawa Bureau Chief. He joined the magazine in its Quebec bureau in 1985.*

Broadway Mark Messier

D'Arcy Jenish

March 30, 1992—After a successful night's work, Mark Messier straddles a bar stool at the Play By Play Lounge in Madison Square Garden. His big hands cradle a bottle of Rolling Rock ale, and his rugged, angular face bears the smile of a man who appears to have everything. The 31-year-old hockey star is savoring another New York Ranger victory. To his left sits Carrie Nygren, a tall, blond Swedish model and actress whom Messier is dating. Across the table are his sister Mary-Kay, 29, and brother Paul, 34, who share his 73rd-floor Manhattan condo and handle his off-ice business affairs. But despite his contented smile, Messier remains restless and ambitious, eagerly embracing a daunting challenge: leading the Rangers to their first Stanley Cup in 52 years. "The players talk about what it would be like to skate around Madison Square Garden with the Cup," he said. "And we talk about what it would be like to have a parade down Broadway. You've got to visualize these things if you want to make them happen."

For many Canadian hockey fans, Messier is best remembered as a critical cog in the Edmonton Oilers juggernaut that captured five Stanley Cups between 1984 and 1990. He was the muscular and menacing centreman who played behind superstar Wayne Gretzky, helping to make the Oilers a formidable offensive machine. But last October 4, the Oilers traded Messier to the Rangers in a deal that made him the highest-paid player in the National Hockey League, with salary and bonuses of $3.5 million. For most of this season, Messier has been the team's leading point scorer—and among the NHL's Top 5—driving the Rangers to first overall in the 22-team league. Messier said that he is eagerly anticipating another run at the Cup, despite immense pressure from the notoriously demanding New York fans and media. "I think that kind of pressure is good," he said, "because winning a Stanley Cup doesn't just happen. Putting a little fear into the players sometimes brings out the best in them."

Messier has already made his mark in the highly competitive New York market.

Sports writer Frank Brown, who has covered the Rangers for 22 years, said that the Big Apple's immense media exposure turns star athletes into "monstrous personalities." Over the past decade, the Rangers have not had a prominent superstar to compete with the likes of former Mets outfielder Darryl Strawberry in baseball, Giants linebacker Lawrence Taylor in football or Knicks centre Patrick Ewing in basketball. But Messier's presence, and the Rangers' run at first place overall, have generated renewed interest. "He's put the Rangers back in the spotlight," said Rangers general manager Neil Smith, a 38-year-old native of Scarborough, Ont. "He's raised the prestige level of the franchise in our market."

Both Smith and head coach Roger Neilson say that they wanted Messier for his on-ice leadership qualities after two straight seasons in which the Rangers had challenged for first place in the NHL's Patrick Division, only to falter in March and fall quickly in the playoffs. There is no doubting his intense desire to win. "I can never shrug off a defeat," said Messier. "I can remember a friend of mine, a rookie and a real competitor, on a team that hadn't done well for years. He'd be upset after a loss and the veterans would say, 'Listen, don't worry about it. There's nothing you can do.' That's why some teams never get turned around. They accept losing."

Messier carries his attitudes off the ice, as well. He rarely fraternizes with opponents, he says, and for 10 years never said a word to some members of the Calgary Flames, the Oilers' archrivals. But among his new teammates, Messier is admired—even revered. Tie Domi describes him as "the best guy in the world," a living legend who offers him candid hockey advice and a big-brother figure who takes an interest in his personal life. Colin Campbell, a Rangers assistant coach, said that Messier's personality is so forceful that he even intimidates the coaching staff.

Several times this season, Messier has given his teammates pep talks when he saw their play slipping. At the end of a recent 90-minute workout—on the morning after a 5–2 loss to the Washington Capitals—Neilson summoned his players to one side of the rink for a brief lecture on puck pursuit in the opposition's end. He then headed for the locker room—and Messier took over. With his teammates gathered around him, the captain spoke quietly for 10 minutes. Neither he nor the other players would reveal what he said. But the next evening, the Rangers ended a three-game losing streak by whipping the Chicago Black Hawks.

It is Monday night, and Paul Messier and his sister Mary-Kay are watching the Rangers battle the Capitals from their usual seats in the family's sky suite at Madison Square Garden. The suite, which is included in Mark's contract, is carpeted and comfortable, and the Messiers have a dozen guests in for the game. But Paul sits alone, elbows on his knees, jaw resting on his hands—deeply immersed in the game. Suddenly, when the referee calls a penalty against the Rangers, he erupts, leaping from his seat and denouncing the whistle-blower with a string of expletives. Paul is not the only one watching intently. In the second period, he is summoned to the phone to take a call from his father, Doug, who is viewing the game via satellite dish from Mark's oceanfront estate in Hilton Head, S.C. "He just wanted to know what happened to Mark on that last play," Paul Messier says after returning to his seat, "and I told him it looked like he jammed his hand."

For the Messiers, hockey and family have always been synonymous. Paul said that he and his siblings grew up watching their father play semi-professional hockey in Portland, Ore. Father Doug, 55, who was also a teacher, coached both his sons when they played Tier 2 junior hockey as teen-agers growing up in the Edmonton suburb of St. Albert. Paul went on to play four seasons in the minor leagues in North America—he only made it up to the NHL for nine games with the now-defunct Colorado Rockies—followed by seven pro seasons in Mannheim, Germany. Mark played just five games in the minors before jumping to the Oilers, where he remained until last October—when the brothers received news of the trade over a cellular phone while golfing at Hilton Head.

For his first couple of months in New York, Messier stayed at the Westbury Hotel and dined frequently at its exclusive restaurant, the Polo. Maitre d' Michel Pimienta said that he assigned Messier a personal table and introduced him to such celebrity clients as former sportscaster Howard Cosell and rock singer Cyndi Lauper. Messier has since leased a luxury condominium in a 78-storey, sleek black-glass-and-metal tower two doors down from Carnegie Hall on West 57th Street. He keeps one of his three cars in the city, a 1989 Bentley that he bought from Gretzky, and uses it mainly to drive to Rangers practices in Rye, N.Y., 40 km northeast of Manhattan.

After Mark's move to New York, Paul and Mary-Kay formed Messier Management International Inc. to handle their brother's business affairs. Paul retired from pro hockey in November, 1990. Mary-Kay left a marketing job at IBM Canada Ltd. in Edmonton in January to move to New York. Their parents, Doug and his wife, Mary Jean, now live year-round at Mark's Hilton Head estate, which includes an A-frame main house, a guesthouse that sleeps 16 people, tennis courts and an in-ground swimming pool.

When he signed with the Rangers, Messier relied on his father and brother to

Mark Messier after winning the 1987 Canada Cup.

negotiate a five-year contract. Although he would not divulge details, he said that the deal contains an escalation clause that will allow him to remain one of the three highest-paid players in the league in each of the next four seasons, providing he meets certain performance targets. The brother-and-sister team also have negotiated product endorsement deals for their famous sibling: one to produce a series of limited-edition lithographs depicting Messier in action—$565 apiece—and the other to endorse a line of sports-card binders and school products. "He's a clean-living guy who works hard every night," said David Tarica, whose New Jersey-based company makes the school products. "This is New York—you don't find that in New York very often."

But Messier's main focus remains playing the game, even as a strike threatens to disrupt the NHL season. In tense talks over a new collective bargaining agreement, the players are demanding fewer restrictions on their ability to move from one team to another as free agents, as well as a better arbitration system in salary disputes and a larger share of playoff revenues. But the owners contend that they cannot afford such changes: according to press reports, they will collectively lose $17 million this year, down from a record profit of $55 million last year. A players' strike would also force the CBC, which has the TV rights to the playoffs, to resort to reruns and old movies.

But for Messier, the contract dispute is just so much background noise. He clearly sees himself, not walking a picket line, but carrying hockey's most hallowed trophy, the Stanley Cup, down a confetti-filled Broadway.

The Rangers lost in the second round of the playoffs that season after finishing first in their division. New York missed the post season altogether the following year, but Messier helped them win the Stanley Cup in 1994.

Mario Lemieux: The Reluctant Superstar

James Deacon

April 8, 1996—A small crowd had gathered under the stands at the ThunderDome in St. Petersburg, Fla., waiting excitedly to meet Mario Lemieux after a game between his Pittsburgh Penguins and the Tampa Bay Lightning. As always, Lemieux was well turned out in a tailored jacket and pants, with his dark hair slicked back from a post-game shower. He did not, however, look very comfortable making casual chat with the well-wishers. But as he finished up, his eyes brightened at the sight of David Boulet, a 12-year-old from St. Petersburg whom he had met earlier in the day. Boulet and Lemieux have something in common: Hodgkin's disease, a cancer of the lymphatic system. Pale and thin from months of chemotherapy and radiation treatment, the boy smiled when Lemieux broke away from the crowd to say hello. They talked quietly for a few minutes, after which the six-foot four-inch, 220-lb. hockey player straightened up and rested a hand on Boulet's shoulder. "You're going to be fine," Lemieux assured him. "If I can do it, you can, too."

The scene was a public relations dream—except that Lemieux has no interest in public relations. In an age of headline-hungry athletes, the 30-year-old Montrealer skates the other way, choosing privacy over celebrity, even though it diminishes his income and often deprives him of his professional due. Timing and geography have also dulled the brilliance of a career in which Lemieux has so often made the play but missed the glory. He is a once-in-a-generation talent whose generation somehow produced two—and the Great One, Wayne Gretzky, arrived in the National Hockey League five years before him. Lemieux works his magic in the media backwater of Pittsburgh, and although he has led the Penguins to two Stanley Cup titles—key components of any legend's résumé—most Americans missed those triumphs because they occurred before the NHL had a U.S. network TV deal. And this season, his heroic return to the NHL from cancer and back problems has been overshadowed on the American sports landscape by the Second Coming of basketball icons Michael Jordan and Magic Johnson.

But as the regular season wraps up and the playoffs approach in mid-April, there is no hiding the fact that Mario Lemieux has fashioned a remarkable comeback story. Take last week, when Lemieux—going head-to-head against Gretzky and the St. Louis Blues—tallied *five* goals and two assists to carry the Penguins to an 8–4 victory (Gretzky had a single assist). The goals propelled Lemieux past Guy Lafleur into 11th place on the NHL's career points list, lengthened his lead in the league scoring race this year, and left little doubt that, like Jordan in hoops, he has returned to dominate hockey as if he had never been away. To complete the tale, Lemieux's scoring blowout of the Blues came on his first night back since his wife, Nathalie, gave birth to the couple's third child, Austin, three months prematurely. Mother and son, Lemieux says, "are doing great."

So is Mario, especially considering that he had been off skates for the equivalent of two full seasons since being diagnosed with Hodgkin's in January, 1993. The man the press dubbed the Magnificent One (his teammates simply call him Big Guy) missed 20 games that year while undergoing radiation treatments. He sat out three-quarters of the next season because of complications following surgery to repair a herniated muscle in his back, and later because of another back injury that was so debilitating he was often unable to tie his own skates. That crippling pain, coupled with strength-sapping anemia caused by the radiation treatments, forced him to miss the entire 1994–95 campaign.

If the public does not fully appreciate his talents, Lemieux himself is partly to blame. At his request, his agents and the team's public relations staff politely but firmly turn down all but a few interview requests and, even when Lemieux does sit with a reporter for any length of time, he deliberately reveals little of himself. "That is the way I want it," he told *Maclean's*. "The less people know about me, the better."

Still, his teammates and old friends say he pays too high a price for his shyness. "There are athletes who get bigger accolades than they deserve just because they are in the public eye all the time, and that's not fair," says Rick Tocchet, an ex-Penguin who now plays for Boston. "On pure hockey ability, he's probably the best player in the history of the game next to Wayne, and Wayne's played six or seven more years."

Such respect comes even from the man who casts the biggest shadow. "I think this season has been his best performance, and not just because he's coming back," says Gretzky. "The game is better now than it was four or five years ago. The players play a more defensive style now, the goaltending is better. His performance in that style of hockey is amazing."

Harry Neale, the former Vancouver Canucks coach who now works as an analyst on *Hockey Night in Canada*, puts it most eloquently. Lemieux, he says, "is one of the half dozen or so players in history who are in the NHL only because there is no better league for them to go to."

That he is still playing at all is a tribute to medical science and his own love of the game. Lemieux had been plagued by back injuries for years, and twice had surgery to relieve the pain. A dangerous infection set in after the first surgery, causing him to miss still more games. In January, 1993, he found a lump on his neck that turned out to be an enlarged lymph node, and a biopsy revealed Hodgkin's disease—fortunately, in its early stages. After six weeks of radiation treatment, he returned to the ice in time to capture the league scoring title once again.

Lemieux's current comeback began a year ago, when he started working with trainer Tom Plasko on a program that strengthened his back, increased his overall flexibility and left him more fit than he had ever been. The program has enabled him to play without pain for the first time in years, so he makes time after every practice to lift weights or ride the stationary bicycle. "I feel better, physically *and* mentally," Lemieux says, wiping the sweat off his face with a towel after working out at the Penguins' practice facility in suburban Canonsburg, Pa., 30 km south of Pittsburgh. Then, with a chuckle, he adds: "Maybe I should have been doing that earlier in my career."

The truth is that Lemieux has fashioned his brilliant career even while being notoriously unfit by NHL standards. His willingness to work now has impressed his teammates. Standing outside the training room where Lemieux was going through his paces, teammate Ron Francis said it was not as if the Penguins' captain had anything to prove. "He has already shown people what he could do, he had won the Stanley Cup twice and he had made a lot of money," says Francis. "He could have said goodbye, but he wanted to come back, to play. That's what makes the great players great—they absolutely love the game." Opponents have been equally amazed. "It's one thing to come back from a serious injury like he had," says Cam Neely, a rugged Boston Bruins winger who has also been plagued with injuries. "But it's another to beat cancer, be off skates for that long and then come back and play at his level."

Lemieux himself is not surprised. He has always been able to rely on the sublime talent he first showed on the streets of Ville Emard, the working-class Montreal

Mario Lemieux in action with the Pittsburgh Penguins, 1996.

neighborhood where he grew up. Every kid playing shinny pretended to be Lafleur or Jean Beliveau, but Lemieux showed right away that he was more than just a pale imitation. His parents, Jean-Guy and Pierrette, made sure of that: family legend has it that they sometimes packed snow onto the living room carpet to create an indoor surface on which Mario and his brothers could practise after dark. His first coaches marvelled at his poise and puck control. Throughout minor hockey he was able to manipulate the flow of the game, scoring at will. And like Gretzky, Lemieux seemed to have 360-degree vision on the ice—his passes were often more exciting than his goals.

Though otherwise reticent, Lemieux is not shy about his athletic talent. At 15, when he was drafted by the Laval Voisins of the Quebec Major Junior Hockey League, he boldly predicted that he would break the league scoring records. Sure enough, in the 1983–84 season he tallied 282 points, obliterating the single season record of 251 set by Pierre Larouche, who went on to star in the NHL with the Penguins and Canadiens. And on the final night of that season, needing three goals to tie Lafleur's record of 130, Lemieux scored six. While the NHL scouts drooled, the prodigy was cool. "I have always been very comfortable with what I do on the ice," he now says matter-of-factly. "I grew up doing it and it came pretty easily to me, so it's nothing special."

Lemieux is equally confident—some say arrogant—in off-ice matters. Both as a junior and as a professional, he has been widely criticized for declining invitations to play for Canada at world tournaments. And at the 1984 entry draft, after the Penguins selected him No. 1, Lemieux refused to honor the tradition of donning a jersey at the Pittsburgh table because the team had not yet signed him to a contract. Incidents such as those made Lemieux appear selfish and unpatriotic, a perception the aloof player did little to dispel. He felt he had good reasons—injuries, mostly—and that his actions were misunderstood.

He has also confounded his sponsors—which early in his career included Gillette, Micron Mega skates and Coca-Cola—by occasionally failing to show up at appointed times. "All that smiling-for-the camera, shaking-hands stuff, that's not him at all," says Tocchet. Nowadays, Lemieux simply turns down most endorsement offers. Unlike Gretzky, who earns up to $8 million a year endorsing everything from soup to insurance, Lemieux lends his name mostly to hockey equipment manufacturers and trading cards. Still, he will not go hungry. With bonuses, he is scheduled to make $15 million next season, which will almost certainly enable him to overtake the still unsigned Gretzky as the league's highest-paid player. "I just tell my agents that I'd rather not do much in the off-season," he says. "I know that is costing me a little bit of money, but I am lucky to make enough that I don't have to do those things." When Lemieux does speak, people listen—which can be a problem. During the run-up to the Quebec referendum last summer, he told an inquiring reporter that the vote was of no concern to him because he lived in Pittsburgh. "Mario has done things his own way," says Marcel Dionne, the former Los Angeles Kings star. "He's the best player in the game, and he rates with the best players of all time, but he'll come out and say things that, in Montreal, would get you killed."

In fact, although he was the logical heir to the mantle worn by Aurel Joliat, Maurice Richard, Beliveau and Lafleur, Lemieux says he would never have survived had he been drafted by the Canadiens and played in the hockey hothouse that is Montreal. "I am such a private person that it would have been very difficult," Lemieux says. "All the media attention and fan pressure demand so much of your time, and I don't think I would have lasted too long in Montreal." In Pittsburgh, Lemieux has found an unlikely but happy home. Steel City fans have embraced their reluctant hero, admiring his performance on the ice and honoring his desire for privacy off it.

Although he is not much of a civic rah-rah type, he does host an annual golf tournament to benefit cancer research—"We collected nearly $100,000 last year," he says proudly. He lives in Sewickley, a leafy community 25 km west of Pittsburgh, with Nathalie and the kids: baby Austin joins daughters Lauren, 3, and Stephanie, 1. Lemieux indulges his passion for golf—he is very good at that, too—as a member at two local clubs, including storied Oakmont Country Club, site of several U.S. Opens. "Mario's idea of a perfect summer day," says Tocchet, "is to play golf with a few friends and then go home to his family for a quiet dinner."

Home life has not always been serene. Lemieux was scarred by a 1992 incident in a Bloomington, Minn., hotel when a friend, Dan Quinn, was accused of raping a young woman in Lemieux's hotel room. The charges were soon dropped, but the revelation that he and Quinn had women in the room while Nathalie was pregnant at home damaged Lemieux's public image, particularly in Quebec. His relationship with Nathalie survived. And Lemieux now credits her with helping him recover from his illnesses. "With the back infection, she was my nurse for three months," he says. "She learned how to do the intravenous and all that other stuff. She was there every day."

At work, certainly, Lemieux appears to be having more fun this season. His competitive fire is more evident, particularly against tougher opponents. In a home game against Eric Lindros and the Philadelphia Flyers, for instance, Lemieux made it clear that he was not about to cede any ground to his younger opponent. With mesmerizing puck control, Lemieux rang up three goals and two assists as the Penguins beat their cross-state rivals 7–4. And while he is still undemonstrative— Lemieux can make scoring a goal look about as much fun as going to the dentist—he took great pleasure in one of his goals, which he banked in off goalie Garth Snow from an impossible angle.

"The thing I like about Mario this year is the sparkle in his eye, the enjoyment of the game that I'd seen slipping when he got hurt," says Neale of *Hockey Night in Canada*. Lemieux agrees. "Every time you get away from something you love, it makes you appreciate it more," he says. "That's what I found out last season. I'm just glad to have the chance to come back to the game."

And the game is glad to have him—especially when he works his wizardry. In February, Lemieux produced what may have been the highlight of the 1995–96 season. Bearing down on Canucks goalie Kirk McLean, he had the puck knocked off his stick by Martin Gelinas. But as it slipped behind him, Lemieux reached his stick back between his legs and astonishingly flipped a shot over McLean's shoulder into the far top corner of the net. No one could recall seeing anything like it. "He's so creative with the puck and something like that catches you off-guard," a stunned McLean told reporters afterward. "You don't mind being on a highlight film when it's a guy like him."

To cap his unlikely comeback, of course, Lemieux would like nothing more than to capture the Stanley Cup again. And he says he hopes to play in this summer's World Cup (the revamped Canada Cup). It was at the 1987 Canada Cup, where he teamed with Gretzky to score the series-winning goal against the Soviet Union, that Lemieux emerged as a leading force in the NHL. At the time, he seemed a good bet to break the Great One's single-season records for goals (92) and total points (215). But his health always got in the way. "What if he'd never been hurt, never been sick?" asks Dionne, the NHL's No. 3 all-time scorer. "People once said that Gretzky's records would not be broken but, I'll tell you, the Big Guy would have beaten them."

Despite the millions awaiting him next season, Lemieux says he will not play only for his paycheque. "If my back's OK, if I'm healthy, I'll play," he says. "But I'll see how it goes this summer." Cancer taught him that he cannot take anything for granted, even in this extraordinary season. In December, he found a lump on his neck near where his Hodgkin's had first appeared. "It can be alarming, especially with what I had gone through before," he now says. "But I kept an eye on it, showed it to the doctors, and did all the tests—CT scans, MRIs and so on. There was nothing serious."

Without fanfare, Lemieux takes time to cheer up fellow cancer sufferers, especially kids. David Boulet, who went to the practice in St. Petersburg hoping for an autograph, got a lot more. Lemieux gave him a signed stick, set aside four tickets so that the Boulet family could attend that night's game, and then invited the youngster into the Penguins' dressing room. Boulet waded through the sweaty, post-practice debris, gathering signatures and getting his hair mussed by the players, and then climbed up on the bench beside where Lemieux sat wrapped in a towel. "He would have been happy just to meet Mario, someone who had survived the cancer," said Boulet's father, Pierre, a native of Magog, Que., who moved to Florida seven years ago. "This means so much." The hockey star, of course, played down his efforts, saying he knew how scared the little boy was, because he had been scared, too. Not that Lemieux showed it, of course. That's not his style.

In 1996, Mario Lemieux won both the scoring title and the MVP award. He played his final game at age 31 on April 26, 1997, and despite being in less than 1,000 games, he is the NHL's sixth leading scorer. He finished his 12-year career as a six-time winner of the Art Ross Trophy as the league's leading scorer and three-time winner of the league's top player award. He holds numerous league records including the highest-goals-per game average—he scored more than eight goals for every 10 games he played—and he led the Penguins to two Stanley Cups. In 1997, he was inducted into the Hockey Hall of Fame after the normal three-year waiting period was waived.

In the Name of Greed

Jane O'Hara

January 19, 1998—"There's the son of a bitch now." The words leaked like sour milk from Bobby Orr's mouth as he strained to watch Alan Eagleson, once his friend and agent, now his despised enemy, enter Courtroom 8 in Boston's Federal Court. Orr, the Boston Bruins legend, was one of about 20 former National Hockey League players who shined their shoes, put on their best suits and flew from all over North America to get a rinkside seat at the trial that would bring down the man they once considered a second father.

They sat shoulder-to-shoulder on the public benches, the greats and the grinders, a phalanx of still-powerful men facing the fact that they had been robbed by the man they had entrusted with their financial affairs when he headed the National Hockey League Players' Association from 1967 to 1991. They all had their stories of betrayal, of how they had been abused and tricked by the Eagle, duped out of money and made to feel like idiots when they questioned his command. They all smouldered inside when this still-smirking godfather of hockey hustled into the sedate Boston courtroom with his typical briskness, as though he was late for nothing more important than a tennis game. But no one hated him more than Orr, who feels personally responsible. For it was Orr, the gifted blond defenceman, who became the first NHL superstar ever to hire an agent when he enlisted Eagleson's services to negotiate his contract with the Bruins in 1966. That started the chain of events that would catapult R. Alan Eagleson from his status as an unknown Toronto lawyer to a position of power, wealth and fame; the friend of prime ministers and Supreme Court justices, whose reach into the top echelons of the Canadian Establishment never exceeded his grasp.

Many of the former players in Courtroom 8 never made big money. They now work in construction or sell sporting goods. But back then, when Eagleson helped organize the 1972 Canada–USSR Summit series and the Canada Cup tournaments that followed, he assured the players that if they competed internationally, did their duty to their game and their country—even if that meant playing for free and playing hurt as many did—the money earned would build big, fat pensions that would take care of them for the rest of their lives.

Orr, who played with knees so damaged that they required 10 operations, watched intently as Judge Nathaniel Gorton looked down at Eagleson's reddening face. He asked the Canadian how he pleaded to the first felony count involving stealing hundreds of thousands of dollars from international hockey that was earmarked for the players' pension fund.

"Guilty," said Eagleson, almost too quickly and matter-of-factly, as though trying to beat the buzzer on *Jeopardy*.

To the second charge: "Guilty."

To the third: "Guilty."

At that, the square Irish face of former Bruins right winger Terry O'Reilly circled into a big smile. And former Toronto Maple Leafs defenceman Carl Brewer, who had spent the past 25 years trying to find the money Eagleson had stolen from the players over the years, started crying. But Orr remained impassive. And when court was adjourned, he hustled into the Boston rain, refusing to say a word. "Bobby feels so bad," said his longtime friend, star defenceman Brad Park. "Cause he's the guy who brought Al in. And he's the guy who personally lost the most."

The next day, Jan. 7, the 64-year-old Eagleson pleaded guilty to another three charges of fraud in a Toronto courtroom. Again, the room was filled to capacity, not with irate hockey players, but with curiosity seekers who came to see the Canadian hockey icon brought down. Watching from the second row of the public gallery was Nancy, his wife of 37 years, wearing widow's black, her white hair cut short, her face showing the strain of the nine-year investigation into her husband's affairs. And there in spirit were many of the rich and politically powerful men that Eagleson had cultivated over the years, some with gifts, airline tickets and hockey junkets. Thirty prominent people—from hockey, politics, the media, even the church—most of whom did not know he was negotiating a plea bargain that would see him plead guilty, had sent glowing letters that were read into the public record, lauding him for being a good friend and a great family man of the highest integrity. "We have often talked about shared values," wrote former Liberal prime minister John Turner. "For him those values are Faith, Family and Friends." Added Bob Clarke, the president and general manager of the Philadelphia Flyers: "Alan is a very Good and Decent Man!"

When the two-hour proceeding had ended, this "good and decent man" had been found guilty of defrauding the players he represented by pocketing advertising revenues from the Canada Cups. Then, with his Order of Canada pin in his left lapel, he was taken away in a paddy wagon to begin serving an 18-month sentence in the Mimico Correctional Centre, a medium-security facility that houses white-collar and other nonviolent criminals. Thus ended a two-day drama that came about after a prearranged and highly unusual plea bargain that Eagleson's legal team, captained by Toronto's Brian Greenspan, had arranged with both American and Canadian prosecutors. "Al being Al," said Brewer, "he managed to cut himself a good deal."

Make that a very good deal. If Eagleson behaves himself in prison, he will likely serve only six months of his 18-month term—although he had been facing 42 charges after three-year investigations by the FBI and the RCMP. If convicted on the U.S. charges alone, which included racketeering and embezzlement, he could have done 15 years of hard time. One senior Canadian jurist, outraged by the deal, told *Maclean's* that a non-celebrity accused of Eagleson's crimes in Canada could have expected 10 to 12 years. And Dave Forbes, a former NHLer who flew from Colorado Springs, Colo., to Boston to witness Eagleson's conviction, said: "It's really disappointing. It was such a slap on the wrist for such a huge betrayal."

As a result of the plea bargain, Eagleson was convicted on six of the lesser charges. In Boston, he paid $1 million in restitution for the money he stole from the players, including a $15,000 disability claim that rightfully belonged to Glen Sharpley when the former Chicago Blackhawks centre was blinded by a high stick that ended his career. Eagleson sold properties he owned in Florida and New York City to raise part of the $1 million, and he has told friends that he has very little money left after paying legal bills. But many doubt that: estimates put Eagleson's net worth at anywhere from $5 million to $50 million. How much of that came from robbing the players? "It's an impossible calculation to make," said Bob Goodenow, Eagleson's replacement as executive director of the NHLPA. "Boxes and boxes and boxes of documents have been destroyed." Boston FBI agent Tom Daley, who amassed 250,000 documents and conducted more than 300 interviews in the seven years he spent investigating Eagleson, says: "If Eagleson's poor, I wish I was that poor."

Despite the players' disappointment at the insignificant sentence, Eagleson's fall from grace has been cataclysmic. The Eagle had chutzpah and hubris and a Rolodex the size of a cement mixer. His dialling finger had callouses from keeping in touch with his vast empire of contacts—and his middle finger made him a hockey hero

Alan Eagleson in his Toronto office, 1997.

when he angrily saluted the Russians during the 1972 Summit Series. Although he could be oozing charm one minute, he could be screaming obscenities the next. There never seemed to be enough hours in the day for all the wheeling, dealing and, we now know, the stealing that Eagleson did.

Now, hockey fans denounce him bitterly on talk-radio shows and call for him to be ousted from the Hockey Hall of Fame and stripped of his Order of Canada. Many in the moneyed classes have begun to shun him as well. On Nov. 18, Eagleson's wife was desperate to rent a one-bedroom coach house for $1,450 a month in Cabbagetown, a Toronto neighborhood of stately Victorian homes. When she came to see the property, she told the owners, Martin McCuaig and Jane Martin, that she and her husband had sold their million-dollar house in Rosedale and were planning to move to London where they still own a flat near Buckingham Palace. But they needed to keep a small place in Toronto for trips home to visit family, including Eagleson's mother, who now lives in the Rekai Centre, a no-frills old folks' home. "She kept telling me they really wouldn't be spending much time in the coach house because they still had a farm in the country." said Martin. But Martin did not want the Eaglesons as tenants. "I'd rather have it sit empty for six months," she said, "than have that crook live in it."

In retrospect, Eagleson's descent from power to prison can be traced back to April 1, 1980. That day, Orr—the player who made Eagleson—severed relations with him. For years, Orr had known something was wrong with the way Eagleson was handling his money. But while the Eagle had once promised to make Orr a millionaire by the time he was 25, an independent accountant now revealed that by the time he retired in 1978, his assets totalled $456,000 (U.S.), while his taxes, legal and accounting bills were $459,000 (U.S.). In other words, Orr—the hockey great whose 12-year NHL career brought him two Stanley Cups and numerous records—was essentially broke.

Orr did not go public with the details of his personal penury. He was too embarrassed. But his divorce from Eagleson rumbled through the players' association with the force of an oncoming avalanche. Increasingly, the players were starting to ask questions of Eagleson, whose many guises of player agent, head of the NHLPA, organizer of international hockey and buddy of NHL president John Ziegler, put him in a huge conflict of interest. But every time the players rose up to ask questions, Eagleson beat them down, made them feel they were too stupid to understand the fine points of high finance. "He treated us like children," said Brewer, the former Leaf.

Brad Park, whose career with the New York Rangers and Bruins lasted 15 years, was a vice-president of the NHLPA in 1981. He remembers all too clearly how Eagleson would use his cunning combination of street-thuggery and glib legalese to demean players who challenged his authority. "In those days, most of the guys had a huge passion to play, but they hadn't finished high school," said Park. "When they'd get up to ask him a question he didn't like, he'd tear them a new rear end. That shut a lot of people up."

Two years ago, Park and four other retired players filed a class-action lawsuit against Eagleson, John Ziegler—NHL president from 1977 to 1992—and Bill Wirtz, Chicago Blackhawks owner and longtime NHL chairman. In it they allege collusion between Eagleson and the NHL management that some estimate cost the players between $500 million and $800 million in salaries and lost benefits. Park, who now works for a manufacturing company that designs graphite shafts for hockey sticks, was content with the money made over the course of his career—his salary was $275,000 (U.S.) when he retired in 1983. He well knows, even accounting for inflation, that it is small change compared with the $1 million that even an average NHL player makes today. But he is not complaining. What angered him was finding out, upon retirement, that his pension would be $13,000 (Cdn), compared with Eagleson's pension, which was set at $50,000 (U.S.). In the 1972 Canada-Russia series, Park was one of the players who escorted Eagleson safely across the ice of the Luzhniki Palace rink after he had been apprehended by Russian guards while charging an offending goal judge. "It sickens my stomach to think of it now," said Park. "Year after year, we played all those Canada Cup games for nothing because Al told us the money was all going to our pensions. It was a lie."

It was only one of a tangled web of lies Eagleson told when he was head of the NHLPA. But that finally began to unravel in 1989, when a group of players hired Philadelphia lawyer Ed Garvey to investigate irregularities in the NHLPA. When Eagleson heard that Garvey was working on the report, he phoned him at home. As Garvey tells it, Eagleson barked: "Back off, I've got you in my sights." Garvey, the former executive director of the National Football League Players' Association, laughed at Eagleson's bully tactics, replying: "Well, I hope you shoot straight."

Garvey's confidential report was a damning 55-page indictment of Eagleson's NHLPA stewardship. Among Garvey's findings: during the 1980s, the NHLPA had gained "no benefits of any significance" for the players, who lagged badly behind those of other sports. He said that Eagleson's conflicts of interest negatively affected every aspect of the players' finances. Of the Eagle's own financial situation, he wrote: "Eagleson may be the most overpaid executive in the labor movement in North America. Not even the president of the two-million member Teamsters union comes close to Alan in wages, benefits, pension and expense accounts." Garvey's conclusion: "What we found can only be described as a scandal."

Garvey's report, which was put together with the help of Canadian player agents Rich Winter and Ron Salcer, was the document that helped topple Eagleson. Two years after it was written, Eagleson was deposed as union leader and replaced by Goodenow, a Detroit lawyer. And Garvey's report was taken up by Russ Conway, the rumpled sports editor of the Lawrence, Mass., *Eagle-Tribune*, who launched a seven-year investigation into Eagleson that culminated in his book, *Game Misconduct*. The book, in turn, was used by the FBI in its three-year investigation, which resulted in 34 felony counts against Eagleson.

With so much evidence against the former hockey czar, why did he get off so lightly? Paul Kelly, the former U.S. prosecutor who built the American case against Eagleson, fumed when he considered the plea bargain. Kelly was hoping to try Eagleson in the United States. In December, 1995, the Boston district attorney filed a three-volume, 800-page extradition request to the justice department in Ottawa. According to Kelly, Canada and the United States routinely extradite criminals back and forth across the border every year: close to 70 alone last year. But the Canadian government never acted on the Eagleson extradition request. Canadian officials explain that cases involving fraud are far more complex and difficult to extradite than drug or even murder charges. But critics speculate that Eagleson's deep political connections may have helped as well. "For two years, the extradition request remained in limbo," said Kelly. "It never left the minister of justice to be publicly filed. We urged the Canadian side to act on it, but we heard nothing from them. Nothing. There was no more the United States could do in terms of getting Mr. Eagleson back to the U.S. short of coming into Canada and kidnapping him. Was it frustrating? Yes."

In many ways, it seemed that right up until he was taken to jail, Eagleson was still acting as though he was above the law. In a move that astonished veteran courtroom observers, he was not handcuffed as he was led away from his Toronto court appearance. In Boston, when the FBI booked, fingerprinted and took his mug shot, one agent reported that he was tinkering with the fingerprinting equipment. "He just didn't get it," said the agent. "He doesn't realize he's a criminal." In the Boston courtroom, when Carl Brewer got up and said: "Thank God for America, because this never would have happened in Canada," Eagleson started laughing.

At the Mimico Correctional Centre, Eagleson now lives in a single-storey dormitory, where he sleeps in a room that smells like stale cigarette smoke mixed with sweet institutional cleanser. In a chilling comedown for a man about to become a senior citizen in three months, he now finds himself bunking with 27 other convicts—break-and-enter artists and petty drug dealers for the most part. He works cleaning offices. There is one telephone available to inmates, usually with a long lineup, and prisoners are entitled to only two visits a week. When he gets out later this year, Eagleson will face a series of civil lawsuits brought by former players. They may take enormous satisfaction from seeing the Eagle finally land in jail, but what they want most of all—and will have to fight mightily to get—is their money back.

Written with files from Stephanie Nolen, John Nicol and Stevie Cameron in Toronto, and John Geddes in Ottawa. Jane O'Hara is a senior writer at Maclean's.
Alan Eagleson was released on parole, after serving one-third of his sentence, on July 7, 1998.

Over the Top: Has Don Cherry Gone Too Far?

James Deacon

May 18, 1998—Ian Cobby and James Harris are excited as heck. Down from suburban Georgetown, they're spending Saturday night at the main CBC building in Toronto, and they've talked their way into meeting Don Cherry. Grapes! The two boys, both 10, and Ian's dad, John, follow a CBC staffer into a private lounge adjacent to the *Hockey Night in Canada* set where Cherry, preparing for "Coach's Corner," is resting before going on camera. The kids step into the dimly lit room and, wham, it hits them. "Hi guys, how ya doin'?" comes the familiar bellow. It's Don, all right, loud and proud. He's wearing grey flannels, red blazer, red shirt and red tie—can't miss him.

Cherry usually keeps to himself before his between-periods sessions with host Ron MacLean, but for the boys he makes an exception. He likes kids, and they like him. "You hockey players?" he asks, rising to greet them. "I am," says Ian, explaining he plays on an atom team. "That's great," says Cherry. He's too distracted for small talk, but he signs a pair of postcards of himself with his beloved English bull terrier, Blue. "Thanks for stoppin' by," he says, "and enjoy the game, eh?" The door closes and the boys pause behind the set to examine their freshly minted autographs. James says it was cool meeting the big TV star. "Yeah," agrees Ian. "My mom doesn't like what he says, but I think he's great."

Out of the mouths of babes, eh? The 64-year-old intermission icon is one of the most-watched men in Canada thanks to a remarkable talent for simultaneously entertaining and appalling millions of viewers who tune into *Hockey Night in Canada* on Saturday nights in season. With hockey on nearly every night during the playoffs, his exposure is tripled—since mid-April, he has been on every second night, and that will continue until the Stanley Cup is awarded in June. The appeal? Watching Cherry is like watching a bonfire burning next to a barn full of hay. Will he keep the blaze contained, or will all hell break loose?

Cherry, of course, thinks fighting is a good thing; European players are stealing jobs away from hardworking Canadian boys; Americans are ruining the NHL; and anyone who thinks differently is un-Canadian or an intellectual, or both. He has a strong rapport with players from atom to the NHL. "There's not a better guy to have on your side," says Toronto Maple Leafs tough guy Tie Domi. "When he talks on TV, a lot of people listen." And when Cherry drops the bombast, he is a keen analyst who can pick apart a videotape replay to show how a goal was set up by an event at the other end of the ice. "Don's strength is dealing with the game," says *Hockey Night*'s executive producer, John Shannon, "and when he sticks to that, everyone is happy."

But he doesn't stick to the game. He is notorious for his right-of-Reform rants on pet peeves ranging from taxes to immigration. And as for Quebec, well, don't get him started. He claims he is simply taking aim at the separatists, but more often than not national unity feels the pain. His tirades often sound anti-French rather than anti-Bloc—at the Winter Olympics last February, he took a cheap shot at Canada's opening ceremonies flag-bearer, 1994 Olympic gold medallist Jean-Luc Brassard, calling him "a French guy, some skier nobody knows about." The truth is, *Cherry* had never heard of Brassard, and knows nothing about freestyle skiing. Later, he compounded the insult, calling separatists "whiners." Réjean Tremblay, the prominent *La Presse* columnist, says Cherry appears to be crossing the line between nationalism and racism. "Don Cherry is a mystery to me," Tremblay says. "The man I've known personally for 20 years seems infinitely more warm, more open than the guy that we see on television."

Perhaps Cherry is self-destructing. He isn't sure himself. The death of his wife, Rose, of liver cancer last June nearly killed him, too. "And he's still not in great shape," worries Shannon. Cherry concedes his attitude about what he will or will not say on camera has changed since Rose died. "I don't give a shit now, I really don't," he says, his voice falling to a whisper. "Why should I care? People say, 'Don, you've gone too far now,' but I don't care."

He is used to people challenging his politics, but lately, they've been questioning something more sacred—his impact on the game. Cherry has come to symbolize Canadian-style hockey—which is to say, Rock 'Em Sock 'Em hockey, the name of Cherry's hugely successful video series—at a time when Canada's finest have suffered soul-searching losses at the World Cup in 1996 and the Olympics last February.

Cherry says the problems are overblown. "To me, there's nothing wrong," he says. "I wish we handled the puck a little more, but that's it." He cannot stomach the oft-repeated suggestion that Canada take a lesson from the slick-stickhandling Europeans. "We're teaching kids to block shots, hit, God forbid *fight*—we're teaching them all the fundamentals," he says. "The Europeans just go out and score. As long as you get 50 goals, you're a superstar."

But in the post-Nagano world, Canadian officials and parents have acknowledged that minor hockey only teaches some fundamentals. Coaches bent on winning put more emphasis on size and so-called system hockey than on imparting puckhandling and skating skills. At the NHL level, the shortfall in skills translates into a scoring race dominated by Europeans, who did not come up in a similarly stifling hockey environment.

Nor are the Europeans' successes limited to scoring. Despite Cherry's insistence that they cannot match Canadians for playoff competitiveness, it was a pair of imports, Russian Alexei Yashin and Swede Daniel Alfredsson, who led the small but swift Ottawa Senators to a stunning first-round playoff upset of the big, intimidating New Jersey Devils. Alfredsson did duck a direct question about Cherry, but it was clear he and the other targets of Cherry's derision were thrilled the Senators beat the Devils. "It feels great to come through like this against New Jersey," he said, "because they're the toughest team out there. Ask any of the other teams—no one wanted to play them."

Howie Meeker, the man Cherry replaced between periods, says Canadians should have begun rethinking the way hockey is taught years ago. "I'd say 1972 was the time to start taking it more seriously, after the Russians showed us how to play the game," Meeker says. The need for that reassessment may have been lost in the euphoria surrounding Paul Henderson's momentous last-minute goal that saved the series for Canada. But now the reformers are having their day, and there is no escaping the shadow of Cherry. His bigger-is-better, take-no-prisoners ethic has become gospel to minor-hockey coaches and players. In that way, he has helped build a generation of competitors who are long on work ethic and size, but short on the stick skills and creativity that define truly great players. "That influence can be detrimental, particularly for people who hang on his every word," says Murray Costello, president of the Canadian Hockey Association. "And there are many who do."

Roy MacGregor, the respected *Ottawa Citizen* columnist, author and one-time minor-hockey coach, says he could see the Cherry effect on kids. "His thinking, and

Cherry working out at home.

his extraordinary influence, has been the single most destructive influence on the development of Canadian hockey," MacGregor says. He adds that Cherry has that power not just because of TV, but "because hockey means so much in Canada, and because people believe in him."

All the outrage and controversy have built quite a little empire. While some may dismiss Cherry as an annoying but harmless redneck, like the loudmouth at the end of the bar who might shut up if people just ignore him, it is a mistake to underestimate him. And even for committed hockey haters, it is almost impossible to escape him. He has an enormous audience—CBC's Saturday night games attracted an average of 1.5 million viewers this season—and he has been allowed to hurl his Cherry bombs unopposed, except when the affable MacLean, the host since 1986, can get a word in edgewise. His Rock 'Em Sock 'Em videos—the series now numbers nine—have

Over the Top: Has Don Cherry Gone Too Far?

sold over a million copies and counting. He does a nationally syndicated radio show and lends his name to a 12-restaurant chain, Don Cherry's Grapevine. Then there are his commercials—for several companies, including Nabisco's Mr. Christie products and Campbell's soup. Don Cherry—the self-styled voice of the regular guy—is a very rich man.

The fact is, Cherry's schtick is not buffoonery. He has an agenda. His high-decibel, over-the-top delivery may be TV-driven theatricality, much like his wardrobe, but the opinions, the issues he tackles, the edge, are genuine Cherry. He does not take calls on game days, using the time to put together a "game plan" for that night's show—"just like when I was coaching." He arrives late to the set so that Shannon and MacLean do not have time to rehearse. He does his own version of the old TV detective Columbo, playing dumb but speaking straight to his core audience—"my people," as he calls them. "He's just giving viewers what they want," says Shannon. "Don would not say the things he says if he didn't think they would be well received. And he knows his constituency better than most politicians know theirs."

Cherry did all the wrong things on his way to the top. A native of Kingston, Ont., he was a career minor-leaguer who laced up his skates for exactly one NHL game—no goals, no assists. He retired from the American Hockey League Rochester Americans at 33 to work on a construction crew at the Kodak plant there. Laid off, he became, by his own admission, the world's worst Cadillac salesman. He fell back on the only thing he knew—hockey—mounting a comeback with the Americans at 35. In midseason, the general manager fired the coach and gave the reins to Cherry. Within 3 1/2 years, he was running the Boston Bruins. "I was coaching Bobby Orr," he says, still incredulous. "Me."

He nevertheless squandered that windfall. Never one to button his lip, he feuded—foolishly, he now admits—with Boston general manager Harry Sinden and got fired after five seasons. He later coached the Colorado Rockies (now the New Jersey Devils) and was fired there, too. Ralph Mellanby, then the producer of *Hockey Night in Canada*, got him a job as a color commentator and, Cherry says, "I was in trouble all the time." He was saved from the unemployment line by Mellanby, who paired him with then-host Dave Hodge between periods. "Coach's Corner," and a star, were born.

A controversial star, of course: his scornful comments about Brassard, and remarks he made during the January ice storm about Quebec's language laws, prompted Bell Canada to pull its sponsorship of "Coach's Corner" in Quebec in April. But it goes against the TV grain to muzzle Cherry—the more outrageous he gets, the higher the ratings go. "The interesting thing about 'Coach's Corner' is that we set out to create intermissions that were entertaining," says Shannon. "What we've done is create programming that is actually more viewable than the games." Ross Brewitt, a Cherry booster from Mississauga, Ont., says "it's his penchant for blurting out what he thinks that has made him a national figure. And 95 per cent of the time, he's right." That may be a stretch, but Ken Dryden, the former goalie who now is president and general manager of the Toronto Maple Leafs, agrees that Cherry has much to offer on the subject of hockey. "There is a lot of wisdom, a lot of knowledge, in what Don says," Dryden concludes.

The way critics see it, however, *Hockey Night in Canada* has allowed its star to get away with what might otherwise be seen as on-air conflicts of interest. He has worn a hat on camera with the logo of his soon-to-be-launched Mississauga Ice Dogs, a major-junior A team that is busy selling season tickets (and that will not include a single foreign player, Cherry vows). He recently supported NHL owners who were making pleas to Ottawa for tax relief that could ultimately help the profitability of his own team. He defends fighting in the game and he includes replays of two major fights in each Rock 'Em Sock 'Em video to boost sales. "Is that correct?" asks MacGregor. "The CBC would not stand for that in any other aspect of their business, presumably."

Worse for the game, says Bruce Dowbiggin, national sports correspondent for CBC Radio, is that Cherry has been allowed to deliver his one-sided message on how hockey ought to be played without rebuttal. "Kids take their messages straight," Dowbiggin says. "That's why I hold *Hockey Night in Canada* accountable. They do not offer a counterpoint. I'm not saying 'Take him off the air.' I'm just saying they should put someone on with a different point of view, someone who will say, 'Don, you're a clown.'"

Sitting back on an old sofa in the studio lounge, his on-air duties done, Cherry is watching two different playoff games on a bank of TV monitors. He's mad at MacLean, who inadvertently wore the same color tie. "It's the first time that's happened in 12 years," Cherry says grumpily. This has not been a happy time for him. It has been a year since Rose died, and he has not yet fully absorbed the hit. He struggled when he and MacLean took their show on the road, to Vancouver for the all-star game in January and to Nagano, Japan, for the Olympics. "I've been lost now for awhile, but I seemed to be more lost over there," Cherry says of his time in Japan. "I used to call Rose every morning, wherever I was, at 8:30 on the nose, and . . ." He doesn't finish the thought.

The real-life Don Cherry—the soft-spoken, painfully private guy rattling around in his now-too-big house in suburban Mississauga—does not want to talk about Rose. Or at least, that's the word before the interview begins. "I think it's a tender subject," explains CBC publicist Susan Procter. "And it may be that way for a long time." But Cherry brings it up himself. She was his best friend, the centre of his daily existence far more than work or hockey. All his adult life, he left the rink or the construction site or the car lot and went home to her, and now she's gone. He hardly knows what to do with himself, says fellow broadcaster Brian Williams, who delivered one of two eulogies at her funeral. "Rose," Williams says, "was his life."

Cherry's children, Cindy, 41, and Tim, 35, both live nearby, which is a help. Cindy has taken on Rose's old job, sorting the huge pile of mail that arrives daily via the restaurants and the CBC. She is also working with a group in Milton, Ont., on what they're calling Rose's Place, a hospice Cherry is helping to fund for families with terminally ill children. Keeping busy helps, but Cherry's loneliness is palpable. "I'm a lone guy. I don't go out. I, ah, I always . . ." His voice trails off. "When I got out of hockey, I never hung around with anybody. I still don't. I don't have a guy to say, 'Let's go fishin' or somethin'.' Maybe Tim, my son, but I don't have a friend like that. If I ever had advice for anybody, it's to have other friends, and don't isolate yourself or just stick with your wife all the time."

Then he remembers a story that cheers him up. Rose, among other things, was Don's censor. "One time on 'Coach's Corner,' I told Ron to shut up," he says. "Rose just hated it." She wouldn't talk about it when he got home that night, but he heard about it at breakfast. "She said, 'You are, without a doubt, the most ignorant human being. I'm embarrassed.'" Cherry laughs a little at the memory. But the smile soon fades.

Without Rose's moderating influence, he has been more provocative on "Coach's Corner," more out on the edge politically. He says he's just saying aloud what other people—*his* people—are thinking. "As far as Quebec's concerned, it's not fair," he says. "Everybody knows it's not fair, but they're afraid to say it. We have French signs, and they don't have any English—is that fair? Is it fair that you can't speak English down there anywhere in government, and we have to speak French for our government in Ontario? Everybody says the same thing. They whisper to me, 'If they want to leave, let them leave.'"

Cherry has turned his attention to the third period of the Montreal Canadiens-Pittsburgh Penguins game. His jacket is off, his tie is loosened, his three-storey collar is undone, and he's ripping into Jaromir Jagr, the gifted Czech centre who led the league in scoring this season, not to mention helping his country win Olympic gold. Jagr is the kind of guy people pay to see—six-foot-two, a powerful skater and larcenous stickhandler—but Cherry claims he's everything that's wrong with the NHL. "The guy can't hit, and never back checks," Cherry sneers. "The joke is that he has to go down and introduce himself to his goaltender. But he'll get all the trophies and stuff like that."

While his private style is toned down from his TV persona, his opinions remain the same. He really does think European players are cowardly, that they take dives to draw penalties—conveniently ignoring the fact that "good, hardworking Canadian boys" do the same. The Philadelphia Flyers' Bill Barber was arguably the most prolific diver in NHL history, and he came from Callander, Ont. Czech defenceman Frank Musil, now with Edmonton, once called Cherry "a total idiot" for painting all imports with the same brush. Cherry has softened a little—he professes to like a pair of Russians, the Senators' Yashin and the Vancouver Canucks' Pavel Bure. But he is adamantly against imports on his junior team. "They call me a racist because I don't want any Europeans coming to play for my Ice Dogs," he says. He doesn't mind depriving his team of a young Yashin and Bure? "If a kid comes over here and becomes a Canadian, I'll put him on in a minute," he says. "But I will not parachute him in so that he can grab the money and run."

That, says Dryden, is where Cherry goes wrong, not just in political correctness, but in hockey, too. By declaring that the old-style Canadian game is best, and that all others are unworthy, he denies his players a chance to learn from the Europeans. "Don gets himself into a box," Dryden says. "The National Hockey League is a far, far better league now that the best players in the world all play here." Harry Neale, a former coach who has become CBC's top game analyst, agrees. "Anyone who thought that Canada was going to be the only supplier of NHL players had blinders on," Neale says. "It's a global game now."

Friends who have watched Cherry take ever-greater risks on camera wonder if he's trying to get himself fired. At times, he seems tired of the effort it takes to be Don Cherry, tired of the constant criticism. "I'd be lying if I said it didn't wear me down," he says. "You wake up in the morning, you're half-asleep, and you look at the paper and they're ripping you. I like to say I laugh it off, but it gets to me, it bothers me."

His approach to hockey and life, however, were forged years ago in the minor-league ice wars. Asked if the Cherry-bashers made him want to quit, he scoffs: "You don't understand—nobody understands. I don't *care* what they think. It's like a fight—I thrive on it." He leans forward, and suddenly his weariness and sadness are gone. He is again the guy on TV, pugnacious defender of all things Canadian, and of all things Grapes. "When somebody criticizes 'Coach's Corner,'" he goes on, "I'll come back twice as strong. That's what I did as a player. If I knew going into a game that the best fighter was on the other team, it got me pumped. I knew, sooner or later, him and me would be at it. It's the second-best rush in the world, fighting. You know what I mean? It keeps life going."

though
Postscript

The Holy Grail

D'Arcy Jenish

April 26, 1993—A century ago, the game of hockey was as raw and unpolished as the country itself. Sparsely populated and spiritually divided, Canada was a gaunt and gangly adolescent in the midst of a long journey from colony to nation. Hockey was also young—a game that was becoming a sport. Invented by British soldiers stationed in Canada in the 1850s, hockey was originally little more than an athletic free-for-all played with skates, sticks and a ball on frozen sloughs, ponds and rivers. Four decades later, rules had been developed, leagues formed and the top teams played indoors before paying audiences. Hockey had also acquired something else: the Stanley Cup, a modest 7-1/2-inch-high silver bowl that Lord Frederick Stanley, the governor general, donated to the people of Canada in 1893—a cup that quickly became the game's Holy Grail.

And hockey became a national obsession.

Some things have changed. Gone is the silver bowl, replaced in 1949 by a gleaming three-foot-tall 30-lb. trophy ready-made for hoisting over players' heads in delirious triumph. Gone, too, are turn-of-the-century teams of seven skaters who played the entire 60 minutes; contemporary clubs dress 20 players, most of them specialists who race through 60-second shifts before taking a breather. Professionals long ago displaced amateurs as the game's best, and the hockey season has stretched from a compact six weeks to an unwieldy eight months. But for all the changes—for all the pads and masks and helmets that have become the modern player's combat gear—hockey remains at heart the same old game, provoking the same intense passions.

In the beginning, teams from coast to coast pursued the Stanley Cup. They came from Halifax, Sydney and Moncton in the Maritimes, and from Quebec City, Smiths Falls and Kingston in Central Canada. They came from Kenora, Winnipeg and Brandon, from Edmonton and Calgary, Vancouver and Victoria. In 1905, the Dawson City Nuggets made an epic journey from the Yukon all the way to the nation's

The first Stanley Cup Champions, the Montreal Amateur Athletic Association, 1893.

capital to compete for the Cup—only to be battered in a two-game series with the Ottawa Silver Seven, the last time by a score of 23–2. Such long-distance quests for the Cup ended in 1927, when the then-10-team National Hockey League took sole possession of the game's premier prize.

In the days before radio and television, the telegraph provided home-town fans with up-to-the-minute accounts of Stanley Cup games. From 1896 until the late 1920s, the Canadian Pacific Railway and the Great North Western Telegraph Co. had operators at rinkside for Cup games. A sports writer described the play, and the telegrapher used Morse code to send the accounts across the country. In Montreal and Ottawa, Winnipeg and Calgary, huge crowds gathered outside newspaper offices or packed the lobbies of hotels and arenas to read the telegraph accounts the moment they were transcribed into English and posted on bulletin boards. When the crowds were too large, someone would broadcast the bulletins with a megaphone. And when the home team scored, the cheering could be heard for blocks around.

Then, as now, the greatest players seemed to find a way to lead their teams to

Stanley Cup victory—and to save their best performances for the occasion. In fact, their reputations rest on it. Fans quickly forget who won a scoring title or who holds an individual record. But neither the fans nor the players forget the sight of Bobby Orr or Guy Lafleur or Wayne Gretzky or Mario Lemieux standing at centre ice with the Cup held high. And—Brett Hull and Eric Lindros, take heed—an unforgiving public will always find stars wanting unless they win the Cup.

That is because the Stanley Cup has become part of the fibre of a hockey-crazed country. It was created in the era of the passenger train and the telegraph and continues to captivate Canadians in the age of the jumbo jet and the satellite dish. It has survived a century of war and depression, boom and bust, increased prosperity and rising expectations. It began life as a simple athletic trophy. It has become a national icon.

Photo Credits

page

6 National Archives of Canada PA-175909

15 Graphic Artists/Hockey Hall of Fame

31 Halkett

36 Ken Bell

56 *Montreal Gazette*/Hockey Hall of Fame

79 Horst Ehricht

86 John Reeves

93 Phill Snel/*Maclean's*

99 Gaby

117 *Montreal Gazette*

129 *Montreal Star*/National Archives of Canada PA-175897

145 Joe Scherschel

150 Graphic Artists

155 Horst Ehricht

163 Graphic Artists/Hockey Hall of Fame

171 Don Newlands

179 Horst Ehricht

203 Brian Willer/*Maclean's*

210 CBC

215 National Archives of Canada PA-112331

224 Brian Willer/*Maclean's*

234 Frank Lennon/*Toronto Star*

255 Scott MacDonald/Canapress

259 Phill Snel/*Maclean's*

271 Peter Bregg/*Maclean's*

277 *Toronto Star*
281 Ray Giguere
291 Gary Hershorn/Reuters
303 Darrell Sandler/AP
308 Chris Schwarz/*Maclean's*
320 Chris Schwarz/*Maclean's*
328 Phill Snel/*Maclean's*
335 Phill Snel/*Maclean's*